# England

## *The Quest for the World Cup*

### A Complete Record

*About the author*
Clive Leatherdale was born in 1949. He is a writer, journalist, lecturer, and publisher, and a person with wide interests. Born with sport in his blood, he has been writing histories and trenchant articles on football for many years. He has backpacked around much of the globe, has lived in Saudi Arabia, China, and Korea, and written histories or travel books on all three countries. He has a Ph.D. in Arabian history and is an international authority on Dracula.

*Author's Note*
An earlier version of this book appeared in 1984 under the title *England's Quest for the World Cup*. Recent matches are the easiest to recall, with the help of memory, video, and saturation coverage in the press. These aids were not available half a century ago, when the researcher is restricted to newspaper coverage of no great objectivity, some blimpishness, and much wishful thinking. Did England really carve out chances by the hatful against the United States in 1950? Or were frustrated football correspondents of the time simply trying to come to terms with that unpalatable defeat? In the absence of alternative sources, historians must tread warily.

My thanks to David Barber of the Football Association, Tony Griffin and Julia Johnson for their assistance in getting this book shipshape.

Clive Leatherdale, April 1994

# England

## *The Quest for the World Cup*

### A Complete Record

*Clive Leatherdale*

TWO HEADS
PUBLISHING

*Published in association with*
**Desert Island Books**

This edition first published in 1994 by

Two Heads Publishing
*in association with* Desert Island Books
12A Franklyn Suite
The Priory
Haywards Heath
West Sussex
RH16 3LB

ISBN   1-897850-40-9


Photograph credits.
Front cover, pages 29, 31, 51, 53, 55, 71, 73, 77, 79, 99, 101, 119, 141,
151, 153, 175, 183, 243, 247, 251, 254, 255, 279, 283, 287, 291, 317,
318 - Popperfoto.
Rear cover, pages 129, 131, 165, 181, 211, 213, 249, 315 - Colorsport.
Pages 145, 195, 205, 219, 272 - Sporting Pictures.
Page 22 - Glasgow Herald.


Cover design by Doug Cheeseman

Printed & bound by Caldra House Ltd., Hove, Sussex

# CONTENTS

# Foreword

I was first vaguely aware of the World Cup in 1950. At the time I was a seventeen-year old greenhorn, uprooting from my home in Durham to sign for Fulham in the Big City. The World Cup didn't mean much in those days, and England's defeat by the United States in Brazil didn't cause much of a stir, to me or to anybody else.

What a difference nowadays. Over the next forty years the competition grew so fast that when I quit as England manager in 1990 it was football's greatest pageant. As I set out on my own journey in 1950 I would never have believed that the World Cup would become the theatre of theatres or that I would lead the England national side to two World Cup finals.

World Cup football is about performing on the greatest stage of all, against players of great skill, pace, technique, courage, discipline, playing under intense strain and pressure with the unforgiving world watching every move.

I have attended the finals of every competition except 1978, when Ron Greenwood asked me to lead an England party to Australia and New Zealand. What memories those finals evoke. 1958 was special to me because they were my first and I played in all three group games. Walter Winterbottom had given me my first England cap in November 1957. That match, against France, was also the last for Roger Byrne, Tommy Taylor and Duncan Edwards, those great Busby Babes. The records show that I never scored a World Cup goal, but I shall always believe I scored two in Sweden. Against the Russians, the Hungarian referee Istvan Zsolt ruled out my goal after a perfectly fair challenge by Derek Kevan on that colourful goalie Lev Yashin. Playing Austria a few days later, Zsolt was a linesman. He flagged against me for handball as I scored, but the ball had hit me on the side. Had he allowed either goal, England would have reached the quarter-finals and a date with Sweden, the hosts.

The 1962 World Cup was frustrating for me for other reasons. England still played 4-2-4 in those days and I enjoyed a long partnership with Johnny Haynes in midfield. The squad lodged with a copper company high in the Andes. You reached the site by scenic railway and the restaurant by a rickety old bridge. There were no televisions or telephones, it was unthinkable for wives to come out, and players easily got bored. We used to read, tell stories, or play cards. I was a reader myself. Anyway, in a kickabout with a local side I chipped an ankle bone. I was fit to return for the quarter-final with Brazil, but by then that whipper-snapper Bobby Moore, called up at the last moment, had seized my place for good.

By 1966 I thought I was playing well enough for Fulham to deserve a recall. Alf Ramsey didn't agree, so I watched the Final with my eldest son, sitting near the royal box. You can't argue with Ramsey's team selection, though I must say I would have recalled that world-class goalscorer Jimmy Greaves.

Brazil in 1970 and West Germany in 1974 were probably the two finest teams ever assembled. Though I missed 1978, I went to Spain in 1982 as Ron Greenwood's lieutenant. I had agreed to succeed him and I learned much.

During my eight years in charge I never lost a World Cup qualifier. Mexico '86 marked my baptism on football's world stage. What traumas lay in store, defeat by Portugal, Ray Wilkins' sending off, Bryan Robson's dislocated shoulder. My namesake was the toughest player I ever knew. But sitting in the changing room at half-time he was ghostly white with pain. I had to say 'get him out of the room!' I could not let the other players dwell on his agony.

No one came to terms with the heat of Monterrey. Dr Vernon Edwards stuck a thermometer in the pitch and said guess the temperature. '90?' 'It's 104!' 'For god's sake don't tell the players,' I said. 'They'll melt thinking about it.'

Diego Maradona stood between us and the semi-finals. Only Pelé could match his genius. Against us, it was so obviously handball that Don Howe and I couldn't believe it. Imagine how Argentina would have reacted had we scored a goal like that. They would have lynched the ref! Maradona's second goal was magic, but an Italian defence would have chopped him down thirty yards out. Had Maradona been on our side I'm sure we would have won that tournament.

And so on to Italia '90 and that thriller with Belgium. On the bench we braced ourselves for penalties. Gascoigne made this little spurt and was brought down. He looked done, his tongue was hanging out. I could see him about to tap the free-kick sideways and waste the final seconds. I yelled at him 'Get the ball in the box!' He heard me, otherwise Platt wouldn't have scored that goal.

I knew the world was rooting for Cameroon in our next match. They were the biggest bunch I have ever seen. Giants all of them, except one, and they took him off and brought on Roger Milla, another big 'un. What a game that was, winning it, out of it, and then Gascoigne's two perfect passes to Lineker, who got chopped down for those penalties.

Gascoigne always needed careful handling. He liked to chase the ball like a dog chases a bird. Against Germany I warned him, 'Look, next to you, Matthäus is the best there is. You can't leave gaps for him to run through and score.' 'Relax boss' said Gazza. 'Go smoke your cigars and leave him to me.' I did. Although that second booking barred him from the Final, he did us proud.

That penalty shoot-out was heart-breaking. Franz Beckenbauer was gracious at the final whistle. 'No team deserved to win,' he said, because no team deserved to lose.'

It is a great pity we shall not be there in the USA but we will bounce back. As someone who has played, watched and managed teams in the World Cup it is an honour to be invited to write the foreword to this excellent book.

Bobby Robson
FC Porto, April 1994

# INTRODUCTION

England's quest for the World Cup began in the austere years following the defeat of Hitler when, along with Scotland, Wales and Northern Ireland, England deigned to enter the first post-1945 World Cup competition, the finals of which would be held in Brazil in 1950. Yet our story begins earlier. The inaugural World Cup was staged twenty years previously, in 1930, but neither England nor the other British nations competed then, nor in 1934 and 1938.

It was back in 1904 that the soccer bureaucrats of Belgium, France, Holland, Spain, Sweden, and Switzerland set up, in Paris, the Fédération Internationale de Football Association – FIFA. The aim was to establish regular international competition, to formulate a set of agreed rules, and to speculate on a future world championship. The English Football Association (the FA) gingerly signed up the following year. The Scottish, Welsh and Irish FAs soon followed, and by 1930 FIFA membership totalled forty-one countries.

Serious proposals for a soccer World Cup were aired at FIFA's 1920 conference at Antwerp. The driving force was Jules Rimet of the French FA, now also president of FIFA. He would retain this position until 1954, giving his name to the World Cup prize – the Jules Rimet trophy. His appointment, however, tallied with one of the FA's endemic disputes with FIFA, as a result of which the British associations spent much of the inter-war years disaffiliated. The very idea of foreigners tampering with the whys and wherefores of a British game rankled the FA, who treated FIFA with aloofness and condescension. They refused, for example, to accede to FIFA's diktat that matches might be played with defeated wartime enemies, Germany, Hungary and Austria. They protested the right of the Irish Free State to separate membership, though this was granted, with the result that independent Ireland participated in the World Cups of 1934 and 1938. Yet even these issues took a back seat compared with the vexed question of 'amateurism'.

In the absence of an official world football championship, the Olympic Games constituted the only internationally recognised title. Amateur soccer had come to dominate the Olympics, and Britain to dominate amateur soccer, winning Olympic gold in 1908 and 1912. These successes stiffened resistance to change, and made the FA increasingly suspicious of FIFA's flirtation with the evils of professionalism.

At the Paris Olympics of 1924, Harold Abrahams and Eric Liddell may have won gold medals on the track, as portrayed in *Chariots of Fire*, but Britain boycotted the football tournament, and did so again in 1928. The dispute had by now crystallised into the issue of 'broken-time' payments, compensation for time off work. Britain was opposed, demanding that sportsmen remain amateur not just in spirit, but to the letter. On this question there would be no swift solution. FIFA ploughed on, finalising plans for the first professional World Cup, to be held in Uruguay. The British associations turned their backs, ostracising FIFA until after the war, when London's staging of the 1948 Olympics compelled compromise. By then, of course, the first three World Cups were part of history.

It is tempting to suggest that Britain's exclusion from the inner councils of world football was a misfortune, a quirk of fate peculiar to a particular sport at a particular time. In truth, of course, the matter went far deeper, into the complex psyche of the British and their attitudes to the rest of the world. Comparisons with Britain's attempts to join the European Economic Community decades later are invidious yet illuminating. There, too, Britain remained aloof at the start, joined too late to have major decision-making power in the formative stages of the organisation, and threatens non-cooperation or withdrawal when decisions taken by her partners are not to her liking.

It has subsequently come to light that politics cast a heavy shadow over British football between the wars. The decision not to play the defeated enemy powers in 1920 owed as much to government injunction as to sporting distaste. By the dangerous 1930s, the Foreign Office was masterminding Britain's sporting fixtures to an extent unrecognised at the time. Matches with European teams were tailored to serve international diplomacy. Decisions over desirable or undesirable opponents were made less and less from Lancaster Gate (home of the FA) and increasingly from Whitehall. If Hitler wished to demonstrate Aryan superiority at the 1936 Berlin Olympics, then the Foreign Office was not above promoting football in the trust that England could tan the hide off any upstart Axis teams. In a celebrated match in Germany in 1938 the Aryan hide was indeed tanned, but not before the English players had given the Nazi salute. This had been insisted upon by the Foreign Office, to preserve protocol.

The government seemed vindicated in its faith in this country's footballers. England's international results from 1919 to 1939 sustained belief that all was well with Britain's principal invisible export. True, the footballing itinerary of that time was largely confined to tours of the dominions, designed to cement the Empire. Such matches do not appear in the official records, though England's inevitable victories kept the 'colonials' squarely in their place.

Uncomfortable, but rare, defeats were easily shrugged off as due to freaks of climate, diet or improper refereeing.

Even by the tougher yardstick of Europe, England fared equally well. European teams were regularly dumped on their backsides. Up till 1939, of almost fifty matches against continental opponents, only seven were lost. Spain first took that honour in 1929, winning 4-3 in Madrid.

Three principal challengers emerged to contest England's claim to be the uncrowned kings of soccer. The first was Uruguay. Benefiting from England's absence, Uruguay claimed Olympic soccer gold in 1924 and 1928. This, coupled with the coming centenary of her independence, and her offer to meet all costs, put Uruguay in an unassailable position amid the lobbying for the right to host the first World Cup, which Uruguay duly won. British insularity, however, precluded tours to South America, ruling out any chance of England putting the official world champions to the test.

The first continental team to take the eye was Austria's 'Wunderteam'. In thirty-odd matches between May 1931 and May 1934 they lost only once, to England, 4-3 at Stamford Bridge.

The third challenge came from Italy, hosts of the second World Cup. Not just the British teams, but Uruguay, too, declined to compete. This was partly in retaliation for only four, second-rate, European teams having participated in 1930, partly the result of a players' strike in Uruguay. Enjoying home advantage, Mussolini's *azzurri* (blues) seized the trophy, overcoming the fancied Austrians in the semi-final. Italy's was an unpopular and dubious success, her players seeking to mirror the physical brutality of the *Duce*'s regime.

They were soon put to the test. In November 1934, just months after raising the Jules Rimet trophy, the Italian team came to London. There, despite Mussolini's inducement of huge bonuses, England triumphed 3-2 in the infamous 'Battle of Highbury'. Italy played most of the game with ten men, and were three goals down at the break. They pulled two goals back and might have achieved more but for the athletic interventions of Frank Moss, the Arsenal and England goalkeeper.

Following the example of Uruguay, Italy would shortly be double world champions, adding the Olympic title. Her stature in the game was assured when, in 1938, in France, she retained football's ultimate prize, this time indisputably and in style. England had been offered a wild card entry, following Austria's *Anschluss* with Germany, but declined it.

To celebrate the FA's seventy-fifth anniversary, Highbury staged 'England v Rest of Europe'. England triumphed by three goals over Europe's best players, and were now set to take on Europe's best team. In May 1939, in Milan, England drew 2-2 with the two-time World Cup winners. The FA thrust out its chest and boasted 'we are the best'.

World War II then threw its heavy shadow over the world. International football went into hibernation, to re-emerge into a new era that would eventually acclaim the World Cup as its footballing pinnacle. Looking back to 1939, domestic British football had never been healthier, league attendances never higher. Radio had brought the game direct to those unable to attend. Buoyed up by a booming domestic game, with no foreign opposition showing themselves superior to the national team, the FA was under little pressure to compete in second-rate tournaments such as the World Cup.

Indeed, a competition ignored by British teams was widely regarded, not just at home, as inconsequential. This was an era when belief in the supremacy of the British game was shared throughout the world, and when England's results confirmed that hers was a privileged position within the game's elite. Even the United States team of 1930, backed by half a dozen ex-British pros, merited being seeded, and repaid that assessment by reaching the semi-finals. On the other hand, self-belief in one's superiority is no substitute for a trophy that confirms it. Circumstances would not again favour an English World Cup triumph until she hosted the tournament in 1966. In the meantime, she would pay the price for her earlier insularity in full, and never more spectacularly than in 1950.

# 1

# THE 1950 WORLD CUP

With the return of peace, Clement Attlee's Labour government presided over a country straining from economic and social dislocation. Sport played a valuable role in the rehabilitation of society. Organised football was prized, as it had been in wartime, both for keeping people fit and for entertaining large crowds cheaply.

Social attitudes in 1945 were incomparable to those of 1918. Following the trench horrors of World War I, Britain had closed its mind to the nightmare and returned to safe, secure, pre-war values. Not so in 1945. The traumas of the Holocaust and Hiroshima demanded that attention be switched forward, not back, to a new, more enlightened world order. In political terms this spelled electoral defeat for Churchill and the coming of the welfare state. In footballing terms war brought in its wake a new spirit of international comradeship and interdependence. British football took steps to end forever the isolationism and fuddy-duddy amateurism of the pre-war years.

To this end, two momentous changes revolutionised the English game. The first was the FA's appointment of a full-time director of coaching. Previously, the FA had lacked an overall supremo accountable for all aspects of the team's preparation, selection and tactics. Overseas tours were administered by one or more members of the FA Council (comprised, in part, of representatives of leading clubs). Each member advocated his own preferred style, team line-up, and even personal choice of trainers. Replacing one member by another meant scrapping the previous team and starting afresh. The values of continuity were not even considered.

With home matches, the situation was even worse. Teams were chosen by the FA International Selection Committee as a whole. It was customary to select a 'team' by going through the positions one by one, if necessary by vote. Inevitably, the eleven names that emerged reflected not their combined strengths and weaknesses, but the prejudices of individual committee members.

The first FA director of coaching, whose voice was added to that of the selection committee, not substituted for it, was Walter Winterbottom. Still in his early thirties and younger than several of the famous internationals he coached, Winterbottom had played centre-half for Manchester United, though he was forced into premature retirement through injury. During the war he had turned his organising talents to the Royal Air Force, where he rose to the rank of wing-commander. Through the same reasoning that appoints retired officers to the umpire's chair at Wimbledon, in the belief that they know best how to deal with errant tennis players, Winterbottom's wings, along with his footballing credentials, were seen as evidence that he knew how to handle men.

It was, however, not for some years that Winterbottom added the duties of national team manager to his coaching responsibilities. Even then the title was a misnomer, for team selection remained the prerogative of the international selection committee. Winterbottom could wield influence and expertise in a bid to field players of his choice, but the final decision still lay with the committee, and would continue to do so until the appointment as England's manager of Alf Ramsey in 1963.

The second change to emanate from the euphoria of peace in 1945-46 was the rejoining of FIFA by the British football associations. In deference to Britain's historical standing in the game, FA chairman Arthur Drewry was appointed vice-president, where he represented the interests of all four home associations. True to type, the Soviet Union accepted FIFA's invitation only on the understanding that privileges granted to Britain were extended to her. In consequence, a Soviet vice-president was also appointed.

For a brief moment it appeared that the old schism over the right to play defeated wartime enemies would lead to the blacklisting of Germany and Japan. This time, wiser counsels prevailed. The rejoining of FIFA widened the horizons of British football, not just through being eligible to compete in the World Cup, but as a tacit admission that Britain had something to learn from the game as well as to give. Although Britain's voice had always carried weight, that voice could now be raised in the inner chambers of the game's international administration.

It seems poignant, the excitement generated by soccer in those grim years. British society faced desperate hardships. By 1950 rationing was even more severe than in 1945. The man who best mirrored the times was Stafford Cripps, vegetarian Chancellor of the Exchequer, who at one stage raised basic income tax to a 'Crippling' 9s 6d in the pound. Cripps was once caricatured as living off water-cress grown on Downing Street blotting paper. Whole sections of the population lived in 'pre-fabs', boxes with flat roofs made of asbestos. Many people, looking at German industry being rebuilt with American finance, while Britain contributed resources she could not afford to an army of occupation, began to wonder if victory had not turned just a little sour.

Against this background domestic football played its greatest tune to the masses. Crowds were so huge they outstripped even those of the heady pre-war years. Total annual attendances, 35.6 million in 1946-47, reached 41.3 million by 1948-49. Nor was public interest confined to the professional teams. The amateur game also lured vast audiences. The likes of Bishop Auckland and Pegasus were household names. In 1949, 95,000 spectators turned up for the Amateur Cup Final. Increasing numbers also wanted to play the game, stretching local resources. Hackney Marshes in east London, for example, was carved into a maze of 111 pitches.

News that the 1950 World Cup, now officially called the Jules Rimet Cup, would be contested in Brazil was a natural consequence of post-war rehabilitation and reconstruction. With much of Europe still ravaged, South America was the obvious venue. Europe had, in any case, staged two finals to South America's one, and Brazil – having sought the cancelled 1942 tournament – applied unopposed.

With hindsight, as with the 1948 London Olympics, the competition came too soon. Economics and politics cast a heavy cloud. Though membership of FIFA had risen to sixty-eight, participation was patchy. The Iron Curtain had erected ideological barriers, behind which sulked the Soviet Union, Hungary and Czechoslovakia, powerful footballing nations. Germany, already a rising power in the game, had yet to be admitted to FIFA. When France learned that her Brazilian itinerary included a 2,000-mile hike from one venue to the next, she tore up her invitation. Other absentees included Austria, citing the youth of her team, Argentina, on the instructions of Juan Peron, and India, because FIFA would not permit them to play in bare feet. From a British point of view the most glaring omission was Scotland's, and there lies a tale.

## Qualifying Pool I

Sixteen final places were up for grabs. In January 1949 the World Cup organising committee convened to establish an eliminating competition. In Britain's case, it was thought expedient to employ the Home International Championship of 1949-50 as a World Cup qualifying zone.

This was practical, but hardly ideal. On grounds of equity, contenders should play each other home and away, unless on neutral ground. In the British Championship the four countries played each other once only. In consequence, two teams enjoyed two home games, the other two just one. Balance was restored every other season by reversing the fixtures. In the season in question, England and Scotland would contest the climax at Hampden Park, hardly a neutral venue with its partisan crowd and famous 'roar'. In part, perhaps, to circumvent this difficulty, the organising committee decreed that both the winners and runners-up of the British Championship would be invited to Brazil. This was illogical, in that it did not overcome the asymmetry of the fixtures. (In 1968, the European Championship qualifiers would employ the Home Internationals over two successive seasons.) It was also generous, bearing in mind that British teams had no formal World Cup credentials.

FIFA's indulgence did not close the matter. Today, appearing in the final stages of the World Cup is a national prerogative. In 1949, however, the Scottish FA (followed by the Welsh and Irish FAs), in a flurry of misplaced pride and discourtesy to FIFA, sniffily proclaimed that second place was not good enough. Unless they were crowned British champions they would not compete in Brazil. As for England, she would qualify whatever, either by skill or default.

## WALES v ENGLAND
*Saturday, 15 October 1949*                                    *Cardiff – 60,000*

England approached their opening World Cup-tie, in Cardiff, having just lost 0-2 to the Irish Republic at Goodison Park. This marked England's first ever home defeat by a non-British team, though by juggling with geography it was decided that Eire was not really 'foreign' at all, and the much-vaunted myth of England's invincibility at home lived a while longer.

England had won all three post-war internationals against Wales without the loss of a goal, and had been defeated on Welsh soil just twice this century. Football was in some ways akin to cricket in those post-war years. The international was played concurrently with a full league programme, those clubs depleted by the loss of their best players having to make do. The England team was reasonably settled. Stanley Matthews was once again out of official favour, his No. 7 shirt being worn by Tom Finney. Newcastle's Jackie Milburn ('Wor Jackie' on Tyneside) returned at centre-forward, as the search continued for a successor to Tommy Lawton. Len Shackleton, the eccentric, non-conformist Sunderland inside-left, was granted the third of his meagre five caps. He would wait five years for the next two.

Despite the handicap of fielding seven players from the English second division, it was Wales who forced the early play. For twenty minutes the English defence creaked and strained. But not for the first time, England, with what passed for good fortune, got the breaks. Cyril Sidlow might have intercepted Finney's corner. He didn't, and Milburn flicked it back for Stanley Mortensen to head home. Within minutes England were three up. Milburn was set up, first, by Finney's lob, then by one of Shackleton's famous dribbles.

The atmosphere at half-time was one of familiar perplexity. How could it be, Welshmen argued, that the better team was losing? The second half promised better things, for shortly before the interval Billy Wright, England's skipper, had been injured. Without substitutes, players did not come off unless dead. Wright spent the second half out of harm's way on the left wing. Mortensen dropped back, disrupting England's attack while not fully compensating for Wright's absence in defence.

Once again Wales pressed, their attacks spearheaded by Trevor Ford. English goalkeeper Bert Williams was soon limping, restricted to throwing out clearances. The siege was broken just once, by Milburn, who beat Sidlow in the air for his hat-trick. The indefatigable Welsh were left with just one moment to savour, when Griffiths earned a late consolation.

| WALES (0) 1 | ENGLAND (3) 4 |
|---|---|
| Griffiths 80 | Mortensen 22, |
| | Milburn 30, 34, 65 |

**WALES:** Sidlow (Liverpool), Barnes (Arsenal), Sherwood (Cardiff), Paul (Swansea), T G Jones (Everton), Burgess (Spurs), Griffiths (Leicester), Lucas (Swansea), Ford (Villa), Scrine (Swansea), Edwards (Cardiff).
**ENGLAND:** Williams (Wolves), Mozley (Derby), Aston (Man U), Wright (Wolves), Franklin (Stoke), Dickinson (Portsmouth), Finney (Preston), Mortensen (Blackpool), Milburn (Newcastle), Shackleton (Sunderland), Hancocks (Wolves).

## ENGLAND v NORTHERN IRELAND
*Wednesday, 16 November 1949*          *Maine Road, Manchester – 70,000*

England went in search of two more points, against Northern Ireland, at Maine Road, home of Manchester City. The Irish and Welsh in those days were never invited to Wembley. As it happened, London had been blacked out for days by smog, and traffic was at a standstill. The poor view could not have assisted sightings of the first commercial jet, the Comet, undergoing test flights between Edinburgh and London.

London, in any case, had more romantic heroes to attend to. Wednesday, 16 November marked the official reception for officers and men of *HMS Amethyst*. Earlier that year the sloop, making her way up the Yangtze river to Nanjing, had come under fire from Chinese communists. The British public waited spellbound as months later, rescue missions having been repulsed, the stricken vessel finally escaped, to have her exploits admired in due course by multitudes of cinema-goers.

Though the sun peeped through for the heroes of the *Amethyst*, Mancunians had to endure continuous drizzle. Still, the England team saw no reason to be depressed. Ireland had not beaten them for twenty-two years. To make matters worse, Scotland had just thrashed them 8-2.

England showed six changes from the side that dealt flatteringly with the Welsh. Bert Williams was still injured, allowing Bernard Streten of Luton Town his one and only cap. Milburn, too, was unfit, his place taken by Jack Rowley of Manchester United. Shackleton had returned to the wilderness, the steelier talents of Stan Pearson, Rowley's partner at Old Trafford, being preferred. The Portsmouth winger, Jack Froggatt, made his debut in the No. 11 shirt.

The match proved to be an Irish nightmare. Shortly after the half-hour England led by four goals. Rowley bagged the first; the impressive Froggatt combined with Finney for the second; Pearson plundered the third, before Finney's flashing centre was spectacularly headed into the net by Stan Mortensen.

The second half provided no respite for the green shirts. Straight from the kick-off Rowley headed England's fifth. Mortensen's ferocious drive made it six. At the other end, Sammy Smyth struck one for Ireland. Rowley replied twice more, and the score was 8-1 with less than an hour played. The assembled press were fast running out of note-paper, but the match had two more goals in store, England's ninth, by Pearson, Ireland's second, by Bobby Brennan. The result sent sports writers scurrying for their reference books to check when Ireland last provided such merriment (England scored 13 in 1899). Poor Hugh Kelly, the Northern Ireland goalkeeper, endured a plague of back passes in the final minutes as his defenders tried to keep the score respectable!

ENGLAND   (4) 9                    NORTHERN IRELAND   (0) 2
   Rowley 5, 47, 55, 58,              Smyth 52, Brennan 85
   Froggatt 28, Pearson 31, 75,
   Mortensen 35, 50

ENGLAND: Streten, Mozley, Aston, Watson, Franklin, Wright, Finney, Mortensen, Rowley, Pearson, Froggatt.
N IRELAND: Kelly (Fulham), Feeney (Swansea), McMichael (Newcastle), Bowler (Hull), Vernon (WBA), McCabe (Leeds), Cochrane (Leeds), Smyth (Wolves), Brennan (Birmingham), Tully (Celtic), McKenna (Huddersfield).

## SCOTLAND v ENGLAND
*Saturday, 15 April 1950*                    *Hampden Park, Glasgow – 134,000*

By the time of the big 'un, in April 1950, President Truman had announced a programme to develop the hydrogen bomb, a doomsday weapon out of all proportion to the atomic devices dropped on Japan; and for some weeks the first McCarthy witch-hunts against alleged communist sympathisers had sent shock-waves through American society. The British government chose match-day to put an end to fish rationing. Housewives celebrated by panic buying, and bulk-purchasing at fishing ports sent fish prices soaring – which defeated the object of the exercise. Fish of a non-edible variety (though in days of rationing one could never be sure) were flooding pet-shops from Italy, heralding a boom in goldfish. The going price was sixpence an inch.

The footballers of England and Scotland did not need the stimulus of a fish bonanza to appreciate what was at stake. The World Cup finals were just two months away. Scotland had defeated Wales 2-0, and the decider was here, now.

Had Scotland backed down, they and England would already be preparing for Brazil, enabling the match to be fought for prestige and nothing else. As it was, Scotland's continuing insistence on travelling only as champions lent the fixture added spice. Interest was world-wide, outside eyes peering at this most private of British ritual skirmishes. Brazilian representatives came to plead with the Scottish FA to reconsider, as well as to indulge in a little spying on their likely rivals.

With Scotland and England both on four points, the Scots required only a draw to share the championship and pack for Brazil. Disingenuous rumours began to circulate. A draw would surely satisfy all parties. Scotland could travel to Brazil on their own terms, England would accompany them, and both countries would share the British Championship. The perpetrators of such rumours did not appreciate the depths to which Anglo-Scottish rivalry plunged. This would be no fix.

The form book was confusing. Scotland were defending British champions, but they had not enjoyed a home victory over the auld enemy since 1937. England, moreover, since hammering nine past Northern Ireland, had recorded a 2-0 victory at White Hart Lane over a makeshift Italian side.

Scotland picked a side containing just four Anglos (players from the English league), and took the field with the weight of Saturn on their shoulders. Nevertheless, in front of 134,000 raucous spectators, they did not dally in pressing forward. Within two minutes Bauld, the Hearts centre-forward, swerved clear to shoot hurriedly straight at Williams. With a cooler head he might have christened his international baptism more rapturously. His effort was to prove memorable chiefly because, as time wore on, Scotland found the England goal an ever-receding target. Half-time arrived, still goalless, but with England beginning to impress. The visitors were matching the Scots' famed ground passing, while the Scottish threesome of McColl (right-half), Moir (inside-right) and Waddell (outside-right) were being short-changed by the probing of Middlesbrough's Wilf Mannion and the covering of Portsmouth's Jimmy Dickinson.

A family outbreak of measles had caused Mannion to miss team-training. Six minutes after the restart he 'scored', but was ruled offside. Scotland, however, were now enjoying their brightest spell, inspired by Billy Liddell, the legendary left-winger of 'Liddellpool'. One sensed that his struggle with England full-back Alf Ramsey would prove the key to the match.

But it was England who took the lead. Mannion slipped the ball to Bolton's Bob Langton and moved wide, dragging McColl and Young with him. Langton cut inside and passed to Chelsea's Roy Bentley, who evaded Woodburn and

Cowans belly flops, but Mortensen's 'goal' is offside. (v Scotland)

shot on the run. The ball cannoned off Cowan's despairing hands and into the Scottish net.

134,000 voices jammed. At that instant Scotland's dreams of Brazil were reduced to just that. England began to assert themselves, though it was Scotland who came nearest to scoring. Williams made a flying save from Liddell's volley that etched itself on the memory of all who saw it. Then Bauld took a pass from Steel but, clean through, he shot agonisingly against the underside of the bar. Only seven minutes then remained and the Hampden roar was curiously stilled. And when Waddell cut inside to shoot over, Scotland's last gesture was spent.

The arguments, and begging, continued a while longer, but the Scottish FA remained adamant. Stanley Rous, secretary of the English FA, tried to intercede, and Billy Wright urged his opposite number, George Young, to use his influence. All was to no avail. Scotland would not compete in Brazil. The Scottish people were understandably miffed. One early casualty was the Scottish vice-president of FIFA, who failed to be re-elected.

Significantly, Scottish and English pundits had predicted an England win. Apart from cries of 'bad luck' from the tartan faithful, most judges credited England with a deserved victory. *The Scotsman* conceded, 'England were just about good value for their win.' One correspondent put his finger on the cause of Scotland's demise. Praising the tartan spirit, he suggested that the navy shirts would 'gladly have chased the ball over the stand and into the carpark'. Their talents might have been put to more constructive use.

| SCOTLAND (0) 0 | ENGLAND (0) 1 |
|---|---|
| | Bentley 63 |

SCOTLAND: Cowan (Morton), Young (Rangers), Cox (Rangers), McColl (Rangers), Woodburn (Rangers), Forbes (Arsenal), Waddell (Rangers), Moir (Bolton), Bauld (Hearts), Steel (Derby), Liddell (Liverpool).
ENGLAND: Williams, Ramsey, Aston, Wright, Franklin, Dickinson, Finney, Mannion, Mortensen, Bentley, Langton.

*Qualifying Pool I*

| | P | W | D | L | F | A | Pts |
|---|---|---|---|---|---|---|---|
| ENGLAND | 3 | 3 | 0 | 0 | 14 | 3 | 6 |
| Scotland | 3 | 2 | 0 | 1 | 10 | 3 | 4 |
| Northern Ireland | 3 | 0 | 1 | 2 | 4 | 17 | 1 |
| Wales | 3 | 0 | 1 | 2 | 1 | 6 | 1 |

*Other group results*
N Ireland v Scotland  2-8   Scotland v Wales  2-0     Wales v N Ireland  0-0

## World Cup finals – BRAZIL                                    June-July 1950

England now found themselves with the chance to put their feet where their mouths were, and show that they were indeed world masters of football. They entered the final competition as joint favourites with the hosts, Brazil. Confidence was high, and with justification. Since international competition resumed after the war, England had claimed some notable scalps. In 1947, for example, Portugal were thrashed by the astronomic margin of 10-0 in Lisbon. Reigning world champions Italy had been beaten twice; the first time, in Turin, comprehensively 4-0. Prior to the second encounter, won 2-0 at White Hart Lane, disaster had struck the Italian team as it would Manchester United's nine years later. In May 1949 seventeen Torino players, eight of them internationals, had perished in a plane crash near Turin. Amid the carnage on an Italian hillside it was clear that Italy would struggle to retain the trophy.

Following victory over Scotland, England squeezed in two friendlies before departing for South America, gaining victories over Portugal (5-3) in Lisbon and Belgium (4-1) in Brussels. Neither victim would be competing in Brazil: Portugal had been hammered by Spain in the qualifiers and Belgium withdrawn from their matches with Switzerland. All told, by the time England set off they had played over thirty internationals since the war, losing only four.

The 1950 World Cup employed a unique procedure for electing the soccer champions of the world. Several permutations had been tried over the previous tournaments, and would be experimented with in future. Back in 1930, a mere thirteen countries had been divided, Procrustean fashion, into four groups, the winners of each then meeting in semi-finals and Final. The 1934 competition preferred a straight knock-out, inviting Brazil and Argentina from the other side of the world, then sending them back home again after their first defeat ninety minutes later. The same format was repeated in 1938.

Apologists for the knock-out versus the mini-league formulae continue their arguments to the present day. The clean-cut knock-out makes for better spectacle, leading to its gladiatorial climax. The FA Cup in England thrives on this heart-stopping, sudden-death atmosphere. Yet, as a means of finding the best soccer nation in the world, the one-off knock-out is unsatisfactory. It is no accident that in the annual Charity Shield match at Wembley between the League champions and the FA Cup winners, the League champions invariably triumph. Any team can have an off-day, or suffer a cruel deflection or critical refereeing error, and find itself dumped from cup competition. To head a league table after a series of matches is much the truer guide to the all-round better team.

There is, furthermore, the economic argument. A league format guarantees more games, and hence greater receipts. The 1930 Uruguay tournament comprised just eighteen matches. That number had risen to thirty-eight by 1974, and the competitions from 1982 onwards reaped the rewards from fifty-two fixtures.

On the other hand, the round-robin process encourages computer soccer, teams calculating before they take the field whether they can afford a 0-0 draw, or must go for a minimum 3-0 win, or whatever. Matches in which only one team needs, and even tries, to win are the curse of football. Furthermore, under the league system, teams may be eliminated though unbeaten (Scotland in 1974) or prosper without winning (Ireland in 1990).

In 1950, FIFA elected to use the league format from start to finish. Four groups of four teams would be followed by the four respective winners contesting a final four-team pool. At least that was the theory. But by the time the tournament opened only thirteen teams were present. Four of these were seeded, Brazil as hosts, Italy as holders, Uruguay as former-holders, and the British champions, England. It would not be the last time England would be seeded in the face of modest – or as now, non-existent – achievements in the World Cup.

England were assigned to Pool II, along with Spain, Chile and the United States. Chile and the United States were completely unknown quantities, untested in a full international. Spain, however, had ignominiously inflicted

England's first ever defeat by a non-British team, in 1929, though they had been made to pay for their impertinence to the tune of 7-1 at Highbury two years later. Fortunately, England would face Spain last. All in all, what with England embarking to an unknown continent, and having to play two unknown teams, there were grounds for proper caution.

To those who would but see them, there were signs that the footballing gap with the rest of the world was closing. In November 1945, before the dust of war had settled, Moscow Dynamo, in effect the Soviet national team, toured Britain, stunning vast audiences with their slick technique and ruthless application. Over a quarter of a million people saw Chelsea and Glasgow Rangers scrape draws, Arsenal lose 3-4 (despite the guest appearance of Stanley Matthews), and Cardiff get thrashed 1-10. The multitudes could not believe their eyes. If this was happening in the Soviet Union, disrupted by war far more severely than Britain, what progress was football making elsewhere? Perhaps it was just as well that Stalin's men declined the trip to Brazil.

England's first and third group matches were scheduled for the Maracanà Stadium in Rio de Janeiro. This massive, three-tiered edifice could accommodate 200,000 people, and it remains the largest amphitheatre of its kind in the world. Surrounding the pitch was a security moat three metres wide, which could be swiftly flooded if necessary. Among the stadium's other innovations were two hundred arc lamps, the precursors of floodlights. In those pre-global TV days, no one had to worry about kick-off times coinciding with peak viewing in Europe. There was talk of England being invited to avoid the heat of the Brazilian summer by playing their matches in the evening under lights, but it appears they refused.

The Maracanà, built in a desperate rush to be finished in time, still had the air of a gigantic builder's yard for the final match, though that did not prevent 199,854 hardy souls packing inside to see it. The stadium's seats were painted bright blue, the explanation being that blue had a calming effect on people, whereas other colours were more excitable. With this insight, one is tempted to ask what colours the Argentines employed in their stadia in 1978.

The welfare of the England players was virtually non-existent. They arrived in this unfamiliar continent with just five days to acclimatise. Winterbottom did much of the cooking for the players. No doctor was taken along to protect them from South America's peculiar health hazards. Instead, the services of a local physician, supplied by the Brazilian Sports Federation, were gratefully accepted. Whether or not this gentleman specialised in sports medicine is not known. What is known is that he advised the England team on everything from diet to vitamin pills. Besides which he possessed a liberal supply of sleeping tablets, which he prescribed willy-nilly to offset the explosions of firecrackers outside England's hotel, the Luxor, on Copacabana beach. During the day, the team's training sessions were admired by flocks of grazing sheep, and through the windows by the Luxor's staff, decked out in smart new uniforms of gold, fawn and blue in honour of their distinguished guests. The chief porter was to be heard earnestly practising his English, muttering 'welcome, sir' *ad infinitum* to all and sundry. Even the Brazilian press seemed awed by the country's star visitors. Banner headlines proclaimed 'The Kings of Football have arrived'.

The England squad of twenty-one players was ageing and, if measured in caps earned per man, inexperienced – both to some extent a consequence of the recent world war.

| Position | Name | Club | Age | Caps | Goals |
|----------|------|------|-----|------|-------|
| Goalkeepers | Bert Williams | Wolves | 28 | 7 | – |
| | Ted Ditchburn | Tottenham | 28 | 2 | – |
| Full-backs | Jack Aston | Manchester U | 28 | 14 | – |
| | Alf Ramsey | Tottenham | 30 | 5 | – |
| | Laurie Scott * | Arsenal | 33 | 17 | – |
| | Bill Eckersley | Blackburn | 23 | – | – |
| Half-backs | Billy Wright (c) | Wolves | 26 | 29 | 2 |
| | Laurie Hughes | Liverpool | 24 | – | – |
| | Jimmy Dickinson | Portsmouth | 25 | 7 | – |
| | Bill Nicholson | Tottenham | 31 | – | – |
| | Willie Watson | Sunderland | 30 | 2 | – |
| Forwards | Jackie Milburn | Newcastle | 26 | 7 | 6 |
| | Stan Mortensen | Blackpool | 29 | 18 | 15 |
| | Roy Bentley | Chelsea | 27 | 4 | 2 |
| | Wilf Mannion | Middlesbrough | 32 | 19 | 9 |
| | Tom Finney | Preston | 28 | 25 | 18 |
| | Eddie Baily | Tottenham | 23 | – | – |
| | Jimmy Mullen | Wolves | 27 | 4 | 2 |
| | Stanley Matthews | Blackpool | 35 | 30 | 10 |
| | Henry Cockburn | Manchester U | 27 | 10 | – |
| | Jim Taylor | Fulham | 32 | – | – |

\* Would not play in the finals or in future.         *Averages  28.2    9.5*

Certain of England's established internationals would have held their own in any company. Bert Williams, the Wolves goalkeeper, who had taken over the responsibilities performed so flamboyantly by Frank Swift, was more highly regarded then than now, principally because the records show he retired with just three clean-sheets in twenty-four internationals. Tall, fair and quietly spoken, his speed off his line had earned him the nickname 'the Cat'.

In front of Williams, right-back Alf Ramsey was a late developer – thirty years old with just one season as a full international behind him. Ramsey was one of the game's thinkers. His was the constructive rather than the destructive approach, forever looking to pass out of defence, though his lack of speed could be cruelly exposed.

England's front line 'W' formation appeared irresistible. England took to Brazil three proven wingers – Matthews, Finney and Wolves' Jimmy Mullen. Challenging for the inside- and centre-forward slots were other great names in English soccer. Wilf Mannion was short and fair, swift of foot, immeasurably graceful, and blessed with a devastating body swerve. An unselfish player, Mannion preferred to let the ball do the work.

Stanley Mortensen was disparagingly known as 'the other Stanley' in Blackpool's side. That Mortensen was playing at all in 1950 was a bonus for club and country, the player having survived head and back injuries from a wartime crash in a Wellington bomber. Though Mortensen was not a ball-player, and limited in the air, with his hunched shoulders and spindly legs he was a goal-poacher supreme. He eventually retired with a tally of twenty-three from just twenty-five internationals.

Tynesiders always reckoned Jackie Milburn worth more than thirteen caps. Wor Jackie was fast. His parents judged well in giving him the initials J.E.T. He, too, overcame physical handicaps, in his case a boyhood attack of fibrositis in the neck, and was another modest header of a ball, but his dramatic acceleration could, and did, turn matches.

In only one position were England short of the best available. Cornelius (Neil) Franklin of Stoke City was indubitably England's finest centre-half, but he had pioneered a posse of mercenary players chasing gold abroad, in his case, in Colombia. For breaking his contract with Stoke, the FA suspended Franklin indefinitely. Even when, disillusioned, he returned home by the end of the year, the international ban stayed.

Franklin had sailed for South America only a month before his former team-mates arrived on a nobler mission. His place at the heart of England's defence was assumed by Laurie Hughes of Liverpool, whose international career began and ended with the 1950 World Cup finals. The void in England's defence would take years to fill. By 1954 eleven players had tried on the No. 5 shirt, before Billy Wright did so and made it his own.

## CHILE v ENGLAND
*Sunday, 25 June 1950*                                    *Rio – 29,703*

As England prepared for their coming ordeal with Chile, events elsewhere threatened to make football an irrelevance. Communist forces had surged across the 38th Parallel that divided North from South Korea. The United

States, which had occupied and financed the South since 1945, was immediately sucked into her first major post-war military entanglement. The world held its breath as the cold war threatened a rapid change in temperature.

The British public had other matters to attend to as England's footballers toiled. Complaints were voiced in the House of Commons about the ease with which nylons 'laddered'; Robert Newton was starring in *Treasure Island*, Walt Disney's first cinematic venture outside cartoons; and London milkmen, used to a morning lie-in, were informed that the ban on deliveries before 7.30 a.m. was to be lifted – a consequence of the ending of petrol rationing.

The most sensitive issue of the day was that of public morality. The press reported the fears and chastisements of an indignant clergy. Brighton was condemned as 'morally dead' for allowing cinemas to open on Sundays. Under the Sunday Observance Act of 1781 it was an offence even to kiss a girl on that day. The BBC was criticised for broadcasting programmes on evolution, which were taken to contradict the teachings of the Bible. The crusade climaxed with the intervention of the King during royal addresses at Canterbury and York, the monarch denouncing the declining standards of moral conduct.

Cosseted in their hotel under the watchful eye of their Brazilian doctor and his ready supply of sedatives, not to mention the restraints imposed by their £2 per day pocket money, the England players were in no grave danger of moral laxity. Otherwise, the elements conspired to make them feel at home. Before the match with Chile heavy rain softened the pitch and doused the ardour of 30,000 curious Brazilians by sprinkling them through the half-completed roof.

Against Chile, Stanley Matthews remained an absentee, not having been asked to pull on an England shirt for a year. Finney and Mullen were the preferred wingers. Bentley kept his place instead of Milburn. The Chilean team had enjoyed a bye to the finals when Argentina, who were surely stronger, refused to take part. Chile boasted just one full-time professional, George Robledo, Milburn's team-mate at St James's Park, but it was the South Americans who impressed with their neat inter-passing. Jack Aston, struggling at left-back, permitted one teasing centre to fly across Williams' goal.

Against the flow of traffic England scored, Mortensen's head connecting with Mullen's cross to net from close range. Muñoz replied by hitting a post. The longer the game progressed the more likely it seemed that Chile would equalise. To boos from the crowd, England resorted to back-passes to relieve the pressure. Then Mannion scored the second, a fine goal, engineered by Mortensen and assisted by Finney.

The woodwork prevented further goals at both ends. Chile came closest when Robledo's thirty-yard free-kick cannoned back into play. The final whistle blew on a patchy England performance, for whom Bentley had been one of the few qualified plusses, roaming hither and thither to the confusion of all. But at least the first hurdle had been safely overcome.

Mortensen, flat out, watches Mannion score England's second. (v Chile)

CHILE  (0) 0                    ENGLAND  (1) 2
                               Mortensen 39, Mannion 70

CHILE: Livingstone, Farias, Roldan, Alvarez, Busquet, Carvalho, Mayanes, Cremaschi, Robledo, Muñoz, Diaz.
ENGLAND: Williams, Ramsey, Aston, Wright, Hughes, Dickinson, Finney, Mannion, Bentley, Mortensen, Mullen.

## UNITED STATES v ENGLAND

*Thursday, 29 June 1950*                    *Belo Horizonte – 10,151*

Four days is a long time in sport. It is also a long time in politics. By the time England took the field against the United States, world peace had taken another lunge backwards. Truman had ordered American air and naval forces into Korea – seeking to appear conciliatory by designating his forces as United Nations 'peacekeepers'. It would not be long before General MacArthur, in command of the US (and UN) forces in Korea, would be threatening the use of the atomic bomb. The day before the first ever United States v England soccer match, Anglo-American peacetime cooperation reached new heights. Attlee put British naval forces in the Far East at the disposal of the United States.

At home, Britain's leaders debated the merits of the Schuman Plan, forerunner of the Common Market. By coincidence, cross-Channel ferries to France were reintroduced for the first time since 1938. The sporting headlines of 29 June made gloomy reading. At Lord's, the West Indies won their first ever test match in Britain – by 326 runs. Sonny Ramadhin and Alfred Valentine did the damage with the ball, Clyde Walcott with the bat. At Wimbledon, Britain's last hope in the men's singles disappeared when Tony Mottram was beaten by Geoff Brown of Australia.

The last week of June was also 'National Baby Week', promoted annually by the National Baby Welfare Council to educate the public on the consequences of the post-war baby boom. Parents were exhorted to cut out expressions such as 'diddums' which were considered to be insulting to a child. Nor should they speak about their indigestion or lumbago in front of children, for fear of inducing similar preoccupation in infants with their own needs. It was also wrong to get angry when a child banged his spoon on the table, for this was no more than an 'exercise in muscular coordination'.

Winterbottom was hoping for better muscular coordination against the USA than was shown against Chile. England's second match was to be played at Belo Horizonte (pronounced 'Bel Orizonch'), a fresh-aired mining town 300 miles from Rio. Translated, Belo Horizonte means 'beautiful horizon'. Today, an impressive stadium adorns Belo Horizonte, but in 1950 the town could provide only a shabby little ground, made worse by a bumpy pitch and long grass. A red cinder track round the perimeter lay in wait for players unwise enough to stumble over the touchline. On three sides the arena was walled in, claustrophobically, making the place reminiscent of a bullring. The stadium lacked proper changing facilities and the England players arrived at the ground in their team bus already kitted out for the match.

Responsibility for team selection during the World Cup rested with FA chairman Arthur Drewry. His decision was to field an unchanged team, again leaving out Milburn – and Matthews, for whom special travelling arrangements had had to be made to make him available. Matthews had been with an FA touring party of USA and Canada. Just two weeks before the fateful encounter in Brazil, an England XI scraped a 1-0 win in New York against the USA World Cup team.

The United States, semi-finalists in 1930, had qualified this time at the expense of Cuba, having lost six goals to Mexico home and away in their other two qualifiers. If those results suggested the Americans were set to be trodden underfoot, Spain had just discovered otherwise. With just ten minutes to play, the United States led 1-0. An almighty shock was on the cards when Spain rallied with a three-goal finale.

With England wearing blue, Wright won the toss and under heavy cloud elected to play into a light breeze. Williams was the first keeper to save – from

Bert Williams gathers the ball to thwart a USA attack. (v USA)

John Souza, scorer against Spain. Several times the sash-shirted Americans, shrugging off the effects of a late-night party, ploughed their way forward. Bentley dallied and was robbed as England began to press, only to be slapped in the face as America dashed upfield and scored. McIlvenny (a Scot who had once reached the dizzy heights of seven games for Wrexham) threw the ball to Bahr, who struck goalwards from twenty-five yards. Williams would have saved, but Joe 'Larry' Gaetjens, the Haitian centre-forward, lunged at the ball with his head. He made contact, but not much, and not as intended, but enough to have Williams moving one way but beaten the other.

England attacked as best they could. Bentley switched to the right, Mortensen to the middle, and Finney to inside-right. Finney hit a post. Mannion did likewise. Finney shot over the bar as, according to one jaundiced commentator, England's forwards tried to walk the ball into the net. American keeper, Borghi, a pro baseball player, declined to make an obliging blunder. In the dying minutes Ramsey's free-kick was met firmly by Mullen's header. The ball, insisted many, was over the line before a despairing limb scooped it clear. By this time firecrackers were exploding around the stadium. A flurry of English shots, too high or too wide, was interrupted by the Italian referee's concluding whistle. The American players were carried shoulder high as inquests began into England's first and most infamous defeat in the World Cup.

During the search for scapegoats, Arthur Drewry was said to be considering an appeal to FIFA on the grounds that the United States had fielded an ineligible player. Though no such appeal was made, the accusation of 'non-Americans' perverting the course of soccer justice persists. In fact, eight of the victorious team were born in the United States, six of them in St Louis. The three exceptions, who qualified under FIFA's 'residency' ruling, were McIlvenny the Scot, Gaetjens the Haitian and a Belgian left-back.

Not that the American public could understand the hullabaloo. What was headlines in London was small print in New York. No ticker-tape reception would greet their heroes. Americans couldn't give a damn.

UNITED STATES  (1) 1          ENGLAND  (0) 0
    Gaetjens 38

USA: Borghi, Keough, Maca, McIlvenny, Colombo, Bahr, Wallace, Pariani, Gaetjens, J Souza, E Souza.
ENGLAND: Williams, Ramsey, Aston, Wright, Hughes, Dickinson, Finney, Mannion, Bentley, Mortensen, Mullen.

## SPAIN v ENGLAND
*Sunday, 2 July 1950*                                    *Rio – 74,462*

England had three days in which to repair their tattered morale and, more importantly, rearrange their standing in Pool II. On the other side of the world the Korean War hummed along, boosted by a contingent of British warships. Further south, in Indo-China, the first American military aid was handed over to the French, and America's inexorable slide into Vietnam had begun. Too fearful to discuss these frightful happenings, and too ashamed to dwell on events in Brazil, people turned for consolation to 'pets'. It was not just goldfish that were enjoying a boom. The latest craze was tortoises, said to be flooding into the country from one firm alone at the rate of 30,000 a week.

Only days previously the England team had been glad to leave behind the rubble of the Maracanà for the mountain air of the 'beautiful horizon'. Now they couldn't wait to be back. At least the Maracanà would remind them of the scent of victory. There were those who feared for Spain should they now take England lightly, and who argued that the jolt to England's esteem was just the tonic to make them pull up their socks.

In fact, England's future in the competition now hung by a thread. Spain had beaten Chile 2-0. With just one team progressing to the final pool, it was imperative that England beat Spain. But as FIFA had at this time no approved means for separating teams level on points, England would have to beat Spain twice, the second time in a play-off, to stay alive. If the United States should beat Chile, thereby also finishing with four points, all manner of complications would arise. (Chile would win 5-2.)

Inevitably, the England teamsheet was torn up. Jack Aston, uncomfortable in both matches, stepped aside for Bill Eckersley. It was the Blackburn full-back's first cap. The front line was completely reshaped. Matthews was at last, irresistibly, brought in for his first World Cup match. Finney, as always when Matthews played, switched to outside-left. The quicksilver skills of Jackie Milburn were restored to centre-forward. English 'spies' had reported a square-looking Spanish defence vulnerable to the through pass which Milburn might exploit. Mortensen switched from inside-left to inside-right, and Spurs' Eddie Baily earned the first of his nine England caps, at No. 10.

This new formula at least won praise from onlookers. For the first time it was England, not their opponents, who began in a rush. Within minutes reserve goalie Ramallets, scrambled away Mortensen's header. Ramallets could do nothing with Milburn's header from Finney's cross, but the Italian referee chalked it off for offside. Press photographs showed Milburn onside, and an English 'if only' was committed to folklore.

England's quiet optimism vanished five minutes after the break. The ball was floated in from the wing, Laurie Hughes bungled his clearance, and Zarra headed past the advancing Williams. Thereafter Spain sat back, packed their defence and played out time.

Supposedly the best in the world, England had been comprehensively exposed. Talk of bad luck, as was heard after the USA match, could find no listeners a second time. Instead it was painfully conceded that England had come to teach but should stay to learn. Not that they did. The England party had been scheduled to depart, revealingly, after the competition's finale. Long before then they had packed their bags and fled.

With hindsight, England might have been grateful to escape while they could, for awaiting Spain in the final pool was a 1-6 drubbing by Brazil, who in due course met Uruguay at the climax. Despite Brazil's home advantage it was Uruguay who triumphed. In the twenty years since the first World Cup, just two names – Uruguay and Italy – were inscribed upon it.

SPAIN   (0) 1                        ENGLAND   (0) 0
Zarra 50

SPAIN: Ramallets, Alonzo, Parra, J Gonzalvo, M Gonzalvo, Puchades, Basora, Igoa, Zarra, Panizo, Gaínza.
ENGLAND: Williams, Ramsey, Eckersley, Wright, Hughes, Dickinson, Matthews, Mortensen, Milburn, Baily, Finney.

*Final positions – Pool II*

|  | P | W | D | L | F | A | Pts |
|---|---|---|---|---|---|---|---|
| SPAIN | 3 | 3 | 0 | 0 | 6 | 1 | 6 |
| England | 3 | 1 | 0 | 2 | 2 | 2 | 2 |
| Chile | 3 | 1 | 0 | 2 | 5 | 6 | 2 |
| United States | 3 | 1 | 0 | 2 | 4 | 8 | 2 |

*England appearances and goalscorers*
*World Cup qualifying rounds and final competition 1950*

| | Apps | Goals | | Apps | Goals | | Apps | Goals |
|---|---|---|---|---|---|---|---|---|
| Wright W | 6 | – | Mannion W | 3 | 1 | Shackleton L | 1 | – |
| Finney T | 6 | – | Bentley R | 3 | 1 | Watson W | 1 | – |
| Mortensen S | 6 | 4 | Hughes L | 3 | – | Rowley J | 1 | 4 |
| Williams B | 5 | – | Mozley B | 2 | – | Pearson S | 1 | 2 |
| Aston J | 5 | – | Milburn J | 2 | 3 | Froggatt J | 1 | 1 |
| Dickinson J | 5 | – | Mullen J | 2 | – | Langton R | 1 | – |
| Ramsey A | 4 | – | Streten B | 1 | – | Eckersley W | 1 | – |
| Franklin C | 3 | – | Hancocks J | 1 | – | Matthews S | 1 | – |
| | | | | | | Baily E | 1 | – |

|  |  |
|---|---|
| *25 players* | *16 goals* |

# 2

# THE 1954 WORLD CUP

Following England's hang-dog return from Brazil, there followed an interval of over three years before they took up their World Cup cudgels again. Those years were traumatic for the future of the British as of mankind. In the field of advanced weaponry, one numbing breakthrough tumbled rapidly over another. The general public became acquainted with a new vocabulary, including 'thermo-nuclear', 'fission-fusion', 'vaporisation'. It was musical chairs with the superpower leadership. Stalin had died, while Eisenhower assumed the US presidency. Britain not only had a new prime minister – the return of Winston Churchill – but also a new monarch, Queen Elizabeth II. The latest spy scandal precipitated the flight to the Soviet Union of the agents Guy Burgess and Donald Maclean. The cold war was well and truly freezing.

All was not well within the British Empire as the stirrings of independence gathered momentum. A militant secret society in Kenya called 'Mau Mau' inflicted terror among blacks and whites alike. Elsewhere in Africa, King Farouk of Egypt was overthrown and power ultimately assumed by Gamal Abdel Nasser, while at the other end of the continent South Africa officially adopted the doctrine of apartheid.

Science and technology were transforming society. The last tram had gone from London's streets; the first jet fighter had broken the sound barrier; and the riddle of the DNA molecule had been solved, giving scientists insight into the genetics of life. The first reel-to-reel tape-recorders were being mass-marketed, while the number of televisions registered in Britain increased from 350,000 in 1950 to two million by 1952. The indoor screen would remain a minority fad until it came of age with the aid of Richard Dimbleby and the coronation in June 1953.

After years of belt-tightening, the nation was coming to terms with affluence. By 1954, Britain had squared the circle and achieved the impossible, full employment without inflation. This was, of course, an illusion, though the jangling of loose change in trouser pockets was a prerequisite for the emerging youth culture. James Dean and Marlon Brando were the young, rebellious anti-heroes of the early 1950s.

English soccer appeared archaic when set against this social and technological upheaval. The national team's humiliation in Brazil accelerated English football's plunging fortunes, as rival forms of entertainment began to compete seriously with the bleak, exposed soccer terraces. From a high of 41.3 million spectators in 1948-49, the number fell to 39 million in 1951-52. A further six million would stay away by the mid-'fifties.

England's international stature could no longer arrest the march of progress. Nevertheless, reading of English defeats in far-off lands – in what were bound to be unfair conditions – was shaky evidence for the insulated doubting Thomases. What the masses needed was to see England defeated on home soil, in front of their own eyes. That had not yet happened. But the day of reckoning was drawing perilously near. Just months after England returned from Brazil, Yugoslavia secured a 2-2 draw at Highbury. A year later France did likewise. 2-2 was again the score when the innovative Austrians turned out at Wembley. Austria modified the classic *metodo* system, pivoting the whole team around Ernst Ocwirk, an attacking centre-half. England softened this latest blow by winning 3-2 in Vienna.

In 1953 England toured North and South America, beating the United States 6-3 (three years too late) and Chile, but losing 1-2 to world champions Uruguay in Montevideo. The tourists also drew 0-0 in Argentina, where Billy Wright carried a wreath at a service for Eva Peron, who had died the previous year – a surprising omission from the Rice – Lloyd-Webber musical, *Evita*.

## Qualifying Pool III

1954 marked the fiftieth anniversary of FIFA. With its headquarters in Zurich, it had been decided back in 1946 that these, the fifth World Cup finals, be held in Switzerland. The country's political neutrality also made her a prudent choice at the height of the cold war. The Soviet Union and Argentina were the only notable absentees. The qualifying arrangements for the British contingent were a repeat of 1950. Once again, two qualifying places were on offer, and once again the British champions would be seeded in the finals. World football, it seemed, still looked up to the English game with a venerable mystique. The curious notion of announcing the seeds before they qualified meant favoured status for Northern Ireland or Wales, should they reach Switzerland. When Turkey qualified at the expense of seeded Spain, Turkey were seeded instead.

As the venues for the Home Internationals were switched each season, the fixtures for 1953-54 were a replica of those for the previous World Cup. The Irish felt particularly aggrieved: with only one home match, Switzerland was surely out of reach. Yet this time FIFA's terms were accepted. Still smarting from the recriminations of her 1950 withdrawal, Scotland announced she would not turn her back again.

## WALES v ENGLAND
*Saturday, 10 October 1953*                          *Cardiff – 61,000*

By the time England opened their World Cup account, another dependency had demanded gunboat remedies. Fears that British Guiana was turning 'red' prompted the despatch of British troops. They duly arrived, only to find hostilities adjourned while the Guianese entertained Trinidad for their annual cricket match.

The English line-up in the autumn of 1953 retained a core of players from 1950, though Bert Williams had lost his place to Birmingham's Gil Merrick. Alf Ramsey had clocked up twenty-nine consecutive caps – but was missing against Wales – and Bill Eckersley was still first choice for the No. 3 shirt.

Wright and Dickinson were unchallenged at half-back, while the latest to experiment with the centre-half slot was Harry Johnston of Blackpool. Finney and Mullen were back in harness on the wing. Mullen had the distinction of playing in the debacle against the United States, then being dropped for three years, only to reappear as soon as the next World Cup came around. Matthews was once again an international outcast. Not surprisingly, many reasoned that his international days were over. He was, after all, nearly thirty-nine.

The one stirring addition to the side had claimed the No. 9 shirt shortly after the Brazilian finals. Nat Lofthouse is remembered as the classic target man, a battering-ram of a player, totally opposed in style to the likes of Jackie Milburn. He was flanked in the middle by two new boys. Albert Quixall, just twenty, a prodigy with Sheffield Wednesday and with what many swore was a golden future, pulled on an England shirt for the first time. In the event, he would win just five caps, all of them before he turned twenty-two. Quixall's inside partner, likewise making his debut, was Wolves' Dennis Wilshaw.

For their part, Wales were handicapped by the loss of Trevor Ford, but such handicaps brought few tears when Wales simply moved John Charles from centre-half to centre-forward. Charles was probably the finest all-round Welsh footballer of his generation.

The weather took its cue. A bright day encouraged Welsh harmonies. So did events on the pitch. Ivor Allchurch's blond head flicked Foulkes' centre, the ball brushing the dust from Merrick's crossbar. Within seconds Allchurch curled a shot past the far upright.

A Welsh score seemed inevitable. The English goal had survived countless near misses before Wales took an overdue lead. The ball sped from Burgess to Charles, to Davies, to Allchurch – who drove it past Merrick. Ninian Park erupted, and not just for the goal. Few Welshmen could recall such glorious football from their team. Startled English journalists enquired whether the echoing verses of *Sospan Fach* and *Cum Rhondda* could be heard throughout the principality.

The torture continued. Within another ten minutes Charles twice grazed an upright. The break England needed owed nothing to their own football. After half an hour, Welsh full-back Alf Sherwood clashed with Finney and was seriously concussed. Up to that point England had not mustered a single attack. The last seconds of the half were expiring when Lofthouse was fouled. Quixall lobbed up the free-kick and Wilshaw was allowed a clean header into goal.

If the first period was memorable for Welsh flair, the second was about to spring immediate surprises. Facing a rearranged home defence, Mullen twice broke clear on the left. When he did so a third time, he chipped the ball onto Wilshaw's head, and to general disbelief England led 2-1. A minute later Mullen fed Wilshaw, who squared for the inrushing Lofthouse to score.

The choristers on the terraces could not believe their eyes. Wales dejectedly kicked off and immediately presented the ball to Mullen. This time his cross was met by Lofthouse's airborne header that ballooned the net. The score defied reason: 4-1 to England after fifty-two minutes.

Thereafter sanity returned, along with the dazed Sherwood groggily playing out time near the touchline, but in the face of what had passed before, the rest of the game could not easily survive in the memory. Merrick was one of the few English players who could hold their head high at the end, along with the Scottish referee, Mr Faultless.

The press was scathing. 'Larceny at Ninian Park', screamed one English headline. Some papers went so far as to doubt the existence of a worse England team. Wales had lost all four goals while reduced to ten men, conceding three headed goals from three Mullen crosses. The other winger, Tom Finney, was berated mercilessly. This was his forty-eighth international and one of his least effective. 'Bring back Matthews!' was the cry. Stanley would come again, unlike Tom Garrett, the Blackpool full-back who had replaced Ramsey. His international career was over.

With Scotland already victors over the Irish in Belfast, both they and England were well set for Switzerland. But, for the moment, tribute was owing to an exalted Welsh performance and one of the most thrilling Home Internationals ever contested. Not that football could command the headlines for long. The following day the Duke of Bedford was found dead, shot in the head, in a clump of rhododendron bushes. 'No foul play' said police.

WALES  (1) 1                    ENGLAND  (1) 4
   Allchurch 22              Wilshaw 45, 50, Lofthouse 51, 52

WALES: Howells (Cardiff), Barnes (Arsenal), Sherwood (Cardiff), Paul (Man C), Daniel (Sunderland), Burgess (Spurs), Foulkes (Newcastle), E R Davies (Newcastle), Charles (Leeds), I Allchurch (Swansea), Clarke (Man C).

ENGLAND: Merrick (Birmingham), Garrett (Blackpool), Eckersley (Blackburn), Wright (Wolves), Johnston (Blackpool), Dickinson (Portsmouth), Finney (Preston), Quixall (Sheff W), Lofthouse (Bolton), Wilshaw (Wolves), Mullen (Wolves).

## ENGLAND v NORTHERN IRELAND

*Wednesday, 11 November 1953*          *Goodison Park, Liverpool – 70,000*

England had four weeks for their blushes to disperse before taking the field against Northern Ireland at Everton. Normally, a fixture against the Irish would be considered a timely pick-me-up, witness their 9-2 trouncing in 1949. Ireland had strengthened their team since that woeful afternoon in rainy Manchester. In 1952 they had had the temerity to draw 2-2 with England in Belfast, avoiding defeat, home or away, for only the second time since 1927. And though recently going down 1-3 to Scotland, the score had flattered the Scots. Wales, too, had underlined their recent promise with a thrilling 3-3 draw at Hampden, a result that meant England could guarantee their place in Switzerland with victory at Goodison Park.

At the time, the Irish visit was viewed not as a vital qualifier but as a warm-up to prepare for distinguished footballing guests due at Wembley a fortnight hence. This was the age of the great Hungarian team – 1952 Olympic champions and unbeaten for twenty-five matches. Those who had seen the great Magyars insisted that Hungary were the best team in the world. England could allow no such claims to go unchallenged. The outing against Ireland was a timely opportunity to weld an effective combination fit to break the Magyars' winning procession.

If the visit of the Irish football team could not arouse public interest, there was much in the news that could. The popular press became mesmerised by the strange activities of youth. Dance-halls up and down the country swayed to the rhythm of the 'Creep'. Teenage boys danced in 'creepers' – drainpipe trousers and Edwardian jackets with velvet collars. The dance-steps consisted of moving two steps back and one to the side. Bemused parents and palais managers were witnessing the first symptoms of the Teddy Boy era.

Another manifestation of social change was reflected in the second Kinsey report – on female sexual behaviour. The activities admitted to, and condoned by 6,000 women interviewees sent shock waves of pious indignation throughout 'decent' folk. The press was vilified for daring to discuss Kinsey's findings. Less controversial 'progress' was manifested through an upturn in the British economy. Car manufacturers surpassed all previous records, turning out 64,000 vehicles in one month alone.

These disparate developments, taken against the dissolution of the Empire, generated much soul-searching on the virtues of being British. A backs-to-the-wall defence of our national character was proffered by the people's voice of the 1950s, Cassandra. Without a trace of tongue-in-cheek he began: 'How any foreigner could think that the British are anything other than generous, wise, courteous, sympathetic, brave, far-seeking, high-minded, intelligent, sensitive and forgiving is beyond me.'

In the days preceding the Ireland game, two prominent deaths were reported. Welsh wordsmith, Dylan Thomas, passed away in New York, having just completed his celebrated radiodrama *Under Milk Wood*. He was not yet forty. In the mountains of Arabia, King Ibn Saud, founder of Saudi Arabia, died in his sleep.

The public clamour for English heads to roll bore no connection, one hopes, to Arabian judicial process. Ramsey had returned to the side for a representative match against FIFA (4-4), but was now left out again. On this occasion his position would be filled, for the one and only time, by West Bromwich's Stan Rickaby. The crusade against Finney saw him 'rested' against FIFA, Northern Ireland, and Hungary. Matthews, now the proud possessor of a Cup Final winner's medal, returned to enjoy yet another Indian summer on the right-wing. Quixall was retained, but Wilshaw, despite his pair against Wales, was not – a fifth and final cap going to Harold Hassall of Bolton Wanderers.

If the spectators who flocked to Goodison came hoping for great things they were soon disillusioned. The ineptitude so apparent against Wales came flooding back – and this after the daftest of gift goals for England. The match had barely kicked-off when Hassall meandered towards the edge of the Irish box. His half-hearted cross-shot was permitted by Smyth to slither obligingly under his body.

England did not deserve to be in front, and nine minutes into the second half they were not. Billy Bingham's probing cross was powered goalwards by Eddie McMorran, the ball ricocheting off Merrick over the line. England now looked good bets to lose, playing without conviction, disorganised, and handicapped by a lifeless front line. The one figure to inspire the crowd was Matthews, who acknowledged his return by assuming the responsibilities of his inside-forward and right-half in addition to his own.

It was Matthews who helped restore England's advantage, jinking down the touchline and flipping the ball to Wright, who centred for Hassall to head his second. This time it was asking too much of the Irish to come back. Lofthouse and Billy Dickson rose to meet Mullen's cross. Lofthouse got there first, the ball flew past Smyth, and Dickson's head opened up Lofthouse's eye. England played out time a man short, and so did Ireland when Smyth broke his nose in a collision with Mullen's boot. Dickson took over Smyth's jersey.

Yet again a scornful public reckoned the better team had lost. No euphoria greeted England's qualification for the World Cup finals. It was, after all, taken for granted. But this England team was still widely canvassed as the worst in memory: 'What a fumbling, foozling flock of footballers' bewailed one newspaper. If the same eleven were picked to play Hungary, one soothsayer warned: 'English football will die a horrible and lasting death.' People could be forgiven for thinking that the flags flying at half-mast from government buildings were commemorating the nadir of English football. In fact, it was an act of courtesy to Saudi Arabia for the loss of her late, great king: and besides, England had another nadir just coming.

ENGLAND   (1) 3                          NORTHERN IRELAND   (0) 1
   Hassall 1, 60, Lofthouse 75           McMorran 54

ENGLAND: Merrick, Rickaby, Eckersley, Wright, Johnston, Dickinson, Matthews, Quixall, Lofthouse, Hassall, Mullen.
N IRELAND: Smyth (Distillery), Graham (Doncaster), McMichael (Newcastle), Blanchflower (Villa), Dickson (Arsenal), Cush (Glenavon), Bingham (Sunderland), McIlroy (Burnley), Simpson (Rangers), McMorran (Doncaster), Lockhart (Villa).

The days before Hungary's visit witnessed a dramatic recuperation of English soccer appetites. Peter Wilson of the *Mirror* spoke for his readers with typical understatement: 'No footballing match in our recollection has created the same bubbling, partisan, out-of-this-world, fantastic, biased, monomaniac, wooden-headed, war-to-the-knife, conservative, communist, labour – but not liberal – attitude as the clash between Hungary and England at Wembley tomorrow.'

Delightful anecdotes circulated concerning Hungary's preparations. The visitors were rumoured to be leaving nothing to chance, even installing a fog-making machine on their training pitch to simulate English weather. In the evening the Hungarians trooped to the theatre to watch the bosom and belly epic *Pardon My French.*

Only the second half of the match was televised live to a spellbound nation, for fear that earlier transmission would affect attendances at a batch of cup replays. But by half-time most of the damage had been done. Hungary demolished England 6-3 in the finest all-round performance this country has ever seen. It might have been 16-3. At long last, England had been vanquished at home, on English grass and under English conditions by a continental team. England's last claim to any sort of elite standing in the game was wiped away. For decades English soccer had consoled itself in the belief that while continental teams might express themselves more artistically, those frills were peripheral to the basic art of the game, striking power, the art of finishing. Hungary had disposed of the prejudice that foreign teams did not know the road to goal.

In World Cup terms, that damp grey November afternoon reduced England's aspirations to rubble. Six international careers were terminated, among them some illustrious names. Alf Ramsey would not play in his second World Cup finals. Nor would Eckersley. Centre-half Harry Johnston, tormented by the withdrawn tactics of Hidegkuti, was another casualty, as was Stanley Mortensen. Two players had been asked to make their debuts against Hungary. Both – Tottenham's George Robb and Blackpool's Ernie Taylor – would be left with just that one numbing experience in England white to savour. A seventh member of the team, Jackie Sewell of Sheffield Wednesday, would gain just one more cap, and was sidelined in Switzerland.

English football was in tatters. The World Cup finals were seven months away and a fresh national team had to be hastily constructed around the four shell-shocked survivors, goalkeeper Merrick, half-backs Wright and Dickinson, Stanley Matthews – plus Finney and Lofthouse, who had mercifully been spared the national humiliation.

## SCOTLAND v ENGLAND
*Saturday, 3 April 1954*                    *Hampden Park, Glasgow – 134,000*

England were excused further exposure of their limitations till the spring, when they journeyed to Glasgow for their final British qualifier. Wales and Northern Ireland had completed their programmes, leaving Scotland and England assured of their representation in Switzerland.

The current match was surrounded by none of the tension of 1950. At stake was simply the Home Championship. But that carried with it a place among the seeds in Switzerland. In view of the sorry state of English football, there were those who doubted the national team's worthiness to be seeded. But the hard facts were that since 1950 England had lost just twice to foreign opponents – to Uruguay (world champions) and to Hungary (Olympic champions).

Because the World Cup draw had been made in advance, the Scots and English already knew the alternative fates awaiting them. The British champions would face Belgium and Switzerland, while the unseeded British runners-up would land in the same daunting group as Uruguay and Austria. Having four points to Scotland's three, England needed only a draw to secure the less intimidating opposition. The form book favoured England, who had extended their winning sequence in Scotland to four matches. It was now seventeen years since Hampden last echoed to a win over the Sassenachs. England were probably glad to be playing over the border; they hadn't beaten Scotland at Wembley since 1934.

Those early days of April 1954 were notable for the grotesque images of American H-bomb tests in the Pacific. Newsreel clips of those now-familiar mushroom clouds were transmitted on small screens and large. The outcry was widespread and impassioned. For weeks, a running debate considered whether the world had a future.

Those unwilling to contemplate Armageddon sought distraction in the first waves of new, popular music from the United States. Deaf singer Johnny Ray flew into London for a three-week tour. The last verse of Frankie Laine's disc, *The Kid's Last Fight*, was banned by the BBC. The lyrics included the words 'climbing through the golden ropes of that big ring way up high', thought to be offensive to many listeners.

Zsa Zsa Gabor did not uplift the American image. She was divorcing George Sanders, her third husband. Homespun agony aunts preferred a more traditional view of marriage. Mary Brown, for one, warned a young girl contemplating sex with her boyfriend that she risked a moral struggle, pain, humiliation, shame, physical damage and, possibly, permanent frigidity if she went ahead.

Those sports buffs not preoccupied by the 100th Varsity Boat Race, won by Oxford, enjoyed a Hampden goal spree in a stadium buffeted by slanting rain and pounding wind. Winterbottom had acted swiftly to seek a fresh blend for Switzerland. His new full-backs were Ron Staniforth of Huddersfield and Roger Byrne, soon to be a key figure in Manchester United's Busby Babes. The one tall and elegant, the other short and tigerish, this partnership would stay together through the World Cup. Less fortunate was the latest stop-gap No. 5, Spurs' Harry Clarke. Up front, back came Finney to patrol one touchline, with Mullen the other – which meant no place for Matthews. The central attackers were Ivor Broadis, then of Newcastle, and the sixty-goal WBA pair, Ronnie Allen and Johnny Nicholls. Little was expected of such an inexperienced side.

The early pressure was Scotland's, assisted by a spate of free-kicks conceded by an anxious English defence. The pressure brought a goal when McKenzie's corner was converted by Brown. Despite being on the receiving end, England shortly drew level. Finney, playing so well that questions were asked about why he had ever been omitted, slipped a pass to Broadis, who in full stride hit a venomous shot high and wide of George Farm. The patter of the rain was the only audible applause.

Still Scotland looked the more dangerous. By the end of the match they had forced thirteen corners to England's one. Yet slowly the Scottish fire was doused. Even with the rain and wind at their backs after the break, the tide was turning. Finney taunted Cox, veered past him and crossed for Nicholls to head England dramatically into the lead. That goal would have dispirited many sides, and worse was to come. Midway through the half, Mullen, out wide, was pulled down. Taking the free-kick himself, he swung the ball in for Allen, soaring with arms outstretched to head goal number three.

The pace slackened on the heavy pitch. Hampden was eerily quiet, and became quieter still when Finney teased his way down the right. His centre fell perfectly onto Mullen's head. 4-1 to England. The final gesture belonged to Scotland. Willie Ormond's swirling centre confused both Merrick and Byrne. As they became entangled under the crossbar the ball, with a mind of its own, wriggled its way behind them. Official records credit the goal to Ormond.

No one could dispute England's four goals, the most scored in Scotland this century. But praise for England had to be measured against Scotland's apparent lack of fight. Long before the end Hampden's renowned roar had been quelled, and dejected, bedraggled fans were streaming for the exits. *The Scotsman* expressed its tears through verse: 'shiver'd was fair Scotland's spear and broken was her shield.'

England might not walk off with the World Cup, but at least the Scots had been put in their place.

| SCOTLAND (1) 2 | ENGLAND (1) 4 |
|---|---|
| Brown 8, Ormond 88 | Broadis 14, Nicholls 52, |
| | Allen 69, Mullen 81 |

SCOTLAND: Farm (Blackpool), Haughney (Celtic), Cox (Rangers), Evans (Celtic), Brennan (Newcastle), Aitken (Sunderland), McKenzie (Partick), Johnstone (Hibs), Henderson (Portsmouth), Brown (Blackpool), Ormond (Hibs).
ENGLAND: Merrick, Staniforth, Byrne, Wright, Clarke, Dickinson, Finney, Broadis, Allen, Nicholls, Mullen.

---

*Qualifying Pool III*

|  | P | W | D | L | F | A | Pts |
|---|---|---|---|---|---|---|---|
| ENGLAND | 3 | 3 | 0 | 0 | 11 | 4 | 6 |
| SCOTLAND | 3 | 1 | 1 | 1 | 8 | 8 | 3 |
| Northern Ireland | 3 | 1 | 0 | 2 | 4 | 7 | 2 |
| Wales | 3 | 0 | 1 | 2 | 5 | 9 | 1 |

*Other group results*
N Ireland v Scotland  1-3   Scotland v Wales  3-3    Wales v N Ireland  1-2

---

**World Cup finals – SWITZERLAND**                                    **June–July 1954**

So England, yet again, had overcome a British challenge in her quest for the Jules Rimet trophy. Scotland, for good measure, would keep them company in Switzerland, on a shoestring budget that accommodated just thirteen players. Nevertheless, the contrast in mood between 1950 and 1954 was palpable. England had flown to Brazil as the 'kings of football', wallowing in the adulation, and certain of their ability to be a major force in the competition. Insular and ill-prepared, England's downfall had been painful.

How different it seemed in June 1954. Never before had an England national team been so maligned. In just four short years, its standing in world football had plummeted from the heights to the depths. The word 'Hungary' wrapped

England in a shroud of gloom and self-doubt. There were many who doubted the wisdom of a return match with the magic Magyars, a week after losing 0-1 to Yugoslavia in Belgrade, and with the finals less than a month away. Maybe, it was reasoned, a better result than 3-6 would lift English spirits for the trials ahead. Instead, Hungary won crushingly, 7-1, England's most devastating defeat to that day or since. Many wondered what further horrors lay ahead in Switzerland, and whether it was worth competing at all. Hungary surely had the Cup wrapped up.

FIFA did its best to ensure that the organisation for the 1954 World Cup finals was the most chaotic ever devised. The procedure adopted in Brazil, of using mini-leagues from start to finish, was discarded. When Uruguay had played Brazil in the final match of the final pool, they both led the group, contesting what was, in effect, a World Cup Final. But it need not have worked out so tidily. In any case, Brazil went into that match with one point more than Uruguay, and would have lifted the trophy with a draw. That would have seemed anticlimactic, and FIFA acknowledged that future world champions be decided by the team that won on the day.

So far so good. But FIFA now applied tortuous logic and doubtful common sense. There would again be four four-team pools, but eight teams were seeded. For reasons which failed to make sense then or now, the two seeds in each group avoided each other. Each team played *two* group matches only: the two seeds played the two non-seeds, and *vice versa*. The top two teams from each pool then progressed to knock-out stages, quarter-finals, semi-finals and final.

This pool system was patently unfair, a sham league. In Pool IV, England faced the unseeded challenge of Belgium and Switzerland, but avoided Italy. Non-seeded Scotland were pooled with seeded Uruguay and Austria, yet missed out on the chance of easier points against non-seeded Czechoslovakia.

Worse was to come. It was apparent to FIFA that such a truncated programme would be likely to leave teams level on points. Though goal average would separate a tie between first and second, play-offs would be imposed on teams tieing for second and third. In a misguided effort to minimise this possibility, draws were banned. Group matches level after ninety minutes would go to extra time to try to break the deadlock. Only if teams stayed level would the result stand.

Grappling with the implications of this nonsense, England opted to send just seventeen of the permitted twenty-two players to Switzerland. The other five stayed at home, awaiting a summons that never came.

| Position | Name | Club | Age | Caps | Goals |
|----------|------|------|-----|------|-------|
| Goalkeepers | Gil Merrick | Birmingham | 32 | 20 | – |
| | Ted Burgin * | Sheffield U | 26 | – | – |
| Full-backs | Ron Staniforth | Huddersfield | 30 | 3 | – |
| | Roger Byrne | Manchester U | 24 | 3 | – |
| | Ken Green * | Birmingham | 30 | – | – |
| Half-backs | Billy Wright (c) | Wolves | 30 | 58 | 3 |
| | Syd Owen | Luton | 31 | 2 | – |
| | Jimmy Dickinson | Portsmouth | 29 | 35 | – |
| | Bill McGarry | Huddersfield | 27 | – | – |
| Forwards | Stanley Matthews | Blackpool | 39 | 36 | 10 |
| | Ivor Broadis | Newcastle | 31 | 11 | 6 |
| | Nat Lofthouse | Bolton | 28 | 19 | 20 |
| | Tommy Taylor | Manchester U | 22 | 3 | 2 |
| | Tom Finney | Preston | 32 | 49 | 23 |
| | Albert Quixall | Sheffield W | 20 | 3 | – |
| | Dennis Wilshaw | Wolves | 28 | 1 | 2 |
| | Jimmy Mullen | Wolves | 31 | 11 | 5 |

* Would not play in the finals or in future.    *Averages   28.8   14.9*

The five stay-at-home reserves were: Ken Armstrong (Chelsea), Allenby Chilton (Manchester Utd), Johnny Haynes (Fulham), Harry Hooper (West Ham), Bedford Jezzard (Fulham).

Averaging almost twenty-nine, this squad would be the oldest England would ever send to a World Cup. It was also weaker overall than in 1950. Whilst on his day Gil Merrick was as good as any goalkeeper, those days did not come around frequently enough. Full-backs Staniforth and Byrne were, of course, international novices. No satisfactory centre-half had yet been found. Equally suspect, at least compared to Mannion and Mortensen, were the current crop of inside-forwards. England's strengths lay up front. Nat Lofthouse was brave and tough, a clatterer of goalkeepers. Defences had to cope, not with close control or stealth, but with a frontal assault. Attrition was the chosen weapon, directness the preferred approach. Above all else, Lofthouse could score. He had already bagged twenty for England, more than one a game.

Five players were set to compete in their second World Cup finals. They were clustered around two positions, half-back and winger. Billy Wright and Jim Dickinson had teamed up as half-backs more than thirty times. Dickinson would eventually earn forty-eight caps over a seven-year international career.

Billy Wright would finish with more than double that number. His was an unlikely success story. As a youth he had been rejected as a professional footballer on account of his small stature. He had to overcome a broken ankle early in his career which required the insertion of a pin. Wright's was an uncomplicated game. A muscular, compact player with a bob of fair hair, he kept within his limits, sticking to the simple things but doing them supremely well. He was competent in everything, outstanding in nothing. Sound at interception, safe in distribution, quick in the tackle, and with natural timing in the air to offset his lack of inches, Wright possessed two added bonuses. He was rarely injured, missing just three internationals in thirteen years, 1946-59, and none since 1951. He was also temperamentally unflappable, never booked for club or country. As a captain, his was the quiet approach, leading by example rather than the shaken fist.

For wingmen, England took to Switzerland the same trio as went to Brazil – Finney, Matthews, and Mullen. The debate over Matthews and Finney's relative attributes probably has no parallel. Both were exceptionally talented, but in quite different ways. Matthews was the maverick of the English team, a winger who demanded that the ball be played to his feet, and who would then freeze the game as the opposing full-back squared up. A nod to the left, a nod to the right, and Matthews was gone, a paralysing sleight of body and feet setting him free to curl in a cross. Matthews wore an expressionless mask as he performed his carnage. He seemed ageless. He and Tommy Lawton were the only players to appear for England before the war and after. His first full cap had been earned back in 1934. With his bowed legs and rounded shoulders he was already a national institution, and would become the only professional footballer to be knighted before retirement. His skills were so feared that, over the years, when opposing teams learnt he wasn't playing they would ask tremulously: 'You mean you have someone better?'

Inevitably, with someone so extravagantly gifted, it was Matthews' ability to fit in with the mortals around him that was in doubt. They, no less than the opposition, often had little idea what he would do next. His inclusion, furthermore, dictated the way the whole team played. As his style was 'stop-go', so was the whole team's.

It was something to boast one such player, never mind two. Tom Finney was a plumber by trade and a one-club man. On the pitch he demonstrated surprising resilience for one so slight. His crouching swerve was a familiar landmark in English soccer. It was to England's fortune that Finney, outside-right for his club, as was Matthews, could perform with equal aplomb on the left. When England first lined up with both wingers, in 1947, Portugal felt the draught to the tune of 10-0. For over a decade, if Matthews played, Finney took the left flank; if not, he took the right.

Finney's game was broader than Matthews', two-footed, good in the air, and not just content to make goals for others. Finney would represent his country on seventy-six occasions (Matthews fifty-four). He would score thirty goals, on a par with Lofthouse, although when he arrived in Switzerland, Finney was still searching for his first World Cup goal. Like Billy Wright, he was never booked, let alone sent off the field.

## BELGIUM v ENGLAND
*Thursday, 17 June 1954*                                                    *Basle – 14,000*

England retained the habit of departing late for the World Cup finals, allowing themselves just two full days before their curtain-raiser. Winterbottom did not approve of arriving too early for matches abroad. Players were thought to become easily dispirited if parted from their families for too long. England were the last squad to arrive, basing themselves in the picturesque town of Lucerne. Combs, soaps and other toiletries were presumably in abundance, for this would be the first World Cup to be televised, benefiting from Kenneth Wolstenholme's commentary and Britain's experimental link-up with the newly created Eurovision.

Switzerland was playing host to diplomacy as well as soccer. The Geneva Conference on south-east Asia dragged on interminably. Foreign Secretary Anthony Eden was present, negotiating with Chinese Premier Zhou Enlai. Elsewhere on the international front, France was still reeling from the collapse at Dien Bien Phu in Indo-China. There was widespread interest in the work of Dutch surgeons performing the first successful separation of Siamese twins. In Britain, teenage girls screamed and wept at the announcement that 'croon and swoon' heart-throb Dickie Valentine was to be married.

Belgium had qualified at the expense of Sweden, whom they defeated home and away. Under normal circumstances, England would have had nothing to fear: Belgium were favourite cannon-fodder for English sharpshooters. One win and one draw was all Belgium could show from fourteen encounters. England had won all three post-war meetings, amassing fourteen goals. The Belgians sensibly ensured that not all the omens were stacked against them. Prior to the match, at Scarborough, they had beaten Britain's tennis players 3-2 in the Davis Cup.

The English selectors faced three positional headaches. Centre-half for the moment belonged to Syd Owen of Luton, cruelly indoctrinated into international football in the warm-ups against Yugoslavia and Hungary. The inside-right slot was given to Ivor Broadis, though dropped to Newcastle's reserves, and the inside-left shirt handed to Tommy Taylor from Manchester United.

The spectators in the St Jakob Stadium and those back home fortunate enough to possess a television set were treated to an exhilarating if mistake-riddled match. With Hungary temporarily banished from English minds, and knowing that Belgium were used to a good spanking, Matthews and company rolled up their sleeves – only to find themselves a goal down after five minutes. Rik Coppens used his backside to impede Owen's challenge. Pol Anoul won possession and scored from twelve yards. It was an inauspicious start for a goalkeeper still suffering from a Hungarian double-whammy. Coppens was only inches away from a Belgian second.

Midway through the half England restored parity. Taylor and Wright combined to create the chance for Broadis, who held off a challenge before thumping home. England now began to treat Belgium with their customary disdain. Finney's fast, low centre was converted by a breathtaking, daisy-cutting Lofthouse header. Despite being caught repeatedly offside, England were well on top. Matthews was irrepressible, highlighting the apparent typeset error in the Swiss match programme which identified England's No. 7 as St. Matthews. The Belgian defence, particularly van Brandt, were unnerved by his seemingly divinely inspired ball skills. Shortly after the hour Matthews embarked on his umpteenth mazy dribble, allowing Broadis to supply the finishing touch. 3-1 was the sort of score expected of an England v Belgium clash, three-quarters through the match. Yet England's defence had of late shipped goals with alarming frequency. The team was still on Cloud Nine when the blond Anoul strolled through to pull a goal back. All of a sudden, England were up against it. To be mauled by Hungary was one thing: to let slip a two-goal advantage over the likes of Belgium quite another, but Coppens somehow levelled with a low shot which Merrick half-saved. There was time for Matthews, the goal-maker, to become Matthews the goal-taker, but the 'saint's' shot was clutched by Gerneay under the bar.

Instead of traipsing off to a well-earned bath, both teams stayed on for the mandatory thirty minutes which FIFA hoped would break the deadlock. Within seconds Broadis had crossed for Lofthouse to power home off the crossbar. But again Belgium snuffed out the deficit. Jimmy Dickinson was playing in his twenty-third consecutive match. He would never score in international colours, except here, in Basle, when his head deflected Dries' free-kick past his own goalkeeper. With Owen limping badly, Wright spent the closing minutes deputising at centre-half, with unforeseen consequences. When West German referee Emil Schmetzer blew the final whistle, FIFA's aversion to draws had failed to prevent one, and left two sets of players unnecessarily exhausted.

| BELGIUM (1) 4 | ENGLAND (2) 4 |
|---|---|
| Anoul 5, 71, Coppens 78, | Broadis 25, 63, Lofthouse 37, 91 |
| Dickinson 93 (o.g.) | *After extra time (3-3 after 90 minutes)* |

BELGIUM: Gerneay, Dries, van Brandt, Huysmans, Carré, Mees, Mermans, Houf, Coppens, Anoul, P van den Bosch.
ENGLAND: Merrick, Staniforth, Byrne, Wright, Owen, Dickinson, Matthews, Broadis, Lofthouse, Taylor, Finney.

## SWITZERLAND v ENGLAND
*Sunday, 20 June 1954*                                         *Berne – 43,500*

By the time England faced Switzerland in their second and concluding pool match, the sporting public had swallowed another disappointment. Ezzard Charles had failed in his bid to become the first man to regain the World Heavyweight Boxing title, having been beaten over fifteen rounds by Rocky Marciano.

The eccentricities of FIFA's pool system meant that England could guarantee a place in the quarter-finals by beating Switzerland. FIFA's obsession with seeds had come unstuck in Pool IV. Not only had little Belgium thumbed their noses at England, but Switzerland, just one month after drawing 3-3 draw with Uruguay in the run-up to the finals, had triumphed 2-1 in a bruising match with the powerful Italians. The shirt-sleeved spectators who packed Berne's Wankdorf Stadium in temperatures in the eighties knew Switzerland required just a draw to send them into the last eight.

Belgian robustness had left England with a number of walking wounded. Two key figures – Matthews, toe, and Lofthouse, throat infection, were ruled out, their places taken by the Wolves pair Mullen and Wilshaw. Finney moved, mandatorily, to outside-right. Tommy Taylor had looked uncomfortable in his twin spearhead role with Lofthouse. Now he could play a more conventional game. Owen's obvious discomfiture at centre-half, injured or otherwise, necessitated a further reshuffle at the heart of England's defence. A first cap was awarded to Huddersfield's combative right-half Bill McGarry, shifting Billy Wright, black eye and all, to centre-half, where he had filled in against Belgium. Against opponents carrying greater firepower than the Swiss – the host team was not even seeded – some alternative solution might have been weighed, but Wright was not expected to be unduly extended. In the event, Wright would wear No. 5 for the rest of his international career. Owen's England days were over.

Switzerland's record against England was better than most, two wins apiece from their first four meetings, though England had won the fifth, 3-0, in Zurich in 1952. The combination of bone-hard pitch, Swiss lack of ambition and English lack of initiative prompted a dreary match. The Swiss were converts to the 'bolt' defensive system favoured by the Austrians, which would evolve into the stifling *catenaccio* dourly practised by the Italians. The bolt method was to employ one full-back as a central defender, with the other covering him. The

Ivor Broadis is almost decapitated in front of the square-framed goalposts. (v Switzerland)

wing-halves moved wide to confront the opposing wingers, leaving the nominal centre-half free to instigate attacks and join them.

The operation of any system, however, needs the right players to operate it, and the Swiss had insufficient talent at their disposal. When Merrick's goal was threatened, Wright, revelling in his new portfolio, quickly defused the danger. Switzerland were almost halfway to their draw when England pulled the rug from under them. It was a goal worth enduring the preceding tedium. Merrick threw the ball to Wilshaw, who sent a pass down the wing for Taylor. The ball was nodded on to Mullen, who dribbled round the full-back and the keeper.

Switzerland quickened the pace in the second half but their uninspiring attacks were easily repulsed. England extended their advantage with a delightful solo goal from Wilshaw. Receiving the ball in his own half, the Wolves inside-forward zig-zagged past three defenders before shooting past Parlier. Both Wolves newcomers had scored. Once Staniforth had cleared Ballaman's attempt off the line (behind it, according to photographs), England ran out comfortable winners. They had, however, failed to set pulses racing. Their progress was described by one commentator: 'England, in a world sense, represent a third division side that has found its way into the last eight of the FA Cup.' The insult was worse than it sounds: there was no fourth division in 1954.

Thanks to FIFA's seeding, and the fact that two teams stayed alive, England had advanced further than in 1950. Italy beat Belgium 4-1, but then lost to the Swiss for a second time, in a play-off. This meant Italy, ridiculously, had to play Switzerland twice and England not at all. Scotland were also on their way home, beaten 0-1 by Austria and pulverised 0-7 by Uruguay.

SWITZERLAND   (0) 0             ENGLAND   (1) 2
                                Mullen 43, Wilshaw 69

SWITZERLAND: Parlier, Neury, Kernen, Eggimann, Bocquet, Bigler, Antenen, Vonlanthen, Meier, Ballaman, Fatton.
ENGLAND: Merrick, Staniforth, Byrne, McGarry, Wright, Dickinson, Finney, Broadis, Wilshaw, Taylor, Mullen.

---

*Final positions – Pool IV*

|                  | P | W | D | L | F | A | Pts |
|------------------|---|---|---|---|---|---|-----|
| ENGLAND          | 2 | 1 | 1 | 0 | 6 | 4 | 3   |
| SWITZERLAND *    | 2 | 1 | 0 | 1 | 2 | 3 | 2   |
| Italy            | 2 | 1 | 0 | 1 | 5 | 3 | 2   |
| Belgium          | 2 | 0 | 1 | 1 | 5 | 8 | 1   |

* Switzerland qualified after play-off with Italy.

---

**URUGUAY v ENGLAND**
*Saturday, 26 June 1954*                              *Basle – 50,000*

FIFA had more organisational malpractice up its sleeve. The eight quarter-finalists found themselves batched up, ostensibly to avoid teams playing each other twice. The survivors from Pools I and II faced each other; ditto those from Pools III and IV. But instead of the winners from one group playing the runners-up in another, as would be employed for the next six World Cups, the groups winners were paired, the runners-up likewise. In practice, this meant that the four favourites – Hungary and Brazil, Uruguay and England – contested two quarter-finals, the respective winners in turn meeting each other in the semis. This would leave unseeded West Germany, newly constituted as a state, newly admitted to FIFA, and newly thrashed 8-3 by Hungary in Pool II, to tiptoe into the Final by the back door.

But all this lay in the future. England enjoyed six days' rest after their weary victory over Switzerland. Knocks had time to heal and bruises to fade before battle commenced against the World Cup holders. The press had time to dwell on matters of less consequence. Laya Raki had performed a nude swimming scene in Jack Hawkins' latest film *The Seekers*. The censor admitted he had had

Knee-padded Máspoli in an aerial duel with Lofthouse. (v Uruguay)

to see the offending clip twice, or was it three times, before passing it. There was also an eclipse of the sun to enjoy. The eclipse was total if viewed from northern Scotland – prompting unkind jibes at Scotland's World Cup results – only the second total eclipse seen from Britain this century.

It was a busy week for other sports, too. Roger Bannister's historic world record for the four-minute mile was just a month old when Australia's John Landy clipped a second and a half from it in Finland. Medical minds gave serious thought as to whether the new record marked the limit of human endurance. Wimbledon unearthed a promising British talent in eighteen-year-old Bobby Wilson; while another eye-catching youngster, David Sheppard, though studying for holy orders, was appointed England's cricket captain for the Second Test against Pakistan at Trent Bridge.

In domestic football, evidence was at hand of the inbuilt resistance to change and progress. The merits of plastic, non water-absorbent, footballs were considered but rejected. Heavy, soggy, leather balls had to be retained for fear of undermining the character of the British game.

Water-absorbent footballs were hardly relevant in the sweltering heat of St Jakob Stadium, where England had recently shared a goal feast with Belgium. Other than Hungary, it was hard to imagine more formidable opponents than Uruguay. This was the South Americans' third World Cup: they had won the first two, and never yet tasted defeat. The present side had just demolished Scotland 7-0. Several of the triumphal 1950 team – Máspoli, in goal, massive defender Varela, now thirty-nine and still captain, Andrade, Míguez, above all Juan Schiaffino, for whom AC Milan would shortly pay a world record transfer fee – would line up against England. English 'spies' key-holed Uruguayan training sessions in an attempt to fathom their secrets. They reported upon a varied regime designed to improve fitness, stamina, subtlety and ball-mastery. The Uruguayans even endured sessions of formal marching, Grenadier style.

For England, Matthews and Lofthouse had recovered and reclaimed their places. Mullen and Taylor stood down. Those pessimists waiting to knock the team were soon vindicated, for Merrick conceded an early, splendid goal. Schiaffino sent Borges away down the left. A one-two with Abbadíe, and Borges netted with a low, right-footed, angled shot on the turn. Uruguay looked good, playing a fluid 'bolt' system, seven men sweeping into attack, then falling back with the ebb and flow of the game.

To their credit, England fought back manfully. Matthews, roaming across the forward line, threaded the ball behind Varela to Wilshaw. A reverse pass found Lofthouse, who snapped a sharply-taken goal.

As play settled down it was noted with surprise that England were more than holding their own. Lofthouse's drive was beaten out by Máspoli, and Wilshaw lobbed sickeningly wide. The interval was beckoning when Uruguay reclaimed the advantage. Dickinson headed away a Uruguayan free-kick; man-mountain Varela cushioned the ball on his chest and struck a floater across Merrick and inside his far post. Pained stares daggered the motionless goalkeeper, who should have saved. Byrne responded with a heavy foul on Varela which temporarily took the Uruguayan from the field.

It was bad enough England going off a goal behind when they could easily have been to the good. But before Winterbottom's dressing-room wisdom had sunk in they lost another goal. Byrne fouled Ambrois. The free-kick was taken by Varela. Unseen by Austrian referee Steiner, Varela drop-kicked the ball, goalkeeper fashion. A nonplussed England defence looked stunned as Schiaffino outpaced Wright and from an acute angle shot under Merrick, rooted to his line.

A two-goal deficit seemed insurmountable. Yet with three Uruguayans – Varela, Andrade and Abbadíe – hobbling badly, and Schiaffino dragged back into defence, the initiative passed to England. They were almost caught out when Ambrois struck Merrick's bar, but otherwise Uruguay were under the cosh. The steadiness of Wright and the magic of Matthews, (der Zauberer 'the Magician', according to the Uruguayans) lit up one of England's finer World Cup displays.

A path still had to be found through Uruguay's massed defence. All of a sudden, Wilshaw crossed, Lofthouse shot, and Finney poached the rebound off

Máspoli, wearing one glove, collects as Finney and Lofthouse threaten. (v Uruguay)

Máspoli for his first ever World Cup goal. England now mounted waves of desperate attacks. Matthews hit a post, but the final, decisive gesture belonged to Merrick. With eleven minutes remaining, England were caught out by a lightning counter-strike. It should have petered out, but Ambrois' ambitious cross-shot was fudged by a flat-footed England goalkeeper, and Uruguay now led 4-2.

England were out of the World Cup. Critics asked whether this was the end of Gil Merrick's England international career. It was. Yet others had also been below par. Broadis' England days were also over, and Finney had rarely imposed himself.

Hungary, meanwhile, disposed of Brazil in the infamous Battle of Berne. They then accounted for Uruguay, 4-2 after extra time, in a momentous semi which should have graced the Final. But Hungary would confound the predictions that theirs would be an inevitable triumph. West Germany overturned that earlier 3-8 whitewash, and overturned a two-goal deficit in the Final, to snatch the trophy when they faced Hungary for the second, decisive time. It was Hungary's first setback in thirty matches, their first defeat in four years. Their five games in Switzerland had produced twenty-seven goals, yet somehow they finished second. Never before or since would a non-seeded team win the World Cup.

The England party packed their bags determined to modernise and think afresh. At least they would no longer blame their diet. They returned home to a nation celebrating the lifting of all remaining peacetime rationing.

URUGUAY  (2) 4                          ENGLAND  (1) 2
  Borges 5, Varela 40,                      Lofthouse 16, Finney 67
  Schiaffino 50, Ambrois 79

URUGUAY: Máspoli, Martínez, Santamaria, Andrade, Varela, Cruz, Abbadíe, Ambrois, Míguez, Schiaffino, Borges.
ENGLAND: Merrick, Staniforth, Byrne, McGarry, Wright, Dickinson, Matthews, Broadis, Lofthouse, Wilshaw, Finney.

---

*England appearances and goalscorers*
*World Cup qualifying rounds and final competition 1954*

| | Apps | Goals | | Apps | Goals | | Apps | Goals |
|---|---|---|---|---|---|---|---|---|
| Dickinson J * | 6 | – | Staniforth R | 4 | – | Garrett T | 1 | – |
| Merrick G | 6 | – | Wilshaw D | 3 | 3 | Rickaby S | 1 | – |
| Wright W * | 6 | – | Matthews S* | 3 | – | Hassall H | 1 | 2 |
| Finney T * | 5 | 1 | Eckersley W* | 2 | – | Clarke H | 1 | – |
| Lofthouse N | 4 | 6 | Johnston H | 2 | – | Allen R | 1 | 1 |
| Mullen J * | 4 | 2 | Quixall A | 2 | – | Nicholls J | 1 | 1 |
| Byrne R | 4 | – | Taylor T | 2 | – | Owen S | 1 | – |
| Broadis I | 4 | 3 | McGarry W | 2 | – | | | |

---

* Appeared in 1950 World Cup.                     *23 players*     *19 goals*

---

# 3

# THE 1958 WORLD CUP

The 1958 World Cup, held in Sweden, has come to be regarded as the first truly authentic world soccer championship. Gone were the days when politics, austerity, travel difficulties and real or imagined slights to national pride could restrict the entry of the major soccer countries into the World Cup. Each of the previous five tournaments had had to contend with the absence, for a variety of reasons, of one or more of the world's best. In 1958 there were no absentees of note, and over fifty countries entered – among them, for the first time, the Soviet Union.

In 1956, the World Cup organising committee drew up the qualifying paths to Sweden. For the British teams, reliance on the Home Internationals was abandoned. Public relations disguised this as a compliment, that it was considered indecent to ask the founders of football to commit fratricide in order to contest the Jules Rimet trophy. In fact, member states had rebelled against two of the final sixteen placings being guaranteed to British teams. In consequence, England, Scotland, Wales and Northern Ireland were allocated to separate qualifying zones. All four might qualify – which would certainly wipe the smile off the faces of those demanding change – or, possibly, none. In view of England and Scotland's combined records in World Cup finals to date – two wins and five defeats – that did not seem out of the question.

England came out of the hat with Denmark and the Republic of Ireland, a feeble combination that brought relief to Lancaster Gate. In past World Cups, qualifiers had been squeezed into the months preceding the finals. From 1958, they would be staged earlier, concluding at least six months before the final tournament commenced. England kicked-off their campaign against Denmark at Wembley in December 1956.

The years since the defeat by Uruguay had seen Britain appoint a new prime minister. Anthony Eden had no sooner come to power than he confronted Egypt's President Nasser, whom he unwisely likened to Hitler. Nasser had nationalised the Suez Canal Co. The confrontation escalated into war in the autumn of 1956. Denmark's footballers arrived during the subsequent political recriminations, by which time Britain's final visions of great power status had vanished: Britain was now a second-rank political and military power.

Simultaneously, a Hungarian uprising had been brutally put down by Soviet forces. In north Africa, Algerian nationalists had begun the struggle for independence from France. Haunting memories of World War II had been revived with the publication of a Jewish girl's wartime diary in Amsterdam. Her name was Anne Frank.

Socially, the mid-'fifties heralded the arrival of commercial television to contest the BBC's self-imposed guardianship of public tastes. Advertisers' obsession with whiteness, from washing powders to toothpaste, spilled into countless homes. A national lottery, known as Premium Bonds, now competed with football pools in offering a fortune for a minimal stake. Marilyn Monroe was at the peak of her fame, although in Europe increasingly rivalled by Diana Dors and the pouting Brigitte Bardot. Literary escapism could be enjoyed through the first of the James Bond books.

By 1956, youthful assertiveness reached new levels. Crime and delinquency escalated alarmingly. Two films took their share of the blame, the late James Dean's *Rebel Without a Cause* and Bill Haley's *Rock Around the Clock*. Elvis Presley dominated the charts on both sides of the Atlantic. He and others – among them Lonnie Donegan and a proliferation of 'doo-wop' groups – offered new identity to the previously uncategorised 'teenager'. Nor was protest confined to the inarticulate. This was the age of the Angry Young Men, when John Osborne's *Look Back in Anger* and Colin Wilson's *The Outsider* lashed out at the Establishment and its public-schooled hierarchy.

Football, too, had its place in the general upheaval. The outcry over England's dismal showings in Brazil and Switzerland prompted the FA to set up technical committees to examine all aspects of the game. Clubs were requested to release players for international duty less grudgingly. European and South American influences gradually permeated English training grounds. The obsession with lapping and cross-country running gave way to greater emphasis on ball skills, such as trapping the ball with chest or thigh. More youth and Under-23 internationals were arranged. By 1958, six of the England side had graduated from the Under-23s.

Innovation was also evident in matters of appearance. In Switzerland, the British teams had turned out in baggy shorts, clod-hopping boots with rigid toe-caps, bulging shin pads. Within two or three years mini-shorts were in vogue; shirts had V-necks, no longer laced, buttoned, or collared. Lightweight boots had arrived, cut away at the heel, and shin pads, if worn at all, were trimmer.

Club football widened its horizons. In 1955, the European Champions Cup and Fairs Cup had been inaugurated, enabling the continent's best to be pitted against one another, increasing international awareness. The FA, typically, refused to permit champions Chelsea to enter, on the spurious grounds of fixture congestion. The following season, the new champions, Manchester

United, insisted upon entering, and did. 1956 also saw England's first floodlit league match (Portsmouth v Newcastle United).

*Qualifying Pool I*

## ENGLAND v DENMARK
*Wednesday, 5 December 1956*                    *Molineux, Wolverhampton – 55,000*

The World Cup clash with Denmark at Molineux marked the Danes' first footballing visit to England. In two previous meetings in Copenhagen, England had drawn 0-0 in 1948 and won 5-1 as recently as October 1955. The World Cup qualifier had to contend with the distraction of the Melbourne Olympics. Chris Brasher had already won the steeplechase in a new Olympic record time. Terry Spinks and Dick McTaggart won boxing golds, as did fencer Gillian Sheen in the foil. On the day of the match Britain's great swimming hope, Judie Grinham, climbed the winner's rostrum after the 100 metres back-stroke, Britain's first swimming gold since 1924. Away from the Olympics, twenty-one year old Floyd Patterson knocked out Archie Moore to become World Heavyweight Boxing champion.

At home, British and French forces were quitting the Suez Canal zone. To stem the run on Britain's gold and dollar reserves, petrol prices rose by almost a third, to six shillings and five pence. Bus fares rose immediately.

TV entertainers softened the blow with a 'spectacular', featuring an all-star cast – Ruby Murray, Ted Heath, Alma Cogan, Anne Shelton, Eddie Calvert and David Whitfield. Viewers tuned into the most captivating of the early quiz shows, *The $64,000 Question*. In the record business, Elvis had three records in the Top 20, Bill Haley two. Guy Mitchell and the Platters were also selling well, but topping the charts were Johnny Ray's *Just Walking in the Rain* and Frankie Vaughan's *Green Door*.

The door to Sweden was beckoning England. Football's various innovations had been translated into impressive performances on the field. In December 1954, the newly crowned world champions, West Germany, left Wembley with their tails between their legs. Come May 1956, England jubilantly departed from Berlin with a repeat, 3-1, score-line. Brazil's scalp had also been claimed, 4-2 at Wembley, and England entertained Denmark a week after disposing of Yugoslavia 3-0, to extend their unbeaten run to fourteen months and ten matches. Denmark were not expected to halt that sequence. They were amateurs, they had already lost 1-2 in Dublin, and had not even dared to send a team to the Olympics. And, of course, England had recently trounced Denmark in Copenhagen. Only three of that side were retained at Molineux.

Four English veterans – Wright, Matthews, Finney and Dickinson – were about to take part in their third World Cup, though this would be Dickinson's last international. The goalkeeper was Tottenham's acrobatic Ted Ditchburn, though this would be his only cap. Roger Byrne was still at left-back, now partnered by Jeff Hall of Birmingham City, who would later die of polio. Tommy Taylor, strong, fast, good in the air, had wrestled the No. 9 shirt away from Nat Lofthouse. Spurs' John Brooks earned the last of his three caps at inside-right. The remaining places were occupied by two youngsters already well established. The first of these, Ronnie Clayton, was right-half with Blackburn Rovers of the second division.

The second youngster was Duncan Edwards. Edwards was then a mere twenty, but had first been capped when just 18½. No full international cap has ever been awarded to a younger English player. He would settle at left-half, successor to Jimmy Dickinson. A prominent Busby Babe, Edwards would not have looked out of place in a rugby second row. He could swashbuckle, he could tease, he could shoot like a howitzer. Edwards and Clayton had first been paired at half-back in the defeat of Brazil, and, who knows, one day might have emulated the long partnership of Wright and Dickinson. On this occasion, another gifted newcomer, Fulham's Johnny Haynes, was unfit, enabling Edwards to slot into Haynes' inside-left position.

England did not have long to wait before piercing the Danish defence. Only two minutes had passed before Finney – playing on the left, following two experiments at centre-forward – skipped past two defenders for Taylor to score from close range. The same combination created the second goal, after Taylor expertly took Finney's cross on his chest.

Early strikes against modest opposition often lead to lethargy, and this was the case against Denmark, who seized the initiative and pulled a goal back when one of three Nielsen's in the side scored from a cross by one of three Hansen's.

Walter Winterbottom was probably not the sort to indulge in half-time rollickings. But within four minutes of the restart Taylor powered his way through flimsy tackles to clinch his hat-trick. Even that failed to subdue the Danes: Nielsen broke away to score his second.

It was then that Duncan Edwards took over. With spectators fearing that the Danes would have the temerity to equalise, Edwards unleashed a blockbuster from Matthews' cross. By the end of the match he had scored a second, from Matthews' flick, struck a post, and come near on several other occasions.

Taylor and Edwards took the applause, Denmark took the moral honours.

ENGLAND  (2) 5                      DENMARK  (1) 2
   Taylor 2, 20, 49, Edwards 67, 80      O Nielsen 29, 65

ENGLAND: Ditchburn (Spurs), Hall (Birmingham), Byrne (Man U), Clayton (Blackburn), Wright (Wolves), Dickinson (Portsmouth), Matthews (Blackpool), Brooks (Spurs), Taylor (Man U), Edwards (Man U), Finney (Preston).
DENMARK: Drensgaard, Larsen, V Nielsen, F Nielsen, O Hansen, Olesen, J Hansen, Petersen, O Nielsen, Jensen, P Hansen.

## ENGLAND v REPUBLIC OF IRELAND
*Wednesday, 8 May 1957*                                    *Wembley – 52,000*

It was a sign that the task of qualifying was not viewed as too exacting when the FA arranged to play England's concluding three matches in the space of twelve days. Such a concentration of fixtures could hardly allow injuries to heal or unexpected setbacks to be properly digested.

Britain had a new prime minister. Eden had resigned over the Suez debacle and Harold Macmillan taken over. The first of Britain's African colonies had lowered the Union Jack: the Gold Coast had been granted independence and renamed herself Ghana. The Treaty of Rome had been signed, setting up the European Economic Community – with Britain turning her back.

Television entertainment in early May saw Gracie Fields topping the bill on *Sunday Night at the London Palladium*. Comedians Charlie Drake and Arthur Haynes enjoyed popular series, and Lonnie Donegan headed the hit parade with *Cumberland Gap*. Wednesday, 8 May is remembered not just for the England v Republic of Ireland match, but as the occasion when uproar engulfed Hughie Greene's quiz show *Double Your Money*. Two contestants going for the £1,000 jackpot argued with the compere over the fairness of the questions. The programme had to be taken off air.

This was England's first World Cup encounter to be played at Wembley. Just four days previously its hallowed turf had hosted one of the best-remembered Cup Finals, when Aston Villa beat Manchester United 2-1. Five of the twenty-two players on view that day returned for the international.

The England team showed some new faces. Goalkeeper Alan Hodgkinson of Sheffield United had recently made his debut against Scotland. Returning at inside-right was burly John Atyeo of second division Bristol City. Johnny Haynes was back, allowing Edwards to switch to left-half.

England had not faced the Irish Republic since losing at Goodison eight years earlier. The present match, lying in the shadow of the Cup Final, attracted little interest. The Irish team were hardly strangers to this country, nine of them playing in the English league. But familiarity did not lend them strength. England were four goals up by the break. Tommy Taylor, unimpressive against Villa on the Saturday, tormented the Irish with a first-half hat-trick – the first set up by Haynes, the second, courtesy of Finney, with a shot that deceived the Ireland goalkeeper, the third a header from Finney's corner. Shortly before

Taylor's third goal, Atyeo had bagged one himself, heading home a rebound from Finney's effort. Finney's contribution to three of the four goals must have been gratifying to the Preston man. Despite his great reputation, Wembley had never been one of his favourite haunts. For his part, Hodgkinson had not been called into action until thirty minutes had passed, whereupon he took a knock colliding with Manchester United's Bill Whelan.

With a handsome lead under their belts, England once again suffered the dithers. Most of the second period belonged to Ireland, who camped for long stretches in England's half. Ireland even salvaged a goal when Haverty's cross struck Dermot Curtis smack in the face and rebounded beyond Hodgkinson. Whelan then had the cheek to vibrate England's crossbar. But England had the last word, Atyeo finishing off another rippling attack by Finney. *The Times'* football correspondent wrote: 'The score looks better on paper than it did in achievement.' Apart from Finney, Haynes and Taylor, few other reputations had been enhanced. Eight-year-old Prince Charles was spared the fuss. He was in hospital having his tonsils and adenoids out.

ENGLAND   (4) 5                         REPUBLIC OF IRELAND   (0) 1
    Taylor 10, 18, 40, Atyeo 38, 89        Curtis 56

ENGLAND: Hodgkinson, Hall, Byrne, Clayton, Wright, Edwards, Matthews, Atyeo, Taylor, Haynes, Finney.
IRELAND: Kelly (Drumcondra), Donovan (Everton), Cantwell (West Ham), Farrell (Everton), Mackey (Shamrock R), Saward (Villa), Ringstead (Sheff U), Whelan (Man U), Curtis (Bristol C), Fitzsimons (Midd'bro), Haverty (Arsenal).

## DENMARK v ENGLAND
*Wednesday, 15 May 1957*                              *Copenhagen – 35,000*

With four points secured, England had only a week to wait before seeking two more in Copenhagen. During that week Denis Compton announced his retirement from test cricket, and the first Ford Zodiac automatic six-seater saloons rolled off the production lines. Previously, American models had monopolised the British large-car market. Sales were boosted by the ending of petrol rationing imposed after the Suez crisis. The Danes had the distraction of a new government being installed on match-day.

Copenhagen's Idraetspark Stadium was not an ideal venue, its pitch being used daily by schools and minor clubs. The Danish team showed three changes from that which had performed creditably at Molineux, while England sent out the same eleven that had beaten the Republic of Ireland.

The game's first impact was supplied by Edwards' studs, which left their mark on two hapless Danes. The young giant was booed loudly thereafter.

England looked as uncomfortable as the press, having to sort out, this time, two Nielsen's, three Hansen's, and three Jensen's. It was midway through an untidy first half that England deservedly fell behind to the lively amateurs. One of the Jensen's, initial J, making his debut, held off Wright's challenge and struck the ball cleanly past Hodgkinson.

Before the cheers had subsided, England had erased the deficit. Finney and Edwards set up the chance with some neat passing. The Danes stopped, thinking the referee had blown for an injury, allowing Haynes to equalise.

For much of the second half Denmark threatened to restore their lead. Attacks were raining down on Hodgkinson when, in a rare English sortie, Taylor clashed with Danish centre-half, O Hansen, who collapsed on his own goal-line. Once again the Danes did not play to the whistle, and a grateful Taylor put England in front.

Hansen was off the field receiving treatment when his over-stretched defenders conceded a third goal, scored by Atyeo. To add insult, Taylor claimed number four, pouncing on Finney's sweet cross. Though Taylor had hit the bar twice, and now netted eight World Cup goals in three matches, the critics were not deceived. England had been second best to the Danes for most of the match. Haynes was the only player to escape criticism. Despite England amassing fourteen goals, there was no satisfying some diehard detractors.

Shortly after the match the Queen and Duke of Edinburgh arrived in Denmark. England's victory enabled the royal couple to avoid jests over the banqueting table at what would have been a soccer sensation.

On the other side of the world, in the Pacific, Britain exploded her first hydrogen bomb. The blast was the equivalent of one million tons of TNT. Another sign of changing times was the demise of *Picture Post*, almost a British institution, whose sales had peaked in the 1930s and 'forties.

DENMARK  (1) 1                ENGLAND  (1) 4
J Jensen 22                   Haynes 24, Taylor 70, 86, Atyeo 75

DENMARK: Drensgaard, Amdisen, V Nielsen, F Nielsen, O Hansen, Olesen, J Hansen, J Jensen, E Jensen, A Jensen, P Hansen.
ENGLAND: Hodgkinson, Hall, Byrne, Clayton, Wright, Edwards, Matthews, Atyeo, Taylor, Haynes, Finney.

## REPUBLIC OF IRELAND v ENGLAND
*Sunday, 19 May 1957*                      *Dublin – 50,000*

England had a mere four days to shake off their lethargy before taking part in the decisive match of Pool I. With Ireland having beaten Denmark and lost to England, a win over England, followed by another in Copenhagen, would produce a tie with England on six points. In that eventuality a play-off would be necessary. England, therefore, travelled to Dublin knowing that a draw would book their tickets to Sweden.

Fifty thousand Irishmen crammed into Dalymount Park. A few might have had an ear for two other sporting occasions. In Stockholm, Ingemar Johansson defended his European Heavyweight Boxing title by knocking out Britain's young Henry Cooper in the fifth round. And in the Monte Carlo Grand Prix three British drivers crashed — Stirling Moss, Peter Collins and Mike Hawthorne. Only six cars finished the course, led by Juan Fangio in a Maserati.

England showed one enforced change from their midweek trip to Copenhagen. Matthews had injured an ankle and Finney switched wings, making room for Manchester United's young winger David Pegg. Matthews, it transpired, had won his last cap, and at the age of forty-two was done with international football.

With both teams setting their sights on Sweden, the match was a cracker, one of England's most stirring post-war internationals. The early pace and passion came principally from Ireland, boosted by a fine goal after just three minutes. Haverty flighted over a cross for Ringstead to hammer past Hodgkinson. Ireland called the tune throughout the first half, inspired by Bill Whelan until he was slowed by a bone-numbing challenge from Edwards. Haverty wasted a marvellous chance to increase the lead.

After the break England were compelled to step up a gear. They forced a plague of corner-kicks. The tackling grew fiercer. Irish centre-half Charlie Hurley kept the English attack at bay and Tommy Godwin in goal gave one of the finest performances of his career. Dunne cleared off the line and, following a lightning Irish break-out, Wright did the same at the other end. As the minutes ticked away the home crowd sensed Sweden beckoning. To a man they urged the referee to call for time. He had already looked at his watch and checked with his linesman when Finney dribbled past Pat Saward. Noel Cantwell backed off, permitting room for the cross. It was met splendidly by John Atyeo, who soared to head England into the World Cup finals. He would never score a more vital goal. A marvellous match had seen England earn a World Cup result which, for the fourth time in succession, many observers felt unmerited on the balance of play. The English press concurred that Ireland had deserved a narrow victory, but it was England who would travel to Sweden a year hence.

REPUBLIC OF IRELAND  (1) 1      ENGLAND  (0) 1
    Ringstead 3                        Atyeo 89

IRELAND: Godwin (Bournemouth), Dunne (Luton), Cantwell (West Ham), Nolan (Shamrock R), Hurley (Millwall), Saward (Villa), Ringstead (Sheff U), Whelan (Man U), Curtis (Bristol C), Fitzsimons (Midd'bro), Haverty (Arsenal). ENGLAND: Hodgkinson, Hall, Byrne, Clayton, Wright, Edwards, Finney, Atyeo, Taylor, Haynes, Pegg.

---

*Qualifying Pool I*

|  | P | W | D | L | F | A | Pts |
|---|---|---|---|---|---|---|---|
| ENGLAND | 4 | 3 | 1 | 0 | 15 | 5 | 7 |
| Republic of Ireland | 4 | 2 | 1 | 1 | 6 | 7 | 5 |
| Denmark | 4 | 0 | 0 | 4 | 4 | 13 | 0 |

*Other group results*

Rep Ireland v Denmark    2-1         Denmark v Rep Ireland    0-2

---

**World Cup finals – SWEDEN**                                    **June 1958**

In 1950 and 1954 England had marched straight from beating Scotland into the World Cup finals two months later. Following the match in Dublin, an interlude of thirteen months beckoned. That provided time for reflection. If England had laboured unconvincingly to pile up a stack of World Cup goals, those performances had to be seen in the context of a sixteen-match unbeaten run stretching back to October 1955. It was Northern Ireland who would end that sequence, in November 1957, beating England 3-2 at Wembley.

Almost as gratifying as England's winning streak was the way the players were stabilising into a powerful unit. The confidence running through the side made future opponents and bookmakers look to England, in the absence of other clear-cut favourites, to have as good a chance as any. By the turn of 1957-58 the England team more or less picked itself, and its average age was under twenty-four.

England could also enjoy the reflected glory of other British teams. FIFA's decision to segregate them in the qualifiers resulted in Scotland overcoming Spain and Switzerland, and Northern Ireland, remarkably, shrugging off the challenge of Italy and Portugal. When Wales finished behind Czechoslovakia in Pool IV, she was handed a welcome second bite. In the Asia-Africa zone, all the Islamic nations had refused to play Israel, who topped that section by default. But FIFA now stipulated that only the hosts and holders could compete in the finals without beating someone first. Consequently, all the runners-up in the European zones were put into the hat for the right to compete with Israel. Wales' name came out. Her footballers disposed of Israel's 2-0 home and away, and the unlikely name of Wales was listed as the Asian-African entry for Sweden. British teams would occupy a quarter of the places available.

When Harold Macmillan said, in another context: 'You've never had it so good,' he might have had in mind the state of English, and British, football as things stood at the beginning of 1958. But if English prospects in 1954 had been dashed in a word – Hungary – so, too, fate had a word in store for 1958 – Munich.

The young Manchester United side of 1957-58 had won the league championship two seasons running and were still an emerging force. The Busby Babes had just reached the European Cup semi-finals at the expense of Red Star Belgrade. Flying home, on 6 February, their Elizabethan aircraft crashed on take-off after refuelling at Munich airport. Britain was still celebrating the Welsh clinching their World Cup place when news of the disaster broke. Twenty-three people died, including eight United players.

The disaster affected the preparations of all four home nations. Matt Busby had recently agreed to take charge of the Scotland team in Sweden. Although he survived the crash, he would be too ill even to attend the tournament. Busby's assistant at Old Trafford, Jimmy Murphy, was by coincidence Welsh team-manager, and had stayed behind to supervise the team against Israel in Cardiff. It now fell to him to minister to the needs of the Manchester club, inevitably to the detriment of his responsibilities to Wales.

Northern Ireland lost their centre-half when Jackie Blanchflower shattered an elbow in the crash. But it was England who, in footballing terms, paid the greatest sacrifice. Four members of the team which qualified in Dublin lost their lives. Roger Byrne, twenty-eight year old skipper and 'grand-dad' of United, had earned thirty-three consecutive caps at left-back. England had no obvious replacement. Nineteen-cap, sixteen-goal Tommy Taylor had been touted as potentially England's finest centre-forward since Tommy Lawton. David Pegg, only twenty-two, had just forced his way into the side, as cover for Finney.

Football-wise, the most tragic loss was that of Duncan Edwards. He had already been earmarked as the man around whom England would construct their team for the next ten years. In December 1957 he had been voted third in Europe's Footballer of the Year (Taylor had been fifth). Edwards battled against death for over two weeks. To England, he was irreplaceable. Losing Byrne, Taylor and Pegg as well, meant each department of the English team – particularly its left flank – had had the guts wrenched from it.

These deaths necessitated the shake-up of a well-settled England team. By the time the World Cup came round the side bore a fresh complexion. Warm-up matches included a 0-5 drubbing by Yugoslavia in Belgrade a month before the curtain-raiser in Sweden, evoking haunting memories of similar humiliation in Budapest in 1954.

In goal, Alan Hodgkinson had given way to Bolton's Eddie Hopkinson who, in turn, was succeeded by Colin McDonald of Burnley. At right-back, Don

Howe of West Bromwich came to the fore. Byrne's position passed temporarily to Jim Langley of Fulham, before being claimed by Bolton's hard-man Tommy Banks.

Two fresh wing-halves were required, one to fill the gap left by Duncan Edwards, the other to replace Ronnie Clayton who, following a long promotion campaign with Blackburn, had burnt himself out. After a tired display against Yugoslavia, he gave way to young Eddie Clamp, who had only recently established himself in the Wolves team. Clamp's versatile club colleague, Bill Slater, assumed Edwards' position. Thus England lined up in Sweden with the half-back line of Clamp, Wright and Slater, all drawn from the new league champions, Wolverhampton Wanderers.

It was in attack that England's selectors suffered their biggest headaches. Pivotal to their concerns was who to play alongside Johnny Haynes. Still only twenty-three, Haynes was already an established international, winning his first cap immediately following the defeat by Uruguay in 1954. His special talent was directing pin-point passes over long distances or short, from any angle; changing the direction of play at a stroke.

The difficulty with Haynes was that, no less than Matthews, his inclusion conditioned the way the whole unit functioned. By seeking to pass into space, young Haynes combined uneasily with the likes of Matthews, who disliked chasing after balls directed behind the full-back. Indeed, Matthews might still have been in the team were it not for the selectors' faith in the Londoner. Haynes had his shortcomings, of course. His game was predictable, which, on an off day, made him appear worse than mediocre. Yet his passing ability made his one of the first names pencilled in.

Happily, a replacement had been found for Matthews in a ball-artist from Blackburn named Bryan Douglas. With Finney and Haynes automatics on the left, there remained just two vacancies to be filled. The names toyed with included Derek Kevan, a burly attacker from West Brom, with less than two seasons' experience behind him; Middlesbrough's dynamic Brian Clough; Bobby Robson, Kevan's partner at West Brom; and a shy youngster, Bobby Charlton, who, with cruel irony, sought to lay claim to the place vacated by his deceased team-mate, Tommy Taylor.

The selectors opted to take to Sweden only twenty players instead of the twenty-two permitted. Of these, ten were forwards, which left a shortage of cover in defence. Clough was not even named in the squad. Neither were Stanley Matthews and Nat Lofthouse, both still in sparkling form with their clubs. Lofthouse, in fact, had just scored both Bolton's goals in the 1958 Cup Final, and would return to international duty after the World Cup.

| Position | Name | Club | Age | Caps | Goals |
|----------|------|------|-----|------|-------|
| Goalkeepers | Colin McDonald | Burnley | 27 | 1 | – |
|  | Eddie Hopkinson | Bolton | 22 | 6 | – |
| Full-backs | Don Howe | WBA | 22 | 7 | – |
|  | Tommy Banks | Bolton | 28 | 1 | – |
|  | Peter Sillett | Chelsea | 25 | 3 | – |
| Centre-halves | Billy Wright (c) | Wolves | 34 | 91 | 3 |
|  | Maurice Norman | Tottenham | 24 | – | – |
| Wing-halves | Ronnie Clayton | Blackburn | 23 | 20 | – |
|  | Eddie Clamp | Wolves | 24 | 1 | – |
|  | Bill Slater | Wolves | 31 | 6 | – |
| Wingers | Tom Finney | Preston | 36 | 73 | 28 |
|  | Bryan Douglas | Blackburn | 23 | 7 | 1 |
|  | Peter Brabrook | Chelsea | 20 | – | – |
|  | Alan A'Court | Liverpool | 23 | 1 | 1 |
| Centre-forwards | Derek Kevan | WBA | 23 | 7 | 4 |
|  | Bobby Smith | Tottenham | 25 | – | – |
| Inside-forwards | Johnny Haynes | Fulham | 23 | 20 | 8 |
|  | Bobby Robson | WBA | 25 | 2 | 2 |
|  | Peter Broadbent | Wolves | 25 | – | – |
| Utility player | Bobby Charlton | Manchester U | 20 | 3 | 3 |

*Averages* 25.2  12.5

With only four of the squad possessing more than seven caps – and of these, Clayton was out of favour – England were taking a very inexperienced party of players to Sweden.

The sixteen teams that had won through to the finals were collectively the strongest ever assembled. Not only had there been no withdrawals among the stronger nations, but none of the footballing non-entities had survived the qualifying rounds. There were, however, two notable absentees: former two-time champions Uruguay and Italy had both been knocked out – by Paraguay and Northern Ireland respectively. Unless West Germany hung on to the Jules Rimet trophy, a fourth name would in due course be inscribed upon it.

The impact of Munich on England's chances was compounded just three days later by FIFA's organising committee. With sixteen nations contesting the most open of tournaments, the task of seeding acquired added complexity. So much so, that seeding on merit was abandoned and replaced by seeding on geography. This solution was encouraged by having four British, four west

European, four east European and four Latin American finalists. One team from each region went into each group. The four teams in each section would play one another, abandoning the 1954 nonsense, and thereafter a knock-out would ensue, group winners playing group runners-up in the quarter-finals. This format would survive for the next twenty years.

Geographical seeding had a compelling logic, yet there was a real fear of disproportionate group strength. From England's point of view, the draw could hardly have been worse. From Latin America they hoped for Mexico: they got Brazil. From eastern Europe they preferred anyone but the Russians, but they got them. And from western Europe the name that emerged was Austria, who had finished third in Switzerland in 1954. Austria protested at being drawn against the three teams widely canvassed as favourites to lift the trophy. Thanks to FIFA's lucky-dip, at least one of the three would not even make the last eight.

On the morning of 6 February England had looked forward with quiet confidence to a sustained challenge for the World Cup. On the evening of 9 February, England faced a mountain to climb even to reach the quarter-finals.

## SOVIET UNION v ENGLAND
*Sunday, 8 June 1958*                                    *Gothenburg – 49,348*

World events in the year prior to the World Cup finals were dominated by the cold war. In the autumn of 1957, the Soviet Union had startled a complacent West by sending two Sputniks into orbit. Their sophisticated technology implied that the Russians could now launch inter-continental ballistic missiles and strike at American cities. The Sputniks provoked frantic US attempts to reassert her missile supremacy. Anxieties of impending Armageddon, exacerbated by the development of Britain's own H-bomb, culminated in February 1958 with the launching of the Campaign for Nuclear Disarmament (CND). The first Aldermaston march took place in April.

In early June Peter Manuel ensured himself a place in the Pantheon of crime when he conducted his own defence against charges including robbery and rape, not to mention seven murders. After a sixteen-day trial he lost his case and was sentenced to hang.

Alfred Hinds presented a picture of gentler notoriety. In 1953 he had been convicted for his part in a furniture store robbery. Despite pleading not-guilty, Hinds was sentenced to twelve years' imprisonment. His appeals (even to the House of Lords) proving unsuccessful, he escaped, not once but three times. His first bid for freedom was from Sherwood Prison, Nottingham, whence he became associated in the public mind with Nottingham's earlier hero, Robin Hood. After his second escape (from a court-room, no less) he now found his way out of Chelmsford Prison. He would remain at large for nineteen months.

Maybe he hid himself in London. The capital was in the grip of a bus strike which provoked fisticuffs among commuters. Or perhaps Hinds fled to France, teetering on the brink of civil war over Algeria.

Concerned not to disrupt family life unnecessarily, Winterbottom made sure England were the last team to arrive in Sweden. Three days' acclimatisation was all he allowed his players. While their various opponents settled into training camps in the Swedish countryside, Winterbottom's squad took up residence in the plush Park Avenue Hotel in the old sea-port of Gothenburg (known locally as 'Little London').

England's first opponents were the Soviet Union. Olympic football champions enjoy a strong tradition in the professionals' championship, and the Soviet Union were no exception. Gold medallists at the Melbourne games, the Soviets now entered their first World Cup, for which they prepared with great thoroughness. Tour matches had been arranged outside the Iron Curtain, and top club sides – including Wolves and West Brom – invited behind it.

Three weeks before the tournament, the national sides had met in Moscow. England deserved more than a 1-1 draw, and McDonald, Banks and Clamp made encouraging debuts. Not unexpectedly, the five FA selectors sent out the same team again, hoping for a similar performance but a better result. Wolves and West Bromwich Albion would boast three England men apiece. Manchester United would boast none. Despite playing in three recent internationals and scoring three goals, Bobby Charlton was thought to be too mentally scarred by Munich to be thrown into the World Cup finals. He would remain on the sidelines throughout.

The Russians, discouraged by that 1-1 score, and by the loss of their left-half and captain, Igor Netto, through injury, summoned four new faces, three of them in attack. In goal they were served by the acclaimed Lev Yashin who, at times, played like a third back, commanding the breadth of his penalty area.

The match was the first in Gothenburg's new Ullevi Stadium, with its futuristic, wire-suspended roof, and which would later host a number of world speedway championships. The evening fixture was played under dark skies and steady drizzle. For an hour, England looked what they were, disorganised, carrying too many novices. The Soviets called the tune, reversing the tacit superiority England had shown in Moscow. Netto's absence was barely missed. Tsarev and Voinov commanded the midfield, while central defender Krijevski blocked English routes to goal.

England had fallen behind early on, when winger Alex Ivanov's shot across goal was only parried by McDonald. The ball fell kindly for Simonian, the short Armenian centre-forward, to flick the Soviets into a merited lead. The red shirts, with CCCP stamped across their chests, continued to dictate play up to and beyond the interval. It came as no surprise when McDonald, to whom no blame was attached, was beaten again. This time Kessarev, the right-back,

Simonian beats Don Howe to a ball that Colin McDonald cannot hold. (v USSR)

ventured forty yards upfield. The ball was passed to Tsarev, then to Alex Ivanov, who rounded the Burnley goalkeeper to score.

Though none could dispute the Soviets' superiority, their physical approach raised a few eyebrows, not to mention lumps on English limbs. By full-time, thirty-three free-kicks had been awarded against the red shirts – the principal victims being the wingers, Finney and Douglas – six against the white.

At 2-0 the contest seemed over, but midway through the second half Wright pumped up a free-kick from inside his own half. Derek Kevan climbed highest to put England back into contention. It was the first clear-cut chance they had created.

The spectators then witnessed a transformation. Finney's thirty-six year old legs began to carry him past obstacles, whereas he had earlier found only cul-de-sacs. Kessarev could find no answer to him. Robson spurned one chance, but did better with his next, smashing home Finney's cross, only to find that the Hungarian referee – Istvan Zsolt – had whistled for an infringement by Kevan on Yashin.

Time slowly ate up England's hopes. Finney shot wide, but in a thrilling climax Haynes burst into the Russian box, his legs were whipped from under him and England had a penalty. The Russians protested that the offence had been outside the area. Yashin grabbed the referee's arm and threw his cap at him in disgust. England, nevertheless, had been given a late reprieve. Several players, Wright among them, could not bear to look. Finney, his legs already swelling from Russian maltreatment, despatched the ball inside Yashin's right-hand post. There was time for a heart-stopping moment when, from McDonald's short throw, Robson was caught in possession. It took a sharp save by the England goalkeeper to make amends.

Had they lost, England would have been as good as out. Instead, they remained vibrantly alive, avoiding the need to contemplate flying discreetly into Gatwick airport, which had opened the same day. With Britain recording a 5-0 win over Germany to reach the semi-finals of tennis's Davis Cup, the flag was still flying.

SOVIET UNION   (1) 2              ENGLAND   (0) 2
    Simonian 13, A Ivanov 56           Kevan 65, Finney 85 pen

USSR: Yashin, Kessarev, Kuznetsov, Voinov, Krijevski, Tsarev, A Ivanov, V Ivanov, Simonian, Salnikov, Ilyin.
ENGLAND: McDonald, Howe, Banks, Clamp, Wright, Slater, Douglas, Robson, Kevan, Haynes, Finney.

**BRAZIL v ENGLAND**
*Wednesday, 11 June 1958*                                      *Gothenburg – 40,895*

Brazil arrived in Sweden endeavouring to become the first team to win the Jules Rimet trophy outside their own continent. As the World Cup approached, the aura which surrounded Brazil's footballers owed more to their exuberant style than to any tangible successes. That they were in Sweden at all was due to a 'falling leaf' banana-shot from Didí that put paid to Peru's stiff challenge. Brazil's one previous meeting with England had seen them lose 2-4 at Wembley in 1956. More pertinently, while England were labouring against the Soviets, Brazil were comfortably disposing of Austria 3-0 to go top of Pool IV.

Brazil brought a clutch of gifted players to a competition that would not otherwise be remembered for individual talent. Two – Garrincha and the seventeen-year-old prodigy, Pelé – would not line up against England. Defenders Bellini and Nilton Santos would. Also included were the Aztec-like centre-forward Vavá and the tricky left-winger Zagalo. Inside-forward Didí lined up, too, despite rumours that he might miss the trip through being too old (thirty) and having married a white woman. Brazil even brought along their own psychologist, more like a witch-doctor from some accounts.

Coach Vicente Feola had a genuine innovation up his sleeve. Few had paid attention to Brazil's unfamiliar playing formation at Wembley and elsewhere on that disappointing European tour. Now, upon the Swedish altar, a revolution

Lev Yashin guesses right, but cannot prevent Finney equalising from the spot. (v USSR)

in tactics was unfurled. Bill Nicholson, the Spurs coach and assistant to Winterbottom, had run his eye over Brazil's defeat of Austria. They had, he reported, cheekily played their nominal left-half alongside the centre-half. The No. 8 joined the centre-forward as a twin striking force, leaving the notional right-half and inside-left to forage as a pair in the middle of the team. Today, this formation is known as 4-2-4.

As Nicholson noted, unless England responded with tactical flexibility, Billy Wright would have to contend with two central attackers. To counter this threat, Don Howe, the taller full-back, moved into central defence. Eddie Clamp assumed the duties of an attacking right-back, and Bill Slater was instructed to stick tight to danger-man Didí.

Billy Wright had enough on his mind, without fretting about obscure Brazilian formations. Back in Britain, the tabloids had published details of his romance with Joy Beverley, eldest of the three singing Beverley Sisters. One paper went so far as to print personal letters he had written to his future wife. Officials became alarmed lest domestic issues affect the form of the team's defensive king-pin. And when, after the Brazil game, the press informed readers that Joy had been married previously, and harangued Wright for his comments, the FA intervened and banned him from giving interviews.

Another problem proved insurmountable. Tom Finney's heavy treatment by the Russians had left him with a torn muscle behind the knee. He would take no further part in the competition. As he was England's one forward of world class, the loss could not be disguised. His place went to Alan A'Court of Liverpool. A'Court's inclusion, together with that of Douglas and Haynes, meant that England took on Brazil with three of their five attackers from the second division.

Whatever the sceptics expected, England rolled up their sleeves for a match they knew might stand between them and the quarter-finals. Millions at home stayed glued to the Eurovision transmission, listening to the wit and wisdom on BBC of Kenneth Wolstenholme, or on ITV of Gerry Loftus and Peter Lloyd. They saw England set about dismantling the mystique of Brazilian football with determination and no little enterprise.

Bobby Robson was presented with one fleeting opportunity. Gilmar then whipped the ball off Kevan's toe, and Bellini received the benefit of the referee's doubt when bringing down Kevan in the box. But Brazilian flair, orchestrated by the midfield mastery of Vavá and the balding Dino, set the theme of the first half. McDonald excelled in the England goal, saving superbly from Mazzola and others. The crossbar then denied Brazil, vibrating crazily after a twenty-yard Vavá effort. Clamp cleared another goal-bound effort off the line, and Mazzola showed his frustration when he too struck the woodwork.

England had performed doggedly, but in the second half it was unmistakably they who were calling the tune. With McDonald and his improvised centre-backs looking secure, the game's centre of gravity moved perceptibly towards Gilmar. Johnny Haynes took to shooting on sight. The final act of a stirring match was supplied by a Haynes shot that looped off Orlando's foot to skim past his own goalpost. Brazil had failed to score for the first time ever in the finals of the World Cup. A draw seemed manifestly fair, the final tally of shots being fourteen to Brazil, thirteen to England.

When pulses returned to normal, the public once more took stock of the world. The Middle East was aflame. UN observers patrolled the Lebanon-Israel frontier, and Britain despatched a parachute battalion to Cyprus, as Greek and Turkish Cypriots clashed again. From Buckingham Palace came news that among the Queen's Birthday Honours was a CBE for Matt Busby, the still-convalescing manager of Manchester United. Young girls fainted at reports that twenty-one year old heart-throb Tommy Steele was to become engaged.

BRAZIL   (0) 0                          ENGLAND   (0) 0

BRAZIL: Gilmar, de Sordi, N Santos, Dino, Bellini, Orlando, Joel, Didí, Mazzola (a.k.a. Altafini), Vavá, Zagalo.
ENGLAND: McDonald, Howe, Banks, Clamp, Wright, Slater, Douglas, Robson, Kevan, Haynes, A'Court.

## AUSTRIA v ENGLAND
*Sunday, 15 June 1958*                                    *Borås – 16,800*

England's two draws lent much importance to their final match, against Austria, who had just gone down to their second defeat, 0-2, at the hands of the Soviet Union. With one match to play, Brazil and the USSR had three points, England two, Austria none. England could not, therefore, ignore the coming Brazil versus Russia match. Provided that result was not a draw, a win over Austria, whose position was irretrievable, would take England through to the quarter-finals. Reports showed Austria to be a shadow of their former selves, making seven changes following their first defeat by Brazil, but looking just as ragged against the Soviets. They had decided against calling up talented defender 'clockwork' Ocwirk, playing in Italy, and were paying the price.

As in 1954, goal average would separate teams finishing first and second, but not second and third – these would have to play-off. Should the deadlock still be unbroken after extra time, then the goal averages at the conclusion of the pool would be invoked. If, heaven forbid, these were identical, a coin would be tossed.

All things considered, England had grounds for optimism as they made the sixty-mile trip to the small town of Borås, with its scenic Ryavallen Stadium set among pine-covered hills. Only one of eight previous meetings had been lost, and Austria's record in Sweden to date showed five goals conceded without reply. Wright and Finney, who had survived the nightmare of Belo Horizonte, knew the dangers of picturesque settings and underrated opponents.

Back home, television's preoccupation with young audiences had seen *The 6.5 Special* break new ground in popular music. Now its successor, Jack Good's *Oh Boy!*, took to the air for the first time. In tennis, Britain reclaimed the Wightman Cup (4-3) from the USA for the first time in twenty-eight years. The British heroine was seventeen-year-old Christine Truman, who beat Althea Gibson, the reigning Wimbledon champion.

England fielded an unchanged team. The press had demanded changes to the right, where Robson and Douglas were not seen to be coordinating. Senior players, among them Finney and Wright, it transpired, had argued against change, endorsing Winterbottom's confidence in the incumbent eleven.

The task of collecting two points was hindered when, after early sparring, Austria netted their first goal of the tournament. Busek gathered the ball on the left as England defenders stopped, arms raised, appealing for offside. Busek bore down on McDonald, who turned the shot over his bar. From the corner, England were not to be so fortunate. The ball was cleared to left-half Koller, twenty-five yards from goal, but was hit back crisply into the top corner.

Considering they were apparent no-hopers, Austria seemed determined to go out with a bang. The crowd applauded their neat footwork, but not their playacting. A bunch of British sailors resorted to bugling *The Last Post*, whether at Austrian histrionics or England's apparent demise we shall never know.

In keeping with previous matches, England started to find their touch after the interval. Within five minutes Haynes might have reaped a hat-trick, but his name on the scoresheet was only to be postponed. Szanwald should have held A'Court's shot, but he did not. The ball came back off his chest for Haynes to smash into an empty net.

Encouraged by the scoreboard showing Brazil beating the Soviet Union, England swung into attack. Each of the forwards missed chances before Austria hit back on the break. Körner's long-range shot was not cleanly struck, but it beat McDonald low to his left and squeezed in off a post.

Elimination was now staring England in the face, but Kevan provided a swift riposte. Haynes and Robson set up the chance for him to fend off a challenge before scoring with a fierce shot. The West Bromwich forward's second-half mastery over the veteran stopper, Happel, hinted at the most probable source of victory.

Bobby Robson's World Cup frustration was not yet over. Having had a 'goal' questionably disallowed against the Russians, he now met the same fate. His shot from six yards struck the advancing keeper, but in netting the rebound Robson was adjudged by linesman Zsolt (who refereed against the USSR) to have controlled the ball with his arm. The player insisted the ball hit his side.

The 2-2 draw would have been fatal had the Soviet Union squared the match with Brazil. But Brazil's 2-0 triumph left England and the Soviet Union tied on three points with identical goal tallies. Consequently, England, who had never previously played the Soviets, were now asked to face them for the third time in a month. The subsequent winners would meet Sweden in the last eight.

AUSTRIA    (1) 2                    ENGLAND    (0) 2
Koller 16, Körner 71              Haynes 58, Kevan 77

AUSTRIA: Szanwald, Kollmann, Swoboda, Hanappi, Happel, Koller, E Kozlicek, P Kozlicek, Busek, Körner, Senekowitsch.
ENGLAND: McDonald, Howe, Banks, Clamp, Wright, Slater, Douglas, Robson, Kevan, Haynes, A'Court.

## SOVIET UNION v ENGLAND

*Tuesday, 17 June 1958*                                    *Gothenburg – 23,182*

Conflict between Britain and the Iron Curtain was not restricted to sport. On the Monday, Moscow announced the execution of Imry Nagy, Hungarian prime minister at the time of the 1956 revolution. Britain condemned the act. Behind the scenes in Sweden, England demanded that Istvan Zsolt not take

Szanwald, in goal, fumbles, and Haynes smashes into the empty net. (v Austria)

charge of their play-off. As referee in one match and linesman in another he had been responsible for chalking off two Robson 'goals'. He was duly withdrawn from the short-list.

Winterbottom and the selectors could no longer resist pressure to make changes. Fresh blood was clearly needed, especially to the right flank. Clamp, Douglas and Robson made way. Clayton returned to right-half. Making their debuts in this, England's most critical match in years, were the Wolves inside-forward, Peter Broadbent, and another Peter – the exciting twenty-year-old Chelsea winger – Brabrook, renowned for his acceleration and shooting power. Although Haynes was suffering from severe blistering on both feet, he retained his place. Tom Finney hoped that nine days' recuperation would be enough for his knee. It was not. Despite a press campaign for his inclusion, Bobby Charlton was again overlooked. He would be one of five unused England players in Sweden. For their part, the Soviets showed two changes from the earlier 2-2 draw. The winger Alex Ivanov was dropped for Apoukhtin, and Salnikov made way for Fallin.

Although opening sluggishly in all their games, the reshaped English team was unable to mend its ways. For half an hour the Soviets held the whip hand, but were mercifully profligate in front of goal. Not till nearly half-time did England threaten, when Broadbent forced Yashin to save smartly, then drew the keeper off his line and slipped the ball to the other Peter. Brabrook had only to tap it in, but poked the ball straight at Yashin. At half-time the tally showed eight Russian and three English shots at goal, and many yawns from spectators lazing in the sun.

Winterbottom's dressing room pick-me-ups must have been potent, for once again his team re-emerged to play out of their skins. England's offside trap now stifled Soviet attacks at birth, while around Yashin's goal white shirts buzzed menacingly. Kevan came close, Brabrook closer, striking the inside of Yashin's right-hand post, not once, but twice – on each occasion the ball rebounding straight to the goalkeeper. When the Chelsea winger did find the net, the effort was wiped out for hand-ball.

England's fast, fluent play was now stretching their opponents to the limit. The harassed Krijevski thumped the ball over his own crossbar to thwart Kevan. It was, then, a vicious twist of fortune when, with their first worthwhile attack of the second half, the Soviets took the lead. McDonald's feeble clearance was picked up by a surprised Fallin out wide. The ball sped quickly to Voinov, then to Simonian, who, as Wright committed himself, laid the ball off to Ilyin. McDonald came out but was beaten to his right. With cruel disregard for the law of averages, the ball rolled in off a post. Soviet discipline gave way to wild jubilation.

The match was not yet over. Kevan burst through, to be foiled by Yashin's athletic save. In shooting, Kevan twisted an ankle and limped out the final minutes. When Albert Dusch of West Germany blew for time, England had lost the one match they emphatically deserved to win, and were out of the World Cup. Wright summoned his players to the centre circle, where they saluted the four corners of the ground. Winterbottom brought his dejected players home two days later, to be received by the fury of the press, who demanded the sacking of the manager, selectors, and certain England forwards. It would be no consolation when, four months later, the Soviet Union left Wembley thrashed 5-0 by a team spearheaded by the overlooked Lofthouse and Charlton.

Two other British teams required play-offs to determine their fate. The sad exception was Scotland, who now boasted the miserable World Cup record of just one draw from five matches. Wales and Northern Ireland, the poor relations of British soccer, overcame Hungary and Czechoslovakia respectively in their play-offs, though they both fell at the next hurdle, played just two days later. Northern Ireland, having circumvented a domestic regulation forbidding matches on Sundays, were put firmly in their place by France. Little Wales, the team most fortunate to qualify for Sweden, lost to Pelé's first World Cup goal for Brazil. The Soviet Union, too, fell tamely at the quarter-finals, and the fact that all three teams surviving play-offs tumbled at the quarter-finals – having to play three matches in five days – drew the curtain down on World Cup play-offs.

Peter Brabrook's effort is ruled out for handball. (v USSR play-off)

Brazil went on to rapturously claim the trophy – presented by Arthur Drewry, now president of FIFA. They demolished Sweden 5-2 to become the first nation to win the Cup outside its own continent. This time, at least, immeasurably the best team in the world had won.

Public reaction in England was full of 'what might have beens'. The pre-Munich eleven was thought to have been as good as any team in Sweden. The loss of Tom Finney had deprived the rump of that side of its one ball-playing genius. Nevertheless, England were the only team to avoid defeat by the eventual champions. In the previous two years, England had faced each of the four would-be semi-finalists. Three had been comprehensively beaten (Brazil 4-2, France 4-0, West Germany 3-1), while the fourth, Sweden, had been held to a goalless draw in Stockholm.

In the debit column, the sum of English achievements in three World Cup finals was a miserable two wins out of ten. Of the players, only McDonald, Howe and Wright were thought to have enhanced their reputations. Critics harped at the workmanlike, utilitarian ideals imported into the national team from league champions Wolves.

With an eye to the future, demands were made to reduce the number of domestic fixtures. Questions were asked about shouldering Walter Winterbottom with all manner of administrative duties, such as booking air-tickets and arranging transport. The introduction of Brazil's 'fourth back' game hinted at a revolution in tactics. TV was criticised for its saturation football coverage: many countries' ticket allocations in Sweden were not taken up.

With the nation temporarily replete from football, television returned to its staple diet of the late 'fifties: *Dragnet, The Adventures of Tugboat Annie, Bronco,* and the pioneer in news coverage, *Tonight.*

| SOVIET UNION  (0) 1 | ENGLAND  (0) 0 |
|---|---|
| Ilyin 66 | |

USSR: Yashin, Kesarev, Kuznetsov, Voinov, Krijevski, Tsarev, Apoukhtin, V Ivanov, Simonian, Fallin, Ilyin.
ENGLAND: McDonald, Howe, Banks, Clayton, Wright, Slater, Brabrook, Broadbent, Kevan, Haynes, A'Court.

---

*Final Positions – Pool IV*

| | P | W | D | L | F | A | Pts |
|---|---|---|---|---|---|---|---|
| BRAZIL | 3 | 2 | 1 | 0 | 5 | 0 | 5 |
| SOVIET UNION * | 3 | 1 | 1 | 1 | 4 | 4 | 3 |
| England | 3 | 0 | 3 | 0 | 4 | 4 | 3 |
| Austria | 3 | 0 | 1 | 2 | 2 | 7 | 1 |

* The Soviet Union qualified after play-off with England.

---

*England appearances and goalscorers*
*World Cup qualifying rounds and final competition 1958*

| | Apps | Goals | | Apps | Goals | | Apps | Goals |
|---|---|---|---|---|---|---|---|---|
| Wright W *† | 8 | – | Hall J | 4 | – | Hodgkinson A | 3 | – |
| Haynes J | 7 | 2 | Byrne R * | 4 | – | Matthews S *† | 3 | – |
| Clayton R | 5 | – | Taylor T * | 4 | 8 | Ditchburn E | 1 | – |
| Finney T *† | 5 | 1 | Edwards D | 4 | 2 | Dickinson J *† | 1 | – |
| McDonald C | 4 | – | Clamp E | 3 | – | Brooks J | 1 | – |
| Howe D | 4 | – | Douglas B | 3 | – | Pegg D | 1 | – |
| Banks T | 4 | – | Robson R | 3 | – | Brabrook P | 1 | – |
| Slater W | 4 | – | A'Court A | 3 | – | Broadbent P | 1 | – |
| Kevan D | 4 | 2 | Atyeo J | 3 | 4 | | | |

---

| * Appeared in 1954 World Cup. | *26 players* | *19 goals* |
|---|---|---|
| † Appeared in 1950 World Cup. | | |

# 4

# THE 1962 WORLD CUP

Following successive World Cups in Europe, the finals of 1962 returned to South America. The privilege of host nation might have gone to Argentina, but for her track record of repeated boycotts in the 1930s and again in the 'fifties under the direction of Juan Peron. Chile's record was not much better, but in the wake of devastating earthquakes in 1960 she pleaded successfully for the right to stage the tournament not to be withheld.

English football was in the doldrums again. Unlike the wake of the 1954 World Cup, no notable innovations were forthcoming, and by the 1960-61 season league attendances had dipped to their lowest post-war level, 28.6 million. The British countries, ostrich-like, turned their backs on the first European Nations Cup (now the European Championship), won in 1960 by the Soviet Union. Restricted to 'friendlies', Winterbottom's team stumbled from defeat to defeat. During a disastrous American tour in 1959 England were beaten by Brazil and Peru. And Mexico! That same year Sweden emulated the Hungarians of 1953 and won at Wembley (3-2). England's initial results in 1960 reaffirmed the dispiriting downward trend. Defeats were recorded in Madrid and Budapest as England prepared for their first qualifying match of the new World Cup.

Away from football, the world had a new Pope, John XXIII. Fidel Castro had seized power in Cuba, and General de Gaulle been installed as President of the Fifth French Republic. Great strides were taken in exploration: the US submarine *Nautilus* passed under the North Pole, and a British expedition spearheaded by Hillary and Fuchs trekked overland to the South. The Soviet Union launched a series of Luniks, which successfully photographed the far side of the moon. New forms of transport replaced old. The last British steam locomotive had been built in 1958, and the London-Birmingham section of the M1 motorway opened. The hovercraft, too, arrived, making its maiden Channel crossing.

*Qualifying Group 6*

## LUXEMBOURG v ENGLAND
*Wednesday, 19 October 1960*                          *Luxembourg – 5,000*

England were pitted against Portugal and Luxembourg in a qualifying group less benign than it had been in 1958. Luxembourg were not expected to ruffle any feathers, but Portugal were. Their team of the immediate post-war years had been a shambles, losing twenty goals to England in three matches between 1947 and 1951. More recently, however, the Portuguese had shown signs of building a capable side, constructed largely around a clutch of players from mighty Benfica. In 1955 England had been beaten 1-3 in Oporto, and three years later had exacted revenge at Wembley by the odd goal in three. So, for the first time, England's qualification for the World Cup finals was by no means assured.

To begin with, the task was to collect two points from little Luxembourg, who had recently lost four goals to a Belgian 'B' eleven. Winterbottom's team was unrecognisable from that in Sweden. Only Bryan Douglas, Bobby Robson and Johnny Haynes remained. Haynes had assumed the captaincy from Billy Wright, whose England career ended with the American tour of 1959. Tom Finney, too, had seen the last of international football. The heavyweight Bobby Smith of Tottenham, and Manchester United's Bobby Charlton, both unused in Sweden, had now forced their way into the side, but the remaining places were filled by comparative newcomers.

The goalkeeping jersey had passed to Sheffield Wednesday's Ron Springett, robust and brave, but suspect with long shots. The new full-backs were Jimmy Armfield of Blackpool and twenty-year-old Mick McNeil of Middlesbrough. The job of replacing Billy Wright had fallen to another Wednesday player, Peter Swan. Left-half remained the property of Wolves, Bill Slater giving way to the fair-haired Ron Flowers, now in the midst of a run of forty successive internationals. The one player not yet mentioned was destined to become a footballing legend. Chelsea's Jimmy Greaves had first pulled on an England shirt eighteen months earlier, when barely nineteen. This line-up played together for the first time less than two weeks before the trip to Luxembourg, when poking five goals past Northern Ireland.

The city of Sheffield may have boasted two England men, but it no longer had any trams, being the last English city to dispense with them. The farthing, too, had disappeared, ceasing to be legal tender. In the cold war, an American U2 spy-plane, piloted by Gary Powers, had been shot down by the Russians, and Britain had agreed to base Polaris-armed submarines at Holy Loch.

In October it was announced that National Service would be wound up, ending the call-up of young men into the armed forces. The takeover was announced of the Liberal paper, the *News Chronicle*, by the Conservative *Daily Mail*. An early soccer bribes scandal caused consternation to the chairman of the Professional Footballers' Association, Jimmy Hill.

In politics, Labour back-benchers, among them Bill Rodgers, campaigned against the 'disastrous trend towards unilateralism and neutralism within the Party'. John Kennedy confronted Richard Nixon in a televised debate during the run-up to the American presidential election. The incumbent president, Eisenhower, abruptly ceased trade with Cuba, inviting speculation of a full-scale invasion of Castro's island fortress.

British television was still reeling from one of the most harrowing interviews ever screened. On *Face to Face*, John Freeman's dogged interrogation on matters relating to pain, failure and suffering reduced Gilbert Harding to tears. Harding's frank wish to die, and its fulfilment some weeks later (from natural causes), provoked an outcry against the inquisitorial use to which television had been put.

In similar vein were the reported reactions to Ricky Valence's Number One single *Tell Laura I Love Her*. The song featured a young man who died on a race-track, but not before proclaiming his love for 'Laura'. Reports of female suicides, brought on by the lyrics, made this one of the most controversial and best remembered records of the period. But by the time Luxembourg entertained England's footballers, Ricky Valence had been displaced from the top spot by the equally memorable, and no less traumatic, *Only the Lonely* by Roy Orbison.

The new chart topper might have referred to Ron Springett, about to endure one of the most uneventful ninety minutes of his career. The amateurs of Luxembourg (their one professional was injured) were no match even for a mediocre English team. A sparse crowd of 5,000 dispersed about the Municipal Stadium witnessed England's second largest victory since the war. Television was blamed for the disappointing attendance.

England were two up inside seven minutes, thanks to Charlton's deadly finishing, and four ahead by half-time. Seven minutes into the second half England carved the best goal of the game when Greaves left three men trailing in his wake before teeing up the ball for Bobby Smith. A luckless Luxembourg defender was caught in his line of fire and had to retire for temporary repairs. The whole Luxembourg team would have welcomed repairs to their morale, for by the end the English tally was nine; comprising hat-tricks for Charlton and Greaves, a pair for Smith and one for Haynes. England had, for once, exhibited a refreshing ruthlessness against poor opposition.

Ron Springett had earned his wages with a minimum of fuss, and probably found time while the game was contested in distant parts to reflect on the obscenity trial of *Lady Chatterley's Lover*, which had just commenced amid much prurient debate. Upon their return home, the whole team might have been deceived into thinking that the thousands of pennants waved by children lining London's streets were to commemorate their continental goal spree. Instead, it was to welcome the King and Queen of Thailand, in Britain on a state visit.

Following the televising of England's romp in Luxembourg, viewers were treated to two of the more original series of the early 1960s – *Chan Canasta* and *The Strange World of Gurney Slade* – and the Queen launching Britain's first atomic-powered submarine, *HMS Dreadnought*.

LUXEMBOURG   (0) 0            ENGLAND   (4) 9
                             Charlton 3, 7, 65,
                             Greaves 15, 75, 80,
                             Smith 22, 52, Haynes 55

LUXEMBOURG: Stendeback, Brenner, Hoffmann, Merti, Brosius, Jann, Schmidt, Cirelli, May, Konter, Bauer.
ENGLAND: Springett (Sheff W), Armfield (Blackpool), McNeil (Midd'bro), Robson (WBA), Swan (Sheff W), Flowers (Wolves), Douglas (Blackburn), Greaves (Chelsea), Smith (Spurs), Haynes (Fulham), Charlton (Man U).

## PORTUGAL v ENGLAND
*Sunday, 21 May 1961*                              *Lisbon – 65,000*

By the time England travelled to Lisbon, in May 1961, Yuri Gagarin had become the first man in space, aboard the soviet spaceship *Vostok*. The United States had a new President, Kennedy, who no sooner had taken office than he authorised an abortive invasion of Cuba at the Bay of Pigs. In Britain, the Temperance Seven with *You're Driving Me Crazy* tried to dislodge American domination of the charts by Del Shannon's *Runaway* and the Marcels' version of *Blue Moon*. On the race track, Stirling Moss won the Monaco Grand Prix.

The fortunes of England's footballers had also taken a sharp upturn. A sequence of six wins, beginning with those over Northern Ireland and Luxembourg, had accumulated a vast haul of forty goals, including nine against Scotland and eight against Mexico. The glut had not been confined to modest opposition. Among the victims had been a Spanish team brimming with the talents of di Stefano, Gento, Suarez and Santamaria from the club sides Real Madrid and Barcelona.

Several factors lay behind this successful run. Winterbottom had adopted a 4-2-4 formation for the first time. The key linkmen, Haynes and Robson, had both been playing at their peak. A nucleus of just thirteen players had been called upon for all six matches, inviting comparisons with the settled, unbeaten team of 1955-57. Winterbottom also benefited from closer cooperation from league clubs, which agreed to release their players more readily. Previously, the manager's face-to-face preparations had been restricted to a few days, or hours, before each match. The new arrangement inevitably fostered better team spirit.

Barring another Munich, the run might even carry on into Chile. No one was rash enough to propose that the present side was as strong as that built around Duncan Edwards, but it was a team with few conspicuous weaknesses.

Portugal had shown few in accounting for Luxembourg 6-0. Despite England's recent run, away results since 1958 were disappointing, showing just two wins (against Luxembourg and the United States) from seven matches. Yet with goal average once again immaterial, England could not afford to lose in Lisbon. Portugal were basking in Benfica's march to the Final of the European Cup – shortly winning it – and had reason for confidence. Eight Benfica players lined up against England and, in centre-half Germano, Portugal possessed one of Europe's outstanding players.

The match was played in the beautiful, marble-built national stadium. The horseshoe-shaped coliseum perched on a hillside overlooking the Atlantic, the sea on one side, luxurious wooded slopes on the other. The pitch's turf had been imported from Cumberland and offered a playing surface comparable with Wembley. The temperature, however, was not comparable, up in the eighties, despite a 4 p.m. kick-off.

A splendid contest saw Portugal seize the early initiative. Germano clamped an iron grip on Bobby Smith, and Greaves seldom escaped the attentions of Cruz. The English defence coped comfortably with Portuguese assaults, and Springett distinguished himself when necessary. Armfield characteristically raided up the right touchline, and it was from one such sortie that England carved out their best chance of the first half. Pereira, the goalkeeper, failed to clear Armfield's cross, but Smith headed wide.

An hour had passed when the home team took the lead. Aguas played the ball down the middle. Robson fudged a pass back to his goalkeeper, and Aguas, following up, thumped it past Springett.

Encouraged by their score, Portugal attacked with fluent menace. But a second goal, which might have sealed the result, would not come and England broke out to equalise. Haynes was upended outside the box. Taking the free-kick himself, he flicked the ball sideways to Flowers who crowned a fine game with a mighty shot. The ball flew off a Portuguese defender and into the goal.

From then on, England pressed for the winner. Portugal's earlier composure evaporated, and only Pereira's alertness secured the draw. The England party flew out of Portugal to continue their European tour (winning in Italy, losing in Austria). Within weeks the long-feared departure of Jimmy Greaves and Gerry Hitchens was finalised: Greaves went to A C Milan, Hitchens to Internazionale.

| PORTUGAL (0) 1 | ENGLAND (0) 1 |
|---|---|
| Aguas 60 | Flowers 82 |

PORTUGAL: Pereira, Lino, Hilario, Mendes, Germano, Cruz, Augusto, Santana, Aguas, Coluña, Cavem.
ENGLAND: Springett, Armfield, McNeil, Robson, Swan, Flowers, Douglas, Greaves, Smith, Haynes, Charlton.

## ENGLAND v LUXEMBOURG
*Thursday, 28 September 1961*                              *Highbury – 33,000*

The new league season coincided with a flagging of the national team. A 1-3 defeat in Vienna put an end to England's year-long unbeaten run. The loss of Greaves and Hitchens complicated Winterbottom's team planning. Although both players' contracts contained release clauses, the experience of John Charles at Juventus, who enjoyed a similar clause but who was forbidden to participate in Wales' qualifiers, led the England manager to cast uneasily around for replacement forwards. But football at large was again in the throes of revolution. The ending of the maximum wage was thought to make players less interested in playing for their countries. Johnny Haynes, the England captain, had become Britain's first £100 per week footballer.

With Bobby Smith struggling for form and Haynes sustaining a thigh injury, a reshaped attack was drafted for the expected formality of thrashing Luxembourg. Haynes' usual understudy was Arsenal's George Eastham, who – while at Newcastle – had been at the focus of a freedom-of-contract row. Eastham had been omitted from the squad, so in his absence a second cap was awarded to Manchester United's Dennis Viollet. As spearhead, Smith and Greaves were replaced by newcomers, Ray Pointer of Burnley and a third player from Hillsborough, John Fantham.

Like England's football team, international peace had suffered setbacks in mid-1961: the Berlin Wall had gone up; British forces had made heavy weather of assisting Kuwait, after the newly independent sheikhdom was threatened by neighbouring Iraq; and the Secretary-General of the United Nations, Dag Hammarskjold, had died in a mysterious plane crash in the trouble-torn Congo.

In Britain, the press was gripped by a sensational murder investigation. Michael Gregsen had been killed and his friend Valerie Storie severely wounded in the so-called 'A6 Murder'. More fortunate, or so it seemed, was Vivian Nicholson, who won £152,000 on the football pools. Announcing a 'spend, spend, spend' philosophy, she was destined to become one of the most publicised pools victims, as the money slipped easily and rapidly through her fingers. Another success story was longer lasting. After twenty-seven years Stanley Rous had resigned as secretary to the FA to become president of FIFA. The one-time games master at Watford Grammar school, who refereed the 1934 FA Cup Final, thereby became the third Englishman to be elected FIFA president out of six to have held that office since 1904.

'England play, or should it be play with, Luxembourg tonight,' scoffed one tabloid. For over half an hour, the amateurs from the tiny principality held out pluckily against a rag-bag of English attacks. Luxembourg forced two early corners, and when Hoffmann was put clean through only Springett's legs prevented a goal. To try to assert themselves, England resorted to brute force, resented by 33,000 spectators concerned to see fair play.

Captained by Armfield in Haynes' absence, England stumbled from error to error. Most of their shots were fired from long range. Pointer lifted the ball over an open goal, Charlton skimmed the crossbar, and when Fantham missed a sitter he was whistled by the crowd. In the midst of England's ill-directed assaults, Springett had to dive at Schneider's feet to keep his goal intact.

Not until the thirty-fifth minute could an embarrassed England side open their account, when Pointer steered home a Douglas centre after good work by Robson. Viollet then pounced when Steffen failed to collect a high cross. Knowing his place in the side would inevitably return to a fully fit Johnny Haynes, Viollet could be forgiven an obsession with John Leyton's smash hit *Johnny Remember Me*.

On the stroke of half-time Bobby Charlton, who had achieved little, climaxed the best move of the match. After the break the visitors tired visibly, yet still mounted vigorous counter-attacks. When McNeil conceded a free-kick just outside his penalty area, Dimmer scored, earning the loudest cheer of the night. Time was played out to a chorus of boos and catcalls whenever England players made a mistake, which was frequent enough. Although Charlton scored a fourth goal for England, hitting back an attempted clearance with a crisp half-volley, his team sought the sanctuary of the dressing-rooms with the jeers of the crowd resounding in their ears.

ENGLAND  (3) 4                    LUXEMBOURG  (0) 1
  Pointer 35, Viollet 37,              Dimmer 67
  Charlton 45, 80

ENGLAND: Springett, Armfield, McNeil, Robson, Swan, Flowers, Douglas, Fantham, Pointer, Viollet, Charlton.
LUXEMBOURG: Steffen, Brenner, J Hoffmann, Zambon, Brosius, Konter, Dimmer, Cirelli, N Hoffmann, Schneider, Schmidt.

## ENGLAND v PORTUGAL
*Wednesday, 25 October 1961*                    *Wembley – 100,000*

A month later, England entertained Portugal at Wembley in the group decider. In the interim Luxembourg had performed England an improbable good turn, inexplicably beating Portugal 4-2. A draw would now be enough to see

England through to Chile. To qualify themselves, Portugal needed to dispose of England twice, first at Wembley, then in a play-off.

Like Portugal, England suffered a disappointing preparation, struggling to hold the Welsh to a draw in Cardiff. In just five months England's performances had deteriorated alarmingly. Tottenham Hotspur were engaged in a protracted tug-of-war with Milan to negotiate Greaves' return to this country. This would shortly be achieved, although Greaves was excluded from the team to face Portugal. John Connelly, the Burnley forward adept on either wing, returned to the side along with Haynes. Dennis Viollet had survived Munich: he had not survived Luxembourg. At left-back, the stylish Ramon 'Ray' Wilson reclaimed his place, despite playing in the second division with Huddersfield Town. Portugal's team was without Germano, Cruz, and Augusto, but included a powerful nineteen-year-old, Eusébio. He, like half the side, hailed from the colony of Mozambique.

The newspapers informed that the Soviet Union had tested two hydrogen bombs. The British government announced contingency plans to supply powdered milk to babies should Soviet bombs contaminate natural milk. James Hanratty had been charged with the 'A6 Murder'. He would eventually be hanged, precipitating a much-publicised campaign to clear his name. In the hit parade, another James – Jimmy Dean – drawled the brave but tragic tale of *Big Bad John*, while teenage sensation Helen Shapiro was *Walking Back to Happiness*. A new dance craze had arrived – the Twist. On TV, millions of viewers saw pint-sized comedian Charlie Drake knock himself out during a slapstick sequence.

Hoping England would not knock themselves out of the World Cup, the BBC provided saturation coverage. The match was televised live in the afternoon, highlights broadcast on *Sportsview* in the early evening, and a further half-hour recording transmitted in a late *Soccer Special*.

As with all cup matches, both teams coveted an early goal. The battle for the quick breakthrough was won emphatically by England. After ten minutes they led by two goals. Portugal failed to clear Wilson's long free-kick, allowing Connelly to pivot and prod into goal. Then Robson centred, the ball was knocked on by Haynes, and the Burnley pair Pointer and Connelly raced to reach it. Pointer won, unleashing a rising shot.

These early goals cemented the outcome of the match, and – as Portugal needed to win – took much of the sting from it. A swirling wind interrupted moves by both sides, but could not prevent Eusébio from demonstrating that here would be one of the world's great players. Both before and after half-time he smashed shots against Springett's post. On each occasion Aguas might have capitalised on the rebound. When Aguas himself headed Yuaca's cross against a post, Portugal realised the gods had abandoned them and that England were destined to travel to Chile. Winterbottom's much-trumpeted 4-2-4 system was no longer producing the goods, and Haynes' insipid showing prompted fresh demands for a new captain.

The next morning Britain woke up to news of further crisis in Berlin. American and Soviet tanks confronted each other along the Berlin Wall. The US garrison had been put on battle alert.

ENGLAND  (2) 2                    PORTUGAL  (0) 0
   Connelly 5, Pointer 10

ENGLAND: Springett, Armfield, Wilson, Robson, Swan, Flowers, Connelly, Douglas, Pointer, Haynes, Charlton.
PORTUGAL: Pereira, Lino, Hilario, Perides, Soares, Vicente, Yuaca, Eusébio, Aguas, Coluña, Cavem.

*Qualifying Group 6*

|           | P | W | D | L | F  | A  | Pts |
|-----------|---|---|---|---|----|----|-----|
| ENGLAND   | 4 | 3 | 1 | 0 | 16 | 2  | 7   |
| Portugal  | 4 | 1 | 1 | 2 | 9  | 7  | 3   |
| Luxembourg| 4 | 1 | 0 | 3 | 5  | 21 | 2   |

*Other group results*
Portugal v Luxembourg     6-0          Luxembourg v Portugal    4-2

## World Cup finals – CHILE                    May-June 1962

Chile were hardly ideal hosts for a World Cup. The earthquakes of 1960 were estimated to have damaged up to a third of all the buildings in the country. There were doubts about Chile's capacity to organise the competition effectively when her economic sense of priorities was obviously governed by earthquake relief. In the event, these arguments proved double-edged. Rather than switch the finals elsewhere, FIFA confirmed the appointment, out of compassion as much as anything else. The devastated country, stretching 3,000 miles from tip to toe, was in need of a boost. She could have her World Cup.

The tournament's return to South America was not cheered by Europe's football devotees. Inter-continental live television had not yet arrived, and match highlights were not shown on British TV until forty-eight hours later.

This inconvenience may have softened the blow to the Scots, Welsh and Irish. This time, England would carry British hopes alone. Northern Ireland lost twice, narrowly, to West Germany; Wales were put out by Spain; and Scotland, after a play-off, by Czechoslovakia. Other notable absentees included Sweden and France (who finished second and third in 1958), and Austria, who pulled out. Once again, Africa and Asia would not be represented. Following their huffy withdrawals last time, these nations were thrown together with European teams in mixed qualifying groups. None survived.

The Italian and Spanish squads arrived in Chile under a cloud of controversy. Both countries had been luring star players from abroad to play in their domestic leagues, whom they then swiftly 'naturalised'. They then quoted FIFA's 'residence' regulation to send out those same players for the national team. Included in the Italian squad were two Argentines, plus Altafini, who had played for Brazil in the 1958 World Cup under the name 'Mazzola'. Spain had the audacity to field the great Hungarian Puskás in their ranks. To put a stop to this, FIFA announced that in future a player could turn out for one country only, that of his father or his birth.

None of this affected England. In any case, one wonders how the public would have reacted to the prospect of, for example, Osvaldo Ardiles playing for this country. In 1962, as in 1958, Winterbottom took just twenty players to the finals instead of the permitted twenty-two, this time with Derek Kevan and Gordon Banks as stay-at-home reserves.

| Position | Name | Club | Age | Caps | Goals |
|----------|------|------|-----|------|-------|
| Goalkeepers | Ron Springett | Sheffield W | 26 | 21 | – |
| | Alan Hodgkinson * | Sheffield U | 25 | 5 | – |
| Full-backs | Jimmy Armfield | Blackpool | 26 | 25 | – |
| | Ray Wilson | Huddersfield | 27 | 11 | – |
| | Don Howe * | WBA | 26 | 23 | – |
| Centre-backs | Peter Swan * | Sheffield W | 25 | 19 | – |
| | Ron Flowers | Wolves | 27 | 32 | 7 |
| | Maurice Norman | Tottenham | 28 | 1 | – |
| Midfield | Bobby Robson * | WBA | 29 | 20 | 4 |
| | Stan Anderson * | Sunderland | 28 | 2 | – |
| | Bobby Moore | West Ham | 21 | 1 | – |
| | Johnny Haynes (c) | Fulham | 27 | 52 | 18 |
| | George Eastham | Arsenal | 25 | – | – |
| Forwards | Bryan Douglas | Blackburn | 27 | 29 | 8 |
| | Jimmy Greaves | Tottenham | 22 | 18 | 19 |
| | Gerry Hitchens | Internazionale | 24 | 5 | 3 |
| | Bobby Charlton | Manchester U | 24 | 35 | 24 |
| | John Connelly | Burnley | 23 | 8 | 3 |
| | Roger Hunt | Liverpool | 23 | 1 | 1 |
| | Alan Peacock | Middlesbrough | 24 | – | – |

* Would not play in the finals or in future.    *Averages*  25.4  15.4

Jimmy Adamson of Burnley made the trip as assistant to Walter Winterbottom, following Billy Wright's resignation from that post to manage Arsenal.

---

One advantage of the current over the previous World Cup squad was the international experience accumulated. Eleven players had earned ten caps or more. Nevertheless, the constitution of the squad was heavily criticised. Many thought the skilful Johnny 'Budgie' Byrne worthy of a place, but the handicap of third division football with Crystal Palace, before being transferred to West Ham in March 1962, proved too great. Rugged Ray Crawford, centre-forward with Alf Ramsey's champions Ipswich, had also been pressing for inclusion. Both he and Byrne had earned recent caps. Other forwards passed over were Bobby Smith and Ray Pointer, both prominent in the qualifying rounds. Included was the untried centre-forward from second division Middlesbrough, Alan Peacock, who had stepped into Brian Clough's shirt at Ayresome Park.

Notwithstanding its shortcomings, Winterbottom's squad comprised players of proven quality. Right-back Jimmy Armfield had to be good to oust his more-than-competent predecessor Don Howe, who was still in his mid-twenties. Armfield started his playing career as a winger, and when moving to defence was considered the prototype of the modern overlapping full-back. He was so cool under pressure on the pitch that it came as no surprise to learn that he was a pipe-smoker off it.

Armfield's full-back partner was destined for a place in England's hall of fame. Ray Wilson shrugged off the handicap of second division football to force his way into the England team. Assured in every aspect of his craft, Wilson, too, began his footballing life as a forward. He would eventually earn sixty-three England caps, a record for a full-back.

In attack, England took along two contrasting world-class players. The balding, harassed-looking Bobby Charlton could play anywhere up front, from direct winger to deep-lying centre-forward, although his customary position at the time was outside-left. When in full stride, his wispy hair streaming behind him, a dip or swerve could take him either side of opposing defenders – or, if necessary, straight through them. Above all, Charlton is remembered for his shooting prowess. He could strike the ball cleanly from any distance or angle and with either foot. His speciality was shooting at goal on the run, and although he was not a complete footballer – he could neither head the ball nor tackle well – his goalscoring record speaks for itself. His forty-nine international goals are more than any other Englishman has managed.

The player who (prior to Gary Lineker), came nearest to surpassing Charlton's tally, had a completely different goalscoring knack. Jimmy Greaves' tally would be forty-four England goals from half as many appearances as Charlton. Greaves' armoury was centred on stealth, speed, killer instinct.

Whereas Charlton scored most of his goals with power from some distance, Greaves preferred to nudge the ball over the line, being always at the right place at the right time. His critics would complain that his instinct for goals was Greaves' only footballing attribute. He was less adept at defending or making goals for others, and should his name fail to appear on the score sheet it was often difficult to find any other positive contribution. Greaves thrived on the long, early ball sent through the middle, but the arrival of twin central defenders as part of the 4-2-4 revolution had tended to bottle up his favourite route to goal. His goalscoring peak had come in 1960-61, when he had bagged eleven goals in five successive matches. After a brief, unhappy spell in Italy, he had returned to London.

Another of England's footballing celebrities was having a rough time with the critics. Johnny Haynes' style of play did not please everybody. Neither did his style of captaincy. Despite, or maybe because of, his well-groomed appearance and his talent for after-dinner speeches, he was widely seen as conceited and intolerant of the mistakes of others. His familiar shrug of the shoulders following a team-mate's error irked many spectators, especially in the north of England where his footballing strengths were never fully appreciated. Haynes had just emerged from a sapping season, steering Fulham away from relegation but into the semi-finals of the FA Cup. When things were going well, England had no finer player, but when the national team was struggling, as of late, Haynes was less than the perfect choice, both as player and captain.

Abandoning the practice of arriving late – as Winterbottom had done with three previous World Cup finals – the England squad departed from London on 17 May, with a fortnight to spare before their opening match. They journeyed via New York, Jamaica, and Peru, where they won their final warm-up match 4-0. Once in Chile, Winterbottom and his party ensconced in a gymnasium in Coya, over 2,000 feet up in the Andes, and accessible only by rail car or narrow path. The site was normally used as a rest centre for executives of the American-owned Braden Copper Company. Facilities included golf course, tennis courts, and a ten-pin bowling alley. A training pitch beckoned from outside bedroom windows, though not all players appreciated the monastic seclusion. Some had to stay in a miners' shack with corrugated roof. To reach the canteen meant crossing a narrow wooden bridge with plunging drop either side. The complex was an hour's drive from Rancagua, the smallest of the four World Cup venues, where England would play their initial matches. Just four stadia would be utilised for the entire competition. Rancagua's Braden Stadium, set against a backdrop of the Andes, could accommodate a mere 25,000 spectators. It would be an unpalatable indication of the esteem of English football that none of their matches would more than half-fill the stadium.

England had found themselves in Group 4 for the third successive World Cup. Their opponents on this occasion were Hungary, Argentina and Bulgaria. The Argentines based themselves seven miles down the valley from the English camp, whereas the two other European squads took over new hotels in Rancagua itself.

## HUNGARY v ENGLAND
*Thursday, 31 May 1962*                                              *Rancagua – 7,938*

For reasons of psychology as much as anything, Hungary were the most unwelcome of opponents. On top of the double humiliations inflicted by the Magic Magyars in the early 1950s, England had lost again, 0-2 in Budapest in 1960. Though the Hungarians were but a shadow of their former selves, England did not approach the match in Rancagua with any great confidence. Morale had not been helped by losing to Scotland at Hampden for the first time in a quarter of a century.

After sixteen years in charge, Winterbottom more or less had his way with team selection. The side he chose to face Hungary was that which had beaten Peru 4-0 in Lima *en route* to Chile. Illness contributed to this selection. Centre-half Peter Swan had travelled to South America with tonsillitis. England still took no official doctor with them on tours, and Swan would become seriously ill before the tournament was over. The Tottenham stalwart, Maurice Norman, gratefully seized his chance. Norman had been included in the 1958 World Cup squad, but had only won his first cap against Peru.

Haynes' usual midfield partner was Bobby Robson, but he had chipped an ankle. Against Peru his normal understudy, Stan Anderson of Sunderland, had been passed over in favour of a young man called up at the last moment. His name was Bobby Moore, and he had served a solid apprenticeship as captain of the England Under-23s. Like Norman, Moore would earn his second cap against Hungary. At centre-forward Winterbottom fielded Gerry Hitchens. Blacked because of his Italian connection, Hitchens had spent a year in the international wilderness before returning to England colours. In all, only four of the team – Charlton, Greaves, Flowers and Armfield – had prior experience of playing in South America.

World events, when not dominated by tensions in Berlin and the Congo, still retained a violent flavour. Following an attempt to assassinate de Gaulle, the streets of Paris reverberated to the sound of gunfire. In Jerusalem, the appeal of Adolf Eichmann, head of the Gestapo's Jewish Affairs, against the death sentence for war crimes and crimes against humanity, particularly against the Jews, was rejected. He was hanged on the day of the match, the first condemned criminal to suffer execution in Israel, and his ashes were scattered at sea to prevent any permanent grave becoming a neo-Nazi shrine.

Up in space, the American astronaut Scott Carpenter, orbiting the earth in *Aurura 7*, lost contact with mission control, but still splashed down safely. At home, the Queen attended the consecration of the new Coventry Cathedral, designed by Sir Basil Spence, after the original had been destroyed by German bombers; the Crazy Gang, pioneers of lunatic radio humour, gave their farewell performance after thirty years; and the contraceptive pill was made freely available through Family Planning Association clinics.

The Catholic Argentines had no truck with contraceptive pills, but during their opening match one feared that the aim of Argentine boots was designed to reduce the number of offspring sired by Bulgarian footballers. With just one venue per group, matches had to be played on separate days. The England party watched Argentina defeat Bulgaria 1-0, with an early lead protected at all costs. The match yielded sixty-nine free-kicks, and the Bulgarians were left with a spate of injuries that included stud marks down one player's spine.

The following day, England felt in need of the *Good Luck Charm* advocated by Elvis Presley from the top of the hit parade. Unlike Argentina, the Hungarians had no need of ale-house tactics. They had qualified for Chile untroubled by the Dutch or East Germans. They retained their goalkeeper, Grosics, from their famous team of 1953-54. He was now appearing in his third World Cup finals. Hungary's defence was composed of six-footers, and their playing formation based on a fluid 4-6 system. As many as six men were directed upfield if the situation permitted. Though deprived of the likes of Hidegkuti and Puskás – the latter playing for Spain – Florian Albert and Lajos Tichy were no mean players in their own right. Albert would one day be voted European Footballer of the Year.

On a chilly day, and on a pitch greasy following heavy drizzle, England came off worse from the opening exchanges. Yet they seemed to be settling when they conceded the first goal. Haynes lost possession. The ball was despatched to Tichy, who ran on to shoot from outside the box. The ball passed over Springett's head and appeared to go through his arms.

The stimulus of Tichy's goal spurred Hungary to long spells of dominance. Wilson was stretched by Sándor's pace, and Norman and Flowers were overworked down the centre. The midfield was effectively surrendered. Rákosi kept a tight rein on Haynes, and Moore was so taken up with defending that he was unable to support an attack where only Charlton created any hope. Greaves and Douglas both endured miserable matches, and Hitchens seemed bemused – expecting the ball to be delivered to feet, Italian style, instead of into space. Hungary's tall defenders dealt easily with the string of high crosses pumped into their penalty area.

On the stroke of half-time only a double save by Springett kept England in the game. It was as well he did, for on the hour England were awarded a penalty. Grosics had dropped Douglas's corner. In the ensuing scramble

Greaves let fly and a defender handled on the line. Though the small crowd whistled in his ears, Flowers was equal to the task.

Douglas and Hitchens squandered half-chances before the Magyars reasserted themselves. None the less, there was a touch of fortune, or maybe magic, about their second goal. England's man of the match, Flowers, raced back to tackle Albert, but was deceived both by the player and the pitch. Flowers lost his footing and landed on his rear. The advancing Springett was also wrong-footed, permitting Albert a fine goal.

That was the end of England. The British Ambassador to Chile politely applauded the players from the pitch, leaving the press to lambast the whole philosophy of English football. Bob Ferrier of *The Observer* reported: 'In top class world competition our players are like children abandoned in a vast forest, lacking in poise, calculation, variety of pace and adaptability of tactics.' Whatever, unless England could overcome Argentina, their interest in the 1962 World Cup finals seemed over almost before it had begun.

HUNGARY  (1) 2                    ENGLAND  (0) 1
Tichy 17, Albert 70              Flowers 60 pen

HUNGARY: Grosics, Mátrai, Sárosi, Solymosi, Mészöly, Sipos, Sándor, Rákosi, Albert, Tichy, Fenyvesi.
ENGLAND: Springett, Armfield, Wilson, Moore, Norman, Flowers, Douglas, Greaves, Hitchens, Haynes, Charlton.

## ARGENTINA v ENGLAND
*Saturday, 2 June 1962*                              *Rancagua – 9,794*

The match with Argentina, just two days later, assumed life or death proportions for England. Just one change was made to the team, Gerry Hitchens standing down to enable Alan Peacock to make his international debut. This was a calculated gamble. Peacock was taller and stronger than Hitchens, with a somewhat military bearing, better able to cope with the physical punishment likely to be meted out by Ruben Navarro. The Argentines, coached by Juan Carlos Lorenzo, had made the trip across the Andes after hammering eleven goals past hapless Ecuador to qualify. Lorenzo made four changes to the team that beat Bulgaria. He gave a World Cup debut to Antonio Rattín, whose name, if not widely known in 1962, would never be forgotten after 1966. Argentina's style still revolved around a free defender, or *libero*, Sacchi being handed the job in Chile. The pervasive violence of the first round matches had prompted FIFA's organising committee to intervene: the managers of all sixteen competing nations were warned of the consequences for future excesses.

Chile's changeable weather was impersonating Britain's, for on this occasion the Braden Stadium was bathed in sunshine. Taking their cue, England gave a performance that invited accusations of schizophrenia. Against all predictions they ran the South Americans ragged. Peacock shrugged off the chasm between second division and World Cup football. It was he who met Charlton's cross with a soaring header that appeared to have already passed beneath the crossbar when Navarro's straining hand pushed it out. Two penalties in two matches. Once again the unflappable Flowers was entrusted with the kick.

Stricter refereeing – by the Russian Latichev – allied to a more constructive Argentine approach, lightened fears that the match would degenerate into a bloodbath. But Argentina's ball-mastery could not disrupt England's overall superiority. Armfield and Wilson were outstanding. Haynes began to show touches of his old self, and Moore not only curtailed the wizardry of Sanfilippo, but also found space to spark attacks of his own. Up front, Charlton tormented the Argentine back line, well supported by Douglas, though Greaves was well shackled by Páez.

With perfect timing, England scored a second goal just before the interval. Another marauding run by Armfield climaxed with a shot against the post. Flowers nipped in, side-stepped a tackle and passed out to Charlton, who from the edge of the box struck the ball right-footed inside Roma's far post.

Argentina visibly wilted in the second half. Bélen was foolish enough to clash with Armfield, and spent much of the second period receiving treatment for damaged ribs. Only once did England fear for their lead. Moore's hand impeded a strong shot at goal, but the referee waved away Argentine claims for a penalty. Even on an off day Greaves was still dangerous, as he shortly confirmed. Douglas made room for a shot, Roma could only parry, and there was Greaves, materialising out of nowhere to drive the ball into the net.

With the game drifting to its tired conclusion, Argentina pulled a goal back. Marzolini touched a free-kick to Sacchi, whose curled pass into the danger zone was dabbed past Springett by Sanfilippo.

With the final whistle, England had won their first match in the World Cup finals since beating Switzerland in 1954.

| ARGENTINA (0) 1 | ENGLAND (2) 3 |
|---|---|
| Sanfilippo 81 | Flowers 17 pen, Charlton 43, Greaves 70 |

ARGENTINA: Roma, Capp, Páez, Navarro, Marzolini, Sacchi, Rattín, Oleniak, Sosa, Sanfilippo, Belén.
ENGLAND: Springett, Armfield, Wilson, Moore, Norman, Flowers, Douglas, Greaves, Peacock, Haynes, Charlton.

## BULGARIA v ENGLAND
*Thursday, 7 June 1962*                                          *Rancagua – 5,700*

Benefiting from five days rest, in which to shake off the knocks and bruises inflicted by Navarro and others, England set out to face Bulgaria with a place in the quarter-finals at stake. Bulgaria might have come from Mars, so little was known about them. The crib-sheet said simply that these were Bulgaria's first World Cup finals, and the national side was based on players from the CDNA Sofia (Army) team. Bulgaria had eliminated France to qualify. France's 3-0 win in Paris had been cancelled out by a last-minute (shades of 1994) 0-1 reverse in Sofia. In the play-off in Milan, Bulgaria won again by the only goal. Small wonder that English eyes took in their every move in Chile. Bulgaria had followed up their creditable 0-1 defeat by Argentina by capitulating wretchedly against Hungary. After twelve minutes they trailed by four goals, ending up losing 1-6.

The fixtures had smiled on England, for they tackled Bulgaria the day after Hungary and Argentina had wound up their own programmes. That meeting, a goalless draw, duly propelled Hungary into the last eight as winners of Group 4. The runners-up position would be filled either by Argentina or England.

FIFA had changed the set-up, yet again, for the 1962 finals. Criticism of play-offs in previous World Cups, plus tight scheduling in Chile, meant quite simply that there was no room for extra matches. From now on, goal average would determine all group placings for teams level on points. Furthermore, and this was less welcome, there would no longer be replays for drawn quarter-finals and semi-finals. In these cases, lots would determine who lived and who died.

The introduction of goal average had worked out well for England, since theirs was superior to Argentina's. A draw against Bulgaria would be enough. There being no reason to disrupt the team, it stayed as it was.

In the meantime the world learned of the worst aviation disaster in history involving a single aircraft, when a chartered Boeing 707 crashed on take-off from Orly Airport in Paris. Better news awaited the players and supporters of Oxford United, whose club were elected to the Football League to replace the defunct Accrington Stanley. Equally jubilant were Mike Sarne and Joe Brown. Sales of their records, *Come Outside* and *Picture of You*, threatened to overtake those of Elvis at the top of the charts.

The match with Bulgaria was an apology for professional football. As in 1958, England left their weakest opponents till last and almost made a hash of the job. Their performance was as slipshod as the Derby the previous day, when seven horses were brought down near Tattenham Corner, leaving Larkspur to win. Bulgaria were widely dismissed as the worst team in Chile, yet England matched them error for error. Indeed, camouflaged by an unfamiliar red strip to avoid a clash with Bulgaria's white, England might have hoped that their worst indiscretions went unrecognised.

Headed for home whatever the result, Bulgaria seemed concerned only that England should not score. The grey skies frowned, the cold gnawed at the bones, and the sparse crowd hooted with derision at the fare set before them. No England player rose above the general ineptitude. Haynes was hustled out of his stride, Peacock was smothered by the attentions of two markers, and Greaves spurned two early chances, though he did wriggle free to strike a post from a tight angle.

As the match wore on, England gradually retreated into a nervous, nine-man defensive cocoon. Even this cordon couldn't prevent Sokolov and Kostov wasting half-chances. Midway through the second half, Bulgaria fluffed the best chance of the game. Kostov beat Armfield on the by-line and crossed for Kolev, who found himself unmarked in front of goal. To undisguised English relief the header sailed wide.

It was a popular theory at the time that the Bulgarians had been so incensed by Argentine maltreatment that they were determined to upstage their savage conquerors. In front of a noisy contingent of Argentine supporters, Bulgaria – so the story went – made sure the English Gentlemen prospered.

With neither side wishing to score, the final fifteen minutes dissolved into a non-event. Bulgaria perfected the knack of passing the ball from man to man in a backward spiral until it reached the goalkeeper. In a later age, FIFA might have cried 'fix'. When the final whistle blew, England had become the first team to progress to the last eight on goal average, having reached that stage for only the second time.

BULGARIA   (0) 0          ENGLAND   (0) 0

BULGARIA: Naidenov, Pentchev, Zechev, D Kostov, Dimitrov, Kovachev, A Kostov, Velitchkov, Sokolov, Kolev, Dermendiev.
ENGLAND: Springett, Armfield, Wilson, Moore, Norman, Flowers, Douglas, Greaves, Peacock, Haynes, Charlton.

---

*Final positions – Group 4*

|           | P | W | D | L | F | A | Pts |
|-----------|---|---|---|---|---|---|-----|
| HUNGARY   | 3 | 2 | 1 | 0 | 8 | 2 | 5   |
| ENGLAND   | 3 | 1 | 1 | 1 | 4 | 3 | 3   |
| Argentina | 3 | 1 | 1 | 1 | 2 | 3 | 3   |
| Bulgaria  | 3 | 0 | 1 | 2 | 1 | 7 | 1   |

---

Ron Springett cannot hold Garrincha's free-kick and Vavá pounces. (v Brazil)

## BRAZIL v ENGLAND
*Sunday, 10 June 1962*                              *Viña del Mar – 17,736*

As Group 4 runners-up, England travelled to meet the winners of Group 3 at the scenic coastal resort of Viña del Mar, with its Sausalito Stadium framed by pine and eucalyptus trees. Taking the field against Bulgaria, England were unsure who lay ahead. Simultaneously, Czechoslovakia were playing Mexico. If the Czechs won handsomely – as expected against a team seeking its first ever World Cup win in thirty-two years of trying – they would head Group 3 and play host to England or Argentina. As it turned out, either Czechoslovakia preferred their chances against Hungary, or else the Mexicans had a surprise in store, for the Czechs were beaten 1-3. That left Brazil on top.

England doubtless cursed this outcome. Twice they had reached the quarter-finals of the World Cup, and twice they had been asked to play the defending champions. Back home, the press reacted philosophically: England had achieved what they could, and all that was left was honourable elimination.

Against Bulgaria, rather than rest key players for the expected quarter-final, and risk a fatal defeat, Winterbottom fielded his strongest eleven. Now several players showed signs of battle fatigue. A thigh strain ruled out the impressive Peacock, permitting Hitchins to return. The rest had to grin and bear it.

Just twelve players had been called upon in four matches. Four of them –
Armfield, Flowers, Charlton and Haynes – survived the 0-2 defeat by Brazil in
Rio in 1959.

For the second successive World Cup England played a Brazilian team
minus Pelé, injured against the Czechs. At twenty-one, he was already touted as
the world's finest player. But Brazil, managed now by Aymore Moreira, would
not miss him. Nine of the 1958 World Cup Final team were still around,
including Garrincha, Gilmar, and the veterans Djalma and Nilton Santos. Vavá
and Didí had acquired European experience since Sweden. The average age of
the side was thirty, one reason why Moreira was now playing a more cautious
4-3-3.

Consistent only in their baffling inconsistency, the England players matched
their Brazilian counterparts thrust for thrust in the most nerve-tingling and
dramatic of the four quarter-finals. Nine minutes into the match Didí limped off
for running repairs to a leg injury. In his absence, England, playing in all white,
laid siege to the Brazilian goal. Charlton danced round Djalma Santos and
whipped the ball across, only for Greaves to volley too high. The Spurs man
continued his undistinguished World Cup, his only notable success being to
crouch on all fours and capture a dog that had strayed onto the pitch.

Flowers thundered a Haynes centre just wide. Armfield created two chances,
the first for Hitchens, the second miskicked by Douglas. As if to celebrate
Didí's return, Brazil swung into majestic attack. Armfield scooped a Garrincha
effort off the line. Amarildo muffed a shot from ten yards but was given
offside. Brazil's 4-3-3 formation gave them an extra man in midfield, where
Zito was running rampant. Ahead of him, Garrincha, the 'little bird', tormented
the English defence with that characteristic hobbling run.

A goal had to come. Zagalo's hard-driven corner was met cleanly by
Garrincha, despite conceding seven inches in height to Norman. A Brazilian
percussion band provided joyous applause.

Vivified by the goal, Brazil threatened to take England apart. Flowers, in a
dream, set up Amarildo, and was grateful for Springett's desperate
intervention. Then England swept upfield to score a dramatic equaliser. Haynes
flighted in a free-kick for Greaves to head against a post. The ball fell to
Hitchens who hooked it into goal.

The pendulum now swung England's way, and it was Brazil who were most
pleased to hear the half-time whistle. More of the same, and England had every
chance of reaching the semi-finals for the first time.

Amarildo reappeared for the second half with a thigh tightly strapped. With
Didí also limping, Brazil were down to nine fit players. Yet nine was enough.
Straight from the restart Vavá's 'goal' was wiped out. England were forced
back on their heels and were soon chasing the game. Flowers was pulled up for
a questionable foul on Vavá. Didí stood over the ball, then stepped aside as

Gilmar clears from Ron Flowers, in front of the commentary gantry. (v Brazil)

Garrincha smashed the ball in a blur through England's defensive wall. The ball exploded from Springett's chest for the in-rushing Vavá to nod back into goal.

Six minutes later, the irrepressible Garrincha looked up and fired a vicious shot that dipped and swerved beyond the perplexed England goalkeeper. Springett appeared nonplussed, although Brazil knew all about Garrincha's spiralling, 'autumn leaf' shooting.

By now, the percussion band was deafening. Brazil snuffed out England's muted response, while at the other end Norman and his co-defenders were permitted no respite from Garrincha. Without Pelé to seize the limelight, the crippled genius was playing to an awestruck gallery. When at last the torture was over, the England team slunk disconsolately from the pitch, Armfield, Flowers, and the splendid Charlton openly distressed.

Brazil, still without Pelé, went on to retain the World Cup, defeating Czechoslovakia 3-1 in the Final, but the tournament as a whole had been a grim affair. Tactics had been more defensive, more cynical, more violent. No player scored more than four goals, and even Brazil were regarded as weaker, if older, than in Sweden. For England, Haynes was singled out for blame. This was the second World Cup in which the team had been built around the Fulham player. Following Winterbottom's conversion to 4-2-4, it was inevitable that, unless the midfield axis performed, England would struggle. Haynes did not, and England did. Only two players drew consistent praise, Charlton in attack, Armfield in defence. The Chilean press voted the Blackpool defender the tournament's outstanding right-back.

| BRAZIL (1) 3 | ENGLAND (1) 1 |
|---|---|
| Garrincha 31, 59, Vavá 53 | Hitchens 38 |

BRAZIL: Gilmar, D Santos, Mauro, Zózimo, N Santos, Zito, Garrincha, Didí, Vavá, Amarildo, Zagalo.
ENGLAND: Springett, Armfield, Wilson, Moore, Norman, Flowers, Douglas, Greaves, Hitchens, Haynes, Charlton.

---

*England appearances and goalscorers*
*World Cup qualifying rounds and final competition 1962*

| | Apps | Goals | | Apps | Goals | | Apps | Goals |
|---|---|---|---|---|---|---|---|---|
| Springett R | 8 | – | Wilson R | 5 | – | Pointer R | 2 | 2 |
| Armfield J | 8 | – | Robson R * | 4 | – | Hitchens G | 2 | 1 |
| Flowers R | 8 | 3 | Swan P | 4 | – | Peacock A | 2 | – |
| Douglas B * | 8 | – | Moore R | 4 | – | Fantham J | 1 | – |
| Charlton R | 8 | 6 | Norman M | 4 | – | Viollet D | 1 | 1 |
| Haynes J * | 7 | 1 | McNeil M | 3 | – | Connelly J | 1 | 1 |
| Greaves J | 6 | 4 | Smith R | 2 | 2 | | | |

---

| * Appeared in 1958 World Cup. | *20 players* | *21 goals* |
|---|---|---|

---

# 5

# THE 1966 WORLD CUP

Back in 1960 FIFA had confirmed that when Europe hosted the 1966 World Cup the privilege would fall to England. In view of the team's Jekyll and Hyde exploits in Chile, it was apparent that if the originators of modern soccer were ever to lift the Jules Rimet trophy, then they would never be more favoured to do so. As Winterbottom had guided England through all four previous campaigns, it would have been a fitting tribute to his years of service had he been granted this one last shot. As it turned out, the managership of the England team was now in other hands.

Upon returning from Chile, Winterbottom resigned his position to become general secretary to the Central Council of Physical Recreation. He might have stayed within the Football Association had he succeeded Stanley Rous – now president of FIFA – as secretary, but the coveted post went to Denis Follows. First choice as Winterbottom's successor was Jimmy Adamson, his assistant in Chile, but Adamson turned the job down. After months of speculation, in February 1963 the new England team manager was announced as Alf Ramsey.

Winterbottom and Ramsey were chalk and cheese. Winterbottom, tall, scholarly, affable, was a soccer theorist, but he had never played at international level, nor enjoyed prior managerial experience. Star names of the 1950s were on record as saying that players of their calibre had no need of coaching, and should be allowed to play their natural game. Professionally and socially a gulf always separated the general from his troops. Winterbottom's duties were onerous. As team manager, director of coaching, tea-boy, travel agent, his was an invidious work-load, without even the guarantee of being able to pick his own teams. The existence of a selection committee blighted the sixteen years Winterbottom gave to the job. Nevertheless, he departed with a creditable record. Of 137 matches under his charge, seventy-eight had been won and only twenty-seven lost.

Whereas Winterbottom had not been an international player, Ramsey had played for his country thirty-two times. He had tasted the World Cup finals at first hand, and had suffered ignominious defeat by the United States and Hungary. Ramsey had been a notable club manager, taking unfashionable

Ipswich Town to the second division and first division championships in successive seasons. With impeccable timing, as Winterbottom tendered his resignation, Ipswich were lording it over the country.

But there was more to Ramsey than managing the best team in the land. It was the manner of his achievement that raised eyebrows. Ramsey had a talent for turning unexceptional players into world-beaters. Few people today can run through his successful Ipswich side – Ray Crawford, perhaps, excepted. If Ramsey could achieve so much with so little, it was asked, what could he do with the resources of the nation?

As a condition of acceptance, Ramsey – a pragmatic, loyal, private man – insisted on full autonomy. If he could work magic with England, he would work it alone. At a stroke he severed the burden under which Winterbottom had laboured for so long. The international selection panel was consigned to history. Ramsey's team would be Ramsey's choice. With players themselves recently freed from the indignity of the maximum wage, he would stand as a professional manager working alongside professional footballers.

One favour bestowed upon the hosts and holders of the World Cup is automatic entry to the finals. This is a double-edged honour. Though England avoided the risk of not qualifying, they endured a four-year quarantine, unable to test the pulse of competitive football. Familiarisation within the team and with likely World Cup opponents was restricted to years of 'friendlies', where results are often deceptive and where players who hide when the chips are down remain undetected. The only competitive practice available to England was through the European Nations Cup, but Ramsey's managerial baptism turned sour with instant elimination, 2-5 in France, in the first round. Undaunted, Ramsey affirmed with disarming frankness that England would win the World Cup.

The England team on that disappointing day in Paris read: Springett, Armfield, Henry, Moore, Labone, Flowers, Connelly, Tambling, Smith, Greaves, Charlton. Ramsey began the task of dismantling at once. Springett relinquished the goalkeeper's jersey to Gordon Banks of Leicester City. Centre-half Brian Labone was 'rested' from international football for four years. Bobby Moore was switched from right-sided midfield to central defence, at the expense of Ron Flowers. George Eastham was brought in for an extended run. Faith was retained in Bobby Charlton on the left wing, while Bryan Douglas, Terry Paine and Peter Thompson were all let loose on the right. Ramsey took a managerial axe to Johnny Haynes. The hub of the England team for two World Cups had played his last match in Chile. Haynes' style was not Ramsey's. A career that had brought fifty-six caps was terminated when Haynes was still just twenty-seven years old.

The world at large saw turbulent times between 1962 and 1966. Before the Brazilian fiestas had subsided the Cuban missile crisis was upon us. By 1966,

President Kennedy had been assassinated, though not before sowing the seeds of the Vietnam War, from which his successor, Lyndon Johnson, was unable to extricate himself. In the Soviet Union, Khrushchev had been ousted by dual leaders, Leonid Brezhnev and Alexei Kosygin. Britain had gone through two prime ministers. Macmillan had handed over to Alec Douglas Home, who proved no match for the wiles of the Labour leader, Harold Wilson. A Labour government would preside over the first World Cup since 1950. Winston Churchill was dead, prompting the grandest public funeral Britain had ever seen. Even the Stars and Stripes flew at half mast, the first ever US salute to a non-American commoner.

This being the missile age, Britain had launched one of her own, Blue Streak. China became the fifth member of the exclusive nuclear club. Quasars had been discovered in distant galaxies, American and Soviet cosmonauts were space-walking, and Valentina Tereshkova had become the first woman in orbit.

Britain had been knocked to its knees by scandals. Kim Philby had been unmasked as the 'third man', his exposure following that of William Vassall. The biggest and juiciest scandal involved spies, call-girls, government ministers and an intricate plot that ate its way who knows where. It came to light in 1963, with a *dramatis personae* that included Christine Keeler, Mandy Rice-Davies, Stephen Ward. By the time the dust had settled, Ward had taken his own life and Secretary of State for War, John Profumo, had resigned. For a time it looked as though Macmillan's government might fall. These succulent melodramas helped divert attention from de Gaulle's refusal to permit Britain into the EEC. Equally newsworthy was the Great Train Robbery, the Glasgow-London mail train having been stripped of a cool £2.5 million. It was a bad time for trains generally: the Beeching Report recommended axing half the stations and one-third of the nation's tracks.

Youth culture reverberated to the Beatles and to 'mods' and 'rockers'. The latest, short-lived, fashion was topless dresses. 'Swinging London' had created household names, David Bailey, Jean Shrimpton, Carnaby Street. Pirate radio flourished. Up-market BBC2 had arrived, offering 'high-brow' programmes as an alternative to the existing channels. Television satire was spearheaded by the trend-setting *That Was The Week That Was* (TW3). Cassius Clay (Mohammed Ali) dominated world boxing.

England's intention to stage the biggest and best World Cup required feverish organisation. FIFA's specification that all pitches should measure 115x75 yards ruled out certain famous stadiums – notably Highbury – whose pitches could not be extended. Goodison Park, the best-equipped league stadium, needed much structural modification, including the demolition of a row of houses behind the Park Stand, before it was deemed satisfactory. Although Wembley could not count itself among the super-stadiums that had staged previous World Cup Finals, England could supply the necessary half-dozen supporting stadiums of a standard few other countries could match. The government contributed almost £500,000 to aid the tournament, the fund directed mainly at ground improvements.

In view of the World Cup's commercial considerations, it came as a bitter disappointment when, yet again, Scotland, Wales and the two Irelands were dumped by the wayside. Scotland proved unequal to Italy, the Soviet Union put out Wales, and Northern Ireland were eliminated by Switzerland. The Irish Republic's group was won by Spain. The clutch of Iron Curtain countries on their way would bring just a handful of spectators between them. Africa's teams withdrew in protest at FIFA's edict that just one place was on offer for the combined African and Asian entry. That place would be filled by North Korea. Of the sixteen nations that competed in Chile, all but three lined up in England.

The draw for the tournament was made in January 1966 at the Royal Garden Hotel, Kensington. The seeding arrangements were simple, to keep England and Brazil (hosts and holders) apart, and to allocate the four South American teams to separate groups. Following precedent, the host nation would play its group matches in the capital, where gate receipts would be highest. Completing Group 1 were Uruguay, Mexico and France. This was a nostalgic assortment. The first World Cup match ever played, back in 1930, had been between Mexico and France in Uruguay. More to the point, England had beaten all three at Wembley in the past few years, and never lost at home to any of them.

The initial rounds would be contested at four centres, each comprising two venues – London (Wembley and White City), the Midlands (Villa Park and Hillsborough), the north-west (Goodison Park and Old Trafford), and the north-east (Roker Park and Ayresome Park). As in Chile, each round of matches would span two days. With thirty-two fixtures to be completed within nineteen days, FIFA retained the principle of no play-offs or replays, except for the Final.

FIFA were grateful that they still possessed a Cup to be handed over. The Jules Rimet trophy had been stolen whilst on display at a London stamp exhibition. National humiliation loomed until the Cup was found, one week later, by a dog named Pickles in someone's garden. With his proven ability to hunt down the trophy, Pickles might have been a better choice of mascot than World Cup Willie, who beamed out from myriads of souvenirs.

Ramsey's long count-down to 1966 was not without its setbacks. In 1964 his team were thrashed 1-5 in Rio by Brazil, and the following year Austria became the third foreign team ever to triumph (3-2) at Wembley. The World Cup was a mere nine months away. The press derided Ramsey and his 'promise' of ultimate triumph.

Hitherto, Ramsey had employed wingers as a matter of course. In December 1965, six weeks after the defeat by Austria, he sent out a side in Madrid, against the Spanish European champions, playing 4-3-3. By replacing a conventional right-winger with the hard-running Alan Ball, and pulling left-winger Bobby Charlton deeper and more central, England looked solid and won 2-0. Although much experimentation remained, nine of the side that beat Spain would play in the World Cup Final.

June was the customary month for World Cup finals, but the organisers deferred the opening match until 11 July, when English soccer appetites would be replenished. The England squad enjoyed two month's solid preparation between season's end and their first World Cup match.

Whereas many rivals opted to take the pressure off, Ramsey budgeted for a month's get-together at Lilleshall before jetting off on a strenuous European tour with the finals just two weeks away. Any injuries now, and it was goodbye Wembley. England won four out of four (Finland 3-0, Norway 6-1, Denmark 2-0, Poland 1-0), and the blend and team-spirit seemed as healthy as anything in recent years. On top of earlier victories over West Germany, Scotland and Yugoslavia, England entered the tournament riding on seven straight wins. Not that they had proved popular tourists. Their winning streak was built on method and muscle. Controlled aggression was the hall-mark of the side, free-kicks conceded with gay abandon. The English press acknowledged that Ramsey's no-nonsense style was unlikely to win friends. None the less, as the final hours ticked away, England could look back on twenty-one matches over two years with just the Austrian defeat against them. Looking through the list of finalists, only Hungary had ever beaten England in this country. The omens were not bad.

Ramsey was required to lodge his twenty-two man squad with FIFA eight days before the tournament commenced.

| No | Name | Position | Club | Age | Caps | Goals |
|----|------|----------|------|-----|------|-------|
| 1 | Gordon Banks | Goalkeeper | Leicester | 28 | 27 | – |
| 2 | George Cohen | Full-back | Fulham | 26 | 24 | – |
| 3 | Ray Wilson | Full-back | Everton | 31 | 45 | – |
| 4 | Norbert Stiles | Midfield | Manchester U | 24 | 14 | 1 |
| 5 | Jack Charlton | Central defence | Leeds | 30 | 16 | 2 |
| 6 | Bobby Moore (c) | Central defence | West Ham | 25 | 41 | 2 |
| 7 | Alan Ball | Midfield/Forward | Blackpool | 21 | 10 | 1 |
| 8 | Jimmy Greaves | Central forward | Tottenham | 26 | 51 | 43 |
| 9 | Bobby Charlton | Midfield/Forward | Manchester U | 28 | 68 | 38 |
| 10 | Geoff Hurst | Central forward | West Ham | 24 | 5 | 1 |
| 11 | John Connelly | Winger | Manchester U | 27 | 19 | 7 |
| 12 | Ron Springett * | Goalkeeper | Sheffield W | 30 | 33 | – |
| 13 | Peter Bonetti | Goalkeeper | Chelsea | 24 | 1 | – |

| 14 | Jimmy Armfield * | Full-back | Blackpool | 30 | 43 | – |
| 15 | Gerry Byrne * | Full-back | Liverpool | 28 | 2 | – |
| 16 | Martin Peters | Midfield | West Ham | 22 | 3 | 1 |
| 17 | Ron Flowers * | Central defence | Wolves | 31 | 49 | 10 |
| 18 | Norman Hunter | Central defence | Leeds | 22 | 4 | – |
| 19 | Terry Paine | Winger | Southampton | 27 | 18 | 7 |
| 20 | Ian Callaghan | Winger | Liverpool | 24 | 1 | – |
| 21 | Roger Hunt | Central forward | Liverpool | 27 | 13 | 12 |
| 22 | George Eastham *† | Midfield | Arsenal | 29 | 19 | 2 |

* Would not play in the finals or in future.    *Averages*    26.5  23.0
† George Eastham had the misfortune to be named in the World Cup final squads in both 1962 and 1966, but never took the field.

Ramsey opted for a numbering system that, more or less, gave his ideal first team Nos. 1-11 and his second string players Nos. 12-22. It is apparent that he had instilled one invaluable commodity – experience. Of his preferred eleven only Hurst had accumulated less than ten caps (and he would, in any case, not feature in England's group matches). No fewer than six of Ramsey's second strings had played in a dozen or more internationals. Whatever lay ahead, the players could not plead rawness as an excuse. As the squad settled into the Hendon Hall Hotel, the bookmakers installed them as second favourites behind Brazil.

Augmenting the experience was the trail of genuine ability that ran through the squad. Gordon Banks had performed in goal without blemish for three years. Now would come his big test. The four defenders in front of him had welded into a formidable unit. Partnering Ray Wilson, now with Everton, at full-back was a chirpy Londoner, George Cohen. Head down as he surged down the line, Cohen was a memorable sight of the mid-1960s. He had to be good: he kept Jimmy Armfield out of the side.

England had at last unearthed a centre-half to rank with Neil Franklin and Billy Wright. Jack Charlton was an unlikely candidate for World Cup hero. Living in the shadow of his famous younger brother, 'our kid', Jack did not force his way into the England team until April 1965, a month before his twenty-ninth birthday. Only when Don Revie arrived at Leeds in 1962 did Charlton respond to the discipline necessary to make him an international player. Tall, with a straining, giraffe posture, Jack Charlton pretended to be nothing other than an effective stopper. Powerful in the air, he was a menace on opposing goal-lines at corner-kicks.

Jack Charlton was helped by playing alongside one of the great names of English football. Bobby Moore had blossomed since moving to central defence and adopting the captaincy into a player of genuine world class. Serene in temperament and cool under pressure, he brought such mastery to his craft that his comparative slowness about the field and his weakness in the air were easily compensated. His footballing mind was as quick as any, and, rather than confine his talents to those of a sweeper, he was always looking to take the ball out of defence and build attacks.

Moore always rose to the occasion, playing best against the best, although his occasional lapses made some commentators wonder whether the more combative Norman Hunter might be brought in to partner his Leeds club-mate, Jack Charlton. But Ramsey knew the World Cup would bring out the best in Moore. Besides, he complemented Charlton perfectly, the one marking, the other covering, with telepathic understanding.

If Jack Charlton's inclusion in the England side was a fairy tale, that of Nobby Stiles bordered on the incredible. Pleasant enough off the field, with his bank-clerk spectacles, Stiles developed meaner qualities on it. No one pretended he could gain international honours through skill. He lacked most of the requisite talents, except one. Stiles hunted the ball as a hound, starved for a week, might chase a hare. Oblivious to opponents foolish enough to get in his way, Stiles ferreted in front of his defenders, cajoling and barking at their shortcomings whenever an assailant broke through. Stiles was the competitor *par excellence*.

**World Cup Finals – ENGLAND**                                    **July 1966**

**ENGLAND v URUGUAY**
*Monday, 11 July 1966*                                    *Wembley – 87,148*

In early July the Queen and the Duke of Edinburgh paid a nervous visit to Northern Ireland. The province was stirring uneasily. The Reverend Ian Paisley was agitating against the policy of economic cooperation with the Irish Republic. Bottles and chunks of cement were thrown at the royal car. Clashes were also reported outside the US Embassy in London over American bombing in North Vietnam.

Dr Emil Savundra was publicly savaged over the collapse of his Fire, Auto and Marine Insurance Company. He had vanished from a Swiss clinic where he was supposedly receiving treatment for a heart condition (he would later be imprisoned). Myra Hindley was convicted along with Ian Brady of the 'Moors Murders' of three children. On the eve of the Uruguay match, Hindley appealed against her conviction.

In the fashion world, 'hipster' trousers were all the rage, except among the beatniks who roamed London's streets. The Beatles, at the height of their fame, flew to Manila in the Philippines to be welcomed by two battalions of marines and 50,000 screaming teenagers. The foursome left in disgrace two days later, having 'snubbed' Imelda Marcos by breaking an appointment. Theirs was the consolation of being top of the pops, this time with *Paperback Writer*.

The sporting highlight of early July was Manuel Santana's crushing of Dennis Ralston in the men's Wimbledon Final. In the ladies' event, Britain's Ann Jones went out in the semis to Maria Bueno after saving eight match points. Young Billie-Jean Moffitt-King beat the Brazilian girl in the Final. On the track, the late, lamented Lilian Board, then only seventeen, was selected for the women's 440 yards at the Commonwealth Games in Kingston, Jamaica. In cricket, England were two tests down to the West Indies, whose captain, Gary Sobers, rebuked Charlie Griffiths for a bouncer that struck tail-ender Derek Underwood on the head. The rest of the series would be put on ice, until after the football extravaganza.

English football mourned the death of Joe Mears, chairman of the FA. Stanley Rous announced that dope tests would be carried out after each match in the World Cup. Two players from each team would have their names drawn at random. The Brazilians asked for confirmation that coffee was not considered a stimulant. Said a spokesman: 'Our team drinks an awful lot of it.' Households with an aversion to football were in for a rough time. Blanket coverage was planned by both BBC and ITV. Live matches and evening highlights were topped up with daily World Cup reports and the 'game of the week' on Sundays.

Uruguay did not set out to hog the airwaves with spell-binding soccer. Nevertheless, they came to London with a tradition in the World Cup second to none. Twice winners – in 1930 and 1950 – Uruguay could boast a footballing pedigree remarkable for a country with a population of less than three million. Since losing 2-4 in the 1954 World Cup quarter-finals, England had enjoyed the fillip of a 2-1 Wembley success in 1964. Six players were retained from that successful eleven – Banks, Cohen, Wilson, Moore, Greaves and Bobby Charlton. The remaining five places were filled by Nobby Stiles, Jack Charlton, the flame-haired, energetic Alan Ball of Blackpool, who had flitted in and out of the side for a year, Roger Hunt, the grafting, work-horse Liverpool striker, and John Connelly, a fast, direct winger now with Manchester United. Although the era of including two wing-men was long gone, Ramsey, for the time being, kept faith in a solitary orthodox winger, with Bobby Charlton now operating as a deep-lying centre-forward. Neither Charlton nor Greaves, who had been laid low with jaundice, had looked sharp during England's recent continental tour. In Charlton's case, his malaise was baffling. For such a gifted player he was prone to under-achievement.

For his part, Uruguay's redoubtable manager Ondino Viera fielded a team based around the club side Penarol. This was, in part, Hobson's choice, forced by the unavailability of players earning their living in Argentina. The team had qualified without hiccup, taking maximum points from Peru and Venezuela. Horacio Troche and Pedro Rocha had been stars in 1962 and would be in 1966. And only Gordon Banks could hold a candle to goalkeeper Mazurkiewicz.

In front of the Queen, who sat patiently through the opening ceremony on a pitch sanctified by Billy Graham's recent evangelistic crusade, England made an urgent start. In warm evening sunshine they forced three early corners. Connelly and Wilson were the instigators, crashing past heavily built, sky-blue shirted South Americans.

Uruguay manufactured attacks of their own. Aware that Banks was facing the setting sun, first Rocha, then Cortes, sent in pot-shots from thirty yards, the latter requiring a full-length save. At the other end Connelly cut in from the right but shot over.

As time wore on it became clear that England would struggle to penetrate a team employing just two men up front, leaving the rest banked in rows in front of Mazurkiewicz. Neither side was slow to use force. Stiles might have become the first player sent off in the tournament after he threw a punch at Rocha. The referee – the Hungarian Istvan Zsolt, whom England had occasion to remember with disfavour from Sweden – contented himself with a monologue. His words went unheeded. Bobby Charlton, then Moore were crudely floored. Dissatisfied with the lack of judicial response, Connelly and Ball retaliated with scything challenges.

With Uruguay looking increasingly confident, England were obliged to shoot from long distance. Bobby Charlton smashed the ball narrowly over. The final gesture of the half belonged to the South Americans. Moore conceded a free-kick for a push on Cortes. The ball was driven across the face of Banks' goal with nobody able to touch it in.

At half-time it was a familiar story. England had huffed and puffed, seen more possession, but the ball had been put to better use when in the care of the Uruguayans. Neutrals delighted in the way they shielded it, caressed it, stroked it about as a thing of beauty, whereas the England players chased, kicked and thumped it with the affection lavished on a punch bag.

After the interval the pattern continued. Connelly and Hunt were crowded out, Greaves smothered. Bobby Charlton was again infuriating, seeming to meander with the ball to no good effect. Only in the final quarter did England begin to press with conviction. Charlton's drive was deflected onto Mazurkiewicz's chest and away for a corner. These late rallies were directed down the gullies, searching for Greaves and Hunt. Greaves, Connelly and Jack Charlton each managed testing headers, and Connelly almost back-heeled a goal. These efforts were cancelled out by Rocha, pivoting to strike a dipping volley just wide.

The whistle blew to the relief of everyone and the ecstasy of the Uruguayans. England had won sixteen corner-kicks against Uruguay's one, and had mustered fifteen shots at goal – none of which seriously looked like breaking the deadlock. Even the foul-count was against England, conceding seventeen free-kicks to Uruguay's fourteen. Georgie Fame's new chart-topper spoke for the yawning spectators who must have wanted to *Get Away*. The bookmakers responded to the general disenchantment, England's odds against winning the Cup rising to 6-1.

ENGLAND    (0) 0                              URUGUAY    (0) 0

ENGLAND: Banks, Cohen, Wilson, Stiles, J Charlton, Moore, Ball, Greaves, R Charlton, Hunt, Connelly.
URUGUAY: Mazurkiewicz, Troche, Manicera, Gonçálvez, Caetano, Cortés, Rocha, Pérez, Ubinas, Viera, Silva.

## ENGLAND v MEXICO
*Saturday, 16 July 1966*                                   *Wembley – 92,570*

The next day France and Mexico served up equally unappetising fare, drawing 1-1, leaving all four teams in Group 1 with one point. When Uruguay beat France 2-1 the following Friday, England knew that victory over the unfancied Mexicans would leave them with one foot in the quarter-finals.

That same week the British economy slumped. A protracted seamen's strike contributed to one of the worst balance of payments deficits on record. Share prices plunged, sterling came under siege on world markets, and cabinet ministers threatened resignation. Not all was gloom in politics. With astute opportunism, Gwynfor Evans capitalised on the jingoism generated by the World Cup to win the first parliamentary seat (at Carmarthen) for Plaid Cymru – the Welsh Nationalists. So unexpected was his triumph, that prior to the tournament it was possible to get odds of 2,000-1 against it.

The United States reported another of its 'crimes of the century' when eight nurses were mutilated in a Chicago hostel. A ninth escaped by hiding under a bed for six hours. A twenty-four year old seaman, Richard Speck, was charged with the murders. It was a week for show-biz marriages: Frank Sinatra proposed to the crop-haired young star of the TV serial *Peyton Place*, Mia Farrow, and Brigitte Bardot wedded German playboy Gunther Sachs in Las Vegas. The American Jim Ryun knocked more than two seconds off Frenchman Michel Jazy's world mile record. Ryun's time was 3 minutes 51.3 seconds. He became the first American to hold the title since 1934.

Mexico's record in the World Cup was atrocious. Appearing regularly, by dint of feeble opposition in the North and Central American qualifying zone, Mexico had lost all but three of fifteen matches in finals dating back to 1930. Mexico had ended their losing run, happily for them, against Wales in 1958.

England had faced Mexico just twice, surprisingly losing 1-2 in Mexico City in 1959, but extracting handsome revenge, 8-0, at Wembley two years later. Only Bobby Charlton of the current England team savoured memories of that goal feast.

Ramsey made two changes to the side that ran out of ideas against Uruguay. Against Mexico, Ball's tireless running was considered secondary, and his role was taken by West Ham's Martin Peters. Having made his international debut just two months earlier, Peters would pose as a bogus left-winger, his brief being to drift into goalscoring positions from midfield. Like Peter Beardsley twenty years on, once Peters was in, he stayed in. Still searching for a winger to thread nine-man defences, Ramsey tried out Southampton's Terry Paine.

Under overcast skies, Mexico declared their intention from the start. Goalkeeper Calderón said his prayers. (He was playing instead of the veteran Carbajal, who would turn out in Mexico's next match, in a record fifth World Cup finals.) From the kick-off Díaz whacked the ball upfield, as if to be rid of it. Faced with defensive barricades, Cohen and Wilson bombarded Calderón with harmless lobs from the halfway line. Paine was concussed early on, giving him a ready excuse for his inactivity. Starved of service, Greaves and Hunt toiled to no effect, while in midfield Stiles looked so out of sorts that he might have been playing with an orange on a beach.

All the incident of the first half was crammed into its final minutes. Greaves and Moore both headed over Calderón's crossbar. Then Hunt steered a header into the net. The effort was disallowed for a push by Peters.

These snippets served as an *hors d'oeuvre* for a fulminating goal. Bobby Charlton collected the ball in his own half. For what seemed an eternity he strode smoothly and purposefully towards the Mexican goal. For an instant he seemed in splendid isolation, as defenders backed away or moved to cover the expected pass. With the goal in his sights twenty-five yards distant, Charlton cocked his right foot and exploded a shot that seared high to Calderón's right. The goal was as emphatic as a fast bowler snapping middle stump – though a flag raised by a linesman was ignored by the referee. In Mexico, a nation dissolved into a passion of grief.

Most of the second-half excitement was generated by the Mexicans' panic when confronted by the towering Jack Charlton in their penalty area. Peters, more impressive than most, glanced a header that was hacked clear by Chaires. He and Bobby Charlton spurned further chances, before the latter slid the ball into the path of Greaves, who shot across goal. Calderón pushed it out, fatally, to Roger Hunt. Hunt could at least point to the record books as evidence that he had taken part in the game. The crowd chorused 'Oh when the Whites go marching in'. Gordon Banks might have joined in: he was idle enough, earning his £60 match fee without breaking sweat.

So England won their fourth match out of sixteen in World Cup finals, but looked so short on invention as to convince few that they could survive for long.

ENGLAND    (1) 2                    MEXICO    (0) 0
  R Charlton 37, Hunt 76

ENGLAND: Banks, Cohen, Wilson, Stiles, J Charlton, Moore, Paine, Greaves, R Charlton, Hunt, Peters.
MEXICO: Calderón, Peña, Hernández, Chaires, del Muro, Jáuregui, Díaz, Núñez, Borja, Reyes, Padilla.

**ENGLAND v FRANCE**
*Wednesday, 20 July 1966*                                    *Wembley – 98,270*

By concluding their group fixtures one day after Uruguay and Mexico had completed theirs, with a goalless draw, England knew what was required of them against France. Even a one-goal defeat would keep England alive. If they won or drew they would head the group, remain at Wembley and entertain the runners-up from Group 2 – either West Germany or Argentina. The Germans needed a draw against Spain to go though as runners-up, and head for Wembley. If Germany won, it would be Argentina to face England. Alternatively, if England were to lose narrowly to France then, as runners-up to Uruguay, they would leave the sanctuary of Wembley for Hillsborough, Sheffield, to play the winners of Group 2.

As for the French, their hopes were slim, to put it mildly. They needed to score twice without reply against an English defence yet to concede a goal. After taking an early lead against Uruguay, France had capitulated in a manner that prompted unkind reminders of the Maginot Line during World War II. Historically, despite the stimulus of that 5-2 victory over Ramsey's baptismal team in 1963, France's record against England was miserable, just three wins (all in France) from sixteen meetings.

The economic news continued to depress. Prime Minister Harold Wilson had flown to Moscow to discuss arrangements for a Vietnam peace conference. He returned to impose desperate deflationary measures, appearing on television to announce an incomes freeze and increases in the cost of alcohol, petrol and much else. The deputy prime minister, George Brown, tendered his resignation, only to retract it some hours later. For some days Wilson's government teetered on the brink of collapse. Unemployment was particularly worrying, though it comes as a sombre reminder of current trends to learn that those out of work in the summer of 1966 numbered just 264,000.

Alf Ramsey must have wondered whether he would shortly be added to that number but, focusing on the job in hand, he made just one team change. Ian

Callaghan of Liverpool would win his second cap, in place of Terry Paine. Three different wingers had been used in as many matches. Peters retained his position, with Ball again sidelined.

The fact that France were compelled to attack made this the most open game of England's three. France took the game by the horns and after ten minutes created their first real chance. Herbin had been receiving treatment on the touchline. He returned to assist in the build-up, and it was his final header that gave England the flutters. Herbin's injury was not illusory, however, and he did no more than limp through the remaining eighty minutes.

It was as well that Banks, Moore and Jack Charlton looked solid, for England's attack continually fell foul of France's offside trap. For most of the first half France had everything but a goal to show for their superiority.

The clock showed seven minutes to half-time when England took the lead. A fierce shot by Greaves was turned away, and when the same player turned the ball back, Jack Charlton at the far post saw his header thump against an upright. The ball rebounded kindly for Hunt to snap up the easiest of chances. French appeals for offside were not just wishful thinking.

That goal established the pattern of the second half. France took control for long periods. Bosquier and Simon unleashed dangerous shots at Banks. The England keeper then plunged to keep out Simon's header, while at the other end Bobby Charlton's scoring volley was disallowed.

But for a second time England scored against the run of play. Stiles had performed to date like a curate's egg. He had been flattened when colliding with the referee, booked for a foul, and assisted his team greatly by harrying and breaking up French attacks. With fifteen minutes remaining he made one final and lasting contribution – a sickening challenge on France's key player, Simon, that merited more than just a caution. The Frenchman was still pole-axed when Artelesa miscued a bicycle kick inside his own penalty area. Greaves and Callaghan capitalised by setting up a chance for Hunt, whose unimpeded effort was firm but central. It flew straight at Aubour in the French goal, but was fumbled into the net.

Oblivious to their plight, the nine mobile French players carried the game to the end. Hausser's fierce drive was acrobatically intercepted by Banks. But the end was inevitable: France were out, England were through; and by virtue of a Seeler winning goal for West Germany six minutes from time against Spain, it would be Argentina, not the Germans, who would contest England's quarter-final. In this, at least, England were being consistent: three times they had reached the last eight of the World Cup, and three times their opponents hailed from South America.

ENGLAND (1) 2          FRANCE (0) 0
Hunt 38, 75

ENGLAND: Banks, Cohen, Wilson, Stiles, J Charlton, Moore, Callaghan, Greaves, R Charlton, Hunt, Peters.
FRANCE: Aubour, Djorkaeff, Bosquier, Herbin, Artelesa, Budzinski, Herbet, Bonnel, Gondet, Simon, Hausser.

*Final Positions – Group 1*

|         | P | W | D | L | F | A | Pts |
|---------|---|---|---|---|---|---|-----|
| ENGLAND | 3 | 2 | 1 | 0 | 4 | 0 | 5 |
| URUGUAY | 3 | 1 | 2 | 0 | 2 | 1 | 4 |
| Mexico  | 3 | 0 | 2 | 1 | 1 | 3 | 2 |
| France  | 3 | 0 | 1 | 2 | 2 | 5 | 1 |

## ENGLAND v ARGENTINA
*Saturday, 23 July 1966*                                    *Wembley – 90,584*

England enjoyed a mere three-day interlude before turning out against Argentina. That was time enough for the pound sterling to slump to $2.79, and for tragedy to strike in Merioneth, north Wales, when the pleasure craft *Prince of Wales* capsized and sank with the loss of a dozen lives. On the subject of lives, Liberal MP David Steel's Abortion Reform Bill was given a second reading in the House of Commons. High above the earth, Michael Collins performed man's first leap in space when, propelled by a jet gun, he 'jumped' from *Gemini 10* to collect dust boxes from an orbiting Agena rocket. A current earthbound fad was the cramming of ever greater numbers of people into Mini cars. Before the month was out, the record stood at eighteen.

The portents for the confrontation with Argentina were grim. Against Germany, Argentine defender Albrecht had been ordered off. FIFA, later, censured the entire Argentine team for 'unethical tackling'. But the displeasure of football's governing body was not restricted to Argentina. Nobby Stiles, too, was warned as to his future conduct following his vigorous contribution to the game with France. The French press had reacted hysterically to Stiles' unpunished assault on Jacques Simon, labelling him a 'beast' – and worse.

Conscious that expulsion from the tournament awaited Stiles' next misdemeanour, the press speculated whether Ramsey would risk fielding him – especially against Argentina – perhaps sending out Norman Hunter instead. Noises were heard from the FA that, for the good name of English football, Stiles should be 'rested'. Alf Ramsey had no intention of allowing FIFA or the FA to pick his teams. Under the threat of his resignation, the FA relented. Stiles played. So did Albrecht. On the political front, talks between the Foreign Office and the Argentine government on the future of the windswept colony, the Falkland Islands, had been adjourned. In view of the coming fracas, this was just as well.

With their luxuriant skills, Argentina were rightly among the World Cup favourites. They had qualified for the tournament in a canter against Paraguay and Bolivia, and so far in the finals had conceded just one goal. Their famous blue and white stripes offered a proud uniform in which to display their talents. With Brazil and Chile already out, and Uruguay dour rather than dazzling, South America's chief hopes rested with Argentina, for whom goalkeeper Roma, Marzolini and Rattín would now face England in successive World Cups. Argentina had already exacted revenge for that defeat in Chile, winning 1-0 in Brazil's 'little world cup' two years later. Banks, Wilson, Moore and Bobby Charlton belonged to that losing side. So had Jimmy Greaves, but now he was absent, with far-reaching implications.

Ramsey may have had few qualms about retaining Stiles, but an injury to Greaves, coupled with a need to reappraise England's spluttering progress, generated a line-up that would change the shape of world football. Greaves had sustained a gashed shin. The injury, slight in itself, was enough to keep the player out of the game with Argentina but not – if England were victorious – thereafter. To the nation-wide Greaves Adoration Society, the loss of the man who, at that time, had scored more international goals than any other Englishman was a bitter blow.

The task of compensating fell on Geoff Hurst. The twenty-four year old West Ham striker had won just five caps. His was a different game from Greaves. Stronger, better in the air and at shielding the ball, he was what today would be termed a target man. Unlike Greaves, Hurst was not a prolific goal-getter. He had scored just once for England, the public apprehension over his inclusion seemed well founded. Not that Greaves had provided the answer. World Cups had not seen the best of him. He had scored but one goal in Chile, and none so far in 1966.

Ramsey's tactical reappraisal affected the role of a winger in his side. Callaghan had not disgraced himself against France, but collectively that had been England's least convincing performance. Bearing in mind Argentina's combativeness and the need for midfield resilience, Ramsey took a bold decision: he would leave out a winger altogether. Back came the tireless Alan Ball to reinforce the midfield. With only Hurst and Hunt stationed permanently up front, England would play a system fluctuating between 4-3-3 and 4-4-2. The 'wingless wonders' had arrived.

The bookmakers were not impressed. With Brazil eliminated and England as exciting as an Andy Warhol movie, new favourites were installed – Brazil's conquerors, Portugal.

Nobby Stiles would not be himself if he was muzzled. Shortly after the kick-off, under a balmy sky, he walloped Ferreiro with such gusto as to direct 90,000 pairs of eyes in the direction of the referee. He, a short, bald, sun-burnt, imperious German named Kreitlein, took no action. Stiles, to be fair, was not the only transgressor. Both sides indulged in an orgy of early fouls. Ball and Hurst seemed singled out for body-checking or the hack from behind. When attention was turned from the man to the ball, it was England who were first to impress. Quick first-time passing earned England (playing in all white) four corners in as many minutes, with Hurst giving notice that he would be a thorn in the Argentine rump.

As the Argentine back row, supported by Rattín, Gonzáles and Onega in midfield, took the measure of their opponents, the home side's early promise faded. England resorted to pumping in high crosses, but even these sterile tactics might have brought reward when, first, Ball was tripped inside the box and then, when Hurst was flattened. At the other end, Artime, the 'phantom', shot over, and Mas' volley from the edge of the area was scrambled away by Banks at the foot of a post.

At the heart of Argentina's efforts was Rattín, the captain, tall, poised, a player who, had he confined his energies to constructive use, might have stamped himself as one of the outstanding talents of the tournament. Alas, he fancied himself as some barrack-room lawyer.

Kreitlein had already scribbled several names in his notebook when, after thirty-six minutes, the match boiled over. Rattín had earlier been booked for tripping Bobby Charlton. This did not deter him, a minute later, from fouling Hunt. Yet the germ of the crisis – which would sour Anglo-Argentine relations for a decade or more – was obscure. With the ball in distant parts, the Argentine captain was suddenly observed gesticulating wildly at the referee. He was, apparently, protesting about the booking of Artime, and, by pointing at his captain's armband, was demanding an interpreter.

Whatever, the *casus belli*, it was soon evident that Rattín had been ordered off. Bedlam ensued. Rattín refused to go; his team-mates refused to let him; then, for a moment, it appeared that the entire team was going to walk off. Play was held up for nine minutes, during which FIFA officials invaded the pitch themselves in an attempt to restore order. When Rattín's expulsion was at last confirmed, he began his long, solitary walk to the dressing-room, unaware as he swapped curses with the crowd that he had become the first player ever to be sent off at Wembley. Back on the pitch there was time before the interval for Hurst to crash-tackle Ferreiro and almost precipitate a second imbroglio. The Argentine, like others before him, gave a performance of such concentrated agony that it was a wonder he ever got up.

The first memory of the second half was of an astonishing save by Roma. Wilson's cross had fallen to Hurst. The ball became entangled between his legs before he wriggled it clear and unleashed a murderous shot towards Roma's near post. The goalkeeper jack-knifed to turn the ball behind. From the ensuing corner, Jack Charlton, Albrecht and the goalkeeper collided in mid-air, and the England centre-half was trampled on the ground.

The classic West Ham goal. Geoff Hurst glances Martin Peters' cross past Roma. (v Argentina)

Roma's save inspired his team, and while the vision lingered Argentina's ten men enjoyed their best spell, contriving attacks of such fluency that England were reduced to chasing shadows. Onega assumed the midfield responsibilities previously entrusted to Rattín, and one was left to ponder England's probable fate had the Argentine captain still directed operations. All hope of England scoring seemed to have disappeared

That is, until the seventy-seventh minute, when the spectre of drawing lots was looming. On the left touchline Peters collected the ball from Wilson, and lofted it into space by the near post. One moment there was nobody there, the next, Hurst was soaring like an airborne statue to glance the ball beyond Roma's groping reach. In conception and execution it was a classic West Ham goal.

The England players and the watching millions could hardly believe it. One intoxicated fan raced onto the pitch, to be rebuked by a rabbit-punch from Oscar Mas. The same player shrugged off his frustrations from the re-start, bursting through and obliging Banks to clear outside his box.

Asking eleven footballers to protect their goal against ten for just thirteen minutes should not have taxed potential world champions. England achieved that objective, though not altogether comfortably. They thereby reached the semi-finals of the World Cup for the first time, saddling Argentina with the distinction of being the first country to lose twice to England in World Cup finals.

The shock-waves reverberated long after the final whistle. Kreitlein was manhandled by furious Argentines and had to be escorted by police from the pitch. Alf Ramsey, incensed by what his players had endured, intervened to prevent George Cohen exchanging shirts with Gonzáles. Then, after threatening scenes outside England's changing room, Ramsey delivered inflammatory words to a press conference. 'England,' he suggested, 'would do better when they play teams who come out to play football and not act as animals.' His remarks struck a chord across the country, but were less than fair. His own players had played their part in an infamous match. Indeed, it still comes as a surprise to many to learn that England conceded almost twice as many free-kicks as Argentina – thirty-three against nineteen.

Allegations of conspiracy were aired when, at Hillsborough, English referee Jim Finney sent off two Uruguayans in their 0-4 defeat by West Germany. The coincidence of an English referee engineering a German victory, and a German referee assisting England's, smacked of collusion. It was rumoured that Kreitlein had it in for Argentina, following their earlier rough-house match against his kinsmen, when Albrecht had been dismissed. The melee of charges and counter-charges sent shock-waves throughout the football world.

The following day FIFA's disciplinary committee exacted retribution. The Argentine FA was fined the maximum penalty, a mere £85. Rattín was suspended from Argentina's next four internationals, Onega and Ferreiro for three – for spitting and abuse of the referee and FIFA officials. As, only days previously, the Argentine team had been castigated *in toto* for their behaviour against West Germany, FIFA recommended that Argentina be refused entry to the 1970 World Cup unless and until assurances were given regarding their future conduct.

Acknowledging that England were not injured innocents, FIFA confirmed cautions issued by Kreitlein against Bobby and Jack Charlton. The FA was instructed to reprimand Ramsey for his 'animal' remarks.

The image of Ramsey's tigers had been further tarnished. One letter to *The Times* suggested that England had only got so far by virtue of one undeserved sending off and the crippling of two French players. International opinion was summed up by this remark made in Prague: 'If England reach the World Cup Final, football will go back a hundred years.' Unpalatable as that might be, that goal was now within reach. The hard facts showed that England had won ten and drawn one of their last eleven matches, and conceded just one goal in the last nine. This marked England's best sequence of results in over half a century.

ENGLAND   (0) 1                    ARGENTINA   (0) 0
  Hurst 77

ENGLAND: Banks, Cohen, Wilson, Stiles, J Charlton, Moore, Ball, Hurst, R Charlton, Hunt, Peters.
ARGENTINA: Roma, Ferreiro, Marzolini, Rattín, Perfumo, Albrecht, Onega, Solari, Artime, González, Mas.

**ENGLAND v PORTUGAL**
*Tuesday, 26 July 1966*                                    *Wembley – 94,493*

The winners of the England-Argentina quarter-final were scheduled to meet those of the intriguing clash between Portugal and North Korea. The North Koreans, as familiar to world football as pygmies were to ice hockey, had unaccountably reached this far by beating Italy – prompting questions in the Italian parliament, not to mention tomatoes and ridicule heaped upon the Italian players. Even more astonishingly, the Koreans at one stage led Portugal 3-0 until their tactical naïveté enabled Eusébio – European Footballer of the Year – to rescue what should have been a lost cause. As Korea's goals kept flashing up on TV screens, interrupting the sordid happenings at Wembley, it appeared as if a fairy-tale semi-final was in store against North Korea. Eusébio restored sanity to the tournament, scoring four of Portugal's five-goal riposte.

In the fourth quarter-final the Soviets overcame the porous Hungarians before falling 1-2 to the drab Germans in the second semi-final. The German team now waited in the wings, ready to take on either England or Portugal for the Jules Rimet trophy.

Not since 1934 had the World Cup thrown up two all-European semi-finals. The demise of the South American contingent had provoked much rancour, controversial refereeing in the case of Argentina and Uruguay, maltreatment of Pelé in the case of Brazil. It was put about that South America might even withdraw from FIFA and stage their own championship. Such nonsense was short-lived, but there was no doubt that world football was in much need of moral uplift.

With hindsight, Portugal seemed the team least likely to bring a belated halo to the competition. In their group matches, Portugal had had no need to read of the thuggery of others. Against Brazil, in particular, they had demonstrated that if they could not win on skill, extra-curricular methods were acceptable. Morais' blood-curdling double-foul on Pelé remains one of the indelible images of the tournament, as Morais lunged once, saw Pelé fleetingly escape, then finished the job with a callousness that made one shudder. Curiously, Morais was allowed to stay on the pitch; less curiously, he was omitted from the team to play England.

Having overcome his most demanding test, Ramsey stuck with the same team. Without being negative, it was difficult to enthuse about anything England had achieved so far, other than the bleak statistic that no goals had been conceded. Cynics opined that if England could not get worse, they could only get better. Besides, with Hungary's elimination, the one competing country able to boast victory here in England had departed. If England were to be deprived of the World Cup, a fourth name needed to be added to that select list of foreign conquerors: Hungary, Sweden, Austria …

Controversy attended the choice of venue for the match. The pre-tournament blurb stated that this particular semi-final (irrespective of who would contest it) would be staged at Goodison Park. Some punters had bought tickets in advance, in the expectation that if England were still in the running they would be heading for Merseyside. FIFA's organising committee now insisted that it had all along reserved the right to reallocate the semi-final venues.

Portugal had been based in the north-west zone, and had beaten Brazil and North Korea at Everton. England, on the other hand, had yet to move from Wembley. Understandably, neither team was enthusiastic about switching. Wembley was eventually selected on the grounds that the national stadium could accommodate more spectators than Goodison.

Like Argentina, Portugal had suffered defeat by England in the 1962 World Cup campaign. A semi-final place was now their reward for their first ever finals. They had taken only one win from England in nine attempts, but had developed a team of rare talent. Their leading club, Benfica, had been knocking on the door of the European Cup in recent years almost as frequently as Real Madrid before them. Portugal had qualified for the finals without ado, recording four quick victories over Czechoslovakia (runners-up in Chile), Romania and Turkey (twice), and approached the clash with England with four wins out of four in the tournament. Portugal's strengths clearly lay in attack – bagging fourteen goals to England's five – and the contest was portrayed with keen over-simplification as the world's best defence versus the best attack. Eusébio had underlined the promise shown at Wembley in 1961. With his panther speed and missile shooting – his nine goals in the tournament would not be surpassed – he was poised to deprive Pelé of his mantle. Defensively, Portugal had yet to replace the mighty Germano, and in goal, Pereira was not as good as his earlier namesake.

With so much at stake, and with few angels on either side, the game took everyone by surprise. It was a tribute to football. England summoned skills few thought they possessed, Portugal forsook temptation to brutalise, and the contest brought a world-wide television audience to the edge of their seats. Not until the twenty-third minute did the referee blow for an infringement (a mild obstruction by Peters on Eusébio), and almost an hour had passed before Portugal conceded their first free-kick. The total foul-count was a mere three by half-time and ten by the end. At no stage was either trainer summoned.

In such an atmosphere, the football was breathtaking. Stiles, among others, went out to play one of the games of his life. Manchester United had recently beaten Benfica twice in the European Cup, with Stiles nullifying Eusébio's influence. He now did so again.

The opening skirmishes were won by Portugal, their cherry shirts pressing forward. England countered on the break. Indeed, the game was not a minute old when Pereira dashed from his goal to hack wildly clear from Hurst.

England, nevertheless, soon settled. With Bobby Charlton at last performing as he can, the Portuguese defence began to creak. It was fitting that the first goal, on the half-hour, owed everything to Charlton. Wilson despatched the ball through the middle for Hunt to chase. Pereira came out and should have won the race with something to spare. But rather than smother the ball at the feet of the inrushing Hunt, Pereira sprawled awkwardly feet-first, knocking the ball back whence it came. For a second it seemed that Pereira had done his job effectively, if clumsily. Yet he reckoned without Bobby Charlton, surging forward and confronted with a heap of bodies twixt ball and goal. Without checking his stride Charlton side-footed the ball through the muddle into the empty net. One wondered whether any other English player could have scored from that situation. The ball was literally 'passed' to its destination, with the dexterity of threading a needle.

Portugal's reaction was awesome. Their swarthy, moustachioed captain, Coluña, bristled with intent, while the 6ft 4in Torres, loping on spindly legs, tested Jack Charlton to the limit. Eusébio's deceptive volley squirmed out of Banks' hands like soap out of a child's, and both Eusébio and Torres shot too close for comfort.

Marching Guardsmen at half-time treated the breathless spectators to a scarcely appropriate slow march. When play resumed Portugal, with scant thought for heart conditions among the crowd, stepped up another gear. For fifteen minutes England lived on their nerves, as Simoes probed here and there, and Torres continued to out-jump everybody at will. Moore and Co. seemed sure to capitulate. The tigerish Stiles marauded wherever danger threatened, and Bobby Charlton, Peters and Ball were driven back to ease the load around him. It was now that Ball's non-stop running was recognised as indispensable to his team. It is a measure of England's defensive resolve that during this, their most testing spell, Portugal were restricted to just one clear chance, when Eusébio directed a header straight at Banks. Amid the tension, Coluña's obstruction of his opposing captain went largely unnoticed as Portugal's first infringement of any kind.

Portuguese pressure did not prevent England threatening on the break. From one such raid the best move of the match saw England double their lead. Jack Charlton headed out of defence. The ball was conveyed from Wilson to Ball to

Moore, across to Cohen, forward to Hurst. Balked by Hilario, Hurst turned, sighted Bobby Charlton steaming in and caressed the ball into his path. Charlton met it on the eighteen-yard line, smashing it with prodigious power into the far corner of the Portuguese net. Charlton had now scored three goals in the tournament, each with his right foot, and each tinged with genius.

It was a sign of the times, perhaps, that several Portuguese players shook hands with the buoyant scorer. But if common sense suggested Portugal were dead and buried, they soon confirmed otherwise. England enjoyed their two-goal cushion for only three minutes before Torres yet again won the ball in the air. Banks, half coming to collect, was stranded and Jack Charlton handled under the bar. Eusébio took the penalty: Banks went left, the ball went right, and Portugal were back in contention. Eusébio patted the dejected goalkeeper on the back in commiseration for England's first lost goal.

The remaining minutes were as nail-biting as England fans had ever endured. Portugal threw caution to the wind. Stiles appeared from nowhere to dispossess Simoes when Portugal seemed sure to equalise. Stiles picked himself up to scream at those responsible for his intervention. In the dying seconds Eusébio surged down the left, then squared to his in-rushing captain. Coluña could never have struck a football more powerfully. It speared under the English crossbar only for Banks to launch himself and turn it to safety.

The chance had gone and with it, for Portugal, the match. Jack Charlton wept. So did Eusébio. Millions at home might have joined them. To the uncommitted, Portugal had done enough to merit extra time, but thankfully no refereeing or other controversies marred the outcome. England had won fair and square. The twenty-two players left the pitch to thunderous acclaim. The world's press was equally impressed. Bobby Charlton was acclaimed as a jewel in the English team and the blight of earlier criticism was, for the moment, forgotten.

Only the magnitude of England's achievement obliterated a smaller sporting triumph at Trent Bridge, where a Gloucestershire medium-pacer by the name of Brown equalled the world record of seven catches in one innings – one of them off his own bowling. Unlike Charlton's virtuosity, Brown's was not enough. Gloucestershire lost.

| ENGLAND (1) 2 | PORTUGAL (0) 1 |
|---|---|
| R Charlton 30, 79 | Eusébio 82 pen |

ENGLAND: Banks, Cohen, Wilson, Stiles, J Charlton, Moore, Ball, Hurst, R Charlton, Hunt, Peters.
PORTUGAL: Pereira, Festa, Baptista, Carlos, Hilario, Graça, Coluña, Augusto, Eusébio, Torres, Simoes.

## ENGLAND v WEST GERMANY

*Saturday, 30 July 1966*                                      *Wembley – 96,924*

For four days England rejoiced at the prospect of appearing in the World Cup Final. The manner, as much as the fact of this accomplishment, transformed the nation's mood from one of embarrassed relief into one of rampant expectation. Before the semi-final, patriotism had been blurred by doubt. After it, the clouds lifted and a buoyant nation could barely wait for Saturday to arrive.

West Germany, World Cup winners in 1954, were themselves no strangers to criticism. Their stern, methodical approach was allied to a tendency to writhe and wriggle at the slightest physical contact. These histrionics had been partly responsible for seeing three opponents sent off in the past fortnight.

Historically, England held all the trumps. Germany had lost all seven past matches, bar a draw in Berlin back in 1930, when West Germany had been Germany. Crucially, England had beaten their opponents twice in the past year or so – in Nuremberg in May 1965 and at Wembley in February 1966. Goals by Terry Paine and Nobby Stiles gave England their 1-0 victories. Only Martin Peters of the current side had not featured in the earlier Wembley encounter.

In the tournament so far, Germany had the edge in goals, scoring thirteen to England's seven, and conceding two against England's one. Both teams had confronted the twin threat of Argentina and Uruguay and emerged with a win and a draw apiece. Taking everything into account, the bookies installed England, a touch surprisingly, at 4-7 on to lift the trophy.

For Germany, the finals must have seemed a long way off when they were held in Berlin by Sweden in the first of their qualifiers; they needed a 2-1 victory in Stockholm to extricate themselves. Moulded by the shrewd Helmut Schoen, the team was an amalgam of technical aplomb and disciplined power. On Schoen's books were some redoubtable talents. Most prized of all was a twenty-one year old midfielder, Franz Beckenbauer, whose contribution so far amounted to four goals and two bookings. The second of these, incurred against the Soviet Union, was erased by FIFA's disciplinary committee. Otherwise he would have sat out the Final.

Beckenbauer's goals had eased the burden on Germany's captain, Uwe Seeler. Equipped with artificial Achilles tendon, Seeler would five times head the Bundesliga's goal charts. This was his third World Cup (in Mexico he would inflict more mischief on England in his fourth). He was joined in attack by the Bundesliga's current top scorer, Lothar Emmerich, plus the blond duo Siggi Held and Helmut Haller. Other key players included left-back Karl-Heinz Schnellinger, sweeper Willie Schulz, and Wolfgang Overath, a gifted, erratic left-footed sprayer of long sweeping passes. Goalkeeper Hans Tilkowski had fended off a challenge from young Sepp Maier. He retained his place, despite injuring his shoulder in the semi-final, only because Maier too was unfit.

Tilkowski, Schulz, Emmerich and Held were part of the Borussia Dortmund side that had just beaten Liverpool 2-1 in the Final of the Cup-Winners' Cup.

England's team selection revolved around one man – Jimmy Greaves. He was now fit, but would Ramsey restore him? At twenty-six, all of Greaves' international career had been tuned to this moment. Ramsey could hardly drop Hurst, who had fully justified his inclusion. Roger Hunt, though, was more vulnerable, his labour-intensive style having its detractors. Yet Ramsey knew his own mind. At 11 a.m. he announced an unchanged team for the third consecutive match. Hunt kept his place, and the World Cup had suddenly turned sour on the most prolific goalscorer English football had known.

One other distinguished England forward would miss the match. Sir Stanley Matthews, general manager of fourth division Port Vale, had been in a car crash. He needed emergency surgery to his chest, stomach and legs.

With one eye on the football, Parliament tried to maintain normal service. A bill was introduced to ban pirate radio. The BBC considered introducing its own all-pop radio station. They would shortly lure pirate disc jockeys, among them Kenny Everett, at the time broadcasting for Radio London off Frinton-on-Sea, Essex. The most frequently played record of the week was Chris Farlowe's *Out of Time*.

The BBC mounted its biggest ever outside broadcast, catering for an estimated world-wide audience of 500 million. This figure would surpass the previous record audience, for the funeral of Sir Winston Churchill in 1965. For those stubbornly uninterested in football, it was a good time to go UFO spotting. The British Unidentified Flying Objects Research Association held a convocation at Warminster, in the land of the druids.

The weather on Saturday, 30 July was conducive neither for UFO spotting nor for good football. Squally showers battled with intermittent sunshine. One moment Wembley was shaken by thunder, the next it was drowned in a curtain of rain, before being soothingly mopped up under a warm blue sky. The atmosphere above made no difference to that below, which was electric. Germany were well represented, with thousands of black, red and yellow tricolours competing for air-room among an ocean of Union Jacks. The Queen, present for the first match, was back to see the last. As both teams normally played in white, one had to change. England wore red. The band boomed *God Save the Queen* (to deafening accompaniment from the terraces), followed by *Deutschland über Alles* and the battle commenced.

Bobby Charlton would not enjoy the space afforded him by Portugal. Schoen and Ramsey had identified Charlton and Beckenbauer as the opposition's key play-maker. Each player was instructed to curb the other, reducing both players to the margins.

The game's first impact arrived in the eighth minute. Tilkowski and Hurst jumped for the ball, the goalkeeper taking a blow that left him briefly gaga.

The next incident was sufficiently dramatic to register on the scoreboard. Held floated a high innocuous centre from the left. It was overstruck, passing beyond the far post and might even have gone out of play. Wilson was so well positioned to head clear that Haller halted in his tracks. It is as well for his team that he did, for with time to steer the ball where he wished, Wilson misjudged his jump and presented the ball perfectly to Haller's feet. No centre-forward's knock-back could have been better executed. Haller was so astonished that he snatched at the shot. Banks might have got down to save. But a touch of confusion proved fatal. The ball rolled between Banks and Jack Charlton. Each left it for the other, and in a trice it was in the net. For all the shortcomings of Ramsey's team, one of its strengths – some would say its only strength – was its reluctance to give away daft goals. It was a bad moment to introduce new habits. Certainly, it was the first mistake anyone could recall of Ray Wilson in the tournament.

England were now trailing for the first time, and no amount of reminders that in every Final since the war the team that scored first eventually lost could lift the depression. What did lift it, six minutes later, was an equalising goal by Hurst. Moore, felled by Overath, took the free-kick quickly. As with the Hammers' combination against Argentina, the ball was aimed at empty space. Hurst, darting forward, was unattended as he powered his header inside Tilkowski's right-hand upright, with the keeper rooted to his line. The Germans muttered half-heartedly that the scorer might have been offside.

All square again, and England in the driving seat. The Germans broke out only occasionally. Following Peters' caution for shirt-pulling, Seeler out-jumped his markers to head Schnellinger's free-kick weakly into Banks' arms. Charlton might have put England ahead, but Tilkowski collected his shot at the second attempt.

Taking their cue from the weather, the Germans wrested the initiative for the closing minutes of the first half. From a corner, Overath's powerful shot from twenty yards forced a punching save from Banks. Emmerich brought the half to a close with another pot-shot that Banks turned capably over the bar.

The abundance of shots, allied to frequent defensive lapses, had made this a pulsating half for the spectators, an irritating one for the purists. Ramsey and Schoen must have been alarmed by the cavalier football. It was their instructions, not the heavy shower, that dampened play after the resumption. The game was becalmed, only to yield an unexpected goal. Ball, whose work-rate caught the eye throughout the second half, bundled the goalkeeper and ball over the line. The corner-kick was expelled with an undistinguished header. Hurst hit it back hard and Höttges, lunging to clear, succeeding only in skying the ball. Before the German defence could recover, it had dropped for Martin Peters to volley home. Jack Charlton, lurking nearby, admitted afterwards that if it had fallen to him he would have hit it into the crowd. Peters' effort put

England in front with just thirteen minutes to hold out. Banks dashed the length of the field to embrace the scorer.

England, professional above all else, now slowed the game, allowing time to take its course. This did not prevent a chance falling to Weber, who headed Emmerich's free-kick meekly past. With the Germans piling forward England were presented with a chance to clinch the trophy. Ball's astute pass sent Hunt away down the left. Schulz's was the only white shirt in sight as Bobby Charlton and Hurst tore into the space behind him. With three against one, it should have brought a goal, but Hunt's pass was askew, and Germany breathed again.

Hunt, and England, were to pay cruelly. The game was in its dying seconds when Held and Jack Charlton contested a high ball on the English right. Charlton leant on the German, encouraged by the 'back' knowingly made for him. The referee blew for a foul in Held's favour, when it might easily have gone the other way. Eleven Englishmen packed their penalty area as Emmerich hammered the free-kick into a red-shirted wall. The ball careered untidily across goal, suspiciously aided by Schnellinger's arm. Weber was first to the far post, sweeping the ball over Wilson's outstretched leg and Banks' despairing dive.

Almost instantaneously the referee blew for time, releasing every emotion known to football. The Germans were delirious, the English stunned. Jack Charlton sank to the grass, head in hands. The Germans in the crowd waved their tricolours and roared their delight; the English stared dumbly at one another in disbelief. The awful prospect of extra time was exacerbated by the sight of the German players, rejuvenated and vital, the English, sagging and despondent. Germany's momentum would surely sweep them to victory. Could it be that England were destined to come within ten seconds of the World Cup, only to lose it? It was at this moment, as his players huddled ashen-faced in the middle of the pitch, that Alf Ramsey capped his 'animals' remark with his second immortal sentence of the week: 'You've won the Cup once. Now go and win it again.'

Whatever the nation's reservations about Ramsey's team, their hearts went out as England shrugged off their dismay to swarm all over their opponents. One might have thought it was England who had just been reprieved. Team-spirit is a vital and often underrated ingredient of every successful side, and England now showed they possessed it in abundance. Ball, playing the game of his life, ran and ran, and Schnellinger's massive experience proved quite inadequate to contain him. Ball surged forward, and Tilkowski was stretched to keep out his twenty yard shot. Only Siggi Held seemed able to disrupt England's iron defensive grip, leaving defenders trailing before despatching the ball across England's goal. None of his team-mates had the energy to keep pace, and the cross proved harmless. But Held's endeavours were as nothing

Peters puts England in front. Jack Charlton might have put it into the crowd. (v W Germany)

compared to Bobby Charlton's low shot that rebounded to safety via the post and Tilkowski's face.

The intervention of the woodwork must have convinced many that England were destined to lose, and before long German wood was struck again. Stiles propelled the ball down the right. It was a cruel pass, for only Alan Ball would have had the reserves to chase and keep it in play. From the by-line he switched it back to Hurst, lurking in a similar position to Haller when Germany had opened the scoring. Swivelling into the shot, Hurst crashed the ball over Tilkowski's head against the underside of the bar. The ball bounced down and up – the backspin directing it out of the goal – and was headed behind by Weber. This was the first World Cup to enjoy televised action replays. The referee and linesman, of course, were denied them – not that they would have proved of much use, for the ensuing argument has gone on to this day. The officials had to make an unaided decision. Goal or corner?

Gottfried Dienst, the Swiss referee, trotted to consult his silver-haired Russian linesman, the one speaking no Russian, the other nothing but. The Russian appeared to nod, point to the centre circle, and that was enough. The goal stood. English jubilation at the time has rightly been tempered by post-euphoric doubts. *Mostly* behind the line? Yes, the ball clearly was. *Completely* behind (as the laws stipulate)? Surely not. Published photographs dispute the referee's decision, and also show Ball offside. Roger Hunt would become the focus of much later controversy. Arms aloft, he had apparently signalled a goal, not bothering to tuck the ball away because it had evidently crossed the line. It is nonsensical to suggest, as some have, that this be construed as evidence of a goal. As a professional, he would have scored if he could, and so avoided all subsequent inquests. Unfortunately, Weber was always going to beat Hunt to the rebound. At the time, however, it was no time for carping. England were in front once more; and besides, had not Germany's equaliser been equally dubious?

England had to hold out for a seemingly eternal twenty minutes. Germany created nothing until, yet again, just seconds remained. Held headed on to Seeler, who narrowly failed to make decisive contact. Moore, patrolling in front of Banks, chested the ball down and, rather than boot it into the crowd as his co-defenders urged, meandered nonchalantly out of the penalty area. Catching sight of Hurst turning away near the halfway line, like a relay runner set to receive the baton, Moore swung a deep pass that Hurst took on his chest before setting off towards Tilkowski's goal. The German half of the pitch was vacant, apart from Schulz, Overath and, beyond them, Ball screaming for the lateral pass. The German goal came within shooting range, Overath too distant to tackle. A few eager spectators were already on the pitch to acclaim their heroes. Who knows what distraction they caused as Hurst, cheeks puffed, hit the ball on the run. It flew high, past the flat-footed goalkeeper, and it was all over. Hurst had completed a hat-trick – the first ever in a World Cup Final – and England were world champions, the first hosts to lift the trophy since 1934.

The England players did not know whether to dance, cry, laugh or collapse prostrate on the pitch. A bit of each, perhaps. The crowd launched into 'Ee aye addio England's won the cup', and then, turning their adulation to the manager, chanted 'Ramsey, Ramsey' as an accolade that none could deny him. Bobby Moore received the Jules Rimet trophy (a symbolic winged statuette no bigger than a milk bottle yet weighing nine pounds), and one hoped he was not becoming blasé. He had now lifted the FA Cup, European Cup-Winners' Cup and World Cup at Wembley in successive seasons. The foreign press voted Moore the best player of the tournament, and Bobby Charlton would shortly be elected European Footballer of the Year. The celebrations that night resembled those of VE Day in 1945; the fact that both occasions rejoiced in German defeat becoming a tool for subsequent jingoistic mania.

In terms of drama, the Final would not be bettered. England's performances against Portugal and West Germany served to erase the memory of their earlier negativism and, it must be said, good fortune. Yet no one can be content when the World Cup Final is settled by disputed goals. No fewer than four of the six (each of Hurst's, and Weber's equaliser) had at least a hint of equivocation about them, and the other two were the product of untidy defence. This is not to

West Ham celebrate winning the World Cup, with Nobby Stiles.

say that, as marginally the stronger and more disciplined team, England did not deserve to win. The statistics, however, suggested otherwise. Germany had more goal-attempts on target – twenty-five to twenty-three; won more corners – twelve to six; and fouled only sixteen times to England's twenty-two. Overall, none of England's six opponents had been taught a footballing lesson. Nor was this a tournament illuminated by great teams. Brazil were in temporary decline, and Germany were not yet the force they would become. When all is said, the sober verdict is that England's team-spirit and defence (three goals conceded equalled the record), allied to moments of virtuosity (Charlton against Portugal; Hurst against Germany) won them the Cup. That these attributes should be to the fore was, perhaps, inevitable. As England could not hope to win on skill and flair, it was natural that their triumph should be based on functionalism: fitness, determination, organisation.

It was as well that English sports fans had their soccer team to cheer. The following week Brian London paid heavily for thinking he could deprive Mohammed Ali of the world heavyweight boxing title; the West Indies overwhelmed England's cricketers at Headingley; and far away in New Zealand the British Lions rugby team looked second-rate against the All Blacks. But for four wonderfully long years England would be the kings of football.

ENGLAND   (1) 4                          WEST GERMANY   (1) 2
   Hurst 19, 100, 120,                    Haller 13, Weber 90
   Peters 77                           *After extra time (2-2 after 90 minutes)*

ENGLAND: Banks, Cohen, Wilson, Stiles, J Charlton, Moore, Ball, Hurst, R Charlton, Hunt, Peters.

W GERMANY: Tilkowski, Höttges, Schulz, Weber, Schnellinger, Haller, Beckenbauer, Seeler, Held, Overath, Emmerich.

*England appearances and goalscorers*
*World Cup finals 1966*

| | Apps | Goals | | Apps | Goals | | Apps | Goals |
|---|---|---|---|---|---|---|---|---|
| Banks G | 6 | – | Moore R * | 6 | – | Hurst G | 3 | 4 |
| Cohen G | 6 | – | Stiles N | 6 | – | Greaves J * | 3 | – |
| Wilson R * | 6 | – | Hunt R | 6 | 3 | Connelly J * | 1 | – |
| Charlton J | 6 | – | Peters M | 5 | 1 | Paine T | 1 | – |
| Charlton R * | 6 | 3 | Ball A | 4 | – | Callaghan I | 1 | – |

* Appeared in 1962 World Cup.             *15 players*    *11 goals*

# 6

# THE 1970 WORLD CUP

England's quest to defend the Jules Rimet trophy in 1970 would be conducted in the unlikely setting of Mexico. The choice of venue had been settled back in 1964, when the alternative had been Argentina, with her questionable attachment to the World Cup and its principles. Having lost out in 1962, she now did so again. The decision to favour Mexico had brushed aside problems of heat and altitude, not to mention social disturbances, which would cast a cloud over the Olympic Games held in Mexico City in 1968.

Mexico was not the only site of violence. The late 1960s saw an epidemic of world conflicts – the Six-Day War in the Middle East, civil war in Nigeria, the invasion of Czechoslovakia by the Soviet Union and of Cambodia by the forces of the United States and South Vietnam. Northern Ireland witnessed its first civil rights demonstrations, while student protest engulfed universities and cities in western Europe. Individuals became bywords for violence: Martin Luther King and Robert Kennedy were assassinated; Lt William Calley would be prosecuted for the massacre at My Lai in Vietnam. Indeed, the first months of 1970 saw armed conflict recorded in a quarter of the world's states. Just before the World Cup commenced, four students were shot dead by US National Guardsmen during campus riots at Ohio State University.

Britain had tragedies of her own. Before the dust had settled in 1966, a small Welsh village lost 116 children and twenty-eight adults when a coal slag engulfed their school in Aberfan. The following Easter the tanker *Torrey Canyon* spilled 120,000 tons of crude oil, much of it onto the beaches of Devon and Cornwall. It could hardly be guessed that Britain, early in 1970, would actually be discovering her own oil, in the North Sea.

It was an age of achievement in communication and medicine. Man had walked on the moon, Concorde had made its maiden flight, colour television had arrived, Dr Christiaan Barnard had performed the world's first heart-transplant, and in the spring of 1970 it was announced that vasectomy would be made available under the National Health Service.

America had a new President, Richard M Nixon, and his country had a new bridge, an American oil company paying £2.4 million to dismantle London

Bridge and resurrect it over the Colorado River. The Royal Mint had withdrawn the halfpenny and introduced a seven-sided 50p piece, Britain's first decimal coin. The death sentence for murder had finally been abolished, but the 'breathalyser' had arrived to deter drink-drivers. International cricket was under threat. South Africa declined to accept a visiting England team that included a coloured player, Basil D'Oliveira.

If trouble loomed for England's cricketers, the state of English football seemed rosy. Alf Ramsey was now Sir Alf Ramsey. Harold Wilson's Labour government had also bestowed 'Sirs' upon Stanley Matthews and Matt Busby. Previous sporting knighthoods, awarded by the Tories, had been confined to cricket, yachting and horse-racing. These footballing honours were just one tangible sign of an English soccer revival. Between 1966 and 1970 domestic attendances soared, boosted by England winning the World Cup, and sustained by Celtic and Manchester United winning the European Cup.

For the second consecutive World Cup England did not have to undergo the rigours of qualifying. Ramsey, however, looked forward to a confident challenge for the 1968 European Championship. Disappointingly for all the British teams, the Home Internationals of 1966-67 and 1967-68 served as their qualifying zone, depriving them of continental experience.

England overcame their British rivals, beat Spain home and away in the quarter-finals and travelled to Florence in June 1968 for a semi-final against Yugoslavia. *En route*, an England team seeking practice were beaten 0-1 in Hanover by West Germany, themselves eliminated earlier by the Yugoslavs. Certain England players had been handsomely rewarded to wear new German football boots, which they unwisely tried out for the first time in the match. In any case, the result gratified Germany's desperate urge to beat England and broke their psychological barrier. Four days later England lost 0-1 to Yugoslavia in an ill-tempered affair, Alan Mullery becoming the first Englishman ever to be sent off for his country. England then beat the Soviet Union, 2-0, in the match for third place. Italy claimed the title.

By this time Ramsey's World Cup-winning side was showing signs of wear and tear. Neither full-back, Cohen and Wilson, would play for his country again – Cohen through knee trouble, Wilson through age. Roger Hunt, too, was now on the fringe of the team, and Nobby Stiles, plagued by cartilage trouble, was more often out of the side than in. Jack Charlton, no spring chicken, had succumbed to a series of injuries, and was no longer first choice centre-half. Bobby Charlton and Martin Peters were still regulars, though both had their detractors. Charlton was subject to several premature obituaries, while Ramsey's managerial love-affair with Peters was a source of bafflement on the terraces. The forgotten man of 1966, Jimmy Greaves, played just three more internationals, all in 1967, before slipping quietly out of international football. To offset this collective decline, four stars of 1966 were getting yet better.

Banks, Moore, Ball, and Hurst would clearly provide the core of the side.

In June 1969, England toured Central and South America in a climatic dress-rehearsal. Ramsey was, presumably, quietly satisfied following a goalless draw in Mexico – though his abrasiveness sowed the seeds of virulent Anglophobia a year later – a 2-1 victory in Uruguay and a defeat by the same score by Brazil. Thereafter, England continued to be methodical rather than exhilarating, but the defence, encouragingly, was rediscovering its near impenetrability of 1966.

To allow adequate acclimatisation, the squad departed for Mexico on 4 May 1970. Final preparation took the form of internationals in Colombia and Ecuador. The capitals of both countries stood at altitudes higher even than those England would have to endure in Mexico. To permit all twenty-eight players match practice (they would be pared down to the requisite twenty-two in due course), fixtures were arranged at 'A' and 'B' level with both countries. The English teams won four out of four, whereupon they returned to Mexico.

| No | Name | Position | Club | Age | Caps | Goals |
|----|------|----------|------|-----|------|-------|
| 1 | Gordon Banks | Goalkeeper | Stoke | 32 | 59 | – |
| 2 | Keith Newton | Full-back | Everton | 28 | 24 | – |
| 3 | Terry Cooper | Full-back | Leeds | 24 | 8 | – |
| 4 | Alan Mullery | Midfield | Tottenham | 28 | 27 | – |
| 5 | Brian Labone | Central defence | Everton | 30 | 23 | – |
| 6 | Bobby Moore (c) | Central defence | West Ham | 29 | 80 | 2 |
| 7 | Francis Lee | Forward | Manchester C | 26 | 14 | 6 |
| 8 | Alan Ball | Midfield | Everton | 25 | 41 | 7 |
| 9 | Bobby Charlton | Midfield | Manchester U | 32 | 102 | 49 |
| 10 | Geoff Hurst | Forward | West Ham | 28 | 38 | 20 |
| 11 | Martin Peters | Midfield | Tottenham | 26 | 38 | 14 |
| 12 | Peter Bonetti | Goalkeeper | Chelsea | 28 | 6 | – |
| 13 | Alex Stepney * | Goalkeeper | Manchester U | 25 | 1 | – |
| 14 | Tommy Wright | Full-back | Everton | 25 | 9 | – |
| 15 | Norbert Stiles * | Midfield | Manchester U | 28 | 28 | 1 |
| 16 | Emlyn Hughes | Full-back/Midfield | Liverpool | 22 | 6 | – |
| 17 | Jack Charlton | Central defence | Leeds | 34 | 34 | 6 |
| 18 | Norman Hunter | Defence/Midfield | Leeds | 26 | 13 | 1 |
| 19 | Colin Bell | Midfield | Manchester C | 24 | 11 | 2 |
| 20 | Peter Osgood | Forward | Chelsea | 23 | 1 | – |
| 21 | Allan Clarke | Forward | Leeds | 23 | – | – |
| 22 | Jeff Astle | Forward | WBA | 28 | 3 | – |

| | | | | | | |
|---|---|---|---|---|---|---|
| * Would not play in the finals or in future. | | | *Averages* | 27.0 | 25.7 | |

The six players left out of the final twenty-two were: Peter Shilton, Ralph Coates, David Sadler, Brian Kidd, Bob McNab, and the only winger available, Peter Thompson. Eight of the World Cup Final side of 1966 were retained, though Jack Charlton was now reserve centre-half to Everton's Brian Labone. Nobby Stiles' inclusion, with little recent first-team football behind him, was seen as psychological – the embodiment of Ramsey's will to win.

If anything, the 1970 squad looked on paper even stronger than its 1966 predecessors. This strength in depth was important; the introduction of substitutes meant that the age of thirteen-man soccer had arrived. Not that Banks expected to be replaced. He was without question the greatest goalkeeper in the world. He would now become the first England goalkeeper to appear in consecutive World Cups. One could discern no weaknesses in his game. Now on the books of Stoke City, his positioning, anticipation, reflexes and temperament were beyond compare. Likewise, Bobby Moore had few equals as a central defender, and Hurst had matured into a peerless target man. With Ramsey abandoning all pretence at wing-play, and his team operating an undisguised 4-4-2, Hurst's was a thankless task in the midst of enemy defenders. He created space by dragging them wide, and retained the ball in the teeth of tackles that threatened to snap his ankles. He would be partnered in attack by the stocky, explosive Francis Lee from Manchester City.

Ramsey's only real problem was at full-back, though there was no shortage of candidates. The loss of Leeds' Paul Reaney with a broken leg just weeks before the tournament was not therefore as critical as it might otherwise have been. He – together with Tottenham's Cyril Knowles, Everton's Tommy Wright and Liverpool's Emlyn Hughes – had all been tried at full-back since 1966, and although Wright and Hughes had made the squad, Ramsey stuck with Keith Newton of Everton and Terry Cooper of Leeds United. In the wingless era, Ramsey looked to these to provide the crosses.

Cooper was the least experienced of a highly experienced first-choice team (only Cooper and Lee of players numbered 1-11 had earned less than twenty caps). Formerly an outside-left, Cooper's weaving sorties down the Leeds touchline were among the stirring sights of the time.

In midfield, England retained three of the triumphal quartet from 1966. The exception was Stiles, now understudy to Tottenham's Alan Mullery, more creative, less savage, but then he could hardly be otherwise. Bobby Charlton's place was increasingly threatened by the inexhaustible running of Manchester City's Colin 'Nijinsky' Bell. Alan Ball, better than ever, had added genuine skill to the energy so prominent in 1966. Ball craved the crowd's attention where Martin Peters did not.

Peters was proving to be one of England's great enigmas. To his critics, he was too often invisible. To his supporters he was a phantom, materialising when it mattered, with exquisite timing. Most of Peters' hard work was done off the ball. He was so versatile that he could, and did, play almost anywhere. Ramsey allowed him to 'float' over the left side of the field. In March 1970 Peters had become Britain's first £200,000 footballer when transferring to Spurs in a move that took Jimmy Greaves in the opposite direction, to West Ham. Peters' reputation had not been helped by Ramsey's earlier remark that he was ten years ahead of his time. What he meant was that Peters' style would not be appreciated for another decade (by which time the Dutch would be fielding a whole team of similar versatility). Instead, the comment provoked terrace wits to suggest that Peters should be dropped for at least ten years.

But if the team looked powerful, it appeared for a harrowing few days as if they would be deprived of their captain. Returning to Mexico from Ecuador, the party stopped off at the Colombian capital, Bogota. It was there that Bobby Moore found himself arraigned for supposedly having stolen a gold bracelet from a jewellers in the hotel where England had recently stayed. The British press reacted to the charges with gung-ho indignation, ridiculing the testimony of salesgirl Clara Padilla. Either she was making the whole thing up, or she was blaming the wrong man. At the time, no one looked beyond the former explanation. The only certainty was that Moore himself was uninvolved. Whatever their truth, the flimsiness of the charges did not detract from their gravity. With no prospect of Moore's early release, Ramsey's preparations were thrown into confusion. Morale plummeted. Even if Moore was shortly released, he would surely bear the mental scars of his incarceration. He would also have lost vital days of intensive training.

Fortunately, the incident that, in Ramsey's words, constituted the lowest moment in his seven-year reign, did not appreciably worsen England's chances of retaining the World Cup. After four days of internment, diplomatic channels secured Moore's release on bail. He undertook to report to the Colombian authorities at a later date.

By this time, England had a stack of other problems with which to contend. Latin America viewed England's 1966 success as nothing more than the product of home advantage and dubious refereeing. In view of the quarter-final fracas with Argentina, England would have been unpopular in Mexico simply because they were England, and because they were the champions. These handicaps were compounded by a series of misfortunes, some of them of England's own making. Ramsey seldom took the trouble to ingratiate himself with the tournament hosts. Added to which, the plane returning the England squad to Mexico passed through heavy turbulence. Jeff Astle, never a good air traveller, had drunk to steady his nerves and had to be supported as he stepped from the plane, a posture gleefully seized upon by the Mexican press. What with the Moore fiasco, England were cast as a team of thieves and drunks. It was clear as final preparations began that England would face more than just footballing obstacles.

**World Cup finals – MEXICO**                                    **June 1970**

Mexico, like Chile before them, was not universally popular as the venue for a World Cup. From the point of view of sports performance, the principal objections related to Mexico's heat and altitude. June temperatures at midday – when the diktats of European television insisted Sunday matches be played – could soar into the nineties. Guadalajara, the westernmost and lowest of the World Cup centres, where England would be based, stood at 5,200 feet. Toluca, the highest, was 8,700 feet above sea level. Aside from its effects on respiration, the thin air caused footballs to deviate alarmingly in flight.

By 1970, membership of FIFA extended to 138 countries, seventy-three of whom entered the competition. Once again, England were the only British survivors. Scotland had, predictably, failed to overcome West Germany; Wales finished pointless in their qualifying group, won by Italy; and Northern Ireland, George Best and all, were put out by the powerful Soviets. The qualifiers had also seen some famous names dumped on their backsides. Portugal, stars in 1966, had collapsed, finishing bottom of their group. Argentina, another of England's 1966 victims, had solved FIFA's exclusion dilemma by finishing bottom of theirs, which was won by Peru. Yugoslavia, conquerors of England and West Germany in the European Championship, were bettered by Belgium. Hungary, quarter-finalists in 1966 and Olympic champions in Mexico '68, lost out to Czechoslovakia. Enterprising North Korea had locked themselves away, refused to play Israel, and were banned.

The Mexico World Cup also began the trend, with scant justification, of opening up the tournament to nations with no footballing claims to be there. In 1966, just North Korea, on paper, fitted into that category. In 1970, three of the sixteen finalists were soccer midgets making their first appearance – Morocco, Israel and El Salvador. Each would finish bottom of their group, having raised the political temperature of the tournament by their mere presence. The qualifiers between El Salvador and Honduras had provoked open war, and one feared for the prospects if Morocco were asked to play Israel.

Once again, geographical seeding determined the composition of the groups, and, as in 1958, England found themselves with the worst possible draw. Brazil were clear favourites for the trophy, with England narrowly behind. They were drawn together in Group 3, the third time they had been paired in the finals of the World Cup. Out of the hat, too, came Czechoslovakia, World Cup runners-up in 1962. The key to the group's overall strength was decided by the identity of the fourth team. The three aforementioned minnows were all allocated elsewhere, leaving Group 3 saddled with Romania, who had topped a tough European section that included Greece, Switzerland, and Portugal.

Equally unsettling from England's standpoint was their recent record against all three opponents. Since that glorious day in 1956 when Duncan Edwards had helped England beat Brazil 4-2, Brazil stood unbeaten in six further meetings. The Czechs had visited Wembley three months after Bobby Moore raised the Jules Rimet trophy and left with a 0-0 draw. And Romania, the supposed weaklings, had faced England twice recently, drawing both times. England would clearly have to improve upon these results even to survive Group 3.

The England party took over one floor of the Guadalajara Hilton, which was otherwise open as normal, denying the England players any seclusion and leaving them vulnerable to the noisy intrusions of mischief-makers.

Brazil proved themselves expert at public relations, distributing gifts and affection with meticulous forethought. Ramsey, by contrast, so caring for his players in other ways, unwittingly saddled them with the fires of Mexican hatred. He did not think it necessary to include in his entourage a Spanish-speaking press officer. He refused to permit his players to give press interviews, and insisted on giving his own tight-lipped statements instead. For once, he had even let his own players down: the six unfortunates left out of the squad learned of their omission through the press before he could break the news to them personally.

Ramsey's hosts were further incensed by his wrapping his players in home comforts, exposing them to local food and conditions as little as possible. The team bus was imported from England, and Findus commissioned to supply all the players' dietary requirements. These included 140 lbs of beefburgers, 400 lbs of sausages, 300 lbs of frozen fish and ten cases of tomato ketchup.

## ROMANIA v ENGLAND
*Tuesday, 2 June 1970*                    *Guadalajara – 50,000*

In June 1970, Britain had more than football on her mind. It was general election time. Prime Minister Harold Wilson evidently thought that the World Cup might distract attention from the ailing economy, for he set the date for Thursday, 18 June – the day after the scheduled semi-finals. It occurred to political commentators that a buoyant electorate would be less inclined to turf out the incumbent government if England reached the Final. But what if they did not?

When Parliament was dissolved on 29 May, no fewer than seventy-seven MPs departed the House of Commons for the last time, among them Bessie Braddock, best remembered for her passionate support of boxing, and her 'drunk-ugly' exchange with Winston Churchill. Eighty-five year old Manny Shinwell had been the last MP ever to strike another in the House, back in the 1930s.

One problem threatening Labour's return to power was the unemployment figure, currently standing at 600,000. Industrial relations, too, were anything but smooth. A bitter strike at the Pilkington glass factory at St Helens had seen much factory-gate violence. Violence of a different kind was reported in Southend, Brighton and other seaside resorts as gangs of skinheads and greasers rampaged during the Bank Holiday. It was as well that hospital casualty departments were open, for hospital doctors were threatening to strike in pursuit of a salary claim. Abroad, massive earthquakes shook Peru, whose footballers had to put the tragedy to the backs of their minds and concentrate on the job ahead.

The 'Stop the Seventy Tour' cricket campaign, spearheaded by Peter Hain, forced the cancellation of the Test series with South Africa. Hannu Mikkola of Finland won the *Mirror* World Cup Rally, 16,000 miles from Wembley to Mexico. Jimmy Greaves was among the competitors. He finished sixth. Ray Wilson, hero of 1966, finally hung up his boots. Given a free transfer by fourth division Oldham Athletic, he entered the family funeral business in Huddersfield. Nearby Bradford Park Avenue were voted out of the Football League, their place taken by Cambridge United.

To remind the nation of the good old days, the BBC transmitted repeats of England's 1966 victories over Portugal and West Germany, followed by another reminder of German-bashing, *Sink the Bismarck*. ITV tried to compete with *The Simon Dee Show*. Football was showing its uglier face in Italy. After Swindon Town took a three-goal lead over Naples in the final of the Anglo-Italian Cup, Italian fans rioted, the game was abandoned and severe damage inflicted on the San Paolo Stadium. The noises emanating from Wembley, meanwhile, had less to do with the thud of leather than with motor-cycle exhausts. Speedway was returning to Wembley for the first time in fourteen years, Wembley Lions being led by Sweden's five-times world champion, Ove Fundin.

Two sporting celebrities died. New Zealand racing driver Bruce McLaren was killed on a practice run at Goodwood, and thirteen-year-old Arkle, arguably the greatest ever steeplechaser, was put down in his native Ireland after developing arthritis in his hind legs. The Guinness-drinking bay gelding had won every major prize except the Grand National, for which on safety grounds he was never entered.

World Cup fever promoted a smash hit for the England squad, who, together with their bulldog mascot 'Winston', soared to the top of the charts with *Back Home*. At the beginning of June they were dethroned by Christie's *Yellow River*. Yellow was the colour of Romania's shirts, important only in that this would be the first World Cup shown in colour. With the match transmitted live at 11 p.m. (4 p.m. in Mexico), breakfast tables the next morning would greet many a bleary eye.

What with the din outside their hotel, a number of England players also sported bleary eyes. They awoke to the news that Ramsey was selecting his favoured eleven. The team, plus around three thousand England supporters,

Geoff Hurst nutmegs goalkeeper Adamache to beat Romania. (v Romania)

sweltered in the Jalisco Stadium. England had been the first country to register their colours with FIFA – all white – but even with the benefit of slow-sodium tablets the heat was enervating. The weather was supposed to herald a rainy spell.

Heat or no heat, the game was but five minutes old when Romania confirmed that they would not wear FIFA's 'minnow' tag lightly. Dumitrache sped away down the left. With England defenders racing to cover, he chipped a perfect centre beyond the far post. Cooper froze, as if auditioning for Ray Wilson's funeral parlour, freeing Dembrowski for a clear pot at goal. Fortunately for Cooper, the ball was too low to head, too awkward to volley. Dembrowski attempted the latter, and the ball sailed harmlessly past. The jolt to Cooper's nerves ensured that he would not err again.

Fears that Romania were getting ideas were quickly dispersed. Despite the prompting of Tataru and Dumitrache, Banks' goal became an ever-receding target. By midway through the first half England had taken quiet control, rarely breaking unnecessary sweat, but playing chess-board soccer with increasing assurance. There was no profit from passing into space. Energy needed conserving; possession of the ball was the most vital commodity. Charlton shot twice, the first deflected for a corner, the second taken by keeper Adamache high on his chest. Newton and Cooper were both breaking down the wings, and

Cooper's cross ten minutes before the break set up England's best chance. Lupescu's misdirected header allowed Lee to drag the ball clear and shoot in one movement. The ball cracked against Adamache's crossbar and went behind.

The match was conducted, as they say in the vernacular, 'hard but fair'. Shortly before the interval Dumitru – Romania's search and destroy, Stiles figure – bulldozed Mullery with sufficient vigour to suggest that the second half might be more intimidating than the first.

By then, the pitch was cleanly bisected into light and shade. This posed a visual problem for players moving in and out of the shadow, just as a man emerging into sunshine from a darkened cinema requires a second or two to readjust. Banks might have feared being taken for a Romanian, for he appeared after the interval having discarded his yellow jersey in favour of a short-sleeved red vest.

Perhaps the sun had gone to Romanian heads. Something evidently had, for they started the second half disdainful of FIFA's warnings about foul play and set about undermining England's psychological dominance with the assistance of unarmed combat. Mocanu scythed knee-high at Newton as though intending to sever his legs. The Belgian referee, Vital Loraux, allowed the Everton player to lie in pain, unattended, for two minutes. The injury forced Newton from the field and England could be grateful for the new rule regarding substitutes. Five from each side could sit on the bench and any two brought into play. Newton had been a key figure, but in Tommy Wright Ramsey could call on an able replacement.

Wright was barely on the field when Mocanu slashed at Lee's legs with a brutality that made one wonder whether he was not in the employ of some sinister organisation. Mocanu was not even cautioned. The Romanians' next contribution was more legitimate, Nunweiller sending a dipping shot that Banks was compelled to turn for a corner.

England's riposte was to sweep to the other end and score. Ball, deep on the right, swung a cross beyond the far post. It fell for Hurst to drag past Salmareanu with his right foot and strike low with his left. From a tightish angle the ball squeezed neatly through Adamache's legs. The man scoring the last goal of the last World Cup had scored England's first of the next.

Romania retorted with heavy fouls on Wright and Cooper. Neagu came on for Tataru, and Osgood for Lee. One wondered how Romania might contrive an equaliser, and the best they managed was a long-range daisy-cutter from Dembrowski that spun out of Banks' hands. With refreshing rain now tumbling down, Bobby Charlton brought the game to a conclusion with a flashing shot just wide.

Romania had been 'nutmegged', and England were ready for Brazil.

ROMANIA   (0) 0                    ENGLAND   (0) 1
                                       Hurst 69

ROMANIA: Adamache, Salmareanu, Lupescu, Dinu, Mocanu, Dumitru, Nunweiller, Dembrowski, Tataru (Neagu), Dumitrache, Lucescu.
ENGLAND: Banks, Newton (Wright), Cooper, Mullery, Labone, Moore, Lee (Osgood), Ball, R Charlton, Hurst, Peters.

## BRAZIL v ENGLAND
*Sunday, 7 June 1970*                          *Guadalajara – 66,000*

The confrontation between Brazil and England promised to be one of the highlights of the tournament. Here were the two teams which had won the previous three World Cups and which were the favourites in 1970. Connoisseurs of world football looked forward to the clash of styles, the irresistible force of Brazil pounding against the immovable object of England. To add yet more spice, revenge was in the air. Brazil had been the last team to beat England in the World Cup – back in the 1962 quarter-finals.

If Brazil learned anything from watching England beat Romania, then England, the next day, learned much from Brazil's dissection of Czechoslovakia. Desperate to erase the bitter memories of 1966, Brazil were out to regain the World Cup and do it in style. They had qualified with a one-hundred percent record from their South American group, banging in twenty-three goals. They had subsequently sacked their manager, the colourful, erratic João Saldanha, who had contemplated dropping Pelé, and brought in Mario Zagalo, star of the 1958 and 1962 Brazilian teams.

While Lester Piggott was winning his fifth Derby, on Nijinsky, Zagalo's Brazil were crushing the Czechs 4-1. The victory was accomplished with such verve that the world watched spellbound. This was the match where Rivelino, with a devastating body swerve, made five yards of space, where Pelé almost scored from inside his own half, above all, where free-kicks awarded to Brazil were about as fatal as conceding penalties. Pelé, Gérson, Rivelino, Tostão, Jairzinho – who could live with the likes of these?

The World Cup organisers had agreed that, to conciliate European TV audiences, Sunday matches would commence at noon (7 p.m. in UK). This deal flew in the face of players' welfare, for it was inadvisable even to walk in the sun at midday, let alone play football. No less considerate were the rabble who assembled outside England's hotel and who sustained a ceaseless honking, drumming, and chanting of 'Bra-zil' throughout the night. The police stood by, unconcerned, and several of the players had to change rooms in the early hours. At least, they could console themselves with the knowledge that the losers would live to fight another day, and that the impending collision had none of the stark finality of the knock-out stages. (As it happened, Romania's 2-1 win over the Czechs kept Romania very much alive.)

Come the morning, both teams announced late team-changes. For England, Newton's damaged knee was still on the mend. Tommy Wright automatically filled the vacancy. Brazil's injuries were more serious. The chain-smoking genius Gérson had strained a thigh and in spite of his protestations he was ruled out. Paulo Cesar took the moustachioed Rivelino's role on the left, allowing Rivelino to assume Gérson's duties behind the front line.

Oblivious to temperatures that, before the match was over, would climb to ninety-eight degrees, England made an encouraging start. For ten minutes they stroked the ball unhurriedly among themselves, creating fleeting chances for Ball and Charlton. The eleventh minute was rather special. The 1970 World Cup is remembered for a handful of special moments. Most of them were provided by Brazil – but not this time. Carlos Alberto fed Jairzinho down the right touchline. With an awesome change of pace, the winger accelerated past Cooper to the by-line and swung over a perfect cross. Pelé, timing his run to the far post perfectly, rose above Mullery to power a lethal downward header. The Jalisco Stadium acclaimed a goal. So did Pelé. But Banks, originally stationed by the opposite post to cover Jairzinho's cross, propelled himself across his goal-line to deflect the ball, as it reared up off the ground, over the crossbar. It was the finest save that many people had ever seen, securing Banks' ranking amongst the greatest goalkeepers of all time.

Aided by an unbeatable keeper, England went in pursuit of goals themselves. Bobby Charlton threatened twice, first, bursting through for Felix to save at his feet, then shooting over. Mullery marked Pelé as diligently as he had in Rio a year earlier, and Moore threw down the gauntlet to those who doubted his credentials as the finest central defender in the world. The game ebbed and flowed, oozing class, but England were more than holding their own. On the half-hour they carved out their best chance of the half. Mullery and Wright combined down the right, and Wright's threaded centre found Francis Lee, six yards out. The goal was at his mercy, but his header flew straight at Felix. Following up, Lee appeared to kick the goalkeeper. Brazilian defenders squared up to the stocky culprit in the game's one ugly incident.

Hurst loitered and squandered an opportunity, while at the other end Mullery and Pelé crashed headlong together, like performing seals. It did not look like a penalty and the referee waved play on. The last incident of a thrilling half stemmed from a free-kick when Cooper floored Jairzinho. Jairzinho positioned himself mischievously in the England wall, with Moore behind him. As Jairzinho stepped aside from Rivelino's thunderbolt, Moore serenely killed the ball and strode upfield.

Brazil delayed their reappearance, and Hurst almost rebuked them but couldn't quite reach Peters' cross. Banks plunged to save from Paulo Cesar,

Spot the ball (above the left post). Gordon Banks has just saved from Pelé. (v Brazil)

and Brazil began to apply mounting pressure. After an hour the dam was breached. That Tostão was playing at all was down to a Texas eye surgeon who had repaired a detached retina. Now Tostão took on Moore on the left. The ball ricocheted between Moore's legs and came out the other side. Tostão, hemmed in, lofted the ball into the danger zone, where it fell to Pelé. Confronted by Labone and Cooper, Pelé brushed the ball to his right. Cooper was off balance and Peters too far to intercede as Jairzinho smashed it past the plunging Banks.

England were now on the ropes, and Jairzinho shot over when he might have scored again. To inject fresh legs, Ramsey took off Lee and Bobby Charlton, replacing them with Jeff Astle and Colin Bell. Astle, accomplished in the air, teed up Ball, whose volley was abortive. Alas, Astle's next contribution was less constructive. Everaldo, his mind elsewhere, presented the ball neatly to him near the penalty spot. Astle had time and room, but he lashed out in haste and it rolled miserably the wrong side of Felix's left post. In a match of such high technique, the error was as incongruous as a wart on the cheek of Venus.

Even so, Astle's miss need not have cost England the match. With ten minutes remaining, Moore's centre from the left was headed on by Astle to Ball, out near the left edge of the Brazilian penalty box. Ball aimed beyond Felix's shoulder, but the ball thudded against the top of the bar and sailed over. Exasperated, Ball soon shot over again. A magnificent match ended with Pelé chipping uncomfortably close to Banks' crossbar. A draw would, perhaps, have been a fairer result, but there remained the prospect of a rematch in the Final.

BRAZIL   (0) 1                    ENGLAND   (0) 0
   Jairzinho 59

BRAZIL: Felix, Carlos Alberto, Brito, Piazza, Everaldo, Clodoaldo, Rivelino, Paulo Cesar, Jairzinho, Tostão (Roberto), Pelé.
ENGLAND: Banks, Wright, Cooper, Mullery, Labone, Moore, Lee (Astle), Ball, R Charlton (Bell), Hurst, Peters.

## CZECHOSLOVAKIA v ENGLAND
*Thursday, 11 June 1970*                    *Guadalajara – 49,000*

The approach to England's concluding match, with Czechoslovakia, was filled with nods and winks. No one doubted that Brazil would sleep more easily with England out of the competition. If Brazil were devious enough to lose to Romania by one goal on the Wednesday, this would leave England needing to beat the Czechs the following day. Thankfully, Brazil aimed to head the group, in order remain in Guadalajara for the quarter-final, and their diluted team won 3-2. England now needed only a draw to go through. The Czechs, returning to the hemisphere where, eight years earlier, they had lost the Final to Brazil, needed nothing less than a three-goal victory.

The British public was spared much of this gossip, for a national strike halted British newspaper production from 10 to 14 June. Ramsey was probably glad of the respite. Team-wise, he faced two alternatives, to rest his key players in order that they be refreshed for the quarter-finals (against Brazil his players had sweated off an average of ten pounds), or take nothing for granted and field his strongest eleven. Ramsey went for the former, making five changes. Keith Newton was reinstated, Jack Charlton replaced Brain Labone, Colin Bell came in for Alan Ball, Lee stepped down for Allan Clarke to made his international debut. Astle – notwithstanding his Brazilian blunder – claimed Hurst's place. The Czechs appeared to pick their side with a blindfold and pin.

One of the Czech newcomers, Pollak – not dissimilar to Bobby Charlton in hairstyle or playing style – took immediate control of midfield. The play was scrappy, the few constructive moments coming principally from the Czechs. Capkovic and Petras both shot over Banks' bar. With the explosive Petras constantly embarrassing Jack Charlton, there was cause for surprise that Czechoslovakia's goal figures were so wretched. England's apologists would later attribute the malaise to colour blindness – their pale blue shirts, worn to avoid a clash with Czechoslovakia's white, could not be easily distinguished in the confusion of dazzling sunlight and deep shade.

The Czechs, not to say the finger-crossed Romanians, must have felt all was not lost. England's midfield was ragged beyond belief and Astle was having one of those days when his claim to be an international footballer brought hoots of derision from all outside the Hawthorns. Only at the end of the first half did England construct an attack of note, when Clarke's shot was cleanly saved.

Three minutes into the second half the fate of England and Group 3 was effectively settled by a refereeing decision calculated to increase England's unpopularity with the Mexicans and everybody else. Kuna made an untidy challenge on Bell, slipped, and found his hand momentarily on the ball. It was as if two half-infringements convinced the French referee, Roger Machus, of the culpability of the sum, though he would insist he had penalised the foul. The only person unconcerned was Allan Clarke, free from nerves, who smashed the penalty high to Viktor's left.

With England seemingly secure, Astle and Bobby Charlton were pulled off, allowing Osgood and Ball to see the job through. Banks suffered the distraction of coins and fruit hurled at him from behind his goal, and fierce shots by Petras from the front. Jokl replaced Capkovic, whose mouth had been bloodied by Mullery. England's best chance fell to Ball, who shot right-footed high onto the bar. Having done the same against Brazil, Ball felt he was owed one.

The game saved up an embarrassment for the England goalkeeper. Full-back Dobias had just been booked for a challenge on Ball. Seeking to enter the records for more praiseworthy reasons, he unleashed a twenty-five yarder straight at Banks' head. As the keeper reached up to collect, the ball flew through his hands and crashed back off the crossbar.

Thus spared, England held on, but on this display few would have put money on their progress. Harold Wilson was banking on it.

CZECHOSLOVAKIA  (0) 0          ENGLAND  (0) 1
                                        Clarke 48 pen

CZECHOSLOVAKIA: Viktor, Dobias, Migas, Hrivnak, Hagara, Pollak, Kuna, F Veseley, Petras, Adamec, Capkovic (Jokl).
ENGLAND: Banks, Newton, Cooper, Mullery, J Charlton, Moore, Bell, Peters, Clarke, Astle (Osgood), R Charlton (Ball).

*Final Positions – Group 3*

|                  | P | W | D | L | F | A | Pts |
|------------------|---|---|---|---|---|---|-----|
| BRAZIL           | 3 | 3 | 0 | 0 | 8 | 3 | 6   |
| ENGLAND          | 3 | 2 | 0 | 1 | 2 | 1 | 4   |
| Romania          | 3 | 1 | 0 | 2 | 4 | 5 | 2   |
| Czechoslovakia   | 3 | 0 | 0 | 3 | 2 | 7 | 0   |

## WEST GERMANY v ENGLAND
*Sunday, 14 June 1970*                                    *León – 24,000*

England knew as they took the field against Czechoslovakia that as runners-up in Group 3 they would travel to León to meet West Germany, already winners of Group 4. The 1966 World Cup Final was about to be replayed.

León was a squalid city, 170 miles by road from Guadalajara. It was also 700 feet higher up and considerably hotter. Likewise, German firepower was likely to be hotter than anything England had known in Guadalajara. In qualifying for the finals ahead of Scotland, Germany had run up a World Cup record score of 12-0 against Cyprus. In Mexico, the Germans had blitzed ten goals to date, seven of them accredited to their new scoring sensation, the short, huge-thighed Gerd Müller. In comparison, England had mustered only a couple, one of them from a doubtful penalty. West Germany were clearly the team in form, even if their past record against England bore the stamp of divine disapproval. One wondered whether their solitary, hollow success in 1968 would convince them they could beat England when it mattered. Current form might favour Germany: history pointed to England.

Like England, Germany took eight of their 1966 team to Mexico. Ten players who lined up under León's midday sun had squared up in the 1966 Final: Höttges, Schnellinger, Beckenbauer, Overath and Seeler for Germany; Moore, Bobby Charlton, Ball, Peters and Hurst for England. The total would have been eleven but for one of the most mysterious and critical illnesses ever to mar a football match. Gordon Banks was suffering stomach cramps when the team arrived in León on Saturday afternoon. Presumably he had eaten or drunk something that did not agree with him. He was experiencing waves of nausea and the need to dash to the lavatory – a complaint known locally as Montezuma's Revenge. As all the England players' food was carefully prepared, the singling out of the England goalkeeper raised suspicions that mischief was afoot. It was ironic that England enjoyed the services of a team doctor, Neil Phillips – a precaution unheard of in Winterbottom's day – yet were still afflicted by a medical disorder of this magnitude.

On the Sunday Banks awoke feeling stronger. He was included in the team, only to suffer a relapse. This gave Peter Bonetti barely an hour's notice that he was playing in his first World Cup match. He had not played a competitive game for a month. Good as Bonetti was, there was something uncommonly secure about Gordon Banks. No team likes to juggle its goalkeepers in a World Cup, and this was the first occasion England had had to do so. Other than Banks, Ramsey reverted to his first-choice team.

Memories of 1966 came flooding back as England once again lined up in red shirts, Germany in white. The first substitution concerned the ball, which had to be changed in the first minute. The replacement was to England's liking, for they took an early grip, helped by an extra man in midfield. Only Lee and Peters were falling short of the standards they had set themselves in Mexico, and Lee was taking out his frustrations on opposing goalkeepers. Having clashed with Felix of Brazil, now he became embroiled with Sepp Maier and was booked by the Argentine referee, Angel Coerezza. The mere combination of England, Germany and Argentina on the same pitch reawakened such nightmares from 1966 that one questioned FIFA's foresight. But Coerezza redeemed himself in English eyes – at least for the time being – when taking the name of Gerd Müller.

If England were the more impressive outfit, neither goalkeeper had yet been extended. That is, until just after the half-hour, when England scored a fulminating goal. Mullery exchanged a one-two with Lee, then speared a pass out wide to Newton. Both players accelerated, Newton down the line, Mullery across-field towards the near post. The full-back's cross synchronised with Mullery's sprint and fused eight yards out. Under pressure from Vogts, Mullery swept the ball high to Maier's left. It was his first goal for his country, and in creation and execution it was stainless. Mullery was having a memorable World Cup and the goal was a fitting tribute.

Germany's attempts to hit back were strangled by Cooper's domination of Libuda, the raiding winger who had created such havoc in earlier rounds. With Löhr similarly ineffective on the other flank, and England hegemonic in midfield, it was difficult to see how Germany could manufacture an equaliser. It was cause for smug satisfaction that the Germans were resorting to the British stand-by of hoisting up-and-unders at the enemy's nerve centre.

For the second half, Germany rearranged their defence, replacing full-back Höttges with Willie Schulz. This did not prevent a swift second goal for England. Newton, having again hared down the touchline, swept over another cross to the far post. It looked to be fruitless, until Martin Peters ghosted behind Vogts to squeeze the ball home. Newton had made two goals, and if the second was Peters' first notable contribution to the tournament, it appeared to have taken England into the semi-finals.

Considering England's renowned defence, and its reluctance to concede goals even when the team was playing badly – which was manifestly not the case in León – logic pointed to a predictable outcome. With nothing to lose, Helmut Schoen played his last, familiar, card. In each of Germany's group matches Schoen had brought on a fresh winger, Jürgen Grabowski, during the second half. Now he did so again. Cooper had deflated Libuda, but at the depletion of his own powers of recovery. Grabowski exploited the tiring full-back mercilessly and soon found room for a dangerous shot at goal. That show of defiance served to revitalise the Germans. Unease seemed to spread throughout the England camp, not to mention among the millions watching on TV back home.

Ramsey, too, must have sensed that something was amiss, for he prepared to inject Colin Bell's energy and save the struggling Bobby Charlton for the semi-finals. But before the substitution could be made, disaster struck. There were only twenty-two minutes left when Beckenbauer's graceful stride carried him within shooting range. The ball struck Lee in a sensitive area but rebounded back to Beckenbauer. As the German closed for a second attempt, Mullery wisely forced him wide to the right, where the angle on goal, allied to the direction of Beckenbauer's run, seemed to pose minimum threat. Indeed, the shot that Beckenbauer unleashed carried little. Alas, Bonetti chose that instant to expose a fragility none suspected. His dive was clumsy and late, and the ball passed under him into the far corner of the net. Bonetti would never live down that moment of aberration. Inspired by one of the cherished TV commercials of the period, he would exemplify a new category of goalkeeping blunder – the 'Weetabix' save.

Undeterred by the goal, Ramsey went through with the substitution. Bobby Charlton came off, having just won his record 106th cap, one more than Billy Wright. What he could not know was that, like his brother Jack, his England days were over. Bell seemed a useful investment, striking one shot towards Maier, then breaking down the right to project a low centre that the diving Hurst met at the near post. Maier was nowhere as the ball brushed past the opposite upright. The miss seemed sure to be expensive when Müller at last squeezed behind Newton. This time, Bonetti saved capably.

Beckenbauer seemed rejuvenated following Charlton's withdrawal – as in 1966 both men had suppressed their creative instincts in the cause of subduing the other. As Grabowski turned the screw on Cooper, Ramsey made a second substitution. Peters was pulled off, rather than the spent full-back, intending that Norman Hunter intercede between Grabowski and Cooper. But within seconds Germany equalised. The ball flew around the English penalty area as on a pinball machine. At last, Labone was given the chance to thump it clear, only to 'pass' it out to Schnellinger, who swiftly knocked it back high across goal. Uwe Seeler, thirty-four years old, was playing his nineteenth match in his fourth World Cup finals (he would shortly retire after his record twenty-first World Cup appearance). Now he crept behind Mullery, but could do no better than strain upwards, with his back to the goal, hoping to keep the ball in play. Cruelly for England, the ball bounced off his head and arced in a slow parabola under the crossbar. Had Bonetti been on his line, he would have plucked the ball out of the air as easily as taking down the washing. But he was stranded in limbo and the ball sank in slow motion behind him. 'England' bellowed David Coleman, 'were throwing it away'.

After that, they did well to merit extra time, Beckenbauer and Löhr both coming close. During the added thirty minutes both sets of players dredged up reserves of strength, yet Grabowski continued to carry the greatest menace.

The nail in Peter Bonetti's coffin. Müller volleys the winner. (v W Germany)

There was no change to the score in the first period of extra time, though Hurst 'scored' from Lee's cross, only for the effort to be mysteriously disallowed. Hurst had had the rub of the green against Germany in 1966, and now paid his dues. Once Bonetti was transferred back to his unlucky goal all the self-inflicted wounds reopened. Grabowski put over yet another cross to the far post, where Löhr climbed above Newton to head back to the middle. Instinctively in the right place, Müller, 'der Bomber' swivelled to hook the ball in a muscular volley past Bonetti.

England had eleven minutes in which to save their crown. They filled them, admirably, piling forward. Mullery, Ball and, at the death, Newton, all came close, but not close enough, and England were out of the World Cup. Back home, the silence was deafening. In an ITV television studio Malcolm Allison tore off his Union Jack tie and threw it to the floor.

With most football matches it is comparatively straightforward to analyse the result, and attribute reasons why one team won and the other lost. With this particular match, no easy explanations suffice. The result was, somehow, unreal. No Ramsey team had previously lost a two-goal lead, let alone to the kind of sloppy goals conceded to Germany. However hard one tries, it is difficult to acknowledge German superiority on the day, particularly in the circumstances of Bonetti's inclusion, and notwithstanding Ramsey's much-maligned substitutions. England, for an hour, seemed set on booking their appointment in the semis, *en route* for the keenly-awaited Final with Brazil. Few in Mexico disputed the proposition that England were the second best team, or that their match with Brazil would stand as the best of the tournament.

In the days prior to the quarter-finals, Mungo Jerry's No. 1 hit *In the Summertime* seemed to harmonise England's relentless march towards the Final. Following the defeat in León, the disc acquired a new, morose connotation, and cannot easily be listened to nowadays without reminders of the wave of disappointment that enveloped the country for days afterwards. To rub in the misery, England's cricketers were being thrashed by the Rest of the World select eleven, and racing driver Piers Courage was killed participating in the Dutch Grand Prix. The only bright news came from the United States, where golfer Tony Jacklin, having already won the 1969 British Open, was on the road to winning the US Open too. Jacklin had to share coverage in the American press with the trial of Charles Manson and his acolytes, who stood accused of the gruesome murder of the pregnant actress, Sharon Tate.

England's footballers, minus those headed on vacation, arrived home in time to cast their votes in the general election. On the eve of the quarter-final, Labour held a seven per cent lead over the Tories. Four days later Labour, like England's footballers, lost a theoretically unassailable lead, and Britain welcomed Ted Heath as prime minister.

There was no happy ending for the Germans. Exhausted by their recovery, they fell 3-4 to Italy in an extraordinary, error-strewn match that also went into extra time. That left the European champions to contest the Final with Brazil, losing 1-4 in a game in which Brazilian virtuosity etched itself permanently on the mind. Having won the Jules Rimet trophy for a third time, Brazil were entitled to keep it outright. A new cup, known simply as the FIFA World Cup, would be the prize from 1974, when England would have to fight her way through the qualifying rounds.

| WEST GERMANY  (0) 3 | ENGLAND  (1) 2 |
|---|---|
| Beckenbauer 68, Seeler 79, | Mullery 31, Peters 49 |
| Müller 109 | *After extra time (2-2 after 90 minutes)* |

W GERMANY: Maier, Schnellinger, Vogts, Fichtel, Höttges (Schulz), Beckenbauer, Overath, Seeler, Libuda (Grabowski), Müller, Löhr.
ENGLAND: Bonetti, Newton, Cooper, Mullery, Labone, Moore, Lee, Ball, Hurst, R Charlton (Bell), Peters (Hunter).

Down and out. Alf Ramsey consoles his players. (v W Germany)

*England appearances and goalscorers (substitute appearances in brackets)*
*World Cup finals 1970*

| | Apps | Goals | | Apps | Goals |
|---|---|---|---|---|---|
| Cooper T | 4 | – | Hurst G * | 3 | 1 |
| Mullery A | 4 | 1 | Bell C | 1 (2) | – |
| Moore R *† | 4 | – | Wright T | 1 (1) | – |
| Charlton R *† | 4 | – | Astle J | 1 (1) | – |
| Peters M * | 4 | 1 | Bonetti P | 1 | – |
| Ball A * | 3 (1) | – | Clarke A | 1 | 1 |
| Banks G * | 3 | – | Charlton J * | 1 | – |
| Newton K | 3 | – | Osgood P | – (2) | – |
| Labone B | 3 | – | Hunter N | – (1) | – |
| Lee F | 3 | – | | | |

\* Appeared in 1966 World Cup.                    *19 players    4 goals*
† Appeared in 1962 World Cup.

# 7

# THE 1974 WORLD CUP

In 1974 the World Cup finals returned to Europe – to West Germany. No longer hosts, no longer champions, England were obliged to earn their place by submitting themselves to the qualifiers for the first time in twelve years. For Ramsey, achievements and all, this was an unknown challenge. In themselves, the qualifying rounds did not appear unduly arduous. England were given the luxury of a three rather than four-nation group – only the winners going though in either case. Being seeded, England were required to overcome the unseeded Wales and Poland, neither of whom were expected to put up much of a fight.

In the interim, death had taken its toll of de Gaulle, Khrushchev and Nasser. World trouble-spots included India and Pakistan, where a bitter war had been fought; Northern Ireland, experiencing its worst rioting in fifty years; West Germany, where the 1972 Olympics had been marred by terrorism; and Uganda, where the newly installed regime of Idi Amin had booted out 40,000 Asians. Britain had converted to decimal currency; unemployment had passed the one million mark; and 'hot-pants' were briefly all the rage. In June 1972 Britain suffered her worst aviation disaster when a Trident jet stalled after take-off from Heathrow.

England's footballers were also stalling of late. Contesting the 1972 European Championship, England had overcome Greece, Switzerland and Malta to land a two-legged quarter-final with, yes, West Germany. The tie was blown up into some kind of best-of-three decider, an opportunity for England to erase the bitter memories of Mexico. But if question marks clouded Germany's triumph in León, nothing clouded their superiority now. At Wembley in the first leg the Germans won in a canter, playing dream football around new stars Günter Netzer and Uli Hoeness. It was this match that ended the international careers of Geoff Hurst and Franny Lee. A new strike-force would have to be moulded. Facing a 1-3 deficit for the return leg, England accomplished nothing more than a meaningless 0-0 draw. But if Germany's star was clearly rising (they went on to win the European title), even the most diehard England supporter had to acknowledge that Ramsey's all-stars were not what they were.

*Qualifying Group 5*

## WALES v ENGLAND
*Wednesday, 15 November 1972*                    *Cardiff – 36,000*

As a prelude to the Wales v England fixture, the IRA despatched a wave of letter-bombs to London. An IRA man was given life for his part in the Aldershot barracks bombings, which had left seven dead. George McGovern had been beaten out of sight by Nixon in the American presidential elections. Chris Finnegan lost his European light-heavyweight boxing title at the Empire Pool, Wembley, to the German Rudi Schmidtke. The week's best-selling single was Gilbert O'Sullivan's *Clair*, which had displaced Lieutenant Pigeon's *Mouldy Old Dough*.

No amount of 'dough' could compensate the England manager, or his goalkeeper, when Gordon Banks was involved in a fearful car crash a month before the Wales match. Banks lost the sight of one eye and his top-class career was over. At thirty-four, he was still the automatic first choice England keeper. With his new understudy, Peter Shilton, unfit, young Ray Clemence of Liverpool now made his England debut.

Of the team that would face Wales, only Bobby Moore, Colin Bell, Alan Ball and Norman Hunter remained of the Mexico brigade. Ball was now with his third club, Arsenal, as he embarked on his third World Cup campaign. Colin Bell's inexhaustible style set him apart as a player on the brink of greatness – the perfect successor to Bobby Charlton. Both favoured full-backs in Mexico had gone: Keith Newton had not played for England since, and Terry Cooper had broken a leg. A string of players had auditioned for the No. 2 shirt – Emlyn Hughes, Paul Reaney, Chris Lawler, Paul Madeley, Colin Todd, Mick Mills, Frank Lampard. The position would have gone to Madeley, but he was injured. Arsenal's Peter Storey, having recently taken on Mullery's duties in midfield, switched to right-back, with Emlyn Hughes on the other flank. Amazing to think, Ball and Storey were the first players on Highbury's books ever to feature in England's World Cup quest.

Three extravagantly talented forwards were seeking to carry the torch passed on by their illustrious predecessors. Twenty-one year old Kevin Keegan was providing Liverpool with a double baptism, in his case after just one season of first division football since transferring from Scunthorpe. He teamed up with Manchester City's mercurial Rodney Marsh, one of those maverick crowd pleasers who looked ill at ease with the strict commands of top-flight football. Marsh was already twenty-eight, rather late to be thinking of setting the England front line ablaze.

The third new forward, Martin Chivers of Tottenham, seemed set to inherit the target-man duties performed with such distinction by Hurst. Hugely built, deceptively skilful, seemingly lethargic, yet immovable when in the mood, much was expected of him.

The centre-half shirt was once again proving too heavy for comfort. Both Labone and Jack Charlton had played their last internationals in Mexico, since when David Sadler, Roy McFarland, Larry Lloyd, Jeff Blockley and Bobby Moore himself had tried it on. Against Wales, Derby's McFarland got the nod, despite being untypically short for an English stopper and uncommonly skilful.

If history was any guide, the result was a foregone conclusion. Just six months earlier England had won 3-0 in Cardiff. Wales had beaten England only once, in 1955 since the war, and in the dim and distant past had lost two World Cup qualifiers heavily, 1-4, in Cardiff. With Wales failing to score in their last six games, all augured well for Ramsey on the occasion of his 100th match as England team manager.

Despite the occasion, the contest was strangely morbid, lacking heart and atmosphere. England's domination was the product of fitness and organisation, rather than superior technique. Wales looked to nineteen-year-old Leighton James from second division Burnley to spur them to victory, but the youngster was ruthlessly hushed by Peter Storey.

The game needed a goal to open it up. An interchange between Bell, Hunter and Chivers preceded a cross to the far post that was turned past Gary Sprake by man-of-the-match Colin Bell. This breakthrough allowed England to relax, and there was time before the interval for Ball to come close to increasing the lead.

The second period witnessed a procession of dull English assaults, interspersed with unimaginative Welsh breakaways. Ball found space but shot straight at Sprake. Chivers spun on a through ball from Marsh to bring the save of the match from the Welsh goalkeeper. With Moore and McFarland snuffing out all hint of a Welsh equaliser, the game's few goalmouth incidents took place at Sprake's end. Keegan tried to dribble round him, but was foiled, and in the closing seconds a slice of Marsh magic almost produced a memorable climax.

England had won as expected, but the performance had been below par. Only Marsh of the forwards had emerged with any credit. Chivers had failed to make his strength tell, and Keegan's debut had been anticlimactic. In previous World Cup qualifiers, the points were all that mattered, but FIFA had now abandoned play-offs for sides level on points and introduced goal-difference. And that might prove costly.

WALES    (0) 0                    ENGLAND    (1) 1
                                       Bell 35

WALES: Sprake (Leeds), Rodrigues (Sheff W) (*sub* Reece, Cardiff), R Thomas (Swindon), Hennessey (Derby), England (Spurs), Hockey (Sheff U), Phillips (Cardiff), Mahoney (Stoke), Davies (Man U), Toshack (Liverp'l), James (Burnley).
ENGLAND: Clemence (Liverpool), Storey (Arsenal), Hughes (Liverpool), Hunter (Leeds), McFarland (Derby), Moore (West Ham), Keegan (Liverpool), Chivers (Spurs), Marsh (Man C), Bell (Man C), Ball (Arsenal).

## ENGLAND v WALES
*Wednesday, 24 January 1973*                         *Wembley – 62,000*

Ten weeks later, Wembley staged the return match with Wales. Those weeks saw Britain join the Common Market, Lieutenant Mark Phillips woo Princess Anne, and President Nixon's decision to quit Vietnam. But as one conflict ceased, another – not quite so bloody – escalated, as Britain and Iceland locked horns in their 'Cod War'. Battles on the entertainment front were being won by *Monty Python*, *Alias Smith and Jones*, which had become a television cult Western, and the Osmonds, who singly or together boasted three records in the Top Twenty.

As match-day approached, Icelandic gunboats menaced British trawlers. Nixon was sworn into his second term, to be informed of the death of his predecessor, Lyndon Johnson. Alexander Onassis, heir to the vast shipping fortune, was killed in a plane crash. World heavyweight boxing champion Joe Frazier was floored three times in the first round by George Foreman in Kingston, Jamaica. The challenger repeated the dose in the second round and took the title.

Sir Alf Ramsey, hoping for a similar k.o. by his footballers, named an unchanged team. England hadn't won at Wembley for twenty months. Pitted against them was a team comprising three first division reserves, three second division players and one from the third. They would surely not have the gall to repeat the result of their last visit, in 1971, which ended goalless.

Regrettably, from England's point of view, they did. Wales defended stubbornly against an England eleven that spent much of the evening battering their heads against a red wall. Indeed, Germany must have seemed a long way off when Wales took a shock lead midway through the first period. Inside his own half, Evans fended off Chivers, Ball and Bell, thereby initiating a move which eventually reached Leighton James out on the right. McFarland and Storey faltered, seeming to expect an offside flag. James reached the by-line and his low cross was turned in by John Toshack.

For all their pressure, England looked incapable of breaking through, and it took a bolt from the blue for them to do so. Bell, the best player on view, drove in a vicious low centre. The ball took an angled deflection and carried into the path of Norman Hunter. Gary Sprake – kept out of the Leeds side by David

Harvey – was helpless as the ball flew past him from twenty-five yards into the top corner.

The second half saw no improvement. McFarland looked frighteningly insecure, Chivers flitted into the game intermittently, Rodney Marsh played to the rhythm of his own drum, and Kevin Keegan was again submerged by the importance of the occasion. It was down to action-men Ball and Bell to try to light a damp touchpaper.

They carved out just one clear-cut chance. Bell rose to meet Hunter's cross and his firm header thudded against Sprake's crossbar. From less than six yards Chivers stabbed the rebound wide. By this time, the crowd were treating England to a slow handclap, which increased in intensity when Chivers snatched at a cross, thwarting Keegan who was excellently positioned behind him. Malcolm Macdonald and Mike Channon, two regular goalscorers, were sitting on the substitutes' bench, and they stayed there.

England had taken three points off Wales instead of the expected four, dropping their first ever home point in a World Cup qualifier. Whether that would prove expensive now depended on Poland. To rub salt in the wound, four months later Wales returned to Wembley in the British Championship. This time they lost 0-3.

| ENGLAND (1) 1 | WALES (1) 1 |
|---|---|
| Hunter 41 | Toshack 23 |

ENGLAND: Clemence, Storey, Hughes, Hunter, McFarland, Moore, Keegan, Bell, Chivers, Marsh, Ball.
WALES: Sprake (Leeds), Rodrigues (Sheff W) (*sub* Page, Birmingham), R Thomas (Swindon), Hockey (Sheff U), England (Spurs), J Roberts (Birmingham), B Evans (Swansea), Mahoney (Stoke), Toshack (Liverp'l), Yorath (Leeds), James (Burnley).

## POLAND v ENGLAND
*Wednesday, 6 June 1973*                    *Chorzow, Katowice – 105,000*

When England travelled to Chorzow for their first encounter with Poland their prospects looked brighter. Wales had defeated Poland 2-0 in Cardiff. A win for Ramsey's team would now eliminate Poland, and even a draw would be more than welcome.

Poland were something of an unknown quantity. They had not appeared in the finals of the World Cup since 1938 and never previously beaten England. The two past meetings had both taken place in 1966, England drawing 1-1 at Wembley in January, then winning 1-0 in Chorzow in July. On the other hand, as current Olympic champions, Poland were clearly an emerging force. Olympic gold medallists had a strong tradition in the World Cup.

England were visiting Poland as part of a close season tour of the continent. A 1-1 draw had already been achieved in Czechoslovakia. After Poland, England would travel to play the Soviet Union and Italy. With the World Cup finals only a year away, England's weaknesses compared with 1966 and 1970 were brutally apparent. Those teams had at their core three or four players of world class. Of that breed only Moore remained, and at thirty-two he was no longer the incomparable defender of old. Speed was never his strongest suit, even in his prime, and now his place was secure principally for his colossal experience – this would be his 105th cap. True, England could point to other useful players, but none of them had any claim to immortality, while some, in the eyes of Ramsey's critics, were simply not worthy of international football.

But the figures, as ever, were with Ramsey. England had not tasted defeat for a year, had lost only to West Germany and Northern Ireland in twenty-three matches since Mexico, and had not been beaten on the continent since Yugoslavia put England out of the European Championship in 1968.

Ramsey fiddled with his team-sheet. Following their inauspicious performances against Wales, he evidently felt that his newest caps, Clemence and Keegan, hadn't the international maturity to cope with the cauldron of Chorzow. They were replaced by Peter Shilton of Leicester City and Leeds' Allan Clarke. The Leeds utility player, Paul Madeley, returned to right-back, enabling Storey to reclaim his slot in midfield. As for Rodney Marsh, he was never the answer to Ramsey's needs, and his international career was over. To bolster his midfield, the manager recalled Martin Peters.

The papers in those first days of June continued to speculate on the royal romance. A new scandal then broke, surrounding Norma Levy and Lord Lambton. The United States was in the grip of Watergate fever. Congress was debating whether grounds existed for impeaching Nixon. The Soviet Union ate humble pie at the Paris Air Show, when the pride of Soviet aviation, the Tupolev 144 – popularly known as 'Concordski' disintegrated in flight, killing all six members of the crew and eight people on the ground.

Wednesday 6 June marked the twenty-ninth anniversary of D-Day, and Ramsey must have been hoping for a similarly successful invasion of Europe. It also saw the death of 4ft 3in comedian Jimmy Clitheroe, the eternal schoolboy whose show had entertained radio listeners for fifteen years. Soccer shared the sporting focus with the Derby. Three-quarters of a million people flocked to Epsom Downs to see Edward Hide win on Morston. Having celebrated or consoled themselves as appropriate, the sporting masses settled back for the 5.30 p.m. live transmission from the Slaski Stadium in the heart of the Silesian coal fields.

What remains vivid, even today, is the degree of pessimism that preceded the match. Without tangible justification, either in England's recent results or Poland's, the almost unanimous verdict of sports writers and pundits was that

England would lose. One wondered whether they knew something the rest of us did not. Such contagious gloom could hardly have lightened the mood of the England players.

As if determined to fulfil the journalists' curse, England conceded a sloppy goal after just seven minutes. Shilton had already been stretched by one free-kick, from the gifted winger, Lubanski, when Poland were awarded another, far out on the left. The decision, itself, was debatable, McFarland being pulled up for impeding Lubanski. Gadocha took the kick, swinging the ball viciously towards the near post, which Moore was guarding. The ball flicked both him and Peter Shilton and into the net. It was the kind of nonsensical goal to leave any manager tugging at his hair.

The goal settled the Poles, who had begun nervously, but lit the fires of an English onslaught. In the light of the result, it is often forgotten how much England saw of the ball in Katowice. Outscored, they were, outplayed, they were not. England dominated the rest of the half, pushing the ball with grinding certainty towards the Polish goal. Time after time their attacks foundered on the home defence, where Balzucki kept a tight grip on Chivers, and Clarke was allowed no space by Rzesny. The giant defender, Gorgon, repelled most of the high balls projected into the Polish goalmouth. Even so, chances came and went. Just three minutes after Poland had scored, Peters wasted an opening with a tame header. A Clarke effort was well saved by the then unknown Tomaszewski, and Chivers drove over the bar from twelve yards. Poland managed nothing at all.

Oddly, the pessimism that preceded the match was just a memory by half-time. The doom merchants had seen nothing to suggest either that Poland deserved to be in front or would stay there. All that was to change within seconds of the restart. The culprit was Bobby Moore. In oceans of space on the halfway line, he gathered the ball and surveyed the landscape, much like a batsman checking field placings. The fastest man on the pitch, Lubanski, advanced to pressure the slowest. Moore tried to side-step, momentarily lost his balance and presented a fleeting sight of the ball. That was enough. Lubanski whipped it away and set off as if with a firework tied to his tail. His shot was low, hard, and perfectly placed, flashing into the net off the base of Shilton's left-hand post. To those for whom the adjective 'majestic' was tailor-made for Bobby Moore, the sight of such a crass error was hard to comprehend. While all players make mistakes, Moore never seemed to – at least not in crucial matches for England. He had just made the greatest and possibly the most costly blunder of his international career, and one sensed instinctively that his England days were numbered.

Ten minutes into the second half, Lubanski, his work done, was taken off and replaced by Domarski. England saw as much of the ball in the second period as they had in the first, but with only two out-and-out strikers – Chivers and Clarke – Tomaszewski was never put under sustained pressure. Channon, Macdonald and Mike Summerbee were ready and willing on the substitutes' bench, but there they remained.

The temperature of battle steadily increased as England 'fought' to get on terms. As the minutes ticked away, their muscle owed more and more to the illegitimate. With a quarter of an hour remaining, Cmikiewicz and Peters went down in a tangle of whirling feet. Alan Ball intervened, grabbing Cmikiewicz by the throat and jerking a knee towards his groin. The Austrian referee, Paul Schiller, had earlier been guilty of bizarre decisions, but could not be faulted for sending the flame-haired Englishman from the field. The melee even extended to both benches, where there were angry scenes.

The second half had fallen apart long before Ball's dismissal. Afterwards, it degenerated still further. There was no further scoring and England had lost their first ever World Cup qualifier. Ball would be automatically ruled out of the return at Wembley. After the match Ramsey suggested that, despite the score, this had been one of England's better performances. And in some respects it was. Certainly, Poland had shown nothing to be feared. Had England not presented them with two goals, Poland might have been hard pressed to cultivate their own.

Group 5 was now wide open. If Wales succeeded where England failed, and won in Poland, England would be left needing to crush the Poles by an improbable four goals to be sure of qualifying. Such a Welsh accomplishment seemed unlikely, but the fact that their survival was now in the hands of others left England facing an uncomfortable summer.

POLAND   (1) 2                    ENGLAND   (0) 0
  Gadocha 7, Lubanski 47

POLAND: Tomaszewski, Rzesny, Gorgon, Musial, Balzucki, Kraska, Banas, Cmikiewicz, Deyna, Lubanski (Domarski), Gadocha.
ENGLAND: Shilton, Madeley, Hughes, Storey, McFarland, Moore, Ball, Bell, Chivers, Clarke, Peters.

**ENGLAND v POLAND**
*Wednesday, 17 October 1973*                    *Wembley – 100,000*

The autumn of 1973 witnessed one of those hot periods in world affairs. Chile's President Allende, the world's only democratically elected Marxist head of state, was overthrown. In the Middle East, the fourth Arab-Israeli war, the Yom Kippur, raged. The United States was still smitten by Watergate, and was further disgraced when vice-president Spiro Agnew resigned amid allegations of tax fraud. Gerald Ford was named as the new vice-president.

Nixon, now facing impeachment, was ordered to surrender incriminating tapes. As shame enveloped the White House, glory was being heaped upon the Secretary of State. Henry Kissinger, together with Le Duc Tho of North Vietnam, jointly received the 1973 Nobel Peace Prize. On match-day, Israeli forces reached the Suez Canal, preparatory to marching on Cairo. One of Britain's most distinguished foreign correspondents, Nicholas Tomalin of *The Sunday Times,* was killed on the Golan Heights. In Kuwait, a conference of oil-producing states, including Saudi Arabia, agreed forthwith to raise the price of crude and cut back production. Britain, with sixty percent of her oil imports coming from the Gulf, took a deep breath. The Arab oil war had begun, and the economies of the Western world would never be quite the same again.

The sports news of mid-October was marked by death and resignation. The driver François Cevert died practising for the US Grand Prix. This prompted the early retirement of his friend and defending world champion Jackie Stewart, who had raced in ninety-nine Grands Prix. Brian Clough and Peter Taylor resigned from the management of Derby County, as a result of Clough's extra-curricular activities, mostly on television.

Though this was England's most critical match for years, the Football League stubbornly refused to postpone the Saturday league programme. The secretary of the Football League, Alan Hardaker, explained: 'If England do lose [against Poland] the game is not going to die. It will be a terrible thing for six weeks, and then everybody will forget about it.' One or two voices went further, suggesting that it would be best if England were knocked out, for only that might stimulate changing the whole antiquated structure of English football. The combined threat to world peace and English football quite overshadowed the first transmissions from Capital Radio, Britain's first commercial, round-the-clock, pop station.

Both England and Poland had enjoyed an encouraging preparation. The Poles had beaten Wales 3-0 the previous month – in a rough-house that saw Trevor Hockey sent off – and a week before Wembley had drawn 1-1 with the Dutch in Rotterdam. England had rounded off their summer tour by winning in Russia, losing in Italy. They then, in late September, thrashed Austria 7-0 at Wembley with a performance that sent the Polish spies home with heavy hearts.

The Poles' own victory over Wales made the issue crystal clear: Wales were out, England had to win, and anything less would see the Poles through. Subsequent talk that England had tied one arm behind their back by drawing with Wales was inaccurate. Even had England won 4-0 at Wembley, they would still have needed outright victory over the Poles to progress. Not that, according to Messrs Clough and Taylor, England had anything to fear. Clough dismissed keeper Tomaszewski as a 'clown', and Taylor labelled the entire Polish team 'donkeys'. The latter comparison contained at least a germ of truth.

Both donkeys and Polish footballers could kick. Few were in any doubt that the game could turn nasty. The referee was the Belgian, Vital Loraux, who had allowed Mocanu's and other Romanian 'tackles' to go unpunished in Guadalajara.

Public excitement was at fever pitch. Should England fail to beat Poland there was little doubt that Yom Kippur would be pushed from the front pages. Ramsey, with no injury worries, had little hesitation in naming the team that had just whacked Austria. Moore was only a substitute, having also been dropped by West Ham. Hunter kept his place, aiming to stifle the threat posed by Deyna in midfield. Storey was again left out. Tony Currie of Sheffield United and Mike Channon kept their places in a side captained by Martin Peters. Poland's manager, Gorski, sent out the same eleven that beat Wales and drew with Holland. That meant no place for the injured Lubanski.

The atmosphere was electric, the play passionate. Straight from the start England laid siege to the Polish goal. The Poles, in their Liverpool kit, erected a human wall in front of Tomaszewski, earning his thirteenth cap. England carved their way into the Polish penalty area seemingly at will, creating one opening after another. Peters chipped a free-kick towards the far post. McFarland headed it back, and Channon, a few feet out, ran the ball against the post. Currie then headed over the top. Tomaszewski, growing in confidence, flung himself to turn aside a low drive by Bell, plunged to keep out Clarke's header, then deflected a Channon effort to safety.

The interval is remembered for the pearls of wisdom from ITV's panel of experts. Brian Clough continued to ridicule Tomaszewski, insisting that all's well that ends well. Malcolm Allison warned that England were vulnerable to a Polish counter-attack. The gut feeling of most viewers was akin to that in León. Something felt wrong. England were murdering the Poles in all but goals. Who was behind the insistence that the ball stayed out, Tomaszewski or a higher, infallible guardian of goalposts?

Direct from the resumption, England resumed their barrage. Peters was relishing the responsibilities of captain, giving a weighty performance. At the heart of Poland's resistance, and masterminding what few attacks they mustered, lay Kazimierz Deyna. With hindsight, England's midfield did tend to crowd the front line of Channon, Chivers and Clarke. With hindsight, England did snatch hurriedly at their shots. Even so, Poland were literally being swamped. No sooner was the ball expelled from their penalty area than it whizzed back with the certainty of gravity. With chances falling England's way by the minute, the law of averages, if nothing else, seemed to command Poland's eventual demise.

The first twelve minutes of the second half saw England continuing to pummel the Polish goal. Then the unthinkable happened. Norman Hunter was pulled over to the right touchline, near halfway, to intercept a Polish clearance.

He might have booted the ball into the crowd, but tried to control it. The ball was spirited away from under his feet in the manner of Moore in Katowice. Lato was the poacher this time. Small, prematurely bald and dazzlingly quick, he had missed the first match, but was destined to be a star in the finals in both 1974 (when he would top score with seven goals) and 1978. Now, Lato hared towards England's goal, aided by an underpopulated defence. In itself, Hunter's error was not fatal. The poison he injected needed two accessories before death accrued. Though Hunter was beyond redemption, McFarland raced back to interpose himself between Lato and goal. Pausing to weigh his options, Lato laid the ball diagonally forwards, to meet Domarski's surging run. Emlyn Hughes turned to confront the new menace and lunged as Domarski's right boot made contact. Accessory number one, the ball travelled between Hughes' straining legs, number two, though struck with sub-sonic velocity, it beat Shilton low to his left. On another day, the ball would have been blocked by the defender or saved by the keeper. But this was today, and Poland had scored. Shades of León. Domarski's shot had carried more venom than Beckenbauer's, but the taint of contributory negligence on Shilton's part has nagged him ever since.

The goal was a mortal blow to England, who now needed to score twice in a little over half an hour. As with a long-playing record that has stuck, white shirts continued to swarm around Tomaszewski's goal, and six minutes after falling behind England were awarded a penalty. Domarski soiled his earlier strike with a sloppy back-pass. Peters won possession and was adjudged to have been pushed by Musial. It was a softish award. Had the same push resulted in a penalty at the other end, there would have been rioting in the stadium. Allan Clarke, for one, was not bothered by just deserts. He smote the ball flawlessly to Tomaszewski's left and England were level.

The bombardment continued apace. Chivers, the one English forward unable to raise his game, laid on a chance for Currie, but the ball was sliced wide. He did better with his next effort, but from twenty-five yards Tomaszewski punched out Currie's shot to Channon, who volleyed into the side netting. A Currie cross-cum-shot then rolled along the Polish crossbar. The 'clown' persisted with his montage of defiant goalkeeping and outrageous good fortune: he settled for the latter when, caught in limbo, he got a foot to Clarke's shot. Hunter's drive was beaten out, Clarke headed just over, Currie's shot was parried, and Bell was flattened in the box. With Vital Loraux deliberating over a penalty, Clarke flailed at the loose ball.

Eight minutes from time Lato broke away, only for McFarland to haul him down by the neck. Today, the professional foul would have produced a red card. McFarland escaped with a caution. Three minutes later the Pole sprinted clear again, with Hunter appealing vainly for offside. This time Lato dithered and the opportunity was wasted.

So near yet so far. Kevin Hector's late header is cleared off the line. (v Poland)

There were just two minutes left to play when Ramsey belatedly took off Chivers – he would not represent his country again – and replaced him with Derby's Kevin Hector. The absurdly late substitution almost saved the day, as Hector met England's twenty-third corner with a header that was scrambled off the line. The rebound fell to Clarke who, off balance, stabbed it wide. The final whistle sounded and England were out of the World Cup. Moore came onto the field to console the disconsolate Hunter. Ramsey told reporters that England had been the better team twice, an extravagant statement with which the jubilant Polish press fully concurred.

Recriminations abounded. Many were directed once more at the philosophy of English football. But in this instance they seemed cruelly inappropriate. England could hardly have created more chances had they played *à la* Brazil. It was not the style of football that was responsible for Channon's shot coming back off a post. It was not the virtues of flair over functionalism that made Hector's last-gasp header hit a defender on the thigh instead of finding the net. In all but finishing, Poland had been mutilated. However reluctant one is to invoke the rub of the green, that priceless commodity had certainly deserted England.

Elimination from the World Cup spelled the end of the Ramsey era. His playing embodiment, Bobby Moore, returned for just one more match, against

Italy at Wembley. Following a 0-1 defeat, Moore stepped from the limelight to reflect on his record 108 caps. In the spring Ramsey was sacked. His achievements as England manager had been outstanding, losing just seventeen games out of 113. Those of his players in their late twenties would not see a World Cup, nor even, with the need to build afresh, have an international future.

England were not the only famous name missing from the finals. France, Spain, Portugal, Hungary and Czechoslovakia also failed to qualify. The sight of Zaire, Haiti and Australia in the tournament raised fresh questions about the whole qualifying procedure. In an age of jet travel, why was qualification still compressed within continents? Developing nations would surely learn more about international football from meeting European or South American sides, home and away, in the eliminators, than Zaire would from three thrashings in Germany.

England's failure was Scotland's success. They made the finals for the first time in sixteen years. Poland, too, gave a further glimpse of what might have been. Having withstood the English challenge, however fortuitously, there was little for them to fear. Playing with a self-belief non-existent against England, Poland would claim a merited third place in the finals, won by the hosts, West Germany.

For England, all was in the melting pot. Ted Croker succeeded Denis Follows as secretary to the FA, with a manifesto to stir up the English game. The world at large flirted with Armageddon: nuclear alarm bells sounded over the Middle East.

ENGLAND  (0) 1                POLAND  (0) 1
   Clarke 63 pen                  Domarski 57

ENGLAND: Shilton, Madeley, Hughes, Bell, McFarland, Hunter, Currie, Channon, Chivers (Hector), Clarke, Peters.
POLAND: Tomaszewski, Szymanowski, Gorgon, Musial, Bulzacki, Kasparczak, Lato, Cmikiewicz, Deyna, Domarski, Gadocha.

*Qualifying Group 5*

|         | P | W | D | L | F | A | Pts |
|---------|---|---|---|---|---|---|-----|
| POLAND  | 4 | 2 | 1 | 1 | 6 | 3 | 5   |
| England | 4 | 1 | 2 | 1 | 3 | 4 | 4   |
| Wales   | 4 | 1 | 1 | 2 | 3 | 5 | 3   |

*Other group results*

| Wales v Poland | 2-0 | Poland v Wales | 3-0 |

*England appearances and goalscorers (substitute appearances in brackets)*
*World Cup qualifying rounds 1974*

| | Apps | Goals | | Apps | Goals |
|---|---|---|---|---|---|
| Hughes E | 4 | – | Shilton P | 2 | – |
| McFarland R | 4 | – | Keegan K | 2 | – |
| Chivers M | 4 | – | Marsh R | 2 | – |
| Bell C * | 4 | 1 | Madeley P | 2 | – |
| Storey P | 3 | – | Clarke A * | 2 | 1 |
| Hunter N * | 3 | 1 | Peters M *† | 2 | – |
| Ball A *† | 3 | – | Channon M | 1 | – |
| Moore R *†‡ | 3 | – | Currie A | 1 | – |
| Clemence R | 2 | – | Hector K | – (1) | – |

* Appeared in 1970 World Cup.                    **18 players    3 goals**
† Appeared in 1966 World Cup.
‡ Appeared in 1962 World Cup.

# 8

# THE 1978 WORLD CUP

On 1 May 1974 Sir Alf Ramsey was sacked by the FA. Joe Mercer took over as caretaker manager and supervised an encouraging England tour of eastern Europe. But by the time the new season commenced a new man was in charge. Don Revie, at the time of his appointment, had no serious rival for the job. His record was even more impressive than Ramsey's. Revie's club, Leeds United, were, like Ramsey's Ipswich in 1962, defending League champions. Leeds' achievement of never being outside the top four since promotion in 1964 had made them the outstanding English team of the time. Whatever their differences, Revie shared with Ramsey the knack of getting the best out of players. Both men regarded themselves as father-figures overseeing a large family. Revie carried homework to new extremes, being forever associated with fulsome dossiers compiled on every aspect of the opposition. Early on in his stewardship, he assembled forty players he anticipated calling upon for the challenges ahead. Those subsequently left out of the final squads had the consolation that they had not been overlooked.

The European Championship provided Revie with an early opportunity to put England through their paces. But by November 1975 his team could only claim second place behind Czechoslovakia in a group completed by Portugal and Cyprus. Disappointment at England's continuing low-key results in this competition was slightly eased when the Czechs went on to win the European title.

In the summer of 1976 England began the business of qualifying for the 1978 World Cup, the finals of which would be held in Argentina. The draw that pencilled in England's opponents was the toughest yet. Failure in 1974 meant that England were unseeded for the first time. Luxembourg and Finland were named as the two lesser nations in Group 2, but the seeded team to emerge was Italy, European champions in 1968, World Cup runners-up in 1970 and European quarter-finalists in 1972. With just one team to qualify, England must either eliminate Italy or be eliminated themselves. Never had England, or Italy for that matter, been presented with such a hurdle to clear. Many commentators thought the draw indefensible, especially as both teams thought themselves assured of victory, seven days a week, against several of the Third World representatives in the finals. Not since 1958 had the Italians failed to qualify: their conquerors on that occasion were Northern Ireland.

*Qualifying Group 2*

## FINLAND v ENGLAND
*Sunday, 13 June 1976*                                    *Helsinki – 24,000*

Between October 1973 and June 1976 – the lull between England's participation in the World Cup – a crop of new statesmen had appeared: Harold Wilson, now followed by James Callaghan, in Britain; Gerald Ford in the United States; Giscard d'Estaing in France; Helmut Schmidt in West Germany. The Vietnamese war was over, the Americans defeated; an Apollo spacecraft had docked with a Soviet Soyez craft; and North Sea oil was on tap.

Early June 1976 saw race riots in Southall and Notting Hill. A spate of trials captured public interest: British mercenaries captured in Angola faced demands for the death sentence; former government minister John Stonehouse and his friend Sheila Buckley were in the dock, the former on charges of fraud, forgery and theft; the case of the Spaghetti House siege continued; in the United States, newspaper heiress Patty Hearst was awaiting sentence after her conviction for bank robbery with members of the Symbionese Liberation Army. Idi Amin of Uganda had survived yet another assassination attempt. Britain was on a full-scale rabies alert after a man returning from Bangladesh died. The Liberal Party was searching for a new leader in the wake of Jeremy Thorpe's downfall.

Jimmy Hill had been recruited to make Saudi Arabia a world soccer power; the English League fell in line with most countries in replacing goal average by goal difference; the West Indies were slaughtering England – Viv Richards scoring 232 in the First Test at Trent Bridge. Musically it was the age of the Wurzels, top of the charts with their *Combine Harvester*.

Some critics suggested that England's qualification might be better entrusted to Wurzels, given the unpredictability of Revie's team selections. The match in Helsinki would be his eighteenth in charge, and he had chopped and changed the side incessantly. The last heroes of 1966 – Ball and Peters – had finally fallen by the wayside.

In goal, Ray Clemence was preferred to Peter Shilton. Colin Todd of Derby County would line up at right-back, partnering Mick Mills of Ipswich. The new central defensive pair were Phil Thompson of Liverpool and Leeds' utility man Paul Madeley. The midfield trio were named as Trevor Cherry of Leeds, QPR's Gerry Francis as captain, and Trevor Brooking of West Ham, who was not thought to possess divided loyalties on account of his Finnish wife. Those entrusted with the search for goals were Stuart Pearson of Manchester United,

Southampton's Mike Channon, and Kevin Keegan, who, four years on, looked a rare jewel. Only four of the team – Clemence, Keegan, Madeley and Channon – had played in the 1974 qualifiers.

For their part, the Finnish team contained only two full-time professionals. Finland had never lost by less than three goals to England, and the aggregate of their three home games over the years was – scored 1, conceded 16. In the recent European Championship Finland had lost all their home games – to Holland, Poland, and Italy. In any language, this had to be an away banker.

Underdogs they may have been, but the Finns showed themselves to be more than just energetic tacklers. The bumpy pitch and the hosts' physical man-to-man marking ruled out a feast of football. Pearson had the ball in the net after just eight minutes, but his diving header was disallowed for offside. His next effort was legitimate. Phil Thompson sent Brooking clear on the right. The cross was headed back by Keegan for Pearson to net at close range.

The lead was wiped out when Gerry Francis lost possession. Rissanen's flighted centre was met firmly by Paatalainen's header. Ray Clemence had seen little action, and despite laying both hands on the ball couldn't prevent it squeezing into the net off a post.

The embarrassment of conceding a goal to the Finns was quickly alleviated. Pearson sprinted to keep the ball in play, and his cross was converted from a tight angle by a spectacular Keegan header.

Eleven minutes after the break Channon put England 3-1 up. Francis had sent him through, and when Channon's first effort came back off Enckelman he had time to juggle with the rebound before netting. England did not have long to wait for a fourth. Thompson cleared his lines, Keegan ran twenty yards with the ball, eluded Tolsa and shot clinically past Enckelman.

The Finns, strangely, continued to defend, though Paatalainen twice gave warning with fierce drives. Channon missed a sitter, Keegan was just off target, and at the death Cherry's snapshot struck a post and the rebound eluded Pearson.

England had reason to be pleased with the margin of victory. It was now down to Italy to match it.

That same afternoon, Britain's Sue Barker won the French Open Ladies tennis championship. The following day, the trial opened of Donald Nielson, charged with the kidnap and murder of a teenage heiress, whose body had been found hanging by wire down a drainage shaft. British sporting interest turned to the Montreal Olympics, which were set to commence. The British team was just fifty-six strong, the smallest for twenty years.

FINLAND  (1) 1                    ENGLAND  (2) 4
  Paatalainen 27                    Pearson 14, Keegan 30, 60,
                                     Channon 56

FINLAND: Enckelman, Vihtalie, Maekynen, Tolsa, Ranta, Jantunen, Suomalainen (Pyykko), E Heiskanen, A Heiskanen, Rissanen, Paataleinen.
ENGLAND: Clemence (Liverpool), Todd (Derby), Mills (Ipswich), Thompson (Liverpool), Madeley (Leeds), Cherry (Leeds), Keegan (Liverpool), Channon (Southampton), Pearson (Man U), Brooking (West Ham), G Francis (QPR).

## ENGLAND v FINLAND
*Wednesday, 13 October 1976*                              *Wembley – 92,000*

Four months later Wembley staged the return match with Finland. That summer Britain had sweltered under the most intense summer heat since records began in 1727. Israeli commandos had spectacularly rescued two hundred hostages held at Entebbe airport. The one hostage left behind – Mrs Dora Bloch – was killed by the Ugandan authorities. In China, the power struggle that followed the death of Mao Tse-tung resulted in the arrest of his widow, Chiang Ching, and the rest of the so-called Gang of Four.

During the second week of October James Hunt won the American Grand Prix at Watkins Glen. He, and his Austrian rival, Niki Lauda, would contest the world championship at the one remaining grand prix, in Japan. British boxing chalked up a double success. In Copenhagen, John Conteh outpointed Alvari Lopez to retain his world light-heavyweight title. In the heavyweight division, at Wembley, Joe Bugner came out of retirement to regain the European, British and Commonwealth titles with a first-round knock-out of holder Richard Dunn. It was the first opening-round victory for the British title since 1915, when Bombardier Billy Wells knocked out bandsman Rice. A Mexican, George Ramares, won the world conker championship, held at Ashton, near Oundle.

Don Revie pioneered the experiment of postponing the first division programme before major matches. A hastily organised 'friendly' between Aston Villa and Glasgow Rangers at Villa Park had to be abandoned following dreadful crowd trouble. More than one hundred people were arrested and thirty-five hospitalised. Colin Carpenter dreamt he was being chased by a mob of football hooligans. He had lashed out in his sleep to find himself stabbing his wife with a kitchen knife. Magistrates at St Albans cleared him of malicious wounding.

Though Italy had yet to open their account, Finland had hammered Luxembourg 7-1, only to come down to earth with a 0-6 defeat in Scotland. Needing a second handsome victory, Revie plumped for a 4-2-4 formation, packed with goalscorers. The ball-winning midfielder, Trevor Cherry, was considered redundant. With Gerry Francis having suffered the injury that would end his international career, young Ray Wilkins of Chelsea shared the midfield responsibilities with Trevor Brooking. Keegan, Channon, and the Manchester City pair, Joe Royle and Dennis Tueart, would forage for goals.

Revie's famous, or perhaps infamous, thoroughness extended to showing his players a pre-match film on motivation. It worked, insofar as England set off as though to drive their opponents into the North Sea. Within four minutes they had forced three corners. The third, taken by Brooking, was met by Royle's header and handled on the line by Heikkinen. Before the Swedish referee could blow for the penalty, Tueart had pounced from close quarters to put England ahead.

Finland had no choice but to weather the storm. After twelve minutes the tally was seven English corners and several fine saves by Enckelman.

Everything was set up for a slaughter, but gradually England lost their way. It was as if the early goal took away not only their nervousness but their motivation too. Finland came more and more into the game. Even without their 6ft 3in central defender, Tolsa, Finland dealt comfortably with England's stream of unimaginative high crosses. Shortly before half-time Clemence rushed out to commit a wild tackle on Nieminen, for which the Liverpool goalkeeper had his name taken.

Revie's pep talk made little difference. England simply got worse and three minutes into the second period Finland were deservedly level. Wilkins failed to keep a tight rein on Heiskanen. The ball was slipped to Nieminen, who neatly side-footed the equaliser.

It was as well that England did not have to dwell on Finland's impertinence. Four minutes later Channon helped restore the lead with a dazzling run that took him past three defenders to the by-line. His cut-back into the goalmouth left Royle with the easiest of tap-ins. English adrenalin surged briefly again, but soon Finland had the game by the scruff of the neck as they pursued their second equaliser. Tueart and Brooking were substituted by Gordon Hill of Manchester United and Mick Mills. Clemence survived some uncomfortable moments. One Finnish effort was kept out by his full-length dive, another by his flailing legs. Long before the end the full house was giving vent to 'What a load of rubbish'.

England held out, but Revie admitted he had no excuses. Not that the press were in a mood to allow him any. 'A hollow, tawdry victory,' declared the *Daily Mirror*, 'a laborious, ineffective and insulting' one, agreed *The Times*. Finland's amateurs had shown themselves better equipped in basic skills than their opponents.

In retrospect, this would be the result that deprived England of a place in the World Cup finals. At the weekend, Italy got off the mark with a 4-1 win in Luxembourg.

ENGLAND  (1) 2                FINLAND  (0) 1
  Tueart 4, Royle 52                Nieminen 48

ENGLAND: Clemence, Todd, Beattie, Thompson, Greenhoff, Wilkins, Keegan, Channon, Royle, Brooking (Mills), Tueart (Hill).
FINLAND: Enckelman, Heikkinen, Vihtalie, Maekynen, Ranta, E Heiskanen, Pyykko, Toivola, Nieminen, A Heiskanen, Paatalainen.

## ITALY v ENGLAND
*Wednesday, 17 November 1976*                                    *Rome – 85,000*

The following month England faced Italy at the Olympic Stadium in Rome. At the time, Britain was undergoing another financial crisis. Sterling collapsed and a huge loan had to be negotiated from the International Monetary Fund. The BBC radio show *Any Questions* was forced off the air by a furious demonstration aimed at Enoch Powell and his views on immigration. Stained glass windows in the church from which the programme was being transmitted were smashed. In the music world, David Essex was in his prime, being voted Britain's outstanding music personality and best male singer for 1976. It was, however, the American band, Chicago, which boasted the best-selling record of the week with their haunting *If You Leave Me Now*. The first strains of punk rock were appearing, spearheaded by the Sex Pistols. In America, the cult figure was Gary Gilmore, a convicted double murderer in Utah State Penitentiary who demanded to be executed. He now attempted suicide by taking a drug overdose.

The only overdose among the England squad was of aspirins, a spate of colds and sore throats delaying team selection. Revie had just celebrated his second anniversary as England team manager and had, once again, obtained the postponement of Saturday's first division programme. In one respect England had done the job against Finland – no points dropped and with aggregate goal figures of +4. The fear was that goal difference might prove crucial, and that Italy would outscore England against the two weaker teams. The best solution was for England to take three (or four) points off the Italians.

This need to avoid defeat in Rome invited a contrary approach from that which had sought a landslide against the Finns. That England team had been Revie's most attack-minded, against Italy he would field his most defensive. Clemence, Greenhoff, Brooking, Keegan and Channon were the only players retained. Taking the field in Rome would be a completely new back four, a ball-winning midfield with Brooking as the only play-maker, and a madcap front-runner – Stan Bowles of QPR. Bowles had been a key figure in his club's (unsuccessful) title chase the previous spring, and had been promoted by the tabloids as England's saviour. His inclusion meant no place for the orthodox strikers, Joe Royle or Stuart Pearson.

Bowles had not before played under Revie. Precociously skilful, his lifestyle was forever getting him into trouble with his club. He had played in Rome's

Olympic Stadium back in 1970, helping Carlisle United win the Anglo-Italian Cup. The Italian camp seemed surprised at Bowles' inclusion. The Italian press dubbed him 'the nasty one'. Enzo Bearzot, the chain-smoking Italian manager, who was pledged to lighten the negativity that blighted Italy's game, promptly withdrew his conventional stopper – Mozzini – for the faster, more mobile and infinitely more ruthless Claudio Gentile. Hindsight reveals the magnitude of England's task. Bearzot was building a formidable team that would not peak until the next, the 1982 World Cup. Five of the team to play England – Gentile, goalkeeper Dino Zoff, Marco Tardelli, Francesco Graziani, and Franco Causio – would in five years be in the thirteen that lifted the World Cup in Spain. Fiorentina's Antognoni would have been a sixth, but for injury in the 1982 semi-final.

Bearzot retained a ghost from the past in the shape of Giacinto Facchetti, whose No. 3 shirt suggested a taller than average full-back, but who played as a driving force down the left and scored more than his share of goals. Now thirty-four, Facchetti was a survivor not just of 1970 – he had captained the side that lost the Final – but of 1966 in England. The man of the present was undoubtedly Roberto Bettega, handsome, chat-show host, and goalscorer supreme.

Up to 1973, Italy had never beaten England in eight attempts, but two Italian successes that year – at Turin and Wembley – had erased the psychological deficit. The most recent encounter had been during the USA bicentennial celebrations in May, when England had transformed a 0-2 half-time debit into a 3-2 credit. Revie now squandered that psychological boost by fielding just Dave Clement, Trevor Brooking and Mike Channon of that winning team. An unseemly clash between Clement and Facchetti in New York hinted at further instalments in Rome.

Seven Juventus players were named in the Italian team. Juventus had just knocked both Manchester clubs out of the UEFA Cup. Naples, too, had beaten Southampton 4-1 on aggregate in the Final of the Anglo-Italian Cup. To combat Italy's formidable home record (only two defeats in fifteen years), Revie was rumoured to have included in his famous dossiers the choicest Italian swearwords.

Neither Italian nor British TV dared transmit live broadcasts of the afternoon match for fear of encouraging mass absenteeism from work. The fact that the referee was Israeli, Abraham Klein (who refereed the marvellous match with Brazil in Mexico), provoked the soccer-mad Arab world into pulling the plug and restricting coverage to brief highlights.

The Italian media harped on the confrontation between Europe's two economically sickest nations, the 'relegation stakes' – Lire v Sterling.

Italy seemed inhibited by the sense of occasion. For half an hour England contained their opponents with growing confidence. Italian ball-artistry was

Is it a bird? No it's Roberto Bettega soaring to head Italy's second goal. (v Italy)

confined to midfield, where it was vigorously countered by Cherry and Greenhoff. Violence simmered – the first half was interrupted by thirty free-kicks – and Graziani was harshly dealt with by McFarland. Thankfully, the match never boiled over.

The man who quickly established himself as carrying the greatest threat was speedy, tricky Franco Causio. Capitalising on a Mills error, Causio surged forty yards towards the England goal before shooting over. Marco Tardelli's shot then left Clemence wringing his hands, and Causio waltzed round Clement to see his inch-perfect cross headed over by Roberto Bettega. The Italian defence was largely untroubled, apart from sporadic high crosses.

Still, England had not suggested they might cave in when, after thirty-six minutes, they did. Causio was fouled five yards outside the England penalty area. Receiving the free-kick, the Fiorentina maestro, Antognoni, let fly, and the ball was deflected past Clemence by Kevin Keegan. It was a less than tidy goal but one that, on the balance of play, could not be begrudged. Italy now paraded their skills. For England, the half-time whistle could not come quickly enough.

Inexplicably, England showed no great urgency to set about redressing the score. It was almost as if a one-goal defeat was acceptable, as it might have been in a two-legged European cup-tie. Goalmouth incident was rare and the sun-kissed crowd had to wait until midway through the second half for a serious attempt on goal, when Antognoni, Graziani and Benetti combined superbly, only for Bettega to fail to connect.

England offered a wasteful shot by Greenhoff before falling further behind. The move was started, inevitably, by Causio, who teased his way past a defender to set Benetti free down the left. His centre was met by Bettega, soaring through the air, to propel a diving header hip-high past Clemence.

Soon afterwards a Channon drive was tipped over by Dino Zoff, the first time the Italian keeper had been called into action. Beattie came on for Dave Clement, but made little difference. Zoff was called upon to make just one more save, from Cherry, while in the dying minutes England were hanging on to prevent a third goal.

A British newspaper suggested that England could run and run all day but they simply could not play football, certainly not against the talents at Italy's command. The Italians had had no need to resort to tough tactics, though one player apiece – Cuccureddu and Channon – was booked. The foul count was twenty-five against Italy, twenty-three against England. Halfway through their programme, England were staring elimination from the World Cup in the face.

ITALY  (1) 2                         ENGLAND  (0) 0
   Antognoni 36, Bettega 77

ITALY: Zoff, Cuccureddu, Facchetti, Gentile, Tardelli, Causio, Benetti, Antognoni, Capello, Graziani, Bettega.
ENGLAND: Clemence, Clement (Beattie), Mills, Greenhoff, McFarland, Hughes, Keegan, Channon, Bowles, Cherry, Brooking.

**ENGLAND v LUXEMBOURG**
*Wednesday, 30 March 1977*                         *Wembley – 81,000*

England were scheduled to meet Italy at Wembley as the climax of Group 2. In between they would face Luxembourg twice, rendering Revie's task starkly simple; beat Italy, but beforehand run up a stackful of goals against the tiny Grand Duchy. Luxembourg were no strangers to England in the World Cup. During the 1962 campaign England had crashed thirteen goals past them. Somehow, it was unlikely that target would be reached.

In March 1977 Britain was celebrating the Queen's Silver Jubilee. Some six hundred people had lost their lives in the world's worst aviation disaster. Two Jumbo jets had collided on the runway at Tenerife. Westminster was consumed by rumours of a Lib-Lab pact, while Dennis Healey's budget put 4p on a packet of cigarettes, 5½p on a gallon of petrol, yet reduced basic income tax by 2p to 33p in the pound. Abba and Manhattan Transfer were vying for top spot in the charts with *Knowing Me, Knowing You* and *Chanson d'Amour*. Gossip columnists were busy speculating about two supposed romances, those of Prince Charles with Princess Marie-Astrid (of Luxembourg, no less) and Malcolm Allison with ex-bunny girl Serena Williams. Margaret Trudeau, wife of the Canadian premier, had scandalously attended a party thrown by the Rolling Stones.

Wembley was also anticipating a party. If Luxembourg could concede seven to the likes of Finland, there was no knowing how many England might accumulate. Seven weeks earlier, however, the national stadium saw England suffer the worst possible preparation, ripped apart by a sparkling Dutch side *en route* to its second World Cup Final. Neighbours they might be, but Holland and Luxembourg were worlds apart when it came to football.

For the task in hand, Revie again abandoned any pretence of sticking to a settled side. This time he went for a 3-3-4 formation, retaining just five players from those who took the field in Rome. This was horses for courses carried to ridiculous lengths. Injuries deprived Revie of ten hopefuls, opening the door to two newcomers. Villa's John Gidman made his debut at right-back and Birmingham's exciting prospect Trevor Francis, having earned his first cap in thankless circumstances against Holland, won his second in easier ones.

When asked for a prediction, the Luxembourg captain, Louis Pilot, intimated he would be happy with a 1-4 defeat. This posed the obvious question. How were his side going to poach a goal? It transpired that Luxembourg had bagged one or more in each of their past seven games.

Unexpectedly, the Wembley crowd cheered rather than jeered, undeterred as England created and missed one chance after another. Luxembourg had the audacity to win the game's first corner, and it took England ten minutes to break through the stifling, man-to-man marking. Royle and Gidman were involved in the build-up, enabling Manchester City's Dave Watson to float the ball in for Keegan to head down past Zender.

As had happened against Finland, the early goal flattered to deceive. England got worse, not better. Over-anxiety provoked players to tackle one another and generally get in each other's way. Aside from the goal, England's first-half accomplishments amounted to a Watson shot that struck the base of a post, a header by Francis that grazed the crossbar, and two attempts by Kennedy scrambled off the line. Long before the interval the crowd had changed its tune and were chanting for Ipswich's Paul Mariner to come off the bench.

The second period saw England grind their way forward, armed with a diet of high crosses. Despite Zender's discomfort in coming for crosses, it wasn't until the hour that England increased their lead, Francis thrashing the ball home from close range. Kennedy then claimed England's third. When Hill's corner eluded Zender, Channon headed number four.

By this time England's physical strength was proving too much for the tiring amateurs. Cherry shot wide from six yards. Dresch tackled Channon near the by-line. The striker, having already lost the ball, picked himself up from among the photographers to find to his surprise that he had been awarded a penalty. Channon took the kick himself. Three minutes from the end Dresch tripped the Southampton player once too often, and having earlier been booked was ordered off – the first player to be expelled from Wembley since Rattín in 1966.

So, yet again, England had had to rely on fitness and strength. But at least the goals had gone in, and England's slim chances of qualifying for Argentina were no slimmer.

ENGLAND  (1) 5                      LUXEMBOURG  (0) 0
    Keegan 10, Francis 60,
    Kennedy 66, Channon 70, 80 pen

ENGLAND: Clemence, Gidman, Cherry, Kennedy, Watson, Hughes, Keegan, Channon, Royle (Mariner), T Francis, Hill.
LUXEMBOURG: Zender, Fandel, Margue, Mond, Pilot, Zuang, di Domenico, Dresch, Braun, Phillipp, Dussier.

## LUXEMBOURG v ENGLAND
*Wednesday, 12 October 1977*                          *Luxembourg – 10,000*

England had to wait seven months for the opportunity to gain more target practice against little Luxembourg. By that time, England had a new manager. Revie, the subject of mounting press hostility, did as he was asked and resigned, taking up a coaching post in the Persian Gulf. His successor, appointed initially to oversee the remainder of the qualifiers, was Ron Greenwood. Greenwood was a purist footballing philosopher whose name was inextricably associated with West Ham, whom he had managed between 1961 and 1975 before moving 'upstairs' at the club. An agreeable, civilised man, Greenwood was not the people's choice, many of whom, if opinion polls are any guide, would have plumped for the abrasive talents of Brian Clough.

Greenwood had to withstand criticism that, though West Ham's brand of soccer might be exciting, it was ineffectual. Ramsey and Revie had both won the League championship with their clubs. Greenwood never came close. In this respect, his was a puzzling appointment, for his club were almost perennially lodged in the bottom half of the first division (they finished above halfway only four times during Greenwood's fourteen-year tenure, and had never been higher than sixth). One had the feeling that, given the murky circumstances of Revie's departure, the FA were seeking an Establishment man, someone who possessed ambassadorial attributes over and above his managerial ability.

As the England squad left for Luxembourg, Betty Williams and Mairead Corrigan, who the previous year had launched the Northern Ireland peace movement, were awarded the 1977 Nobel Peace Prize; a violent industrial relations dispute at the Grunwick factory embroiled several MPs; and President Carter's brother, Billy, was cashing in on his family connection, mixing with bad company and generally bringing embarrassment to the White House. The strange case of Joyce McKinney was seized upon by the tabloids after she had kidnapped a Mormon missionary and, it was claimed, 'raped' him. The music world was still grieving over the death of Elvis Presley; cricket was in the throes of the Kerry Packer revolution.

England's trip to Luxembourg had now taken on critical dimensions. In June, Italy had won 3-0 in Helsinki. That meant that anything less than a whopping victory, of the order of five goals or more, would be regarded as failure. Anything less, and England might be needing to massacre Italy.

The fixture with Luxembourg was Greenwood's second as England's boss. His baptism had come the previous month with the visit of Switzerland. For that match he had sought instant teamwork by fielding six players from European champions Liverpool, plus Keegan, who had recently left Anfield for Hamburg. The result had been a drab goalless draw. Undeterred, Greenwood now repeated the exercise. Keegan was missing, unwell, and full-back Phil Neal omitted. Otherwise, five Liverpool players lined up for World Cup duty. The side would be captained, from the sweeper position, by Liverpool's Emlyn Hughes in his forty-ninth international appearance.

England had toured South America in the summer, in what looked like a fruitless dress rehearsal, drawing with Brazil, Argentina and Uruguay. These creditable results were the only bright spots in what was now a six-game sequence without a win, in which England had contrived to lose at home to both Wales and Scotland. Those six games had yielded just two goals, hardly the stuff to suggest England would let rip in Luxembourg.

With ominous finality the Football League refused to postpone Saturday's first division fixtures. Luxembourg, with a population of just 350,000, must have fancied their chances, though their regular goalkeeper, Zender, was not included and their capable centre-half, Pilot, had retired.

England justified all the prognostications. Playing 3-3-4 in their quest for a cricket score, they were a disaster. Though Luxembourg only rarely caught a glimpse of Clemence's goal, they kept England at bay with contemptuous ease. New centre-half Rohmann headed away the dull procession of crosses hurled in. For half an hour England sunk in their own inadequacy. Mariner got into a tangle under the Luxembourg crossbar, Hill's twenty-five yarder was tipped over, and at the other end Clemence couldn't hold a fierce shot from Michaux.

When England at last scored the relief was palpable. Paul Mariner's header went askew but the ball fell kindly for Ray Kennedy who volleyed past Moes. Not even this small mercy could settle England's nerves on a day when only Wilkins and Francis looked remotely like international footballers. Two Ipswich players, Beattie and Whymark, came on for Watson and McDermott, but this only denied them the excuse of having had nothing to do with the whole degrading spectacle.

Luxembourg refused to wilt, and only seconds remained when England scored a face-saving, but not life-saving, second goal. Ian Callaghan had played in the World Cup in 1966. Now, eleven years later, it was his centre that was headed down by Kennedy for Mariner to crash into the net.

The newspapers the following day told of an unfortunate sequel. Disgruntled and drunken English hooligans had run amok after the match, smashing seats and fencing in the tiny Luxembourg stadium and rampaging through the town to seal one of England's most shameful European episodes. This marked the first occasion that supporters of the national, as opposed to club sides had disgraced themselves on the continent. At Anfield, Joe Jordan's handball, that won Scotland a penalty – and qualification – against Wales capped a night that British football would long remember, for the wrong reasons.

Golfing in Spain, Bing Crosby died of a heart attack, and following the kidnap of German industrialist Hans Martin Schlayer, Baader Meinhoff and Palestinian guerrillas hijacked a Boeing 737 and forced it to Dubai. At the weekend Italy swept six goals past Finland, and England, barring divine providence, could forget about Argentina.

LUXEMBOURG   (0) 0                    ENGLAND   (1) 2
                                      Kennedy 30, Mariner 90

LUXEMBOURG: Moes, Barthel, Fandel (Zangerie), Mond, Rohmann, Zuang, Michaux, Phillipp, Dussier, Moncelli, Braun (di Domenico).
ENGLAND: Clemence, Cherry, Watson (Beattie), Hughes, Kennedy, Callaghan, McDermott (Whymark), Wilkins, T Francis, Mariner, Hill.

**ENGLAND v ITALY**
*Wednesday, 16 November 1977*                    *Wembley – 92,500*

Five weeks later came the crunch. Italy and England both had eight points, Italy from four matches, England from five. Italy's goal-difference was better by four, and would be even better after they entertained Luxembourg in their one remaining match.

With brutal simplicity Italy would qualify without ado if they avoided defeat at Wembley. Defeat wouldn't bother them much, unless improbably heavy. A

A permed Kevin Keegan heads England into an early lead. (v Italy)

one- or two-goal England win would leave Italy with the simple task of beating Luxembourg. If England won by three goals, Italy would need a three-goal cushion of victory. To have any sort of a chance England had to beat Italy by at least four, requiring Italy to dispose of Luxembourg by five.

Away from the World Cup, Britain had to contend with a national firemen's strike. ITN newscaster Gordon Honeycombe quit his job to champion the firemen's cause. In South Africa an inquest had opened on the death of Steve Biko, the 'Black Consciousness' leader who had died in police detention. Television reached the end of an age with the last episode of *Dad's Army*, which series had run for ten years. Princess Anne and Mark Phillips had a baby son. 'Master Phillips', as he was known, was the Queen's first grandson, and the first royal baby to be born a commoner for five hundred years. Anti-royalist MP Willie Hamilton reacted: 'How charming; another one for the payroll.'

For Ron Greenwood, the *Name of the Game* (in Abba's chart-topping words) was to pay lip-service to the prospect of slaughtering the Italians, but in reality to bow out with dignity. The Liverpool experiment was abandoned. Greenwood kept faith with Revie's defenders, but remodelled the attack, giving first caps to Peter Barnes of Manchester City, Bob Latchford of Everton and Manchester United's Steve Coppell. It surprised many that Trevor Francis was named only among the substitutes.

Blind to the inevitable, football fever bubbled to the surface. England took an early lead when Brooking's diagonal cross from the right was deflected by Keegan's header beyond Zoff's right shoulder. Hope surged through the nation's breast. If England could quickly come up with another, who knew what might happen. Twice in two minutes Peter Barnes might have scored. Life for the Italians was becoming distinctly uncomfortable and Benetti was booked for a crude challenge on the young winger. Keegan was the next to enter the referee's book, retaliating after Tardelli had given him too close a view of his elbow. Barnes was a constant victim, as when scythed down by Gentile.

The match throbbed with a sense of the unexpected. Although Neal had to clear off the goal-line with Bettega in attendance, England looked a class act, seeking to break down their opponents with guile rather than the bulldozer. Brooking sparked innovative attacks from midfield, and Keegan ferreted into all manner of threatening situations. If Barnes and Latchford took time to adjust to international soccer, Coppell looked like he'd played nothing else.

The interval arrived with no further goals. When the teams reappeared Graziani, who had played with a bandaged head for much of the first half, was missing, replaced by Sala. With each minute Italy moved nearer their objective. Before long they were playing possession football, passing back to Zoff to waste seconds. This did not prevent chances falling to England. Hughes shot over the top, then Zoff had to fist away Watson's volley.

With a quarter of an hour remaining Latchford was pulled off in favour of Stuart Pearson, and within minutes England scored. Keegan was impeded by Benetti, but the ball ran to Brooking who turned to side-foot past Zoff. One more goal just *might* make Italy sweat, and England filled the dying minutes pressing forward. Keegan limped off to a rapturous reception, to be replaced by Trevor Francis. Cuccureddu came on for Facchetti, who had played his ninety-fourth and last international. Two minutes from time England fired their last arrow. Barnes' corner, Watson's header, Zoff's save. A smiling Greenwood said the performance had restored pride, and Enzo Bearzot confessed his team had been beaten by the best England team for several years.

England were out of the World Cup in all but name, but the reaction was notably more sanguine than on that crushing night when Tomaszewski broke a nation's hearts. Italy duly beat Luxembourg 3-0 to qualify. England's exit on goal difference was a bitter pill (they were the only country to be eliminated in such fashion), especially when Italy went on to finish an impressive fourth in Argentina. The fact that England's conquerors in 1974 and 1978 managed third and fourth place respectively softened the blow. Had England reached the finals on either occasion, there was no reason to suppose that they would not have acquitted themselves reasonably well. They had, after all, drawn 1-1 in Buenos Aires with Argentina a year before they won the 1978 World Cup.

As for Ron Greenwood, his team had failed to concede a goal in three

Captain Facchetti, playing his last international, pleads his side's innocence. (v Italy)

matches under his care. In view of the enlightened display against Italy, his elevation from caretaker to full-time manager was a formality. But one thing was sure. In seeking to qualify for Spain in 1982 England would need a settled side. Between them, Revie and Greenwood called upon no fewer than thirty-three players – three complete teams – in six matches. Only the goalkeeper was ever-present.

ENGLAND  (1) 2                    ITALY  (0) 0
  Keegan 11, Brooking 81

ENGLAND: Clemence, Neal, Cherry, Wilkins, Watson, Hughes, Keegan (T Francis), Coppell, Latchford (Pearson), Brooking, Barnes.
ITALY: Zoff, Tardelli, Mozzini, Facchetti (Cuccureddu), Gentile, Zaccarelli, Benetti, Antognoni, Causio, Graziani (Sala), Bettega.

*Qualifying Group 2*

| | | | Home | | | | Away | | | | |
|---|---|---|---|---|---|---|---|---|---|---|---|
| | P | W | D | L | F | A | W | D | L | F | A | Pts |
| ITALY | 6 | 3 | 0 | 0 | 11 | 1 | 2 | 0 | 1 | 7 | 3 | 10 |
| England | 6 | 3 | 0 | 0 | 9 | 1 | 2 | 0 | 1 | 6 | 3 | 10 |
| Finland | 6 | 1 | 0 | 2 | 8 | 8 | 1 | 0 | 2 | 3 | 8 | 4 |
| Luxembourg | 6 | 0 | 0 | 3 | 1 | 7 | 0 | 0 | 3 | 1 | 15 | 0 |

*Other groups results*

| | | | |
|---|---|---|---|
| Finland v Luxembourg | 7-1 | Luxembourg v Finland | 0-1 |
| Luxembourg v Italy | 1-4 | Italy v Finland | 6-1 |
| Finland v Italy | 0-3 | Italy v Luxembourg | 3-0 |

*England appearances and goalscorers (substitute appearances in brackets)*
*World Cup qualifying rounds 1978*

| | Apps | Goals | | Apps | Goals |
|---|---|---|---|---|---|
| Clemence R * | 6 | – | Pearson S | 1 (1) | 1 |
| Cherry T | 5 | – | Mariner P | 1 (1) | 1 |
| Keegan K * | 5 | 4 | Madeley P * | 1 | – |
| Channon M * | 4 | 3 | Francis G | 1 | – |
| Brooking T | 4 | 1 | Tueart D | 1 | 1 |
| Hughes E * | 4 | – | Clement D | 1 | – |
| Wilkins R | 3 | – | McFarland R * | 1 | – |
| Watson D | 3 | – | Bowles S | 1 | – |
| Mills M | 2 (1) | – | Gidman J | 1 | – |
| Hill G | 2 (1) | – | Callaghan I | 1 | – |
| Francis T | 2 (1) | 1 | McDermott T | 1 | – |
| Todd C | 2 | – | Neal P | 1 | – |
| Thompson P | 2 | – | Coppell S | 1 | – |
| Greenhoff B | 2 | – | Latchford R | 1 | – |
| Royle J | 2 | 1 | Barnes P | 1 | – |
| Kennedy R | 2 | 2 | Whymark T | – (1) | – |
| Beattie K | 1 (2) | – | | | |

* Appeared in 1974 World Cup.                    *33 players    15 goals*

# 9

# THE 1982 WORLD CUP

During the interlude in England's World Cup commitments the world came up with its usual quota of wars, disasters and individual feats of accomplishment. 1978 saw the first floods of Vietnamese boat-people refugees, thousands of whom had been expelled because of their ethnic (Chinese) origins. In 1978 the Vatican elected a Polish Pope, John Paul II. It was also the year that Mohammed Ali won the world heavyweight boxing title for a record third time.

1979 was a year of upheaval, heralding revolution in Iran, the creation of an Islamic republic by the Ayatollah Khomeini, and the seizure of the US Embassy and its staff in Teheran. The Shah was not the only international leader to be ousted that year. Idi Amin of Uganda met a similar fate, and James Callaghan had to yield to Margaret Thatcher, Britain's first woman PM. British political casualties included Earl Mountbatten and Airey Neave, both murdered by the IRA, and Anthony Blunt, unmasked as the Fourth Man. In sport, Sebastian Coe broke three athletics world records, and Trevor Francis became Britain's first £1 million footballer when transferred from Birmingham City to Nottingham Forest. The year closed with the Soviet invasion of Afghanistan.

1980 witnessed the Saudi furore over the dramatised documentary *Death of a Princess*; the eruption of Mount St Helens in the United States; the election of Robert Mugabe as prime minister of an independent Zimbabwe; the SAS storming the besieged Iranian Embassy in London; America's abortive attempt to rescue her hostages in Iran; and Bill Beaumont captaining England's Rugby Union team to the Grand Slam. Britain's newest aircraft carrier, *HMS Invincible*, was commissioned into service, and the Moscow Olympics took place despite the boycott of the US and many other teams.

While history was running its course, Ron Greenwood concentrated on the task of making a decent challenge for the 1982 World Cup. For almost three years his preparations seemed to be bearing fruit. England qualified for the finals of the 1980 European Championship by dropping just one point from a group comprising Denmark, Bulgaria, and the two Irelands. Defending world champions Argentina were beaten 3-1 at Wembley. All told, England lost just three of their first thirty matches under Greenwood's care.

The bubble burst, at least in the public mind, during the final stages of the European Championship, held in Italy in June 1980. England's results were far from disgraceful (Belgium 1-1, Italy 0-1, Spain 2-1) but three points from three matches was not enough to progress. Greenwood's honeymoon was over.

And so it was that three months later England embarked on their quest for the 1982 World Cup. Not for twenty years had they been asked to go through the qualifying stages and succeeded. As it turned out, the world-wide soccer expansion worked to England's advantage. FIFA had enlarged the number of finalists from sixteen (the allocated number for all previous tournaments) to twenty-four. Essentially, this was to accommodate a greater number of finalists from the Third World, but an increase of fifty percent in the final places available was good news for England and for all World Cup aspirants.

Spirits lifted higher when the teams comprising Group 4 were announced. England would compete against Hungary, Romania, Switzerland and Norway. England would have fancied their chances with just one team to go through. In fact, the top *two* would progress. Armchair pundits were comforted into thinking that England and Hungary had an open door to the finals.

The FA followed its traditional scheduling preferences, arranging for England to start off against one of their less-fancied opponents, and conclude by taking on their main rivals at home (Portugal in the 1962 campaign, Poland '74, Italy '78, and now Hungary).

*Qualifying Group 4*

**ENGLAND v NORWAY**
*Wednesday, 10 September 1980*                                    *Wembley – 48,000*

By judicious selection of opponents, England had never failed to win their opening qualifier. Neither had they ever failed to thrash Norway, who had yet to come within three goals of England. Yet the confidence of the English squad had been shaken by their early exit from the European Championship and the malign criticism that followed. It was imperative to get off to a good start.

Away from football, the British economy was grinding to a halt. 2.5 million people were out of work. Switzerland, of all countries, was experiencing riots on her streets. The British papers were full of the case of Helen Smith, the British nurse who had been 'murdered' in Saudi Arabia, and the efforts made by her father to uncover the truth. The Centenary Test between England and Australia at Lord's fizzled out into a tame draw, and Middlesex won the last Gillette Cup (in future it would be replaced by the Nat West Trophy). Fulham introduced Rugby League to Craven Cottage, while in the Ullevi Stadium, Gothenburg, where England had contested the 1958 World Cup, Michael Lee became England's youngest world speedway champion. He was twenty-one.

Saturday's Football League programme was left intact. Greenwood was unconvinced of the wisdom of wholesale postponements, and had undertaken to seek them only when imperative. With hindsight, it might have been better had league football been cancelled for the day. Soccer violence exploded in one of the worst days on record. Rioting Sheffield Wednesday fans at Oldham reduced Jack Charlton, the Owls' manager, to tears. In Middlesbrough, a youth died of brain injuries after the match with Nottingham Forest. Ron Greenwood expressed the thoughts of many when he despaired for the future of the game.

In the absence of the injured Keegan – twice European Footballer of the Year, and back in harness at Southampton – the team was captained by Phil Thompson. First caps awaited Arsenal's Graham Rix and Eric Gates, who would partner his Ipswich club-mate Paul Mariner up front.

If Norway were overawed by their first visit to Wembley, they did not show it. Perhaps they felt slighted that the historic stadium was less than half full. On a blustery evening, England employed a patient, continental approach, constructing moves from the back. This was partly in imitation of Ipswich's recent successful style. Under manager Bobby Robson's guidance, Mariner and Gates were no longer used to long ball tactics. England had a let-off when Hareide's close-range header was tipped over by Shilton, before they took the lead. Rix's free-kick was half-volleyed by McDermott from twenty yards.

No further goals arrived until midway through the second half when the full-backs – Kenny Sansom (Britain's first £1 million full-back) and Viv Anderson (the first black footballer to play for England) – took advantage of the tiring opposition by pushing forward. Mariner knocked down Thompson's cross for Cologne's Tony Woodcock to hook past Tom Jacobsen. Norway hadn't given up. Striker Paal Jacobsen had earlier burst past three static Englishmen only to shoot wide. Now he forced a memorable save from Shilton.

On the run of play, the score flattered England, but their lead was shortly extended. Einer Aas (thankfully pronounced 'Orse') was dubiously convicted of fouling Mariner. The penalty was converted by McDermott. England had one more goal in store, this time an inventive one. Mariner dispossessed Kordahl and finished off the move with a comprehensive finish.

Britain had the thumbs down on Scandinavia that night, Scotland winning 1-0 in Sweden. World Cup worries over, the British public turned their attention to the romance between Prince Charles and Lady Diana Spencer, who were holidaying at Balmoral. Much newspaper space was given over to Hercules, the forty-stone grizzly bear who had gone missing for three weeks on the Hebrides while filming a TV commercial. He now turned up safe and well.

ENGLAND  (1) 4                    NORWAY  (0) 0
  McDermott 32, 77 pen,
  Woodcock 68, Mariner 85

ENGLAND: Shilton (Forest), Anderson (Forest), Sansom (Arsenal), Thompson (Liverpool), Watson (Southampton), Robson (WBA), Gates (Ipswich), McDermott (Liverpool), Mariner (Ipswich), Woodcock (Cologne), Rix (Arsenal).
NORWAY: T Jacobsen, Berntsen, Kordahl, Aas, Grondalen, Albertsen, Hareide, Dokken, Larsen-Okland, P Jacobsen, Erlandsen.

## ROMANIA v ENGLAND
*Wednesday, 15 October 1980*                                    *Bucharest – 75,000*

Five weeks later England, lined up in the August 23 Stadium, Bucharest, to take on Romania in their fiftieth World Cup fixture. The world had a new war to worry about, between Iraq and Iran, the world's second and third largest oil-exporting states. In Los Angeles, Welsh bantamweight boxer Johnny Owen lay in a coma, knocked out by Mexico's Lupe Pintor. Owen would die without regaining consciousness. Back home, a man-eating tigress, Zeya, had been put down after savaging to death two keepers at Howlett's Zoo in Canterbury.

Señor Pérez Esquival, leader of the Latin American Christian peace movement, received the 1980 Nobel Peace Prize. Another God-fearing man, Cliff Richard, celebrated his fortieth birthday, having enjoyed seventy-five hit singles and ten Number Ones. He could not, however, claim the current top spot. That honour went to Police with *Don't Stand So Close to Me*. That must have been how Manchester City chairman Peter Swales felt about Malcolm Allison and Tony Book, who were both sacked.

Wednesday, 15 October was newsworthy in many ways. James Callaghan announced his resignation as Labour leader. More poignant was the downfall of Lady Isobel Barnet, best remembered for her role in the 1950s TV series *What's My Line?* She now found herself accused of shoplifting. Her 'loot' consisted of a tin of tuna and a carton of cream worth 87p, which had been secreted inside her coat. The following week she was fined £75, and within days she had taken her own life. ITN newsman Jon Snow helped rescue Britons trapped on a tanker on the Shatt-al-Arab waterway.

England were in need of comparable heroics. Although Romania had never beaten England (drawing twice, losing twice), a mood of pessimism assailed pundits, reminiscent of 1973 when England had set off to defeat in Poland. Romania had beaten Yugoslavia 4-1 in Belgrade, and seen their Under-21s crush England's by four goals, their heaviest defeat at that level. Romania's seniors had drawn in Oslo: a win over England would put them top of Group 4.

Greenwood made several changes. Seeking to avoid a repetition of 1970, when Peter Bonetti had been caught cold in León, Greenwood pursued a policy of alternating his goalkeepers, Ray Clemence and Peter Shilton. In Romania it was Clemence's turn. Phil Neal replaced the injured Anderson, and Gary Birtles, despite being omitted from Nottingham Forest's team, pending an expected transfer to Old Trafford, was recalled at the expense of Mariner (hamstring). Also missing through injury were Keegan, Wilkins, Francis and Brooking. Mick Mills had a dental appointment and almost missed the plane.

Greenwood's young, inexperienced team found themselves under the cosh. Right-winger Zoltan Crisan tested Sansom sorely, and the strong, fast Rotin Camataru repeatedly flustered Thompson and Watson. A goal for the home team seemed inevitable. Ten minutes before half-time six Romanian passes set up Raducanu to wrong-foot Thompson and strike the ball past Clemence. Within two minutes the damage was almost doubled, but Camataru, shrugging off some harsh treatment from English defenders, shot wide.

All things considered, England were grateful to reach their dressing-room only one goal in arrears. When they reappeared Gates, enervated by a tummy bug, had been replaced by Coppell. England improved, but still made little impression. With Birtles looking rusty (he had played just once in ten days, against Bury's reserves), it was left to Woodcock to bear the brunt of England's attacking aspirations. All seemed rewarded when Woodcock took a return pass from Birtles, drew the goalkeeper and equalised, with the Romanian defence appealing forlornly for offside.

Birtles was substituted by the trickery of Laurie Cunningham, playing for Real Madrid. England looked to have stabilised, but Romania soon struck back. Crisan was nudged by Sansom and lay prostrate as if shot. The penalty was as dubious as England's against Norway, but this one could affect the outcome. It did, Clemence diving the wrong way from Iordanescu's spot-kick.

There was no way back. Romania might have bagged further goals. The defeat's one saving grace was the performance of West Brom's young Bryan Robson, while Dave Watson's nightmare ninety minutes provoked a rash of obituaries. The Queen was not for long depressed by England's defeat. She had more important business, off to the Vatican to meet the Pope.

ROMANIA (1) 2                                  ENGLAND (0) 1
   Raducanu 35, Iordanescu 75 pen        Woodcock 65

ROMANIA: Iordache, Negrila, Munteanu, Sames, Stefanescu, Beldeanu, Crisan, Iordanescu, Camataru, Ticleanu, Raducanu.
ENGLAND: Clemence, Neal, Sansom, Thompson, Watson, Robson, Rix, McDermott, Birtles (Cunningham), Woodcock, Gates (Coppell).

**ENGLAND v SWITZERLAND**
*Wednesday, 19 November 1980*                          *Wembley – 70,000*

The Labour Party was in crisis, new leader Michael Foot appealing to right-wingers not to desert. It was scandal-time in the Miss World competition, when newly crowned eighteen-year-old Gabriella Brum of West Germany renounced her title after it was revealed that she had appeared in naughty films. Her crown was presented to the runner-up, Kimberley Santos of Guam. Ex-film star Ronald Reagan was now President-elect of the USA; Solidarity, the Polish trade union, was born. In this country, a student at Leeds University became the thirteenth victim of the Yorkshire Ripper. The pop charts were topped by Blondie's *The Tide is High*.

The tide would be going out for Ron Greenwood if his team failed to beat Switzerland. Saturday's fixtures had deprived him of five of his squad through injury. Keegan was missing, as was Thompson, the alternative captain. Leadership responsibilities were entrusted to Mick Mills for the third time in a long international career. Eric Gates was also unfit. Rix and Birtles lost their places to Brooking and Mariner. It was Shilton's turn to keep goal.

Little was expected of Switzerland. They had just lost their opening fixture – 1-2 at home to Norway! – though on their last two visits to Wembley had forced draws. They now experimented with an untried sweeper, Geiger, while Greenwood switched Bryan Robson to that position to replace Thompson.

England's reshuffled team quickly found their rhythm, and Burgener in the Swiss goal faced a mounting tide of English pressure. Not until midway through the half was that pressure translated into a goal, and even then it needed an assist. McDermott had already spurned two good chances and had just flicked Brooking's centre over the bar when Coppell drove the ball in fiercely from the right. Tanner steered it past his own goalkeeper.

Even an untidy goal was little more than England deserved. They had less than ten minutes to wait for a second and this time there was no need to call upon Swiss aid. Brooking was flattened for the umpteenth time. Picking himself up, he floated a free-kick for Mariner to time his run perfectly to glance home. If his team-mates showed restraint in celebrating the goal it was doubtless due to the warnings of Sir Harold Thompson, chairman of the FA, who had publicly criticised the kissing that follows the scoring of a goal. Persistent offenders, Thompson proposed, should not represent their country.

Inexplicably, England's control wilted in the second half. Marti had earlier replaced Schonenberger, and now Egli came on to partner Geiger at the heart of the Swiss defence. Stiffened at the back, Switzerland gradually prised open England's grip. Ludi and Barberis closed down the space previously filled by intelligent English running. Ludi skipped round Shilton, only to be thwarted by a fine Mills tackle.

Switzerland now began to press. Robson, revelling in his *libero* responsibilities in this, his fifth international, kept England from capsizing. With the crowd's appreciation turned to apprehension, full-back Wehrli broke down the left and set up a cross which Pfister volleyed past Shilton. Brooking immediately made way for Rix and confidence gave way to panic.

On the same night Wales beat the Czechs 1-0 in Cardiff, while Northern Ireland lost by the same score in Portugal. The trial opened of Chiang Ching and the other members of China's 'Gang of Four'. For millions, however, the highlight of the week was *Dallas*, tuning in to learn who shot J R Ewing.

ENGLAND    (2) 2                    SWITZERLAND    (0) 1
   Tanner 23 (o.g.), Mariner 32          Pfister 76

ENGLAND: Shilton, Neal, Sansom, Robson, Watson, Mills, Coppell, McDermott, Mariner, Brooking (Rix), Woodcock.
SWITZERLAND: Burgener, Wehrli, H Hermann, Ludi, Geiger, Barberis, Pfister, Tanner (Egli), Schonenberger (Marti), Elsener, Botteron.

## ENGLAND v ROMANIA
*Wednesday, 29 April 1981*                    *Wembley – 62,500*

International football hibernated for the winter months and reawakened with England's return fixture with Romania. In the United States, the hostages freed from Iran had returned home to a ticker-tape reception. President Reagan was recovering from a would-be assassin's bullet that had pierced his lung. In Belfast, Bobby Sands, the IRA man elected to Parliament, was in the last days of his fatal hunger strike. Londonderry was seeing its worst rioting in years. Brixton was clearing up after suffering its own waves of rioting and looting.

Britain was looking forward to a new Princess, for the Royal Wedding was definitely on. Prince Andrew hadn't yet found a wife, but he had qualified as a Royal Navy helicopter pilot. The country had a new political party – the Social Democrats. One lady not joining them was Mrs Harriet Orton of Peterborough, who died aged 103. She left a widower after eighty-one years of wedlock, thus ending the longest surviving marriage in Britain. Newly-weds Ringo Starr and actress Barbara Bach had some way to go. Lester Piggott suffered ear injuries at Epsom when dragged under the starting stalls by his mount, Windsor Boy. Blizzards on Dartmoor trapped five cadets, precipitating a massive rescue operation. They were recovered, safe, thanks it is said to 'dowsing' rods.

Ron Greenwood could expect more than a dousing if England lost a second time to Romania. The previous month Spain had won 2-1 at Wembley. The England manager was having a hard time with the tabloids. The country had rejoiced in Liverpool and Ipswich reaching the finals of the European Cup and UEFA Cup, yet with Greenwood's nominated twenty-two decimated by injuries, the task of *making his mind up* – as Bucks Fizz urged from the top of the charts – was greatly simplified. He plumped for an experienced eleven, handicapped by the absence of Keegan for the fourth successive World Cup match. Encouragingly, England's Under-21s beat Romania's on the Tuesday.

England's seniors did not find matters so easy. Perhaps they were confused by having to play in red. England began promisingly, but Romania grew in confidence and opportunities for the home team dried up like puddles in the desert. The visitors had left out gifted winger Raducanu as a sign of their intention to play for a draw. Early English moves, especially those involving Anderson and Coppell, hinted at better things, but the best chance of the first half fell to Russell Osman, who smacked Brooking's cross hard against Iordache's chest. At the other end, Camataru's gentle header was looping into Shilton's arms when the keeper lost his footing. Sitting on his bum, he had to reach up and pat the ball out of goal with one hand, as a child might a balloon.

By the end of the opening half, Woodcock and Francis had been blotted out. It was as well that Dave Watson, captain for the day, was solid in defence, for the Romanians, satisfied that a draw was within their grasp, might have been motivated to seek a win. Indeed, Osman's desperate tackle on Crisan probably earned England their point. By the end the crowd were taunting 'What a load of rubbish'. Romanian players and officials danced on the pitch as if they'd won the World Cup itself. The result made them favourites to qualify and left England's prospects bleak, particularly with three away fixtures coming up. For Romania to take three points off England was bad news indeed.

Greenwood and his team must have been grateful for the distraction afforded by the opening of the trial of Peter William Sutcliffe, the Yorkshire Ripper.

ENGLAND (0) 0                                    ROMANIA (0) 0

ENGLAND: Shilton, Anderson, Sansom, Robson, Watson, Osman, Wilkins, Brooking (McDermott), Coppell, Francis, Woodcock.
ROMANIA: Iordache, Negrila, Munteanu, Sames, Stefanescu, Beldeanu, Crisan, Iordanescu, Camataru, Stoica, Balaci.

**SWITZERLAND v ENGLAND**
*Saturday, 30 May 1981*                                    *Basle – 40,000*

By the end of May, Greenwood's team were sunk in an almighty trough, having gone five games at Wembley without a win, and scoring just one goal. After Spain (1-2) and Romania (0-0), May brought Brazil (0-1), Wales (0-0), and a 0-1 defeat at the hands of the Scots. This dismal sequence contrasted with the fortunes of England's leading clubs. Ipswich had already won the UEFA Cup. Then, on 27 May, Liverpool kept the European Cup in this country for the fifth successive year, beating Real Madrid.

Now, after a long, hard season, the trips to Basle and Budapest took on critical proportions. Group 4 was wide open. Only Switzerland seemed out of contention, and even they would be back in if they won. England were disadvantaged by having consumed three home fixtures as against one each by Hungary and Romania. Switzerland had been beaten on each of England's five previous visits, and Greenwood's players could at least recall the scent of victory – they hadn't beaten anybody else since defeating the Swiss six months previously. Still, Hungary had been held 2-2 in Basle after fourteen consecutive wins over Switzerland. England had been knocked out of the 1954 World Cup in the St Jakob Stadium.

As the England squad prepared for their make-or-break week, the Pope was recuperating in hospital, shot by a would-be assassin. Peter Sutcliffe had been jailed for thirty years. In Belfast, the fourth IRA hunger-striker had died. London hosted the last ever reunion of Boer War veterans. The youngest of those attending was now ninety-seven. Amazing to think that Jack Warner was not that much younger. The star of *Dixon of Dock Green* for over twenty years died of pneumonia, aged eighty-four. The younger generation were captured by Adam and the Ants, with *Stand and Deliver*.

Similar sentiments must have been in the minds of the FA, for they had just handed Ron Greenwood a vote of confidence. He made six changes from the team beaten by Scotland, Keegan appearing in his first qualifier of the current campaign. The team was experienced, winning the approval of pundits.

As of late, it was impossible to fault England's early play. Clemence was a spectator through the opening phase as play was conducted purposefully towards the opposite goal. The contest was approaching the half-hour when the Swiss countered spectacularly. Sulser – well known to Nottingham Forest supporters in European Cup clashes with Grasshoppers Zurich – flicked a cheeky pass with the outside of his boot over defenders' heads. Osman and Sansom stood stultified as Schweiller fired past Clemence.

The England team looked stunned. They scarcely deserved to be trailing, yet the goal had been so incisive as to take their breath away. Their lungs were still empty when Switzerland scored again. Keegan and Watson exchanged pleasantries with the referee on the merits of a free-kick and were slow to take up position. The ball was played to Sulser, who strolled through to sweep low to Clemence's right. The keeper got the barest touch and looked annoyed with himself. He had saved more difficult shots in his career. Yet the culpability was collective. Two goals down, England were in dire straits.

They were also facing disgrace. English hooligans set about Swiss spectators with fists and anything handy. The interval was consumed by fearful scenes inside the stadium. Back on the pitch, Keegan pushed up to partner Mariner and, with McDermott replacing Francis, England pressed for a quick riposte. The sub quickly scored, which quelled the mayhem on the terraces. England failed to score another and failed to win sympathy by resorting to unseemly challenges. Peter Barnes, now with WBA, replaced the chief culprit, Watson, but saw little of the ball. England departed in shame.

SWITZERLAND   (2) 2          ENGLAND   (0) 1
Schweiller 28, Sulser 30          McDermott 54

SWITZERLAND: Burgener, H Hermann (Weber), Ludi, Egli, Zappa, Wehrli, Schweiller, Botteron, Sulser, Barberis, Elsener (Maessen).
ENGLAND: Clemence, Mills, Sansom, Wilkins, Watson (Barnes), Osman, Keegan, Coppell, Mariner, Robson, Francis (McDermott).

**HUNGARY v ENGLAND**
*Saturday, 6 June 1981*                                    *Budapest – 65,000*

Following defeat in Basle, the England party remained on the continent. The enforced confinement may have compounded their misery. They could not even enjoy the Derby, won on Wednesday by Shergar, the hottest-priced favourite for many years. That same day Romania beat Norway 1-0 to go top of Group 4. Hungary and England were one point behind, but England had played two games more and were within one match of their longest ever sequence without a win – seven, set back in 1958. Hungary were poised both to extend that dismal record and extinguish England's flickering hopes of qualification. England had not triumphed in the imposing Nep Stadium since winning 8-2 in 1909. It must have been galling for Ron Greenwood that Hungary, whose performance at Wembley in 1953 had shaped his football philosophy, looked set to provide the *coup de grace*. Like Revie, Greenwood seemed incapable of finding a settled side, calling upon twenty-eight players this season alone.

Kenny Sansom and Russell Osman had been scapegoated for the shattering defeat by Switzerland. Peter Shilton was not in the England party, enabling Ray Clemence to continue in goal. Mills switched to left-back, Neal partnered him, and Phil Thompson, unavailable against Switzerland because of European Cup commitments with Liverpool, teamed up with Watson in the middle. Only a victory would do, but the safety-first team Greenwood named further angered the tabloids. Appropriately, the match was played on D-Day. England's last World Cup qualifier on 6 June had seen them slump 0-2 to Poland in 1973.

With a sense of occasion, the Hungarians invited Puskás to return to his homeland and indulge in a brief pre-match kick-about. His mere name was enough to send a previous generation of English footballers all a-shiver. But not, apparently, the present England side. The large, billiard-table-smooth pitch was evidently to their liking. Having made a recent habit of starting well, only to be kicked in the teeth, many observers anticipated a predictable loss of momentum. But England scored a neat goal. Coppell fed McDermott on the right, who slipped the ball to Trevor Brooking ten yards out. Brooking had missed England's previous four games and was semi-resigned to being omitted now. But the team's setbacks brought him back into Greenwood's calculations.

Take that! Brooking hammers his unforgettable goal in Budapest. (v Hungary)

He repaid that faith by screwing the ball past Katzirz. Though mishit, it was a vital goal for Brooking and country. It was missed by countless viewers back home, who had switched over to a nail-biting finish at Edgbaston. England's cricketers lost a Prudential Trophy match with Australia by two runs.

The football match, too, was nerve-tingling. England may have enjoyed the lion's share, but the Hungarians, fragile at the back, were no slouches going forward. Keegan's searing shot bounced off Katzirz's chest like a tennis ball off a wall. Then the elegant Nyilasi planted a header firmly against Clemence's crossbar. If the England goalkeeper enjoyed that slice of luck, he was shortly to atone. The interval was seconds away when Garaba pushed up to support Torocsik, the temperamental but gifted striker. Clemence raced out to claim the through ball, but it somehow squirmed behind him, inviting Garaba to sweep it past helpless defenders on the line.

It is as well the half-time whistle sounded when it did, and not a few minutes later, for England were spared the wave of attacks that are the reflex response of a home team that has just scored. By the time the players reappeared, Hungarian adrenalin had had time to congeal. England set off as if Clemence's boob had never happened. On the hour Brooking stamped his name on one of the great goals of English football. Keegan had found him in space near the right corner of the penalty box. Squaring his sights, Brooking unleashed a left-footed drive that speared like an arrow towards the far junction of post and bar. It flew past Katzirz and stuck defiantly in the '>' stanchion. The ball stayed there, mocking, until punched out. Couch potatoes treasured the goal because the ball's trajectory was on a plane with the TV cameras.

Brooking shortly took a knock and, his work done, was substituted by Wilkins. Could it be that the Pope, appearing in public for the first time since leaving hospital, had blessed Trevor Brooking? It was certainly his time. His 'double' was scored on his wedding anniversary; the following week he was awarded the MBE in the Queen's Birthday Honours list.

Garaba shortly lunged at Keegan, who tumbled convincingly and the referee gave him the benefit of the doubt. Keegan took the penalty himself.

England won 3-1 a match that could easily have finished 6-4. 'Yesterday's men' had triumphed, nine of the twelve employed having performed against Bulgaria in the European Championship two years earlier. The transformation in England's group fortunes was dramatic. Wins over Norway in Oslo and Hungary at Wembley would take them to Spain. The 1980-81 season was at long last over, and England could sleep easy.

HUNGARY  (1) 1              ENGLAND  (1) 3
  Garaba 45                      Brooking 18, 60, Keegan 73 pen

HUNGARY: Katzirz, Martos, Balint, Varga, Muller (Komjati), Garaba, Fazakas (Bodonyi), Nyilasi, Kiss, Mucha, Torocsik.
ENGLAND: Clemence, Neal, Mills, Thompson, Watson, Robson, Keegan, Coppell, Mariner, Brooking (Wilkins), McDermott.

## NORWAY v ENGLAND
*Wednesday, 9 September 1981*                              *Oslo – 28,500*

The soccer close-season saw Ian Botham demolish the Australians, Bjorn Borg relinquish his Wimbledon crown after five years, and Coe and Ovett indulge in a frenzied burst of breaking and re-breaking world records. The Royal Wedding in July brought the country to a virtual standstill. Inner-city riots had threatened briefly to spread out of control, an incongruous backdrop to Britain's greatest pageant since the Coronation. Those with a penchant for obsessions fiddled maddeningly with Rubik Cubes, seen everywhere, on trains, buses, on the streets.

Consternation swept the Navy at reports that twenty of the seventy ships of the battle fleet would be auctioned off. The carrier *HMS Hermes* had completed a £30 million refit and was now put up for sale. The death was announced of Albert Speer, Hitler's Armaments Minister in World War II. Derbyshire County Cricket Club set new standards in brinkmanship. They lifted the first

Nat West Trophy at Lord's, having tied with Essex in the semi-final and then repeated the act against Northants in the Final. Fewer wickets down rescued Derbyshire on both occasions. The Football League was in the throes of revolution: winning teams were now to be awarded three points instead of two; and Queen's Park Rangers had had the audacity to lay down an artificial pitch.

At least the Astroturf was smooth, which was more than could be said of the pitch in the Ulleval Stadium. Greenwood had declined the Football League's offer to postpone Saturday's key fixtures, reasoning that so early in the new season match practice was more important than the risk of injury. The team he named showed three changes. Brooking was unfit, permitting Spurs' Glenn Hoddle his first World Cup outing. Injury also ruled out Watson and Coppell, their places going to Osman and Francis – the latter now with Manchester City. With Peter Shilton still out of sorts with his club, Ray Clemence continued to keep goal, despite a discouraging first month with his new club, Spurs.

The last time England had played in Norway was in 1966, on that occasion scoring six. But those heady days had long gone. Norway were no longer a bunch of amateurs. They were now in the business of exporting their best players. Aas had been transferred to Nottingham Forest for £250,000, and Hareide was expected to sign for Manchester City. There was, thankfully, still room for romance in Norway's football. Antonsen, who pulled on the goalkeeper's jersey, was in real life Oslo's chief telephone engineer.

Greenwood would have reminded his players that no English team had ever failed to score less than four against Norway. Once again, England opened strongly. The uneven pitch did not help, but Norway looked out of their depth. Mariner and Francis had already come close when Keegan flicked the ball on to Robson. It bobbled like a rugby ball until Robson, off balance as he fended off two defenders, prodded it past the advancing telephone engineer.

The goal should have settled any residual nerves. Instead, collective atrophy set in. The midfield of Robson, McDermott and Hoddle – playing out of position on the left – first lost cohesion, then lost control. Russell Osman, so promising for Ipswich, began to fret. Clemence found himself in the position of someone enjoying a snooze behind a brick wall, only to wake up to see the mortar crumbling. He soon moved smartly to smother Hareide's header.

The effort spurred Norway more than the save spurred England. Tommy Lund's low cross to the near post was touched by Albertsen between the goalkeeper and the post. 1-1. The covering of the English defence was woeful.

But the worst calamities come in pairs. Switzerland had spilled England's entrails with two quick goals and now Norway followed their example. Okland's wayward centre should have been whacked away by McDermott. Alas, he misdirected the ball backwards, for Thoresen to sweep past Clemence.

The second forty-five minutes saw England grind forward with the consistency and wit of a steamroller. Norway marked man-to-man as they sensed history in the making. Trevor Francis looked uncomfortable out on the right wing. Geske's legs got in the way of one of Hoddle's 'specials'. Hoddle retired forthwith to see if Peter Barnes (now with his third club, Leeds) could unpick the Norwegian defence. After a couple of early runs he, too, faded. Indeed, it was Norway who came closest. Jacobsen, the Norwegian junior sprint champion, was put clean away, only to be foiled by Clemence.

The final whistle provoked extraordinary scenes. Norway had not known anything like it since Amundsen became the first man to reach the South Pole, back in 1912 (beating the English team led by Robert Scott). An ecstatic Norwegian commentator croaked into his microphone: 'Lord Nelson, Lord Beaverbrook, Sir Winston Churchill, Sir Anthony Eden, Clement Attlee, Henry Cooper, Lady Diana, Maggie Thatcher, your boys took a hell of a beating!'

Previous English setbacks were as nothing compared to this. Losing to Norway was worse, far worse, than losing to Switzerland, and infinitely worse than losing to the United States back in 1950. It was akin to Val Doonican knocking out Mohammed Ali, Lord Carrington hitting a six off Dennis Lillee and Gary Glitter outrunning Sebastian Coe. Simply inconceivable.

After the traumas of Basle, the euphoria of Budapest and the nightmare of Oslo, the English patient was very sick indeed. England were as good as out of the World Cup, and one would not have liked to be in Ron Greenwood's shoes as the dejected party flew home to face the music.

NORWAY  (2) 2                          ENGLAND  (1) 1
  Albertsen 36, Thoresen 41             Robson 16

NORWAY: Antonsen, Berntsen, Hareide, Aas, Grondalen, Albertsen, Geske, Thoresen, Larsen-Okland, Jacobsen, Lund.
ENGLAND: Clemence, Neal, Mills, Thompson, Osman, Robson, Keegan, Francis, Mariner (Withe), Hoddle (Barnes), McDermott.

**ENGLAND v HUNGARY**
*Wednesday, 18 November 1981*                          *Wembley – 92,000*

The debacle in Oslo had opened the door for Hungary and Romania to step leisurely into the World Cup finals, especially following their goalless draw in Bucharest in late September. It was on the afternoon of Saturday, 10 October that *it* happened; *it* being the announcement that Romania had lost at home to Switzerland. The commentators on Radio Two's *Sport on Two* hardly dared to trust their ears – Switzerland had scored! Romania had equalised! Switzerland had scored again!! That heaven-sent result meant that England yet again, without kicking a ball, had had their fate thrust back into their own hands. Within five days of the Swiss bombshell ticket sales for the Wembley match with Hungary soared from 32,000 to 90,000. And when Romania completed their programme with a 0-0 draw in Berne, England were left within sight of the Golden Fleece. Hungary had already clinched Group 4 and would lack motivation. All England needed was a draw to claim second place ahead of the frustrated Romanians. And England had never lost at home in the World Cup.

The foreign news was dominated by Solidarity in Poland, civil war in El Salvador, and the safe return to earth of the space shuttle *Columbia*; home news by the murder of Ulster Unionist MP Robert Bradford and the gauntlet of hate run by Northern Ireland Secretary James Prior at the ensuing funeral. Protestant leader Ian Paisley threatened to render Ulster 'ungovernable'.

Greenwood did an about-turn, postponing first division matches for the first time. His only selection headache was centre-half. Dave Watson, now thirty-five, had been relegated to Southampton's reserves. Rather than risk him, Greenwood opted for West Ham's young Alvin Martin, who added a second cap to that awarded against Brazil a year earlier. Hungary were without the semi-fit Nyilasi, an absence which did England no harm at all.

Fortified by Hungarian apathy, England scored a comical goal after just sixteen minutes. The ball broke to Brooking, directly in front of goal, who duly tried his luck. As a shot, it was laughable, as a pass, inspired, for the ball trundled to Mariner, unattended beyond the far post. If Brooking's contact was untidy, Mariner's was worse. The Ipswich striker had to extricate the ball from between his feet with a sweeping movement of his leg. Fortune favoured him. Though the goal was untenanted, the ball rolled an inch inside a post. Mariner had almost perpetrated the miss of the century, and one wondered painfully why England hadn't enjoyed such benevolence against Poland in 1973.

Hungary now had to score twice to stop England joining them in Spain. This they never looked likely to do. With their own qualification assured, they saw no need to roll up their sleeves and risk injury. Besides, they could settle scores with their Romanian neighbours, enemies from years back. Hungary's attitude was summed up by Torocsik, who kicked off for the second half with his arms folded. Only the combative Sallai, brought in to curtail Keegan, did more than go through the motions. Shilton had just two shots to save, both from far out. The only mystery was how England failed to build on their lead and ease the nibbling of finger-nails. Meszaros gave England all possible encouragement, punching or missing every high ball that came his way. Mariner was the principal culprit, failing to register the easiest hat-trick likely to come his way. In the second half he somehow headed wide from underneath the bar.

A troublesome knee took Coppell from the field, allowing Tony Morley, the fitful Aston Villa winger, his first taste of international football. Morley would have scored had not Meszaros pulled off an exciting save two minutes from time. But no matter, England were through to the finals of the World Cup for the first time in twelve years, having overcome the qualifying hurdle for the first time in twenty. For good measure, on the same evening Northern Ireland joined Scotland in qualifying too.

The jubilation was understandable. England's reprieve, following defeats in Bucharest, Basle and Oslo, was a piece of escapism of which Houdini would have been proud. Underneath the sense of relief, however, lay a tacit admission of England's inestimable good fortune. Nine points from eight matches in a poorish group was shameful. In their groups, the Republic of Ireland and Wales both secured ten points but missed out. Four years earlier England had taken ten points from six matches and been eliminated. Moreover, for all the inability of Revie's teams to thrash weaker sides, at least they had *beaten* them. The defeat by Switzerland and Norway (neither of whom beat anybody else at home), put Greenwood's failures into an altogether new dimension. It had been Revie's misfortune to have England paired with Italy with just one to survive. Greenwood could take no credit for being manager in more generous times. Such is the margin between success and failure.

ENGLAND    (1) 1                    HUNGARY    (0) 0
    Mariner 16

ENGLAND: Shilton, Neal, Mills, Thompson, Martin, Robson, Keegan, Coppell (Morley), Mariner, Brooking, McDermott.
HUNGARY: Meszaros, Martos, Balint, Toth, Muller, Garaba, Fazakas, Csapo, Torocsik, Kiss, Sallai.

*Qualifying Group 4*

|  |  | Home |  |  |  |  | Away |  |  |  |  |
| --- | --- | --- | --- | --- | --- | --- | --- | --- | --- | --- | --- |
|  | P | W | D | L | F | A | W | D | L | F | A | Pts |
| HUNGARY | 8 | 3 | 0 | 1 | 9 | 4 | 1 | 2 | 1 | 4 | 4 | 10 |
| ENGLAND | 8 | 3 | 1 | 0 | 7 | 1 | 1 | 0 | 3 | 6 | 7 | 9 |
| Romania | 8 | 2 | 1 | 1 | 4 | 3 | 0 | 3 | 1 | 1 | 2 | 8 |
| Switzerland | 8 | 1 | 2 | 1 | 5 | 5 | 1 | 1 | 2 | 4 | 7 | 7 |
| Norway | 8 | 1 | 2 | 1 | 5 | 5 | 1 | 0 | 3 | 3 | 10 | 6 |

*Other group results*

| | | | |
| --- | --- | --- | --- |
| Norway v Romania | 1-1 | Norway v Switzerland | 1-1 |
| Switzerland v Norway | 1-2 | Romania v Hungary | 0-0 |
| Switzerland v Hungary | 2-2 | Romania v Switzerland | 1-2 |
| Hungary v Romania | 1-0 | Hungary v Switzerland | 3-0 |
| Norway v Hungary | 1-2 | Hungary v Norway | 4-1 |
| Romania v Norway | 1-0 | Switzerland v Romania | 0-0 |

**World Cup finals – SPAIN**                                    **June-July 1982**

On Saturday, 16 January 1982 the draw for the World Cup finals was beamed from Madrid to the far corners of the earth, the whole pompous pageant degenerating into side-splitting farce.

The organising committee had installed revolving silver-wired lobster pots, into which were placed miniature footballs. The obligatory empty gesture to some noble cause was satisfied by recruiting young orphans who stood dressed in blue cassocks by their allocated lobster pots, with scowls on their faces and a collective look of contagious ennui. The wrong balls were put into the wrong drums; the first ones pulled out were put into the wrong groups. Then one ball actually broke, choking the trap-door and requiring manual extrication. Herr Neuberger, senior FIFA mandarin, stared icily at the smirking 'ball boys'.

Even when order was restored it was apparent that Spain's humiliation could have dire repercussions. Snide whispers were overheard that a nation that could bungle a World Cup draw would hardly prove a worthwhile partner in NATO or the EEC. Wars have been waged as a result of national slights no more substantial than those inflicted on Spain that Saturday afternoon. It might have been a good time for Britain to think about reinforcing Gibraltar.

The serious business of the draw was to give shape to a radical innovation. Hitherto, the magic number of finalists had always been sixteen, beloved of mathematicians for its easy division into eight, then four, etc. That number had now been upped to twenty-four to appease the World Cup's record entry of 109 nations. The genesis of the change belonged to the Brazilian, João Havelange's bid for the FIFA presidency in the 1970s. As with the floor of the United Nations, FIFA is disproportionately weighted in favour of Third World states. Theoretically, the nations of Asia and Africa could, if they acted in concert, revolutionise the game. On the eve of the 1974 finals they voted out Sir Stanley Rous in favour of the extra carrots being dangled by Havelange.

The Spain tournament yielded the first fruits of Havelange's wind of change. Six places were set aside for countries outside Europe and South America. The objections to the inflated finals rested with organisation, over-exposure, and lowered standards. A bumper fifty-two match programme required the use of seventeen stadia; twenty years earlier Chile had got away with four. The tournament would extend over twenty-nine days. Even the most avaricious soccer appetite ran the risk of repletion. Not the least of the criticisms was the knowledge that several of the teams participating had no hope of avoiding an early homecoming. As a football fiesta designed to promote the highest standards, the tournament was bound to be marred by tedium and anticlimax.

FIFA seemed to be enmeshed in a fundamental schism. Was the World Cup about parading the strongest teams in the world, or ensuring the widest geographical spread of contestants? In whose interests was it that Holland, runners-up in 1974 and 1978, should be excluded, while El Salvador, having overcome Panama and Cuba, should take the stage? One could foresee geographical egalitarianism running amok, European teams competing for one semi-final place, the Latin Americans another, the African states for a third and Asians the fourth. By the 1990s, there was no question that the Third World merited increased representation, though whether their skills improved because, or in spite of, the exposure of their standard-bearers remains a moot point.

One obvious problem was how to derive two finalists from twenty-four starters, that number not having a square root. It was solved by commencing with six groups of four, the top two from each then being split into four pools of *three*. This second phase would provide four semi-finalists. The schedule required the two finalists to play a total of seven matches, as in 1974 and 1978, but one more than England had contested in 1966.

As with all World Cups, there arose the question of seeding, and on what basis. The draw from Madrid confirmed what had been rumoured for some weeks, that FIFA would seed six countries, allocate one to each group and use past performance in the World Cup finals as the sole arbiter – apart from Spain, seeded as hosts. All but Uruguay of the six previous winners had qualified, and these five were taken to constitute the remaining seedings.

This announcement provoked a barrage of indignation. It meant that Italy were seeded, despite finishing second to Yugoslavia in their qualifying group, on the basis of their grandfathers having won the World Cup in the 1930s. In the case of England, cheeks blushed and eyes lowered. Seeding a country that had just scraped into its first World Cup for twelve years, and trailed behind Hungary to boot, solely on the grounds of winning in 1966, bore the logic of seeding Ann Jones at Wimbledon '82 on account of her triumph in the 1960s. Hungary had every reason to feel sore; so had everyone else.

Greenwood, in effect, prospered from Ramsey. Seeded teams counted on three distinct favours. They avoided the other seeds, they enjoyed one venue for all three matches, and they opened and concluded their group, knowing the precise score needed to be sure of progressing. Yet another bonus was basing England in the northern city of Bilbao in the coolest part of Spain. The San Mamés Stadium, home of Athletic Bilbao, would stage all England's matches, provided they were not disrupted by the activities of Basque separatists.

The four South American teams were kept apart, and the six 'tiddlers' were allocated, like the six seeds, one to each group. There was no bar on Scotland and Northern Ireland being dumped with England – thankfully that dreary prospect did not materialise – nor on teams that had qualified together being pooled again. This fate awaited West Germany and Austria, a soccer *Anschluss*.

As the lobster pots coughed up their contents, England found themselves pitted against France, Czechoslovakia and Kuwait, in that order. This was yet another touch from Lady Fortune, who clearly wanted England to go all the way. The French and the Czechs had qualified by margins even narrower than England's, edging out Wales and the Irish Republic on goal difference. As for unknown Kuwait, England would face them last, having learned their secrets.

Everything seemed to be in England's favour. As the count-down for Spain got under way Greenwood's team even began to win the odd football match. But unbeknown to everybody ominous developments lurked. In the spring of 1982 the world was jogging comfortably along, the harmony smudged only by martial law in Poland and sporadic attacks on northern Israel by Palestinian strongholds in Lebanon. Britain was troubled by nothing more newsworthy than the collapse of Laker Airways.

Then, without warning, the world was pitched into darkness. On 2 April Argentine forces invaded the Falkland Islands. When it became clear that Margaret Thatcher was bent, if necessary, on recovering them by force, it became apparent that world peace was nudging the precipice. The violence in Lebanon and Poland ushered reminders of 1956 for then, as now, a Middle Eastern conflict escalated in tune to gunfire elsewhere, the Hungarian uprising then, the Falklands now. For many, it was the nightmare of Suez revisited. The age of electronic warfare had arrived, ships sunk by remote-controlled weapons and aircraft pursued by missiles that wiggled eerily and irresistibly after them. A new vocabulary was born – 'exocets', 'hunter-killers', 'type 42s' – and a new television personality, the ghoulish bringer of bad tidings, Ian McDonald.

Little wonder that football should appear to many as a vulgar irrelevance. With British servicemen dying, the prospect of British participation in Spain, playing in the same tournament as Argentina, began to be viewed with distaste. Following the Soviet invasion of Afghanistan, hadn't the Prime Minister pressured British athletes (unsuccessfully) not to compete in the Moscow Olympics? Well-known players now went on air to urge the British teams to withdraw. The England manager, too, made resigned noises. It is curious to note that even as British casualties mounted, rumours of British non-participation gradually abated and finally died in their own silence.

With hindsight, arguments in favour of a British boycott always appeared insubstantial. The British government took the view that Britain had been a victim of aggression by Argentina: where was the sense in being a victim in Spain? The argument about British forces suffering appallingly while footballers wallowed in the spurious glamour of the World Cup was equally baseless. It was soon appreciated that success in Spain would lift the morale of British troops and sailors, and that to deprive them of even that outside interest would benefit no one but the Argentines.

A government enjoying much-needed popularity through its firm handling of the crisis would not wish to jeopardise that goodwill by depriving the British of their football, particularly when timing was all-important. This was always likely to be a swift war. By the time the finals commenced, the Falklands might be back in British hands, and precipitate withdrawal would leave a sour aftertaste. It is probable, too, that FIFA would have threatened severe sanctions should the British Associations withdraw at such late notice, perhaps expelling them from the next, 1986 World Cup.

One final factor to be considered was the likely behaviour of trouble-makers determined to go to Spain. 'Bulldog Bobby', the controversial England mascot, was already being tagged to less desirable English fighting qualities. If the British teams withdrew, embittered fans, fed on a diet of cheap booze, excessive sun and 'Galtieri-itis', might congregate around Barcelona and Alicante, where Argentina were based, with mischief in mind. Far better they were cooped up in Bilbao where the local police were well trained to deal with them. As the draw had made it almost impossible for Argentina's path to cross England's or Northern Ireland's, and unlikely to cross Scotland's, it made sense to allow the home countries to compete and hope for the best.

None of this increased the confidence of the England party. What did raise spirits was Greenwood's recent winning ways. Beginning with the victory over Hungary, England embarked on a run of six wins and a draw (in Iceland), conceding just two goals. The victims were the three home nations, plus Hungary, Holland and Finland. This upturn coincided with the appointment of Don Howe as Greenwood's assistant and coach, following the untimely death of Bill Taylor. Howe's importation of Arsenal's renowned defensive resolve had done much to stem the flow of goals leaked. Following a 4-1 victory in Helsinki, Greenwood named his final squad. Ramsey's preference had been to allocate his ideal team with the Nos. 1-11 shirts. Greenwood went for a straightforward alphabetical notation with just four exceptions, his captain (Keegan) and the three goalkeepers.

| No | Name | Position | Club | Age | Caps | Goals |
|----|------|----------|------|-----|------|-------|
| 1 | Ray Clemence * | Goalkeeper | Tottenham | 33 | 59 | – |
| 2 | Viv Anderson * | Full-back | Nott'm Forest | 25 | 10 | – |
| 3 | Trevor Brooking | Midfield | West Ham | 33 | 46 | 5 |
| 4 | Terry Butcher | Central defence | Ipswich | 23 | 4 | – |
| 5 | Steve Coppell | Midfield | Manchester U | 26 | 36 | 6 |
| 6 | Steve Foster | Central defence | Brighton | 24 | 2 | – |
| 7 | Kevin Keegan (c) | Midfield/Forward | Southampton | 31 | 62 | 21 |
| 8 | Trevor Francis | Forward | Manchester C | 28 | 27 | 6 |
| 9 | Glenn Hoddle | Midfield | Tottenham | 24 | 11 | 4 |
| 10 | Terry McDermott * | Midfield | Liverpool | 30 | 25 | 3 |
| 11 | Paul Mariner | Forward | Ipswich | 29 | 21 | 10 |
| 12 | Mick Mills | Full-back/Midfield | Ipswich | 33 | 37 | – |
| 13 | Joe Corrigan * | Goalkeeper | Manchester C | 33 | 9 | – |

Say cheese! The England squad for Spain '82.

| 14 | Phil Neal | Full-back | Liverpool | 31 | 37 | 3 |
| 15 | Graham Rix | Midfield | Arsenal | 24 | 8 | – |
| 16 | Bryan Robson | Midfield | Manchester U | 25 | 19 | 3 |
| 17 | Kenny Sansom | Full-back | Arsenal | 23 | 23 | – |
| 18 | Phil Thompson | Central defence | Liverpool | 28 | 35 | 1 |
| 19 | Ray Wilkins | Midfield | Manchester U | 25 | 47 | 3 |
| 20 | Peter Withe * | Forward | Aston Villa | 30 | 6 | – |
| 21 | Tony Woodcock | Forward | Arsenal | 26 | 22 | 7 |
| 22 | Peter Shilton | Goalkeeper | Nott'm Forest | 32 | 37 | – |

* Did not appear in the 1982 World Cup finals.    *Averages*    28.0 26.5

One aspect of Greenwood's selection raised a few eyebrows. He had reverted to the Ramsey era, abandoning conventional wing-play. This meant no places for the wingers who featured in the qualifiers – Cunningham, Barnes and Morley. Instead, reliance was placed on midfield players such as Coppell, Brooking and Rix who could play wide. As Greenwood had been such a passionate advocate of wingers, his reaction against them at the eleventh hour took most commentators by surprise.

Otherwise, the composition of the twenty-two met with general approval. The two first-choice goalkeepers, Peter Shilton and Ray Clemence, had been custodians of English goalmouths for a decade, and the debate over their relative merits was reminiscent of that between Matthews and Finney. Of late, however, a fallibility had been detected in Clemence's performances both for Tottenham and for his country. Tellingly, he had kept goal in all four away qualifiers, Shilton the four Wembley games, which meant Clemence had contributed to three defeats. Few doubted that when the time came for Greenwood to come off the fence he would plump for Shilton.

Peter Shilton came out of the same stable as Gordon Banks, succeeding his predecessor at Leicester and Stoke before moving on to Nottingham Forest. Hugely built, Shilton's part in Forest's success (winning the European Cup in 1979 and 1980) was incalculable. Now was the occasion for Shilton to put the stigma of Poland in 1973 behind him.

Not many England teams could admit to a shortage of world-class defenders. This one could. The possible exception was Kenny Sansom at left-back. Just twenty-three, and with the same number of caps, Sansom had been dropped following defeat in Basle. Now he was back, looking good, and ready to challenge for Ray Wilson's record number of caps in his position.

There were three contenders for right-back, Phil Neal, Viv Anderson and Mick Mills. Greenwood eventually opted for Mills, who could play either side, as well as midfield. At thirty-three, he was approaching the end of an international career that had begun inauspiciously with a roasting by the Yugoslav, Dragan Dzajic, at Wembley back in 1972.

It was in the centre of defence that Greenwood faced his greatest problems. Twelve months earlier one of the slots would have gone to Dave Watson, now too old. His replacement was bound to lack experience. The best of them, Terry Butcher, had recently received a fearful nasal injury that briefly threatened not so much his playing career as his life. Few doubted that by 1986 Butcher, towering, slightly stooped, would be a very fine centre-half indeed. He would be partnered now by Liverpool's gutsy, reliable Phil Thompson, caricatured by an abundance of nose and knees, a scouse through and through.

The midfield was more settled. Steve Coppell would double as a right-sided midfield man, cum right-winger. Coppell seldom took the eye but rarely let his country down. His Manchester United colleague, Ray Wilkins, was once a teenage prodigy at Chelsea. He had shone in the 1980 European Championship, but was prone to the safe, square pass, leaving the real incisive midfield work to others. While many saw him as a natural international, others did not.

The third England midfielder on United's books was on the verge of greatness. Not even breaking his leg three times in one season had impeded Bryan Robson's rise. He had been the only ever-present in the qualifiers. Whether in midfield or as sweeper, Robson could defend, tackle, and score from deep with head or foot. With consistency another of his hallmarks, he was Britain's most expensive player, costing £1.8 million when Ron Atkinson persuaded West Bromwich to part with him.

Filling the left-hand slot would be either Trevor Brooking or Graham Rix. Brooking was probably England's most popular footballer. Serene and elegant, he was a player good on the eye. His second goal in Budapest stood to haunt those who claimed he couldn't shoot. But as an elder statesmen in a squad containing nine players the wrong side of thirty, there were doubts about his stamina and ability to shrug off a recurring groin strain.

Rix had not yet staked himself a regular place and had missed much of the season through injury. He was not renowned for scoring goals – missing the penalty that cost Arsenal the Cup-Winners' Cup in 1980. Rix and Sansom would be Arsenal's first ever players to appear in the finals of the World Cup.

As for goalscorers, the most famous England footballer of the time, Kevin Keegan, hoped to bag his share, but was transparently in decline. Three seasons with Hamburg had turned a sprightly, resourceful Liverpool forward into a superstar, the first English 'European Footballer of the Year' since Bobby Charlton. Since signing for Southampton he had looked sharp enough, but now he was uncertain even of his place.

His likely replacement as England's free-roaming forward was Trevor Francis, like Wilkins a teenage star. Francis was often crocked by injury and seldom produced the exhilarating pace that terrified first division defences. He had netted just six goals in twenty-six outings, and needed to improve on that.

The inheritor of the old-fashioned centre-forward shirt was Paul Mariner. He took a while to convince managers he could survive in the first division, and many insisted that he was not the stuff of an international. With deft timing he had begun to find his touch, scoring in each of England's last four games.

## FRANCE v ENGLAND
*Wednesday, 16 June 1982*                                   *Bilbao – 44,172*

The England party flew to Bilbao on 10 June, allowing six days to acclimatise in the Los Tamarises Hotel. Sited on the Playa de Ereaga, it permitted a perfect view of unsightly beach pollution. The players left behind a Britain that had opened up Parliament to President Reagan; getting used to a new 20p coin; and taking advantage of a Goodyear airship to hunt for the Loch Ness Monster. 100,000 CND demonstrators had congregated in Hyde Park, lightning strikes were hitting hospitals, and TV audiences were reminded how West Auckland had defeated Juventus to become the first 'world champions' back in 1910.

Spain had joined NATO and Israeli forces had invaded Lebanon. The news from the South Atlantic was grim, no one knowing, or saying, the extent of the casualties on the landing ships *Sir Galahad* and *Sir Tristram*. From China came the news that two of Britain's foremost mountaineers, Joe Tasker and Peter Boardman, had lost their lives attempting to conquer Everest without oxygen.

The World Cup commenced on Sunday, 13 June, though not for British TV audiences. Both channels blacked the opening ceremony and the first match, between Belgium and defending champions Argentina. British teams could play Argentina if and when the time came, but the British public could not watch the South Americans playing anybody else, at least, not for the moment. In the circumstances, the champions' 0-1 defeat was greeted in this country almost as rapturously as if we'd done the damage ourselves.

Monday brought startling developments. Whitehall had imposed a news black-out as the final push for Port Stanley began. Millions were settled in front of their tellies, waiting to see if the Brazilians were as good as everybody said, when news flashes, tentative at first, implied that the Argentine garrison had surrendered. The BBC's panel of experts forgot their brief and took on the jobs of political analysts and flag-wavers. In Argentina, where the Mundial had even pushed the Malvinas from the front pages, losing wars on two fronts, to Belgium's footballers and to British soldiers, sent the world topsy-turvy.

In Britain, the news from Port Stanley seemed unreal. The House of Commons roared its approval. Nothing could have been better stage-managed to lift the spirits of Britain's footballers, not even victory over the Indians in the Lord's Jubilee Test Match. Scotland were ripe for celebration, sticking five past New Zealand. The Kiwi government had had the decency to lend Britain two frigates, doubtless the reason for their two consolation goals.

France may not have had a war on her hands, but she was doing pretty nicely out of the South Atlantic conflict. She was strapped for cash and had devalued the franc. Yet French military hardware was receiving the kind of boost dreamed about by sales promoters. In British playgrounds children were no longer human Spitfires and Hurricanes, but Mirages and Super Etendards. The French Exocet had taken on a fearsome symbolism, a computerised, sea-skimming harbinger of destruction. Whether the shooting power of France's forwards could match it would have to be seen.

France were expected to provide the toughest opposition. Over the years England had played their near neighbours more frequently than any other foreign country. On past results there were few grounds for French optimism, just three wins from eighteen. The two countries' paths had not crossed since 1969, when France had gone down 0-5 at Wembley. The teams had faced each other in the 1966 World Cup, England winning a trifle dubiously.

During the 1970s the French game had enlivened itself, largely due to the fortunes of Nantes and Saint-Etienne. Their national team was blessed with outstanding players, among them the tousle-haired Michel Platini and the ebony sweeper Marius Trésor. The side tended to unpredictability, full of Gallic flair when the mood suited them, lethargic and undisciplined when it did not. During the 1978 World Cup France had performed well, though failing to survive a tough group, including Argentina, Italy and Hungary. The 1982 qualifiers had been equally unkind, asking France to withstand the challenge of Belgium, Holland, Ireland, and Cyprus, which they barely did. Having been dealt two consecutive 'bad hands', France did not take kindly to the decision to seed England. More worrying for Michel Hidalgo, the French team manager, was his team's recent form. Following a 4-0 canter over Northern Ireland, they had lost in Paris to Peru (0-1), Wales (0-1) and drawn 0-0 with Bulgaria.

In masterminding his fiftieth international, Ron Greenwood had to omit Brooking and Keegan, two senior players. Brooking's groin strain was public knowledge, but Keegan's malaise was more dramatic. He had suffered a mystery back spasm in training. Not even the birth of his second daughter and an OBE in the Queen's Birthday Honours could ease his dismay. It was early days, but the injuries to both players could keep them out for the duration. Room-mates, and both decorated by the Queen, they must have been a picture of dejection, knowing they would never see another World Cup. Their places were taken by Francis and Rix. Mills was handed the captaincy.

Though there was no colour clash, both teams wore their second strips, France in white shirts, England in red, with blue and white shoulder blazes. The San Mamés Stadium was a cauldron of noise, English fans holding their own against the thousands of French who had journeyed across the Pyrenees.

England kicked off under a blazing sun. Wilkins conveyed the ball to Coppell down the right, hidden in deep shade. Bossis steered the ball into touch. Coppell flung the ball into the box, where Butcher's head flicked it back. Robson, lurking unattended in the danger area, was suddenly presented with a gaping goal. The ball reached him awkwardly, bouncing almost shoulder high, but with a gymnastic swing of his left foot he hooked it past Ettori. The third-choice French keeper's first touch was to pull the ball out of the net. England were ahead, and only twenty-seven seconds had elapsed. Robson, it transpired, had scored the quickest ever goal in the World Cup finals.

When the euphoria subsided, the mind was assailed by the unhappy fate of teams scoring very quick goals in the World Cup. In the 1974 Final, Holland had done so, but lost. Four years later the French, themselves, had scored after just thirty-one seconds against Italy. They, too, were defeated. An early breakthrough can disrupt as easily as it can settle. The losing side has no choice but to attack. For the scorers, the options are contradictory. Prearranged tactics are at once redundant. Should the team attack or defend? Caught in two minds, the initiative is often surrendered. That was certainly the case with the Dutch in 1974, for whom Neeskens' early penalty turned out to be a false gift.

England's defence soon indulged in mock suicide, armchair fans watching through fingers. Seeking to play keep-ball, Mills and Butcher got tangled. The ball broke to Soler who hit it over. Mills and Butcher exchanged compliments.

France gradually began to impose. The tiny Giresse projected a long searching pass to synchronise with Soler's run. With Butcher trailing in his slipstream, Soler shot cleanly across Shilton, the ball whizzing inside the far post. It was France's first goal in four matches. Butcher shortly felled the goalscorer and was booked by Antonio Garido, the Portuguese referee.

At half-time, France had cause for greater satisfaction, especially in midfield. It was that area that Greenwood sought to strengthen. Rix dropped deeper, seeking to make life difficult for Giresse and Platini, while allowing Robson and Wilkins to forage upfield.

England's tactical change reaped dividends. Encouraged by a layer of cloud, the red shirts began to dictate. With the crowd distracted by disturbances at the other end and news of an Algerian goal against West Germany, Francis floated in a cross and Robson soared salmon-like to plant a header beyond Ettori. It would have been a super goal for an old-style centre-forward, let alone a midfielder slowed by a calf-knock and exhausted by the heat and his running.

England needed to hold on to their lead for twenty-four minutes. Only four had been consumed when Butcher brought Platini crashing down on the cusp of the penalty area. The referee might have awarded a penalty or sent Butcher off, but did neither. France were now labouring. Didier Six and Jean Tigana replaced Rocheteau and Larios, but the introduction of fresh legs could not interrupt England's massive control.

Rix's cross beyond the far post was laid back by Wilkins to Francis, whose shot glanced off Trésor and fell for Mariner to net at close range. The scorer stood motionless, arms raised as he milked the applause from English supporters behind the goal. Mariner deserved the acclaim. He had scored in five consecutive internationals, equalling the feat of Jimmy Greaves in 1961.

France had seven minutes in which to make inroads. For all their frills, they had still managed just the one shot on target, and now that the pressure was on they had little to offer. In the dying seconds cramp took Sansom from the field. Neal came on, lined up for a French free-kick, and the referee blew for time. Neal had won a cap without touching the ball.

The England players were all smiles as they gulped fluids to make up their weight loss (Mariner had sweated off eleven pounds). They had contrived six goal attempts on target to France's one, but committed nineteen fouls against nine. The only doubt concerned the enormity of Bryan Robson's contribution. One-man bands don't make good orchestras. Still, if he was happy now, he was even happier the next day when his wife completed his hat-trick, presenting him with a baby girl.

As Groups 2, 4, and 5 were in the same half of the draw (odd though that sounds), England were looking to the next round. In Group 2, the Germans had been sensationally beaten by Algeria. In Group 5, Spain had been held 1-1 by Honduras. It was looking good.

Bryan Robson, salmon-like, leaps to head past Ettori. (v France)

| FRANCE  (1) 1 | ENGLAND  (1) 3 |
|---|---|
| Soler 25 | Robson 1, 66, Mariner 83 |

FRANCE: Ettori, Battiston, Bossis, Trésor, Lopez, Larios (Tigana), Girard, Giresse, Rocheteau (Six), Platini, Soler.
ENGLAND: Shilton, Mills, Thompson, Butcher, Sansom (Neal), Coppell, Wilkins, Robson, Rix, Francis, Mariner.

## CZECHOSLOVAKIA v ENGLAND
*Sunday, 20 June 1982*                                    *Bilbao – 41,123*

Following victories for Scotland and England, it was Northern Ireland's turn to impress, holding Yugoslavia to a goalless draw. On the Friday, British football was brought down to earth when Brazil overwhelmed Scotland 4-1. Elsewhere the tournament was throwing up the unexpected. In the first batch of matches only New Zealand and El Salvador of the minnows had been beaten. In Group 4, Kuwait had drawn 1-1 with Czechoslovakia after falling behind to a fantasy penalty. An English win would now guarantee progress to the next stage.

By the time England took the field, *HMS Glasgow* had limped into Portsmouth sporting a hole where a bomb had passed through. In Argentina,

President Galtieri was peremptorily toppled from power.

One could foresee a similar fate befalling Dr Josef Venglos, the Czech manager, should his team fail. He made four changes from the side that had fortuitously escaped defeat by Kuwait. Out went stars such as Antonin Panenka and Marian Masny. Out, too, went keeper Hruska, who had allowed Kuwait's long-range equaliser to pass through his hands. Venglos sensibly retained the services in attack of Zdenek Nehoda, now winning his eighty-eighth cap.

It was hard to place the Czechs in the European football hierarchy. Like England, they had last appeared in the World Cup finals in 1970, when England had won a shambles of a match 1-0. The teams had squared up four times since then, the Czechs winning just the once, when eliminating England *en route* to becoming the 1976 European champions. Though they lifted the 1980 Olympic title and hung on to third place in the European Championship, they were clearly a waning force, notching just one win in seven games.

Greenwood announced an unchanged team, his first for three years. The players came out to sympathetic weather, the sun screened by heavy clouds. England played in familiar white, Czechoslovakia red. Whereas England had to overcome French flair, the current task was to break down a one-paced team set on a goalless draw. The danger was that, the longer the game wore on, England might settle for the same, yet Robson might have had a first-half hat-trick.

Unfortunately, he strained his groin. Rather than risk him Greenwood sent out Hoddle for the second half. The arrival of England's glamour boy would have pleased almost everyone were it not for Robson's irreplaceable qualities.

Indeed, England took time to regroup and Czechoslovakia enjoyed their best spell. But then a sweet reverse pass from Rix to Francis earned England their twelfth corner. Wilkins took it, swinging the ball under the crossbar. The ball should have been Seman's, but the goalkeeper allowed the ball to pass through his hands for Francis to hook into the net from two yards.

Francis' seventh goal for England was punished by a Barmos elbow to the solar-plexus. The pain was forgotten as England scored a double-quick second. Seman's goal-kick was headed back by Thompson. Francis chested the ball down to Mariner and set off for the far post. Mariner tried to thread a pass to him, but Barmos, facing his own goal, slid in and prodded the ball inside Seman's left post. Francis raced to retrieve it, as a mother might a child that has strayed on to the M1, and sat cuddling it in the back of the net. Two gift goals suggested that somebody up there liked England.

The Czechs never threatened. Seman, his pride and his hand aching, was replaced by Stromsik, which meant the Czechs had called upon three goalkeepers in less than three hours of football. But not even the introduction of Masny, winning his seventy-seventh cap, in place of Janecka, could raise the Czech tempo, and the game concluded with Francis' sizzling shot on the turn flashing over the bar. With the referee's whistle, English fans danced a conga.

Seman fails to collect Ray Wilkin's corner and Trevor Francis scores. (v Czechoslovakia)

Brazil had already ensured their place in the second phase. Now England joined them, never before having won their opening two games in the finals of a World Cup. Mariner blotted his copy-book with a ludicrous claim to be credited with England's second goal, to extend his scoring sequence to six games. Jimmy Greaves, whose record was at stake, gave a wry smile.

CZECHOSLOVAKIA  (0) 0      ENGLAND  (0) 2
                           Francis 63, Barmos 66 (o.g.)

CZECHOSLOVAKIA: Seman (Stromsik), Barmos, Radimec, Vojacek, Fiala, Chaloupka, Berger, Jurkemic, Janecka (Masny), Nehoda, Vizek.
ENGLAND: Shilton, Mills, Thompson, Butcher, Sansom, Coppell, Robson (Hoddle), Wilkins, Francis, Mariner, Rix.

## KUWAIT v ENGLAND
*Friday, 25 June 1982*                    *Bilbao – 39,700*

By the time England entertained Kuwait, Scotland were on their way home, eliminated for the third successive World Cup on goal difference.

Away from football, the biggest headlines were made by yet another birth.

Following on the heels of daughters for Kevin Keegan and Bryan Robson came a son for the Prince and Princess of Wales. The future King was born just after 9 p.m. on the Monday. Perhaps a sixth sense distracted the Northern Ireland players from hanging on to their lead against the Hondurans, who, with evident disrespect for a British team with its guard down, snatched an equaliser.

General Bignone was named as the new President of Argentina, and Rex Hunt, the former Governor of the Falklands, returned in the renamed capacity of Civil Commissioner. The Spanish government deferred the long-awaited opening of the border with Gibraltar. In the United States John Hinckley had been acquitted on grounds of insanity of the attempted murder of President Reagan. There was a century for Ian Botham at Old Trafford against the Indians – with the assistance of a runner. Allan Clarke was sacked as manager of Leeds United, while his contemporary, George Best, successfully fended off a bankruptcy petition. Wimbledon 1982 had opened its doors to Annabel Croft, at fifteen, the youngest British female competitor this century. Bjorn Borg and Ivan Lendl had declined to enter, and Britain's John Lloyd and Sue Barker had fallen at the first hurdle, the latter despite the loving encouragement of Cliff Richard. London commuters were unable to get home to enjoy Wimbledon or the World Cup on TV because of strikes crippling public transport.

Cliff Richard was not the only 1960s pop star in the news. Paul McCartney had celebrated his fortieth birthday, and the Rolling Stones were engaged in a sell-out tour to commemorate their twentieth anniversary. Their concert at St James's Park, home of Newcastle United, brought in twice the gate of an average Magpies' league match. The present musical scene was dominated by Adam Ant's *Goody Two Shoes* and Charlene's *I've Never Been to Me*.

England had only their pride at stake against the Kuwaitis. France had drawn with Czechoslovakia, so England would top the group whatever. France would accompany England into the next phase unless the Kuwaitis put four past Peter Shilton. Brian Clough put that possibility into perspective, suggesting it could only happen if Kuwait bought Spain.

Kuwait had reduced their match with France (1-4) to pandemonium, stopping play at a phantom whistle and allowing the French to score. After a delay of several minutes, the game was restarted only when the Soviet referee astonishingly annulled the goal. For their impertinence, Kuwait were fined by FIFA; and for his incompetence the referee was suspended.

Kuwait were regarded as the strongest of the six lesser footballing nations in Spain, though she had only 1,600 registered players – fewer than the population of the Falklands. During the 1970s no stone was left unturned in the attempt to make Kuwait a soccer power. Under the custody of Mario Zagalo, star of past Brazilian teams, Kuwait reached the last eight of the 1980 Olympics and won the 1980 Asian Championship, when their World Cup preparations were entrusted to Carlos Alberto, namesake of the 1970 Brazilian captain.

Although England and Kuwait had never met at international level, the Kuwaitis were far from strangers to British football, having been weaned on it ever since the days when Kuwait was a British protectorate. Kuwait had drawn twice with Wales in 1977. Several British coaches were plying their trade with Kuwait club sides, among them Dave Mackay, the old Tottenham and Derby war-horse. Kuwait's World Cup squad even arranged warm-up matches with English clubs. Now came their moment of truth.

Their players were inconvenienced by the requirements of Ramadan, the Islamic fast, which in 1982 coincided with the finals. The most devout were allowing no food or liquids to pass their lips except at night. To offset this, the Kuwaitis had imported their own mascot, a camel from north Africa which would in due course be donated to Madrid Zoo.

Greenwood's problems were more practical. He could either rest key players and pander to his reserves, or keep his winning side together. He opted for the latter, his three changes all enforced. Sansom (thigh) and Robson (groin) stood down, as did Terry Butcher, recipient of a yellow card against France. Another would entail his missing a match. Steve Foster was brought in for his first World Cup action, the first Brighton player so honoured. Glenn Hoddle filled Robson's position, Mills switched flanks, and Phil Neal assumed Mills' duties.

The England team took the field wearing new lightweight shirts, specially flown out after they had complained about the heavy old ones. Learning from Ramsey's lack of PR, Greenwood's players playfully kicked footballs into the crowd before the start.

Taking the hint, Mariner quickly headed a corner into the crowd – where the ball stayed. A couple of minutes later the would-be thief relented and threw it back, alongside its replacement in the Kuwait goalmouth. When the referee blew for a bounce-up on the six-yard line, to revert back to the original, the Arabs must have been convinced that FIFA was gunning for them.

Perhaps the referee – Mr Aristizabal from Colombia – realised he was courting the wrath of Allah, for he appeased the Kuwaitis by ensuring his 'bounce' fell kindly, and for the rest of the match, in harness with his linesmen, made life so difficult for the England team that if any of them so much as breathed the same air as an opponent, a free-kick would be awarded, and any England player venturing across the halfway line without the ball was liable to be summarily given offside. Needless to say the game flowed as smoothly as treacle down a pipette. The first act of wanton violence was committed by Mr Aristizabal, stooping to prick a balloon that was minding its own business.

Mariner now turned the ball back for Francis, who must have feared being mistaken by the referee for a balloon, for he set off in the direction of the Kuwait goal as if his life depended upon it. Riding a half-challenge, Francis shot from sixteen yards. Tarabulsi, the thirty-five year old Kuwaiti goalie, got a touch, but not enough to prevent the goal.

Just before the break, Mr Aristizabal punished England for a novel offence. Blowing for free-kicks with the frequency of expletives emanating from Don Howe's lips was not enough to appease Allah. Rix shaped to pass to Mariner, with the referee hovering between them like some malign piggy-in-the-middle. Mariner thought he had every right to reach the ball. Hauling the official out of the way with the determination of a doctor fighting his way to the scene of an accident, Mariner found himself staring at a rectangular yellow card.

With the referee halting every English attack (England were caught offside twenty-two times and committed twenty fouls to Kuwait's seven), play became desperately scrappy. Afterwards Greenwood readily conceded that his team had not performed. Francis' one goal did not obscure the fact that he ought to have had three and might have had six.

KUWAIT   (0) 0                    ENGLAND   (1) 1
                                        Francis 27

KUWAIT: al Tarabulsi, Naeem Saed, Mayoof, Mubarak, Jasem (al Shemmari), al Buloushi, al Houti, Kameel, al Anbari (al Dakhil), al Suwaayed.
ENGLAND: Shilton, Neal, Mills, Foster, Thompson, Coppell, Hoddle, Wilkins, Mariner, Francis, Rix.

---

*Final positions – Group 4*

|               | P | W | D | L | F | A | Pts |
|---------------|---|---|---|---|---|---|-----|
| ENGLAND       | 3 | 3 | 0 | 0 | 6 | 1 | 6   |
| FRANCE        | 3 | 1 | 1 | 1 | 6 | 5 | 3   |
| Czechoslovakia| 3 | 0 | 2 | 1 | 2 | 4 | 2   |
| Kuwait        | 3 | 0 | 1 | 2 | 2 | 6 | 1   |

---

**WEST GERMANY v ENGLAND**
*Tuesday, 29 June 1982*                           *Madrid – 75,000*

The twelve surviving nations were now divided into four new clusters of three. The teams would play one another and the winners would constitute the semi-finalists. This change had removed any advantage for group-winners, whose perks in previous World Cups included playing in their accustomed stadium and/or facing the runners-up of other groups. These incentives had encouraged teams to go out and win their groups, rather than be satisfied with merely qualifying. None of this applied in Spain. The venues for the second round were elsewhere from those of the first round. England would meet a group winner and a runner-up irrespective of whether they headed Group 4 or come second. France, in other words, were not disadvantaged in any way. Far from it, as things turned out.

England were lumped with the winners of Group 2 and the runners-up in Group 5 in Pool B, playing both matches in Madrid's Santiago Bernabéu Stadium, where the Final itself would be staged. Group 2 was headed by West Germany, following their 1-0 win over Austria, when both teams all but lay down for a siesta. Northern Ireland's sensational win over Spain in Group 5 sent Spain into the same pool as England and West Germany.

This was not what the organising committee had in mind. All six seeds now found themselves clustered into two pools, Italy, Argentina and Brazil in the other. Two semi-final places would now be filled by non-seeds, while four seeds would be toppled beforehand. In Pool D, France had to face only Austria and Northern Ireland, opponents to make English players' mouths water.

The England party decamped from Bilbao and set up residence in a hotel complex at Navacerrada, in the hills outside the Spanish capital. The royal baby had been named – William. The name, announced Buckingham Palace gravely, was 'not to be foreshortened in any way'. The FA confirmed that Robert Robson, otherwise known as Bobby, would succeed Ronald Greenwood at the conclusion of the World Cup. George Schulz also had a new job, succeeding Alexander Haig as US Secretary of State. A new fashion craze was sweeping America, 'bonce boppers', bouncing headgear like human antennae.

Helmut Schoen wore a natty line in headgear in his time as German team manager. Not so his successor, Jupp Derwall. It was Derwall's heavy duty to sustain the high standards of his predecessor. Twice in the not so distant past world football had reverberated to the clash of England and Germany. Germany were world champions in 1974, European champions in 1972 and 1980, and had lost just one of their last six matches with England. They were co-favourites for the current World Cup with Brazil. Since taking charge in 1978, Derwall had guided his team to a twenty-three match unbeaten run that ended in January 1981. After four years in the hot seat he had yet to see his team lose to European opposition.

Such, on paper, was the magnitude of England's task. Yet the form book was looking tattered. Germany's defeat by Algeria ranked among the greatest sporting upsets of all time, the win over Austria the greatest fix. German morale was said to be low. The team might have peaked too early, and were being asked to face an England team at the top of their game.

The Germans had more to fear from England than *vice versa*. And so it proved. Whereas Greenwood eagerly reverted to his favoured eleven, Germany's normal formation was castrated and replaced by one designed to stifle England in midfield. This was especially surprising: in order to avoid 'dead' games, the losers were scheduled to play Spain next; but if the current match was drawn, Germany would have that disadvantage.

In any case, out went Pierre Littbarski, the fleeting, elusive winger who had been expected to torment Mills and Sansom; out went Horst Hrubesch, the tall, powerful centre-forward; out went the diligent Felix Magath in midfield. When asked for a prediction, Bobby Charlton said he could not imagine England v Germany matches ending in draws. But both the 1966 and 1970 games were draws after ninety minutes. There would be no extra time on this occasion.

As if to relive past battles, England once again took the field in red. The 75,000 spectators were joined by millions of prying Spanish eyes, eager to weigh up their heroes' future opposition. Shilton re-acclimatised himself to the stadium where he had helped Nottingham Forest defeat Kevin Keegan's Hamburg in the 1980 European Cup Final.

Paul Breitner carved out an early opening. A full-back in the 1974 World Cup Final, Breitner had drifted into political activism and left the Fatherland to play for Real Madrid. He was eventually tempted back to Bayern Munich and reconstituted as a midfield general for the national team. Now, accelerating past Sansom, he drove a fast, low centre across Shilton's goal which Karl-Heinz Rummenigge missed by a whisker. Shilton held his arms wide in supplication. The German captain and European Footballer of the Year may have been slowed by a thigh strain, but the gamble over his inclusion had almost paid off.

The half-time whistle arrived to the relief of everybody. But if an expectant audience crossed their fingers for better things they were to be disappointed. Both teams packed the midfield and goalmouth activity was non-existent. Reinders was pulled off for Littbarski, Klaus Fischer came on for Hansi Müller, and Tony Woodcock, used to German man-to-man marking with Cologne (he had signed for Arsenal on the eve of the tournament), replaced Francis. The contest nevertheless died of self-inflicted asphyxia. Robson was cynically chopped by the German sweeper, Stielike, playing on his home ground. Stielike was booked by Brazilian referee Coelho, and Rix's best-forgotten free-kick trundled into Schumacher's arms.

Just three minutes remained and the game was yawningly receiving the last rites when Rummenigge unleashed a murderous shot that veered wickedly and smashed against Shilton's crossbar. England were within two inches of defeat.

Since the win over France, England had scored fewer goals with each match. They were now down to zero, and it was hard to see how the slide could be reversed. Still, carping seemed unwarranted given that England had just drawn with, and in no way been inferior to, the reigning European champions. Both sides had managed eight nominal goal attempts and had earned three corners.

WEST GERMANY   (0) 0          ENGLAND   (0) 0

W GERMANY: Schumacher, Kaltz, K-H Förster, Stielike, Briegel, Dremmler, B Förster, Breitner, H Müller (Fischer), Reinders (Littbarksi), Rummenigge.
ENGLAND: Shilton, Butcher, Mills, Thompson, Sansom, Coppell, Robson, Wilkins, Francis (Woodcock), Mariner, Rix.

Rummenigge (No 11) rattles Peter Shilton's crossbar. (v W Germany)

## SPAIN v ENGLAND
*Monday, 5 July 1982*                                    *Madrid – 75,000*

With almost a week to spare, conversations could turn to other subjects – like Wednesday, 30 June being one second longer than all other days of the year, and the largest census in world history ascertaining whether the population of China had reached one billion. Princess Diana, who had added an extra one to Britain's population, enjoyed another celebration, her twenty-first birthday.

Others with reason to celebrate were Roy Jenkins, elected leader of the Social Democratic Party, and Jimmy Connors and Martina Navratilova, who between them cleaned up the Wimbledon singles titles. Billie-Jean King, back at Wimbledon at the age of thirty-eight, had been unable to overcome Chris Evert in the semi-finals. Other sporting casualties included Argentina, beaten by Italy and Brazil and out of the World Cup, and Wolverhampton Wanderers, forced to call in the receiver. The British public faced the hardship of a rail strike, called by ASLEF over the introduction of flexible rostering.

It was rumoured that the train drivers had timed the stoppage so that they could be at home to watch England play Spain. In the meantime, the result most dreaded from Germany's match with Spain was a heavy victory for the Germans. If Spain won or fought a scoring draw, then a simple England victory would see them into the semi-finals. But a victory for the Germans would need to be bettered by England.

When Germany led Spain 2-0 with fifteen minutes remaining, the odds on England's survival looked slender. But a spectacular header by Zamora pulled a goal back and eased the task required. Spain were out. England now needed a victory by two goals, or by one goal in a high scoring match (3-2 or above). A 1-0 win, however, would not be enough since Germany had scored an extra goal. Such a score would see England knocked out of the competition with a playing record of played 5; won 4; drawn 1; lost 0.

The FA sought clarification about FIFA's intentions should England, too, win 2-1. The regulations stated that in such an eventuality the 'classification' from the group matches would be brought to bear. As England's record in Group 4 surpassed Germany's in Group 2, the England camp assumed that this would count in their favour. Instead, FIFA intimated that only the group position would count, and as Germany had also finished top, lots would be drawn, on the pitch, shortly after the final whistle. The captains of England and Germany would first toss a coin for the right of first go, then dip trembling hands into a bag containing six small balls. Four balls would be unmarked; the other two would contain the names of either Germany or England. The first named country to emerge would proceed to the semi-finals. The prospect did little to ease the tension felt by Mick Mills, who publicly expressed his terror at the thought of picking out the wrong ball. A 'sensible' captain he might be, but this was hardly the *Happy Talk* referred to on the week's best-selling record.

Anyway, Spain had nothing to play for except pride. Steve Coppell was ruled out with a knee injury, his touchline-hugging duties assumed by Trevor Francis. Into the side came Tony Woodcock, who had twice previously scored against Spain. Kevin Keegan and Trevor Brooking were on the bench.

The match would kick-off at 9 p.m. The players took their minds off the ordeal by watching Italy's 3-2 defeat of Brazil. With Argentina and Brazil out, and Germany removed along with Spain if England did the business, the field would be laid bare of four of the favourites. France had already reached the semi-finals, and now awaited either England or Germany. If England could beat the French once, they could beat them again. Awaiting them in the Final would be Italy or Poland. The way looked clear for a triumph against the odds.

Not that the outgoing England manager would allow himself to be distracted by such visions. England and Spain had clashed once before in the World Cup – in 1950 in distant Rio – Spain winning on that occasion 1-0. Otherwise, the whip hand clearly lay with England, who had won seven out of seven between 1960 and 1980. In March 1981, at Wembley, seven players now lining up against England were in a team that won impressively 2-1.

Spain were managed by José Santamaria, defender for Uruguay in 1954. Spain's record in World Cups was appalling. Since 1950 they had either failed to qualify or been sent packing after the first round. By such standards Santamaria's achievement in guiding his team to the second phase was remarkable enough, though they needed two daft penalties even to get that far.

England's unpopularity – Spain sympathising with her Argentine cousins – was manifest when the rendition of *God Save the Queen* was roundly whistled.

Robson was soon treated to a discreet forearm smash from Tendillo. Rix's shot was patted down by Arconada, the Spanish keeper and captain, like a lobbed beachball. This was accomplishment enough, for Arconada had much to atone for. Before the tournament, learned football magazines tried to convince readers that here was a great goalkeeper. Such was the myth: the reality resulted in gifted goals to the Irish and Germans. If Arconada possessed an ounce of fairness he would be equally charitable to his present opponents. Alonso showed charity, flashing a shot wide from eight yards. Belgian referee Ponnet waved a yellow card at Wilkins after a tackle on Camacho.

After the break, Wilkins began shooting from such prodigious distances that he must have taken advice on the curvature of the Earth. A lightning Spanish break from Zamora to Satrustegui left Alonso with just Shilton to beat. Again, he scorned the gift, screwing the ball wide. The game was slipping away when Rix and Woodcock were pulled off, allowing Brooking and Keegan their first taste of the World Cup finals. The transformation was remarkable. Brooking's poise immediately caught the eye. He now jinked round a defender to earn a clear sight of goal. Had Brooking's accuracy with the gun matched his deftness in loading it, he must have scored, but eyes down he shot straight at Arconada.

Butcher then fired a shot so close to Arconada's post as to decapitate any basking woodworm. It was now Spain's turn to panic, and Santamaria threw on Uralde for Saura. The substitute arrived just in time to witness Keegan's agony. Robson chipped the ball onto Keegan's waiting head, bang in front of the posts. Alas, the player who had looked to this moment as the climax of an illustrious career headed wide. Keegan sank to his knees and buried his head in his hands.

England were spent. Alexanco – bane of Spurs in Cup-Winners' Cup clashes with Barcelona – was twice within inches of a goal. By the end, England had forced twenty-three shots, seven on target, against one from Spain. England, as ever, even out-fouled the opposition, twenty to twelve. An insensitive TV commentator tracked Mick Mills and tactlessly reminded him that this was probably his last international. Mills excused himself with dignity, when he must have wanted to stuff the microphone down his tormentor's throat.

The last time England had been eliminated from a World Cup, Ramsey had faced stiff questions concerning his substitutions. Greenwood's belated introduction of Brooking and Keegan ensured that his own managership would be blighted by similar controversy. Brooking looked the best player on the field. If he was fit to be sub, he must have been fit to start. Greenwood insisted that the pair could inflict more damage on a tiring Spanish defence.

Only once before, in 1966, had England won more matches than they lost in the finals of a World Cup, and their results in 1982 – three wins and two draws – were second only to 1966. The fact that one semi-final would be contested by France and West Germany, the former roundly beaten, the latter held to a draw, showed what might have been. In the Final, Italy overcame the Germans 3-1.

SPAIN  (0) 0                              ENGLAND  (0) 0

SPAIN: Arconada, Urquiaga, Tendillo (Maceda), Alexanco, Gordillo, Saura (Uralde), Alonso, Zamora, Camacho, Satrustegui, Santillana.
ENGLAND: Shilton, Mills, Butcher, Thompson, Sansom, Wilkins, Robson, Mariner, Rix (Brooking), Francis, Woodcock (Keegan).

---

*Final positions – Group B*

|              | P | W | D | L | F | A | Pts |
|--------------|---|---|---|---|---|---|-----|
| WEST GERMANY | 2 | 1 | 1 | 0 | 2 | 1 | 3   |
| England      | 2 | 0 | 2 | 0 | 0 | 0 | 2   |
| Spain        | 2 | 0 | 1 | 1 | 1 | 2 | 1   |

---

*England appearances and goalscorers (substitute appearances in brackets)*
*World Cup qualifying rounds and final competition 1982*

| | Apps | Goals | | Apps | Goals |
|---|---|---|---|---|---|
| Robson B | 12 | 3 | Keegan K *† | 4 (1) | 1 |
| Mariner P * | 11 | 4 | Butcher T | 4 | – |
| Thompson P * | 10 | – | Clemence R *† | 4 | – |
| Mills M * | 10 | – | Osman R | 3 | – |
| Coppell S * | 9 (1) | – | Hoddle G | 2 (1) | – |
| Shilton P † | 9 | – | Anderson V | 2 | – |
| Sansom K | 9 | – | Gates E | 2 | – |
| Francis T * | 8 | 2 | Birtles G | 1 | – |
| Rix G | 7 (1) | – | Foster S | 1 | – |
| Wilkins R * | 7 (1) | – | Martin A | 1 | – |
| McDermott T * | 6 (2) | 3 | Barnes P * | – (2) | – |
| Neal P * | 6 (1) | – | Cunningham L | – (1) | – |
| Watson D * | 6 | – | Morley A | – (1) | – |
| Woodcock A | 5 (1) | 2 | Withe P | – (1) | – |
| Brooking T * | 4 (1) | 2 | (own goals) | | 2 |

---

\* Appeared in 1978 World Cup.                    *29 players     19 goals*
† Appeared in 1974 World Cup.

# 10

# THE 1986 WORLD CUP

While Greenwood's players were wiping their tears, back in London a certain Michael Fagan slipped uninvited into the Queen's bedroom at Buckingham Palace and chatted with Her Majesty at the foot of her bed while supping from the choicest royal wine.

World headlines in the two-year hiatus between World Cup campaigns spoke of wars in the Caribbean and the Levant. Margaret Thatcher looked on in fury as American troops invaded the British colony of Grenada. The Lebanon's once beautiful capital, Beirut, became a byword for civil strife, religious bigotry, and a quicksand facility to drag Western powers to their doom. Two infamous Soviet spies, Donald MacLean and the recently unmasked 'Fourth Man', Anthony Blunt, met their maker, as did two of Britain's best loved comics, Tommy Cooper and Eric Morecambe. Michael Jackson's *Thriller* broke records of one kind, while Torvill and Dean's *Bolero* broke others at the 1984 Winter Olympics. The Summer Olympics at Los Angeles were scarred by the tit-for-tat withdrawal of much of the Soviet bloc, while York Minster was scarred by fire just days after the appointment as Bishop of Durham of the outspoken Dr David Jenkins. The hand of God, some said. Durham was miners' country, heartland of a bitter and protracted miners' strike that aimed to topple Margaret Thatcher's Government as its predecessor had toppled Ted Heath's.

Australia was coming to terms with the crime of the decade – Lindy and Michael Chamberlain standing accused of the so-called 'dingo baby murder' – while the British were coming to terms with their newest coin, a fat, heavy, £1 piece that holed trousers and turned handbags into weapons. The great hoax of the mid-'eighties concerned Adolf Hitler and his phantom 'diaries'.

It was, apparently, no hoax when Colombia, crippled by banditry and drugs, was formally granted the 1986 World Cup. But when the accountants did their sums it was soon clear that debt-ridden Colombia could not cope. Brazil's fleeting interest was upstaged by that of the United States who, despite her place on the outer margins of the game, somehow calculated that loadsa-dosh, plus the formidable negotiating skills of Henry Kissinger, might twist the arm of FIFA President João Havelange. They did not. He preferred the credentials of Mexico who, just sixteen years after staging one of the most memorable Finals, would become the first nation to host a second World Cup. With the torch passing from coloniser to colony, Spanish would remain for the time being the *lingua franca* of world football.

Lancaster Gate, meanwhile, had a new helmsman. Ron Greenwood had always intended retiring after the 1982 World Cup. Bobby Robson last featured in England's World Cup quest in October 1961, against Portugal. He had partnered Johnny Haynes in England's midfield in Sweden, but was kept out of the side in Chile by that young pretender, Bobby Moore. As a manager, Robson trod the same path as Alf Ramsey. Aspirants to the top job have long turned their backs on the Liverpools and Manchester Uniteds. History shows that it's the reins at Upton Park and Portman Road (and latterly Vicarage Road) that apprentice the national Boss. Robson had been managing Ipswich even before the 1970 Mexico World Cup, though success took its time coming. Not till his fifth season did Robson's Ipswich make any impact. Club and manager then embarked on a ten-year assault on the championship, finishing in the top six all but once – when they lifted the FA Cup in consolation. As with all top jobs, timing was crucial. In 1982 Ipswich finished runners-up for the second successive year, having also won the UEFA Cup in 1981.

In the tabloid press, if not the corridors of Lancaster Gate, Robson had to withstand the challenge of the 'people's choice', Brian Clough. But Robson was already an FA insider, working with the England 'B' team and leading tours abroad, and he held the inside track. Continuity with Greenwood's regime was maintained by retaining Don Howe as assistant, a partnership unaffected by Howe's later promotion at Highbury from coach to manager.

Robson's was no easy baptism, either on or off the pitch. National icon Kevin Keegan had no place in the new regime – he was playing in the second division – and Tyneside turned its wrath on Robson, one of their own. On the field, the new manager was thrown straight into the qualifiers for the European Championship. Qualification from a group comprising Greece, Hungary, Luxembourg and Denmark might have been assured but for running up against an emerging Danish team about to burst into the sunlight. Their 1-0 victory at Wembley left England chasing shadows, insofar as they chased anything, on an evening Robson would describe as the blackest of his international career. Elkjaer, Laudrup, and Olsen went on to storm the European Championship (penalty kicks denying them a place in the Final) and in due course the World Cup.

The press hounded Robson for losing to nobodies. Little did they know. Little did he know that his teams would never again lose a qualifier, in any competition, home or away – an unbeaten sequence of twenty-two games spanning the next seven years. But at the time, all was gloom and despair.

England's lunatic fringe did their worst, running amok in Luxembourg, yet again, when the fading hopes of European qualification were finally extinguished.

All eyes to the future, to the World Cup, the draw for which found Robson understandably touching wood and crossing his fingers. Europe had been allocated twelve places in Mexico, plus the holders, Italy, plus one possible play-off winner. Groups were divided into four or five teams, only one guaranteed qualifier emerging from the former, two from the latter, clearly the better option.

The draw smiled on Robson. England's seeding, which infuriated Scotland and others, kept away the other big fish in the five-team Group 3. The opposition seemed unthreatening and were well-equipped through politics or geography to deal with English hoodlums. Northern Ireland needed no lessons in security, and the film *Midnight Express* showed what Turkey had in store for the unruly. Visa problems would restrict those travelling to Romania, and sheer cost of living those headed for Finland.

It would ordinarily be hard to foresee England finishing third or worse in such company. But these were hard times for the national side. Defeat amid rampaging yobs in France (European champions elect), was followed by another in Wales, yet another by the Soviet Union at Wembley. The tabloids were screaming for the embattled manager's head as he set off with a party depleted by call-offs for a testing summer tour of South America. Given the mood of the country, one feared what damage a rampant Brazil might inflict on English spirits.

What happened, of course, was that England triumphed 2-0 in the Maracanà, in a match illuminated by a virtuoso goal from Watford's John Barnes. With hindsight, that goal, and that match, transformed the prospects of player, manager, and team. Barnes was instantly transported to stardom, Mark Hateley, scorer of the second goal, was transported from Fratton Park (with second division Portsmouth) to the San Siro (with AC Milan), and England – the first foreign team to win in Brazil for a generation – sent tremors around the football world, not least to their forthcoming opponents in the World Cup.

*Qualifying Group 3*

**ENGLAND v FINLAND**
*Wednesday, 17 October 1984*                    *Wembley – 47,234*

The wreckage of England teams lies strewn upon September pitches. That month, so soon into the new season, encourages incohesive performances, exemplified most recently by the Denmark debacle that scuppered Robson's hopes in the European Championship. He was therefore pleased to defer

England's World Cup opener, beating East Germany 1-0 in a September friendly, and entertaining the Finns a month later when his players had started to gel. By then, Finland had secured two points from Northern Ireland, who in turn had notched an impressive 3-2 win over Romania. These results meant that England's principal challengers, the Irish and the Romanians, had dropped two points already. Victory now, in Helsinki, would poke England's noses ahead of the pack.

Finland ought not to provide an upset. They had come away empty-handed from six previous matches with England, including World Cup qualifiers in 1976, and their largely part-time team had been recently dumped at home by the Soviet Union, Poland and Mexico. One wonders whether the insight offered to his team-mates by Notts County's Aki Lahtinen could dampen Robson's assessment that Finland had the capacity neither to threaten the English goal nor defend their own.

Complacency is always an enemy. It was said that the IRA hadn't the capacity to wipe out the British government, but in the days before the match they came close, destroying much of Brighton's Grand Hotel where Margaret Thatcher and her ministers were staying during the Tory Party Conference. Four people died. The unrelated death was announced of Leonard Rossiter, popular star of *Rising Damp*. In Moscow, Anatoly Karpov and Garry Kasparov were head to head in the first of their world chess title duels. Karpov was the overwhelming favourite.

And so were England. Robson had settled on much of his team, but brought in the Southampton pair, Mark Wright and Steve Williams. The No. 9 shirt was up for grabs, having been tried by seven different players in a little over a year. After his exploits in Brazil, Mark Hateley stamped his claim ahead of ageing rivals Paul Mariner and Peter Withe. It was hoped that playing alongside Ray Wilkins in Italy would broaden Hateley's game, despite his being saddled with the sobriquet 'Attila' by the Milanese, a product of his warrior style and their unspoken 'haitches'.

In the event, the match went as expected. Wembley's smallest crowd for a World Cup fixture endured a floodlight failure beforehand, while the Finns were warming up, after which the visitors were truly extinguished. By half-time England led by two messy goals. Hateley, accompanied onto the pitch by his famous father, Tony, bundled in the first after Barnes had hit the crossbar, and Woodcock claimed the second after two defenders fluffed chances to clear.

With the game safe it was simply a matter of piling on the agony. Hateley, more Seb Coe than Attila, ran forty yards to claim England's third. Goals four and five were the fruit of lateral crosses into the box. Barnes' centre was seized upon by Bryan Robson, before substitute Mark Chamberlain, in the closing seconds, set up Kenny Sansom for his first international goal.

Longevity was the theme of the next days. Radical socialist Lord Shinwell, the oldest active peer in history, celebrated his 100th birthday, while Kenyan scientists discovered the oldest complete skeleton. It belonged to a boy aged about twelve, who lived some 1.6 million years ago.

ENGLAND  (2) 5                    FINLAND  (0) 0
  Hateley 30, 50, Woodcock 41,
  Robson 70, Sansom 88

ENGLAND: Shilton (So'ton), Duxbury (Man U) (*sub* Stevens, Spurs), Sansom (Arsenal), Williams (So'ton), Wright (So'ton), Butcher (Ipswich), Robson (Man U) (*sub* Chamberlain, Stoke), Wilkins (AC Milan), Hateley (AC Milan), Woodcock (Arsenal), Barnes (Watford).
FINLAND: Huttenen, Pekonen, Kymalainen, Lahtinen, Petaja, Haaskivi (Turunen), Houtsonen, Ukkonen, Ikalainen, Rautiainen, Valvee (Hjelm).

**TURKEY v ENGLAND**
*Wednesday, 14 November 1984*                    *Istanbul – 45,000*

Finland picked themselves up to win in Turkey, dark horses in Group 3, but followed up by losing in Belfast. Everyone had now tasted defeat, bar England, and dog was merrily eating dog.

It is one of the quirks of international football that up to November 1984 England and Turkey had never squared up. Nine years later the two countries' footballers knew every freckle, having met eight times in European or World Cup eliminators. Turkey would be the more distressed by this bizarre sequence, shipping twenty-nine goals with none returned. They would become fodder to the English lion.

But this is to see with hindsight. Indeed, Northern Ireland's recent defeat in Ankara in the European Championship suggested a rough ride in prospect. For England's manager and players this rare peep behind the Islamic Curtain represented a voyage to the unknown. Bobby Robson did not yet enjoy league postponements before key internationals. He nevertheless announced a team unchanged except at right-back and centre-forward, where injuries to Hateley and Mariner meant an unexpected recall for Peter Withe. The thirty-three year old striker was speechless, not from the shock of his selection, but from being kicked in the throat on the Saturday.

The Under-21s' sterile goalless draw on the eve of the senior match seemed only to underline the difficulties impending, and did little to forebode the coming deluge. The caption – 'slaughter' – was for the moment reserved for Ronald Reagan's presidential trouncing of Walter Mondale, and perhaps the plight of British toads. The spring carnage on the roads as these warty creatures migrated in search of ponds to spawn prompted the Department of Transport to commission 'Toads Crossing' signs to warn careless motorists. The Turks would fare no better than the toads.

In 1915-16, not too far west from Istanbul's Inonu Stadium on the banks of the Bosphorus, British forces had fallen foul of Ottoman resistance at Gallipoli. Alas, Turkey's present-day footballers hadn't the punch of her latter-day soldiers. Before the kick-off elderly cheer-leaders whipped up an already excited crowd, but the angst turned to gasps at the mere sight of Sansom's long throws, and Turkish players ran around dazed, awed out of their skins.

England scored from their first corner, courtesy of Bryan Robson at the far post, and tripled their lead by the interval, whereupon the only question facing these Saxon crusaders was whether to close down the game or hunt for double figures. Shilton hadn't so much as touched the ball for thirty minutes, and his team-mates urged to be unleashed. Before the hour they had run up four more goals, the best of them Bryan Robson's third, an exchange of passes with Wilkins ending with a contemptuous shot. John Barnes trebled his meagre pre-match tally, which stood at one (unforgettable) goal from fourteen internationals.

Minds turned to record scores. Luxembourg had lost by nine in 1960, the USA by ten in 1964. Both targets were now surpassable, but Woodcock and Withe squandered simple chances, leaving Viv Anderson to claim his first England goal, the eighth on the night.

The group table proclaimed England to have four points: in effect they had five, for their thirteen goal haul from two matches could hardly be bettered. Nevertheless, two England careers perished in Istanbul, those of Peter Withe, who to Turkish delight couldn't score, and Steve Williams, who to Robson's fury kept drifting out of position. As for Turkey's West German coach, Jupp Derwall, he was a man more relieved than shamed, for his team should have lost by a dozen and could have lost by twenty. Bobby Robson smiled: 'It is not often you score eight and feel you have let your opponents off the hook.' His players had perhaps felt charitable, capturing the spirit of Chaka Khan's No. 1 hit *I Feel for You.*

| TURKEY   (0) 0 | ENGLAND   (3) 8 |
| --- | --- |
| | Robson 15, 42, 58, Woodcock 19, 60, |
| | Barnes, 48, 55, Anderson 86 |

TURKEY: Yasur, Ismail, Yusuf, Kemal, Cem, Rasit, Mujdat, Ridvan, Ahmet, Ilyas (Hasan), Erdal.
ENGLAND: Shilton, Anderson, Sansom, Williams (Stevens, *of Spurs*), Wright, Butcher, Robson, Wilkins, Withe, Woodcock (Francis), Barnes.

## NORTHERN IRELAND v ENGLAND
*Wednesday, 27 February 1985*                    *Belfast – 28,000*

It would be three and a half months before Bobby Robson reconvened his players to prepare for the trip to Belfast's Windsor Park. By then Britain was lurching towards another economic crisis, the pound sliding inexorably towards parity with the American dollar. British eccentricity was also taking a battering. Sir Clive Sinclair's battery-powered C5 tricycle was achieving more derision than sales. It claimed its first recorded victim when a sixty-five year old woman overturned in one and broke her elbow. A sporting triumph was needed to lift spirits and Dora duly obliged. Dora was a pike measuring 4ft 1½in, a British record.

Pat Jennings was set for records of his own. This would be the Irish goalkeeper's 108th cap, equalling Bobby Moore's British total. Jennings, as always, would present a formidable last line of defence. Though England had triumphed in Belfast the previous year, the Irish had gone on to win that, the last Home Championship. They had beaten West Germany twice in the European Championship, performed famously in the last World Cup, and already accounted for the talented Romanians in this. Though drawing on a small reservoir of players and therefore vulnerable to injuries, the Irish squad was settled in manpower and tactics and unlikely to be intimidated by England or anyone else. Since Billy Bingham took charge in 1980 he had overseen just one home defeat. For all this, England had still not lost in Belfast since 1927.

That being the case, and with history firmly behind him, one might have expected a more bullish England approach. Instead, Robson candidly admitted that all things considered he would settle for a draw. His captain was out, injured. So was Mark Wright, disciplined by Southampton. Trevor Steven won a first cap and Mark Hateley, the prodigal son, returned for his seventh.

Bobby Robson may have been willing to share the spoils, but his team gobbled them all on a filthy, misty evening when the ball lived in the sky and players craned for a sight of it amid the glare of the floodlights. The Irish had the lion's share of a leonine match but their muscular attacks – spearheaded by a duo plucked from the English and Spanish second divisions – floundered against the imposing Butcher. Their best moment came when Jimmy Quinn's header from Donaghy's cross bounced off the bar. The Irish were still pressing when Hateley seized upon a belted clearance, burst clear and side-footed past Pat Jennings.

After the match, while the England party escaped through narrow, pre-dawn streets, through a whirl of fog, car bombs and flashing blue lights, sports hacks railed against the rubbish they had witnessed and the injustice of the result.

In Ulster, life and death went on. An IRA mortar attack on Newry police station the next day killed nine members of the Royal Ulster Constabulary.

NORTHERN IRELAND   (0) 0          ENGLAND   (0) 1
                                       Hateley 76


N IRELAND: Jennings (Arsenal), Nicholl (WBA), McClelland (Watford), O'Neill (Leicester), Donaghy (Luton), McIlroy (Stoke), Ramsey (Leicester), Armstrong (Real Mallorca), Stewart (QPR), Quinn (Blackb'n), Whiteside (Man U).
ENGLAND: Shilton, Anderson, Sansom, Martin, Butcher, Steven, Wilkins, Stevens (*of Spurs*), Woodcock (Francis), Hateley, Barnes.

**ROMANIA v ENGLAND**
*Wednesday, 1 May 1985*                                    *Bucharest – 70,000*

Three wins out of three. England were sitting pretty, whatever the outcome of May's potentially hazardous trips to Bucharest and Helsinki. Romania remained the outstanding threat, but with *two* nations qualifying it was hard to see who else might leapfrog over England. Turkey? Hardly. Finland? Ditto. Northern Ireland? Improbable, with two defeats already and trips to Bucharest and Wembley to come.

A 2-1 Wembley victory over the Irish Republic in March enabled Bobby Robson to blood Gary Bailey and Newcastle's Chris Waddle in the ways of international football. Having arrived, Waddle would stay, literally Robson's right-hand man, through the coming World Cup and the next.

Romania over the years promised more than they produced. Their only post-war appearance in the finals of the World Cup was in 1970, when they were undone in Guadalajara by Geoff Hurst's nutmeg. In 1974 they were denied by East Germany, in 1978 by Spain, and in 1982, improbably, by England, when set to qualify until that shock defeat by Switzerland. 1984, however, saw the Romanian national side expel Italy from the European Championship, and Dynamo Bucharest stretch Liverpool in the semi-finals of the European Cup. Bobby Robson was right to be wary: Romania had a proud post-war record against England, robbing Greenwood of three World Cup points, and losing only once, in Guadalajara.

May Day in Romania witnessed a football match. May Day in Moscow witnessed the birth of a revolution. Presidents Brezhnev, Andropov and Chernenko had died in quick succession, paving the way for a younger man, Mikhail Gorbachev, who reviewed the parade with a smile on his face and polished wife, Raisa, by his side. The fuse was lit, and Romanian President Nicolae Ceausescu's fate would soon be sealed.

With its huge terracing and leaning floodlights, the August 23rd Stadium was hardly an arena for novices, and the England manager posted an unashamedly experienced team. The afternoon match was shown live on English TV, and the viewing public saw Romania win the artistic argument but not the one that mattered. Once Bryan Robson's header had come back off the junction of post and bar England had little choice but to defend. Romania's fluid attacks were orchestrated by diminutive Gheorghe Hagi, described by Bobby Robson as one of Europe's brightest talents. The longer the match went on the more England were forced to retreat. In midfield, Robson and Wilkins were outgunned, and out wide Barnes and Steven disappeared. At one stage all five England substitutes jogged up the touchline in an effort to inspire their labouring colleagues. In a rare attack, Mariner responded by shooting feebly wide. Leicester's exciting Gary Lineker took his place, but the star of tomorrow had little chance to shine. As the match tailed away England looked to have weathered the storm. But in a trice Hagi was clear, shooting with his right foot instead of his favoured left. The bench held its breath as Shilton saved.

As in Belfast, the critics argued that England had stolen a point they scarcely deserved. But at the halfway stage in the programme, with three home fixtures to come, only a sudden storm could rock the boat to Mexico.

ROMANIA   (0) 0                          ENGLAND   (0) 0

ROMANIA: Lung, Negrila, Stefanescu, Ungureanu, Rednic, Iorgulescu (Iovan), Coras (Lacatus), Klein, Camataru, Boloni, Hagi.
ENGLAND: Shilton, Anderson, Sansom, Butcher, Wright, Wilkins, Robson, Steven, Barnes (Waddle), Mariner (Lineker), Francis.

## FINLAND v ENGLAND
*Wednesday, 22 May 1985*                              *Helsinki – 30,000*

England had to wait just twenty-one days for their next match, by which time the domestic game had been savaged by a new and ghastly tragedy. Bradford City's promotion celebrations at Valley Parade went up in smoke, along with the main stand. More than fifty people died in the inferno. Wembley duly bowed its head before the Cup Final between Everton and Manchester United, a match that provoked headlines of its own when United's Kevin Moran was sent off, the first player ever to be expelled from the Football Association's annual showpiece. Not that football's shame was confined to Britain. In far off Beijing, crowds ran amok outside the Workers' Stadium when tiny Hong Kong won 2-1 to expel China from the World Cup.

Finland's home record against England was barren. England had won by eight in 1937, on which occasion the referee had turned out in silk coat and spats, since when the Finns hadn't come within sight of so much as a draw. They were by no means out of contention in Group 3, but needed to prosper from back-to-back home games against England and Romania to keep their hopes alive.

It is one of football's mysteries that a five-goal thumping counts for nothing on the next meeting. In front of Finland's largest ever crowd, the hosts unleashed an opening salvo that threatened to sweep England into the Baltic. The recalled Fenwick struggled early on to acclimatise with Butcher, and the whole team took time to acclimatise to the chilly conditions. When Shilton nudged Lipponen's header against the bar, the giant Rantanen, who towered even above Butcher, was swiftest to react to put his team in front. The Finns might have doubled their lead when Lipponen struck the ball past the advancing goalkeeper. On this occasion Butcher intervened with a desperate clearance.

Though Finland's surge was soon spent, it took England till the fiftieth minute to equalise. To Trevor Francis fell most of the frittered chances, before Anderson's precise pass found Hateley, who, half-stumbling, lifted the ball wide of the sprawling Huttunen. Finland, ever abrasive, mixed it to the end, hanging on to secure their first ever draw against England. Viewed against history, it was a wretched result for Bobby Robson. Viewed against Group 3, it was a handsome point won.

The players returned home to join the great debate. Now that Britain's first professor of parapsychology had been appointed, would science soon get to the bottom of poltergeists and things that went bump in the night?

| FINLAND (1) 1 | ENGLAND (0) 1 |
|---|---|
| Rantanen 7 | Hateley 50 |

FINLAND: Huttunen, Lahtinen (Petaja), Kyrnalainen, Ikalainen, Nieminen, Turunen, Houtsonen, Ukkonen (Hjelm), Lipponen, Rautiainen, Rantanen.
ENGLAND: Shilton, Anderson, Sansom, Fenwick, Butcher, Steven (Waddle), Wilkins, Robson, Francis, Hateley, Barnes.

On the following Saturday England lost 0-1 to Scotland at Hampden Park, provoking a fresh crusade against Bobby Robson from a couple of tabloids. He was able to turn his back by flying out with his players for an acclimatising summer tournament in Mexico.

It was clustered round a television set in Mexico City that the England party learned of the shocking happenings inside the Heysel Stadium in Brussels, where Liverpool were due to play Juventus. The screen had blanked out, and it took worried phone calls home for the grisly truth to unfurl.

For Bobby Robson and the mandarins of the Football Association, it was clear that the fall-out from the tragedy might extend to an international ban on English clubs. The arguments against their continued participation in Europe had been vociferous even before Heysel. Now, as the world rushed to condemn the English and their animal supporters, the England national team, too, suddenly found itself on the brink of exile. Though Robson's players had virtually guaranteed their place in Mexico, that place was suddenly hanging by a thread. With grim irony, England were set to face Italy in their opening Mexican fixture. That, too, was momentarily in doubt. Never was the ambassadorial aspect of the England manager's job so paramount as in the days to come.

Fortunately the need to build bridges overcame baser instincts. The tour went ahead, the England players under almost intolerable strain, for the mildest foul might invoke the severest sanction. Defeats by Italy and Mexico were cancelled out by victories over West Germany and, in Los Angeles, the United States. By then, an indefinite club ban had been announced. Everton would be unable to compete in the European Cup, nor Manchester United the Cup-Winners' Cup. For the time being, the national side was spared.

## ENGLAND v ROMANIA
*Wednesday, 11 September 1985*                    *Wembley – 59,500*

A new season. New hopes, new fears. An unseeded seventeen-year-old German tennis genius, Boris Becker, had won Wimbledon, and Wembley Stadium had been packed to the rafters for Live Aid's concert for the relief of Ethiopian suffering. The *Titanic* had been discovered in the Atlantic's icy depths, while in the shallower waters of Loch Ness, a Wellington bomber that crashed in 1940 was raised to the surface. A gripping Nat West cricket final at Lords saw Essex beat Notts on the final ball. The Handsworth district of Birmingham witnessed pitched battles between police and rioters. At the final whistle of Scotland's World Cup eliminator in Cardiff, Jock Stein collapsed and died. British football mourned afresh.

Bobby Robson had hoped to turn the Heysel ban to advantage. With leading clubs having fewer demands, more time could be spent preparing for World Cup-ties and other internationals. Instead, new domestic cup competitions were hurriedly introduced to compensate for the shortfall in gate receipts. Disparaged by most supporters as 'Mickey-Mouse' competitions, they did little for the image of the game, or the standing of the national side.

Fortunately, these disruptions came too late to affect England's chances of reaching Mexico. Two more points would guarantee qualification. If England didn't pick them up against Romania, they would surely against Turkey. Bobby Robson brought in Everton's Peter Reid in place of Wilkins with instructions to tag Romanian playmaker Boloni. Glenn Hoddle was picked for the sixth time on the trot, his longest run in the national side.

Romania had drawn on both their previous visits to Wembley and were far from overawed. One flowing attack culminated with Hagi striking Shilton's crossbar from long range. Yet it was England who claimed a half-time lead.

From a free-kick, Hoddle, architect of everything England created, drifted into space from a free-kick to swivel and bend the ball past Lung. That lead might have been cancelled on the stroke of half-time; with only Shilton to beat the Romanians struck wood again.

Few begrudged Romania's second-half equaliser, as Camataru fended off two defenders to score. Thereafter the game deteriorated. The visitors had the point they wanted, but might yet have left empty-handed had Barnes' late effort not been disallowed.

It was the Romanians who were *Dancing in the Street* – as Jagger and Bowie trilled from the top of the charts – when learning that Northern Ireland had merely drawn in Izmir, handing the Turks their one and only point in Group 3. For their part, the Irish had been praying for an English victory. They appeared now to have blown their chances, having to conclude their campaign with daunting trips to Bucharest and Wembley.

| ENGLAND (1) 1 | ROMANIA (0) 1 |
|---|---|
| Hoddle 23 | Camataru 58 |

ENGLAND: Shilton, Stevens, Sansom, Hoddle, Wright, Fenwick, Robson, Reid, Hateley, Lineker (Woodcock), Waddle (Barnes).
ROMANIA: Lung, Negrila, Stefanescu, Ungureanu, Rednic, Iovan, Coras (Gabor), Klein (Mateut), Camataru, Boloni, Hagi.

**ENGLAND v TURKEY**
*Wednesday, 16 October 1985*                                   *Wembley – 52,500*

England trooped off against Romania still needing one more point. They trooped out against Turkey needing nothing, for Northern Ireland's heroic victory in Bucharest earlier that same day meant that Romania (barring a double-digit victory in Turkey in their final match) could no longer overtake England.

In the meantime, the World Cup itself had been thrown briefly into doubt. Mexico City had been racked by an earthquake that killed thousands but not the country's determination to stage the tournament as planned. Hollywood mourned the loss of Orson Welles and Rock Hudson, the latter the first celebrated victim of AIDS. The latest Middle Eastern crisis saw Palestinian terrorists board the Italian cruise ship *Achille Lauro* and toss overboard a wheelchair-bound cripple. Tottenham was the scene of England's most recent urban rioting, during which PC Keith Blakelock was hacked to death.

Turkey must have been grateful that England were now playing for pride and not points, for otherwise there is no knowing what damage might have been inflicted on them. The nightmare of Istanbul clearly still pained, for the

Turkish team showed seven changes. Not that this was likely to discomfit Peter Shilton, about to snatch the first of many records to come his way. He was winning his seventy-fourth cap, overtaking the goalkeeping record held by his predecessor, Gordon Banks.

Shilton could not have spent a more relaxing evening. Facing an England team playing in an unfamiliar all red strip, Turkey found themselves five down after fifty minutes. Chris Waddle bagged his first international goal (after drifting past two defenders), and Gary Lineker helped himself to his first England hat-trick (including two headers from Stevens' crosses). A massacre was in the offing.

But, as in Istanbul, England failed to turn the screw against prostrate opponents. Indeed, Bobby Robson hurried from the pitch at the end wearing a frown. His captain, having claimed his customary goal, had wrenched a hamstring so severely its effects would still bother him in Mexico eight months hence. Bryan Robson's early departure robbed England of their driving force, after which they floundered, rarely threatening a sixth goal, never mind a tenth. The crowd, starting to cheer, stayed to boo.

Afterwards, the talk was of bans. The House of Lords ruled against Mrs Victoria Gillick. This mother of ten children had long campaigned to ban GPs prescribing the pill to under-sixteens without parental consent. The Football Association cheered the news that the England national team had escaped a threatened ban from the 1988 European Championship.

ENGLAND  (4) 5                    TURKEY  (0) 0
   Waddle 14, Lineker 17, 40, 50,
   Robson 34

ENGLAND: Shilton, Stevens, Sansom, Hoddle, Wright, Fenwick, Robson (Steven), Wilkins, Hateley (Woodcock), Lineker, Waddle.
TURKEY: Yasur, Ismail, Yusuf (Rasit), Sedit, Abdulkerin, Huseyir, Mujdat, Senol, Hasan, Unal, Selcuk.

## ENGLAND v NORTHERN IRELAND
*Wednesday, 13 November 1985*                    *Wembley – 70,500*

The i's were dotted and the t's crossed. The visit of Northern Ireland was meaningless from England's point of view, an unnecessary aggravation. That such a healthy crowd should descend on Wembley for a non-event was down to the feasibility of sabotage. Having snubbed their noses at England's own feeble efforts by beating Romania twice, Northern Ireland were also poised to qualify – provided they avoided defeat at Wembley. That same night Romania were playing in Turkey, where it was safe to presume an away victory.

It was lost on no one that such a scenario smacked of collusion. No amount of denials from high places would convince Mircea Lucescu, former skipper, now coach of the Romanian team, that fraternal Britishness would not coax the Irish through. *The Power of Love* was the name of the game, as of the chart-topper by Jennifer Rush.

Surprise, surprise, the game ended goalless. The Irish fought for everything but created nothing. The English fought for little but created enough. The first half an hour was Mogadon stuff. Pat Jennings, winning his 113th cap (despite being dropped on his return to Spurs), had become the most capped goalkeeper in world football. He kept out what apologetic efforts came his way. Hoddle tried his luck with one curler, which Jennings flicked away. Before the final whistle news came through that Romania had won as expected in Turkey. Ireland needed to hang on a little longer. They would have failed to do so had Kerry Dixon, playing his first Wembley international and with his family cheering him on, not squandered two chances. The first required a tip-over from Jennings, the second – the simplest tap-in – a hole for Dixon to hide in.

Chants of 'What a load of rubbish' were switched to cries of 'fix'. The FIFA representative present was satisfied with the outcome, but was Kerry Dixon? Afterwards he was the toast of Ulster. Paul Bracewell, replacing Bryan Robson, would also look back on the match with mixed feelings. A later, dreadful, injury meant this would be his last cap.

For the moment, however, he and his team-mates could relax in the bath, chatting happily about the revolution in crime detection promised by genetic fingerprinting, about Garry Kasparov, at twenty-two the youngest ever world chess champion, and about Terry Waite, who had flown to Beirut to free some hostages. On this occasion he would come back.

The players turned a deaf ear to the press. Despite the flak, England had qualified in a canter and remained unbeaten, the only European team to post such an achievement. Two British sides were now through to Mexico. The other two, Scotland and Wales, were likewise fighting it out in the same group. Scotland would in due course overcome Australia in the play-offs to become the twenty-fourth and final nation to qualify.

ENGLAND  (0) 0                    NORTHERN IRELAND  (0) 0

ENGLAND: Shilton, Stevens, Sansom, Hoddle, Wright, Fenwick, Bracewell, Wilkins, Dixon, Lineker, Waddle.
N IRELAND: Jennings (Spurs), Nicholl (WBA), Donaghy (Luton), O'Neill (Leicester), McDonald (QPR), McCreery (Newcastle), Penney (Brighton) (*sub* Armstrong, WBA), McIlroy (Man C), Quinn (Blackburn), Whiteside (Man U), Stewart (Newcastle) (*sub* Worthington, Sheff W).

*Qualifying Group 3*

| | | | Home | | | | Away | | | | |
|---|---|---|---|---|---|---|---|---|---|---|---|
| | P | W | D | L | F | A | W | D | L | F | A | Pts |
| ENGLAND | 8 | 2 | 2 | 0 | 11 | 1 | 2 | 2 | 0 | 10 | 1 | 12 |
| N IRELAND | 8 | 3 | 0 | 1 | 7 | 4 | 1 | 2 | 1 | 1 | 1 | 10 |
| Romania | 8 | 2 | 1 | 1 | 5 | 1 | 1 | 2 | 1 | 7 | 6 | 9 |
| Finland | 8 | 2 | 2 | 0 | 4 | 2 | 1 | 0 | 3 | 3 | 10 | 8 |
| Turkey | 8 | 0 | 1 | 3 | 2 | 13 | 0 | 0 | 4 | 0 | 11 | 1 |

*Other groups results*

| | | | |
|---|---|---|---|
| Finland v N Ireland | 1-0 | Finland v Romania | 1-1 |
| N Ireland v Romania | 3-2 | Romania v Finland | 2-0 |
| Turkey v Finland | 1-2 | Turkey v N Ireland | 0-0 |
| N Ireland v Finland | 2-1 | Finland v Turkey | 1-0 |
| Romania v Turkey | 3-0 | Romania v N Ireland | 0-1 |
| N Ireland v Turkey | 2-0 | Turkey v Romania | 1-3 |

## World Cup finals – MEXICO                    May-June 1986

By the time the finals came around, high-tech, superpower explosions had hijacked our television screens. The first blew up the space shuttle Challenger, with its civilian school-teacher aboard. The second blew the top off a nuclear reactor at Chernobyl in the Ukraine, spewing radio-active fall-out across much of Europe. Even as the World Cup finals got under way, lambs in Cumbria and elsewhere were being slaughtered for their high radiation levels. The biggest political explosion occurred in the Philippines, prompting the dramatic flight from the country of Ferdinand and Imelda Marcos, and the installation as president of Corazon Aquino.

The 1986 World Cup, following the precedent established in Spain, would comprise twenty-four teams. The only change in format saw the demise of Spain's dreary second-round group system, which among other sins had sent England home unbeaten. This was scrapped and replaced by an extra round of knock-out ties to precede the quarter-finals. With excruciating logic, sixteen of the original twenty-four teams would progress, the top two from each group, plus four of the third-placed teams. Put another way, just the six wooden-spoonists and two others would be sent packing after the group rounds.

Either way, Mexico's second World Cup would be greatly inflated compared with her first – twenty-four teams instead of sixteen, fifty-two matches compared with thirty-two, spread over six groups instead of four. This expansion would incorporate several venues unused in 1970, among them the city of Monterrey to the north. Whereas all other centres were located in the high central belt, Monterrey stood at just 1,700 feet and boiled, whereas the higher cities merely simmered. Teams surviving the Monterrey furnace then faced the extra hazard of moving to higher altitudes for the later stages.

1986 remains the only World Cup in which England were excluded from the batch of top seeds. The chosen few were named as: Mexico (hosts), Italy (holders), West Germany (beaten finalists in 1982), France and Poland (beaten semi-finalists), and Brazil (because they were Brazil).

England's exclusion from the seeding list meant that Bobby Robson had no idea where his team would be based. The grapevine, however, had for weeks been peddling the rumour that for security reasons they would be banished to the northern outpost of Monterrey, worst of all possibilities. In fact, not till the draw itself did England's fate become clear, by which time Monterrey in the blink of an eye had transformed from hell to heaven. With just two names left in the bowl – Uruguay and England – one would end up in Group E with the daunting trio of West Germany, Scotland and Denmark. The fearsome Danes, one of Europe's strongest sides, found themselves classified as 'minnows' on account of these being their first finals. The other team would be posted to Group F, Monterrey, in the company of the more congenial Poland, Portugal and Morocco. Of a sudden, Monterrey had lost its terrors, and sighs of relief accompanied the announcement of Uruguay's destination in Group E. England, last out of the bag, were thrown into the hottest, yet weakest, group of all.

In 1970, Alf Ramsey had made the mistake of basing his players in a city-centre hotel, whose peaceful nights were easily wrecked by revellers and agitators. In the search for tranquillity *and* altitude – in case they progressed to the knock-out rounds – England based themselves fifty miles outside Monterrey in Saltillo, high in the Sierra Madre, some 5,000 feet above sea level. All three of England's matches would kick off at 4 p.m. (11 p.m. in Britain), avoiding the noon kick-offs elsewhere, while creating a nation of nocturnal sports-lovers back home. Monterrey boasted two World Cup stadia. England would play their first two fixtures in the Tecnológico Stadium, their last, against Poland, in the larger and better-equipped Universitario.

Diplomacy required that the FA proclaim Monterrey's delights to the world, though even Mexicans knew it for a flat, grimy, industrial city of three million inhabitants, beating to the drum of the United States, just one hundred miles to the north. Monterrey was the least Mexican of Mexican cities. Its citizens, for their part, were less than ecstatic about their English visitors. Local newspapers splashed the insults 'animales' and 'hooligans' across their front pages.

Bobby Robson filled the half-year between qualifiers and finals with the friendliest of friendlies. Wins in Egypt and Israel were followed by victories against four fellow World Cup finalists – the Soviet Union, Scotland, Mexico, and Canada. Six successive wins was just one short of the English record, set in 1966. All told, England's unbeaten run now stretched to eleven matches. Some notable scalps had been seized: England had become the first team to score, never mind win in the Soviet Union for six years. That win paired Lineker and Peter Beardsley for the first time, yet was accomplished without the supposedly irreplaceable Bryan Robson. This combination of players, though far from the manager's ideal, would later reassemble to striking effect.

The England party would acclimatise in the American Rockies. Some flew out bearing the scars of the season's climax. Bobby Robson and Terry Butcher were depressed by Ipswich's relegation, West Ham's Alvin Martin by missing out on the championship. The four-man Everton contingent, whose departure was delayed by the FA Cup Final with Liverpool, arrived in Colorado Springs even more miserable, having ended up with nothing after chasing the league and cup double.

In total, Bobby Robson had experimented with sixty-one players. Just twenty-two of these remained available or in favour. These he announced prior to leaving Britain, and before the friendlies against Mexico and Canada.

| No | Name | Position | Club | Age | Caps | Goals |
|----|------|----------|------|-----|------|-------|
| 1 | Peter Shilton | Goalkeeper | Southampton | 36 | 79 | – |
| 2 | M Gary Stevens | Full-back | Everton | 23 | 8 | – |
| 3 | Kenny Sansom | Full-back | Arsenal | 27 | 63 | 1 |
| 4 | Glenn Hoddle | Midfield | Tottenham | 28 | 31 | 8 |
| 5 | Alvin Martin | Central defence | West Ham | 27 | 14 | – |
| 6 | Terry Butcher | Central defence | Ipswich | 27 | 38 | 3 |
| 7 | Bryan Robson (c) | Midfield | Manchester U | 29 | 50 | 17 |
| 8 | Ray Wilkins | Midfield | AC Milan | 29 | 78 | 3 |
| 9 | Mark Hateley | Forward | AC Milan | 24 | 16 | 6 |
| 10 | Gary Lineker | Forward | Everton | 25 | 12 | 6 |
| 11 | Chris Waddle | Forward | Tottenham | 25 | 14 | 2 |
| 12 | Viv Anderson † | Full-back | Arsenal | 29 | 20 | 1 |
| 13 | Chris Woods | Goalkeeper | Norwich | 26 | 3 | – |
| 14 | Terry Fenwick | Central defence | QPR | 26 | 14 | – |
| 15 | Gary A Stevens | Defence/Midfield | Tottenham | 24 | 4 | – |
| 16 | Peter Reid | Midfield | Everton | 29 | 5 | – |
| 17 | Trevor Steven | Midfield | Everton | 22 | 9 | 3 |
| 18 | Steve Hodge | Midfield | Aston Villa | 23 | 2 | – |
| 19 | John Barnes | Forward | Watford | 22 | 25 | 3 |
| 20 | Peter Beardsley | Forward | Newcastle | 25 | 3 | – |
| 21 | Kerry Dixon | Forward | Chelsea | 24 | 5 | 4 |
| 22 | Gary Bailey * | Goalkeeper | Manchester U | 27 | 2 | – |

* Would not play in the finals or in future.          *Averages*    26.2  22.5

† Viv Anderson had the misfortune to be named in the World Cup final squads in both 1982 and 1986, but never took the field.

---

Players on stand-by until the FIFA deadline of 23 May were: Martin Hodge (Sheff W), Dave Watson (Norwich), Paul Bracewell (Everton), Stewart Robson (Arsenal), Trevor Francis (Sampdoria), and Mick Harford (Luton).

This final list embraced some newish faces, while omitting established names prominent in the qualifiers. Up front, Tony Woodcock had fallen victim to illness and injury, and Trevor Francis had failed to recover in time from a fractured cheekbone. He had scored just once in an injury-interrupted season with Sampdoria, and was in any case, at thirty-two, probably too old to function as a front-line striker in the heat of Mexico. Southampton's Mark Wright had been first choice to partner Terry Butcher in defence until breaking a leg in an FA Cup semi-final. Paul Bracewell's role as understudy to Bryan Robson was claimed by Steve Hodge. Though Alf Ramsey had dispensed with wingers, and Ron Greenwood unexpectedly followed suit, Robson had persevered. To keep faith with his favoured 4-3-3 formation, he took along two wide men, John Barnes and Chris Waddle. When two 'Gary Stevens' were listed in the squad FIFA presumed a clerical error; that England would arrive one player short and unable to call up another.

The backbone of Robson's team picked itself, injuries permitting. Peter Shilton, now thirty-six, had joined Southampton for a bargain £250,000 after the 1982 World Cup. Four years later his place was still not seriously challenged. The same could be said of Kenny Sansom at left-back, to the extent that Robson had brought along no cover. Terry Butcher was in his prime, strong and powerful, but more vulnerable without the nifty Wright alongside him. In midfield, Bryan Robson and Ray Wilkins would be automatic starters. Wilkins, the vice-captain, had progressed in Italian football into the classic anchorman, always involved, a natural 'getter and giver'. But doubts remained over his compatibility with Glenn Hoddle, Tottenham's super-talented creator. Hoddle was enjoying an extended run in the England team, but he and Wilkins rarely gelled. Hoddle's passing ability, his shooting prowess, particularly from set pieces, and his almost feline grace when moving forward had long set 'Glenda' in a class apart. Hoddle's was a languid, long-passing style. He had a tendency to fade out of matches and besides, his speciality, long balls designed to drop beyond defenders for the front runners to chase, was hardly suited to the tactics appropriate to Mexico. The last time England had built a World Cup team around a long-pass specialist was in the era of Johnny Haynes. Such teams were fragile: cut out the key man and the side was impotent.

In Bryan Robson, England now boasted a player of awesome gifts, who motored inexhaustibly, tackled like a demon, and scored goals in the manner of a super-striker. He was the probably the closest England had ever come to producing the perfect player. At twenty-nine, he should have been in his prime. Unfortunately, he exuded such foolhardy courage on the pitch that he had become worryingly vulnerable to injury. Knocks, strains, breaks, Robson had had them all. He had missed half the season with Manchester United, and flew out with England having weakened his shoulder through dislocation. Only an operation could guarantee to prevent a repetition, but United manager Ron Atkinson insisted that surgery take place after the World Cup, not before, while the club were chasing titles and cups. Cruelly, the player dislocated the shoulder again, in Los Angeles, against Mexico. The joint was now so weakened it was liable to pop out again at any time. With 'Captain Marvel' cosseted in a shoulder harness, he proceeded to aggravate his old hamstring injury, preventing serious training. Bobby Robson had to face a critical decision. Should he play his namesake for his psychological impact, though not fully fit, or leave him out from the start? If the latter, the whole team would have to be remodelled, stiffened in midfield, probably at the expense of a winger. With no winger, there need be no Mark Hateley to feed off non-existent crosses. Understandably, rather than pull his team to pieces, the elder Robson banked on the fitness of the younger.

Hateley, himself, had undergone knee surgery, and needed to prove himself. His likely partner, Gary Lineker, entered the 1986 World Cup with a reputation as a rabbit-killer – scoring freely against Turkey and the United States – not yet a lion-slayer. In domestic football, he had transformed himself from a promising striker with Leicester to a prolific one with Everton. His forty goals in one season had earned him both the football writers' and the professional footballers' Player of the Year award, and had quadrupled his transfer value. Barcelona were rumoured to be eyeing him keenly. He had been introduced gently to the senior team by Bobby Robson and was still an international novice. Nevertheless, with his blistering pace in the box, he was a key weapon. Any injury to Gary Lineker would have been an injury to England.

So it was that during England's final friendly against Canada, in Vancouver, Lineker landed badly on his right wrist and feared a break. Luckily it was only a sprain, which could be protected by strapping. First Bryan Robson's shoulder, then Gary Lineker's wrist, finally Vernon Edwards' heart. The long-standing England team doctor was taken ill shortly before the match with Portugal. He was soon flown home, to be replaced by Arsenal's physician, John Crane.

## PORTUGAL v ENGLAND
*Tuesday, 3 June 1986*                    *Tecnológico Stadium, Monterrey – 23,000*

For historians of English football, Portugal are synonymous with that rip-roaring Wembley semi-final in 1966. That match, in fact, stands as the pinnacle of Portugal's accomplishment. Though Benfica remain a mighty name on the club scene, and rivals Porto would lift the European Cup in 1987, the national side was prone to under-achievement. They hadn't even reached the World Cup finals since 1966. That they did so now was credited to one extraordinary result. Portugal looked dead and buried as they travelled to face West Germany in their final match in Group 2. The records show that Portugal won 1-0, to this day West Germany's only home defeat in the World Cup in forty years. Even that shocker would have failed to save Portugal had not Sweden, their minds on Mexico, gone down in Czechoslovakia that same night.

Portugal had been more impressive during the European Championship. With England sidelined, they had woven a pretty path to the semi-finals, where they were six minutes from beating France, the eventual winners.

Though England had only lost once – in 1955 – to Portugal in fourteen meetings, the post-1966 record was nothing to brag about, one win and three draws, two of them in the 1976 European Championship. These had been low scoring affairs, but Portugal's worry nowadays was the defence, likely to spring a leak at any time. The team was coached by José Torres, Eusébio's towering sidekick from 1966. They were not a happy crew, judging from mutinous protests about their puny perks. The Portuguese FA called their bluff, asking FIFA to permit twenty-two reserves to be flown out. President Soares publicly intervened, reminding his players that Portugal expected each man to do his duty. The strike melted away.

Few of Portugal's players were household names. Bento, in goal, seemed to have been around forever, though unlike other long-life keepers – Shilton, Jennings, Zoff – was rated coolly by outsiders. Pacheco looked accomplished in midfield, and Fernando Gomes, twice Europe's leading goalscorer in recent years, was billed optimistically as the new Eusébio. He, and fellow striker Futre, played for Porto, and would contest first-team slots with Carlos Manuel, scorer of the vital goal against West Germany.

Torres' opposite number gambled on his strongest team, including Lineker and Robson, though as an eleven they had never played together before. Alongside Butcher, Robson preferred Terry Fenwick, an all-purpose defender, to Mark Wright's obvious replacement, Alvin Martin.

Monterrey had been cloudy for days. It had been cloudy for Poland's insipid goalless draw with Morocco, the ideal result for England, and remained overcast as the armed escort accompanying the England team-coach whizzed through Monterrey's cordoned off streets to the stadium. But already the clouds were lifting. By kick-off time, the sun was burning with a vengeance. Back home, in a Britain racked by the Wapping print dispute, viewers settled expectantly. Millions had been gripped by the dramatisation of Jeffrey Archer's *Kane and Abel*, and were trusting that the technical gremlins affecting World Cup transmission around the globe would steer clear.

Carlos Manuel has just scored Portugal's winner. (v Portugal)

Video replays of the first seventy-five minutes of the match show England comfortably in control, on a pitch with grass too long and a under a sun too bright. England's attacks were patient and measured. Had Hateley not spurned a half-volley in the first half, and had Gary Lineker – who overcame an attack of nausea just before kick-off – converted either of two chances early in the second, all might have ended well. But these are 'ifs' and 'buts'. Instead, the game ended in bitterness and shattering disillusion. Peter Shilton was just fifteen minutes from keeping a clean sheet in the finals for five consecutive matches, a World Cup record, when Portugal scored from their first direct attack. They were abetted by Sansom's gauche tackle on Diamantino, whom he might have shepherded out of harm's way. Instead, the ball rebounded inside the full-back to Diamantino's feet. Butcher froze in disbelief, and Fenwick and Stevens were nowhere as Carlos Manuel swept in at the far post.

The remaining minutes passed in a nightmarish blur. Bryan Robson, having hardly trained for days, trudged off to be replaced by Steve Hodge, and Waddle swapped places with Beardsley. It made no difference. Futre bamboozled Fenwick, who felled him without penalty, and the same player forced a sharp save from Shilton.

So England, losing by one, might have lost by three. They committed twenty-three fouls to Portugal's eight, and had both central defenders, Fenwick and Butcher, booked at the close by West German referee Volker Roth.

Several proud records had been shredded. England had lost their first match in twelve, their first in a year, and their first World Cup game, including qualifiers, in fifteen – since the debacle in Norway in 1981. In Lisbon, motorists banged their horns deep into the night. But their moment had come – and gone. Goalkeeper Bento would break his leg in training and Portugal would lose their next two games.

| PORTUGAL (0) 1 | ENGLAND (0) 0 |
| Carlos Manuel 75 | |

PORTUGAL: Bento, Álvaro, Frederico, Oliveira, Inacio, Diamantino (José Antonio), Pacheco, André, Sousa, Carlos Manuel, Gomes (Futre).
ENGLAND: Shilton, Stevens (*of Everton*), Fenwick, Butcher, Sansom, Hoddle, Robson (Hodge), Wilkins, Waddle (Beardsley), Hateley, Lineker.

## MOROCCO v ENGLAND

*Friday, 6 June 1986*                    *Tecnológico Stadium, Monterrey – 20,200*

Damaging as the defeat was to England's morale, better it came in the finals of the 1986 World Cup than in any of its predecessors. Losing the first group match had traditionally proved a stiff handicap to advancement. But the new format – sixteen teams going through – reduced the pressure. Teams would now stay alive even if losing their first *two* games.

For Bobby Robson the question was clear-cut. Did he send out the same team, as merited by the first hour and a quarter against Portugal, or did he tear it up, as warranted by that desperate closing fifteen minutes. In his heart, the manager knew all along he needed to keep faith. A good team did not become a bad one overnight, as they say. Despite his captain's troublesome hamstring, Bryan Robson was desperate to play, and so was his manager. Above all, Bobby Robson did not wish to send out panic messages to his opponents. Wholesale changes would do just that. The team would stay intact.

However much respect was granted Morocco, there can be no disguising the fact that England expected to win this one. Morocco had appeared in the finals only once before, in Mexico no less, when in their first game they had taken an audacious lead against West Germany, before losing 1-2. It was part of World Cup wisdom that lesser nations traditionally inflict their damage in their first match, as Morocco had just illustrated against Poland, and that their powder was now spent.

England had never previously faced Morocco, nor, come to that, any African nation – other than Egypt, whom Morocco put out of the African qualifiers. With the present match in mind, England had excursioned to Cairo in January and won 4-0. Under the guidance of Brazilian coach Faria, the current Moroccan side had reached the finals of the African Nations Cup, the Pan-Arab Games, and now the World Cup. They could call upon at least one estimable player, Mohammed Timoumi, former African Player of the Year, while Ezaki Badou – guardian of Moroccan goalmouths one hundred times, so he claimed – had lost just one goal in the African qualifiers. Buoyed by their draw with seeded Poland, Morocco received a further fillip when neighbours Algeria scared the life out of Brazil, though losing 0-1. So adept was the Algerian performance that Bobby Robson privately wished he had not permitted his players to view it.

Determined to disarm their critics, an unchanged England team took the field, only to scatter to the winds their last vestige of credibility. They began tentatively and steadily degenerated. In temperatures disagreeably hot even for Africans, Morocco looked more comfortable by the minute. Though they never threatened, neither did England, and for Bobby Robson the interval could not come quickly enough. That opportunity to rethink and regroup was still seven minutes distant when the world caved in on the England manager. Bryan Robson cartwheeled in the Moroccan penalty area, landed on the point of his elbow, and bang went his shoulder. Though it was quickly relocated, there could be no question of Robson carrying on. Steve Hodge took his place and Ray Wilkins his mantle. The England captain was still trudging disconsolately away when his deputy grappled with Timoumi and was cautioned by Paraguayan referee Gabriel Gonzalez. Moments later, near the site of Robson's mishap, Wilkins considered himself fouled, only to be penalised for offside. In a moment's frustration that would forever haunt him, Wilkins hurled the ball down. It bounced against the referee's leg and the red card was flourished. Never previously dismissed in his life, Wilkins had become the first England player ever to be sent off in the World Cup finals. His team were now shorn of both captain and vice-captain, and little wonder Wilkins buried his face in his shirt. Should England now be eliminated, as seemed probable, he would have nowhere to hide. The FA, furthermore, had warned of an early flight home for any player heaping disgrace on the national team. That threat, at least, proved hollow. Wilkins stayed in Mexico. Back on the pitch, Peter Shilton became England's third captain in two minutes.

England had been second best even with eleven men. Down to ten, the second half threatened a humiliation. Bobby Robson's pre-match target of two points was instantly halved. But whatever was said at half-time in the Moroccan dressing room, it could not have been 'go and take them apart'. England, it seemed, would be saved by their reputation. Unable to countenance a momentous victory, Morocco threw adventure to the wind.

Tottenham's Gary Stevens came on to partner Everton's: he replaced Mark Hateley who, having earned a yellow card was charging around looking for a red. Glenn Hoddle, promoted in midfield from trooper to general, orchestrated the second half as he had never done the first. All around him, white shirts rolled up their sleeves, earning their draw with an ease no depleted team had a right to expect.

MOROCCO  (0) 0                    ENGLAND  (0) 0

MOROCCO: Zaki, Khalifi, El Biaz, Bouyahyaouni, Lamriss (Oudani), Dolmy, Mustapha Merry (Souleymani), Bouderbala, Timoumi, Khairi, Krimau.
ENGLAND: Shilton, Stevens (*of Everton*), Fenwick, Butcher, Sansom, Hoddle, Robson (Hodge), Wilkins, Hateley (Stevens, *of Spurs*), Lineker, Waddle.

## POLAND v ENGLAND
*Wednesday, 11 June 1986*            *Universitario Stadium, Monterrey – 22,700*

Doomsday merchants beat the drum of England's demise. In terms of performance, they had a point; in terms of arithmetic, they did not. Despite the gloom, all that had really happened was that, for England, the knock-out stages had come one match sooner than expected. Poland had beaten Portugal 1-0. All four teams could still finish in any position. Victory over Poland would see England through to the second round – though should a 1-0 victory accompany a scoring draw between Portugal and Morocco, then lots would be cast. Nor would a draw with Poland necessarily close the curtain. In that case, a two-goal win for either Portugal or Morocco would dump the losers to the bottom of the pile and send England through in third place. Both matches, as with the final games in all groups, would kick-off simultaneously to avoid dead contests and allegations of fixing. Not that the long-suffering people of Monterrey cared much. With two measly goals from four matches, Group F was disparaged as the 'Group of Sleep'. It was virtually ignored by the world's sporting press, dismissed as a footballing backwater dragging its heels to its own dreary tune.

Be that as it may, the 'reward' for topping Group F was to stay in Monterrey to play the runners up in Group E (Denmark or West Germany). Those finishing second would head for Mexico City's Aztec Stadium to face the runners-up in Group B (now known to be Paraguay). Identifying the opponents of the side finishing third required a mastery of star-gazing and FIFA's arithmetic tables.

Though Robson and Co. were busily computing the possibilities, the main task was somehow to field a team equipped and fired up to win. Poland's victory over Portugal – belated revenge for twin defeats in the European Championship – was scarcely merited and scarcely welcomed by Robson. He had hoped that Poland would lose, forcing them to come out and attack England.

Gary Lineker sweeps the ball over Mlynarczyk for England's first. (v Poland)

In the same way that Portugal will always be identified with 1966, so Poland are irrevocably tainted with the events of Wembley 1973, when their divinely assisted draw put England out of the finals and Poland into their first since the war. Poland had finished third, four years later they also reached the last eight, and in 1982 had finished third again. This was an impressive pedigree. Now coached by Anton Piechniczek, Poland qualified for Mexico top of their group, ahead of Belgium, and their squad was not short of star names, Zmuda in defence, young Dziekanowski – later to play for Celtic, and Roma's lightning-fast, flame-haired Zbigniew Boniek, who had helped Juventus beat Liverpool in the ill-fated 1985 European Cup Final. Despite the quality at their disposal, Poland's first two matches in Group F exhibited an emphasis on defence.

Behind the closed doors of England's retreat at Saltillo, the atmosphere was thick with protest and frustration. Players apparently hit out at the tactics being foisted upon them. Dare the manager send out the same team – Wilkins apart – for a third time? (Wilkins was automatically banned for one game, but FIFA doubled the punishment for 'abusing the referee'.) Bryan Robson pronounced himself fit and eager to play, though Manchester United were pleading for his immediate return home. They wanted him operated upon and fit for the new season. But playing Robson meant keeping Steve Hodge in reserve on the bench, in case Robson broke down, denying England wider tactical options.

To his credit, Bobby Robson did not flinch. His captain was dropped; so was Mark Hateley, whose bruising English style was impotent in the context of a World Cup; so was Chris Waddle, whose infrequent crosses now had no target. The manager's preferred three-man midfield could only function when shored up by Bryan Robson and Ray Wilkins. Without them, it was back to 4-4-2. Hodge, Peter Reid and Trevor Steven were drafted in to stiffen the midfield around Hoddle, and Peter Beardsley teamed up with Lineker for the first time since the victory over the Soviet Union in Tbilisi. Injuries to others that day had given Beardsley his chance. Had they been fit, it is doubtful he would have been in Mexico at all.

England had not faced Poland since that fateful evening in 1973, had had no chance to wipe the slate clean, and trooped out for the present match – in the more imposing Universitario Stadium – with the ghost of Tomaszewski hanging over them like a pall. Another massive television audience back home ceased chatting about Bob Geldof's knighthood, Ian Botham's test match ban, imposed for smoking cannabis, India's victory at Lord's and the consequent sacking of David Gower as captain, and Ian Rush's agreed transfer to Juventus in a deal part financial, part fence-mending. They settled down for their third middle-of-the-night vigil, contemplating the 'John 3:16' placards at corner flags and other strategic sites, and wondering whether once again Poland would direct England's appointment with the grim reaper.

The doubters were shamed. England were simply transformed, though an early scare – when Fenwick let in Boniek – might have undone all that was to follow. Swiss referee André Caina, traumatised a year previously by officiating at the ill-fated Liverpool v Juventus European Cup Final, was treated to a glittering exhibition of English football. The first goal originated with a chipped pass by Hoddle from near Shilton's left hand corner flag. Lineker carried on the move, which switched right to Stevens, whose low cross was swept home by Lineker in a manner reminiscent of Alan Mullery's goal against West Germany in León. Before the game was fifteen minutes old England had scored a second, Beardsley linking with Hodge, who provided Lineker with a sweet half-volley.

England were playing with speed and inventiveness, unrecognisable from those earlier displays, leaden in foot and mind. Before the interval they had even scored a third. Steven's corner squeezed like soap through Mlynarczyk's hands, dropping for Lineker at the far post. His World Cup hat-trick was England's first in the finals since Geoff Hurst's.

With Fenwick and Butcher both carrying knocks, the second half was not quite the formality it appeared. Shilton twice saved sharply from Boniek. But England were not to be undone, and Lineker and Beardsley were the toast of the land. The team's only black mark was earned by Terry Fenwick, booked yet again, and now forced to miss a game. England had come good at last, but

England players and fans celebrate Lineker's first goal. (v Poland)

to whom should go the credit, Bobby Robson or player-power?

Meanwhile, Morocco had whipped Portugal 3-1 to head the group, the first feat of its kind by any African team.

POLAND   (0) 0                    ENGLAND   (3) 3
                                   Lineker 8, 14, 35

POLAND: Mlynarczyk, Pawlak, Majewski, Wójcicki, Ostrowski, Komornicki (Karas), Matysik (Buncol), Urban, Dziekanowski, Boniek, Smolarek.
ENGLAND: Shilton, Stevens (*of Everton*), Butcher, Fenwick, Sansom, Hoddle, Steven, Reid, Hodge, Lineker (Dixon), Beardsley (Waddle).

*Final positions – Group F*

|          | P | W | D | L | F | A | Pts |
|----------|---|---|---|---|---|---|-----|
| MOROCCO  | 3 | 1 | 2 | 0 | 3 | 1 | 4   |
| ENGLAND  | 3 | 1 | 1 | 1 | 3 | 1 | 3   |
| POLAND   | 3 | 1 | 1 | 1 | 1 | 3 | 3   |
| Portugal | 3 | 1 | 0 | 2 | 2 | 4 | 2   |

## PARAGUAY v ENGLAND
*Wednesday, 18 June 1986*                    *Aztec Stadium, Mexico City – 98,728*

Scotland and Northern Ireland failed to make the second round. The Irish were sunk in Group D, while Scotland endured elimination by the thuggish brilliance of the Uruguayans. For the moment, sporting obituaries for Bobby Robson and his team had to be ripped up, if only to be rewritten a week later. If fortune favours the brave, there is no doubt that fortune favoured England as the dust settled on Group F. Had Portugal's match with Morocco ended all-square, England would have topped the group and been paired with West Germany. Now that joy awaited Morocco, poor reward indeed. England's was a trip to the capital to face Paraguay, one of the least convincing teams left in the competition.

Like Morocco, Paraguay were complete unknowns. They had last reached the World Cup finals in 1958, when they beat Scotland 3-2. Their coach, Cayetano Re, ruled over a squad whose stars had migrated for foreign gold. Julio Romero had been voted South American Player of the Year for his performances for the Brazilian club Fluminense. Paraguay's four goals in the tournament to date had been shared by Romero and Cabañas, of New York Cosmos. English spies Howard Wilkinson and Dave Sexton had cast a critical eye as Paraguay emerged unbeaten from Group B, coming from behind to earn creditable draws with Mexico – in a match of seventy-seven fouls – and Belgium. The duo were nevertheless of the opinion that Paraguay were defensively brittle and not nearly as dangerous as Argentina or Brazil.

Just to breathe the polluted air of Mexico City was said to be the equivalent of smoking forty cigarettes a day. Noise obliged the England squad to change hotels in mid-preparation: they were grateful for the sporting and recreational refuge offered by the Reforma Club, built by British expatriates in 1890.

Though Bryan Robson – in the circumstances – was as fit as he was ever going to be, this time there was no going back. His personal World Cup was over. Bobby Robson could do nothing other than stick by the players who dealt so convincingly with Poland. The only change was forced by Fenwick's suspension – he was in any case unfit, a groin strain. Alvin Martin, not the swiftest of defenders, was chosen to replace him. Against a team fielding two fast, direct wingers, his selection was a calculated gamble. It was offset by Martin's record alongside Butcher: nine unbeaten games, only two goals lost.

The Aztec Stadium, magnificent as it was, had no pitch to match. The England team knew as they lined up for the national anthems that if they could dispense with one South American side they would face another – Argentina – in the quarter-final, in the same stadium. It was a prospect to pump the adrenalin, and in the heady post-Poland euphoria the Paraguayans found themselves, in the media if nowhere else, somewhat under-valued. Defeat at

Lineker is off the pitch, injured, so Peter Beardsley scores instead. (v Paraguay)

their hands was unlikely to be accepted graciously by the sports desks of Fleet Street.

This was a noon kick-off. Within a minute Reid was whacked on his weak ankle by Cañete, the effects of which he never really shrugged off. Paraguay's delicious Latin skills might have belonged to another planet, so dazed did England appear. Four times the dashing red and white stripes threatened the English goal in the first half-hour. Martin's weak clearance was whacked back by Cañete and turned over by Shilton. Then Butcher's heart-stopping back-pass set up Cabañas, forced wide by Shilton, who somehow blocked the subsequent cut-back.

As with Poland, within seconds of almost falling behind, England were ahead. Chasing Hoddle's diagonal ball from the right, Lineker barged over his marker, who was still picking himself up when Hodge squared from the left. Lineker stretched out a leg to score from close in, depriving Beardsley who was queuing behind him. From the restart, Lineker's scorching volley was tipped over by Fernández. The match had turned, and Hoddle was once again basking in the responsibility afforded by the absence of Robson and Wilkins. Hoddle would shortly figure in two more goals as well. In the meantime, Martin kicked out at an opponent while play was stopped and was booked. For this rush of blood, Bobby Robson would drop him from the quarter-final.

Once behind, the Paraguayans displayed less admirable qualities: elbows jabbed, shirts were tugged, ankles tapped, referees intimidated. An off the ball elbow to the throat by Delgado after half-time sent Lineker to the touchline to recover. It was while briefly down to ten men that England scored again. Fernández couldn't hold Butcher's shot: the ball sprang from his grasp for Beardsley to pounce. Always generous in his praise of others, Beardsley must have been secretly grateful for Lineker's momentary absence. Otherwise, England's scoring machine would surely have got there first.

The Paraguayans now lost their heads completely. They berated the Syrian referee without respite, tumbling like gymnasts every time they caught sight of England's penalty box. With a two-goal cushion, Robson was at last able to bring off the courageous, limping Reid. The end of his ordeal marked the start of the commentators', for Reid was replaced by Spurs' Gary Stevens. There were now two Gary Stevens and one Steven on the same pitch. To those in the dark, Stevens was having one hell of a match, so much did he see of the ball.

The substitute's reward was to manufacture England's third goal. Receiving Hoddle's astute pass, his low cross was despatched with ease by Lineker, whose marker had given up the ghost. It was his fourth carbon-copy goal and his fifth in two games.

England's achievement even exceeded the computer forecast. When fed all salient facts, it had predicted an England win, but only by 2-0.

PARAGUAY  (0) 0                    ENGLAND  (1) 3
                                   Lineker 32, 73, Beardsley 57

PARAGUAY: Fernández, Torales (Guasch), Schettina, Delgado, Zabala, Cañete, Romero, Núñez, Ferreira, Cabañas, Mendoza.
ENGLAND: Shilton, Stevens (of Everton), Martin, Butcher, Sansom, Steven, Reid (Stevens, of Spurs), Hoddle, Hodge, Lineker, Beardsley (Hateley).

**ARGENTINA v ENGLAND**
*Sunday, 22 June 1986*                    *Aztec Stadium, Mexico City – 114,580*

England were through to the last eight. To reach the quarter-finals constituted some small success. Given England's handicap, it was par for the course. From now on they would be excused the thrown eggs and doomsday headlines should they lose, especially to the tournament favourites and the best player in the world. For the first time, England would step out as underdogs.

The match had all the ingredients of war. For one thing, England were something of a bogey team for Argentina, who had beaten them only once (shakily, in 1964) in eight attempts. England had triumphed in both previous World Cup meetings, in 1962 and '66. That latter fiasco, also at the quarter-final stage, had seen the Argentine captain, Rattín, dismissed from the pitch and the whole team dismissed as 'animals' by Alf Ramsey.

But it was not sport that gave the current match its edge. The Falklands War was but four years old. Sporting links were still cut: this was the first England v Argentina clash, in any sport, in any context, since 1982. Diplomatic relations also remained severed, and real and imagined wrongs seemed set to be righted on the football pitch. Soldiers, sailors and airmen had done their bit. Now it was down to the footballers to re-fight the war and, in the case of Argentina, redress the outcome. One wondered at the reception in store should her players return home in defeat. Knowing the pressures, both managers wisely sought to lift the burden from their players, who would perform better if setting their sights on the semi-finals and not the rewriting of history. In this, the urgings of Bobby Robson and Carlos Bilardo were successful. Whatever the hype, the conduct of the match was civilised, even if ultimately disfigured by Maradona's sleight of hand.

Today, Diego Maradona cuts a sorry figure, tainted by association with Mafioso and drugs, and widely regarded – at least in Britain – as a common cheat. In 1986 his reputation was unsullied. He was simply a genius, the greatest player since Pelé, and the whole world yearned to see him play. At twenty-five, he was still short of his peak. In 1980 he had graced Wembley as a highly promising nineteen-year-old, in a match lost by Argentina 1-3. Physically, he was an improbable superstar. He stood 5ft 4in of squat muscle and mountainous thighs. His aerial ability – use of his hand, notwithstanding – was modest, and his right foot could have been fitted with a horseshoe, for all the use he made of it. But his left had an adhesive quality that tied the ball to it whether at the trot or the gallop. Allied to his prodigious strength and balance, his searing pace and lightning turns, Maradona could destroy teams on his own. Though scoring just once in the competition so far, he had single-handedly destroyed Uruguay in the second round. Terry Venables once managed him at Barcelona, but the Catalan club was not big enough for both of them, and Venables sold him to Napoli. Without Maradona, Barcelona took the Spanish title. With him, Napoli would shortly take Italy's.

For Bobby Robson, there was no escaping the Maradona factor. Four years earlier, Italy's Gentile dealt with it by kicking him black and blue. Robson did not have a Gentile or a Nobby Stiles. Man-marking was not the English way, it tended to destroy a team's shape. On reflection, the manager declined to alter his team's pattern, restricting himself to just one change, Martin out, Fenwick in. Reid's ankle had mended, presenting him with the perfect thirtieth birthday present. He played, to the natural disappointment of the now-eligible Ray Wilkins. Wilkins didn't know that had Reid failed his fitness test, Bobby Robson would have bypassed Wilkins and gambled on recalling his captain. *A propos* Maradona, the team was told to cope with him as they thought fit.

The Hand of God. (v Argentina)

Carlos Bilardo appeared more worried by the need to counter Lineker's goal deluge, for he withdrew forward Pusculli in favour of an extra midfielder, Enrique. Bilardo, in any case, had problems of his own. Full-back Garré was suspended and veteran stopper Passarella still injured. The former captain's replacement went by the unlikely name of Brown.

A global television audience of one billion tuned in for the match, transmitted live in the UK by BBC and ITV, following Jimmy Tarbuck's *Winner Take All*. In the stadium, 'God Save the Queen' was heard in respectful silence by all but a handful of Argentine mischief-makers, calling themselves 'Las Barras Bravos' ('the Wild Gangs') and waving flags proclaiming 'Las Malvinas son Argentinas'. Apart from the odd scuffle, the explosion of violence the world feared failed to materialise.

Argentina had forsaken their customary blue and white stripes in favour of pale blue. The minutes ticked away as in a dream, with neither goalkeeper remotely troubled. The Argentines compressed the English midfield, cutting off the supply to Lineker and Beardsley. The only action of note centred on the referee's notebook. It took just ten minutes for Fenwick to topple Maradona and earn his third yellow card in four games. It had been England's first foul of the match. If Fenwick was inhibited thereafter he did not show it, elbowing Maradona in the face without punishment.

Step aside Fenwick! Maradona is on his way to scoring his wonderful second. (v Argentina)

Half-time arrived without any serious goalmouth incident, but with the nagging feeling that Argentina had yet to show their all. Those back home who shot off to the kitchen or the lavatory were wise not to dally, for they might have missed the second-half's opening drama, one of the most debated goals of all time. Maradona threaded the ball deep into England's defence. His lay off should have been cleared, but Hodge inadvertently played it over his own head, back towards the penalty spot. Maradona would have been yards offside had the ball been delivered by an Argentine and not Hodge. Shilton raced out to punch clear, only for Maradona to gain precious inches by flipping the ball with his hand over the goalkeeper's head and into the empty goal. The movement was so expertly coordinated that it deceived many at the time, not only the referee (a Tunisian, chosen for his impartiality) and linesman, who, without the benefit of action replays, allowed the goal. England players, under rigid orders not to show dissent, made muted gestures, showing none of the hysteria that would surely have been unleashed had that same goal been scored at the other end. 'The Hand of God', Maradona later explained, blasphemously, had scored the goal.

It is often the case that a scrappy goal paves the way for a classic, and within four minutes England were treated to the full extent of Maradona's genius, following up his goal from hell with a goal from paradise. Picking up the ball in his own half, he shimmied clear of Beardsley and Reid. In a sequence of bewildering feints, Maradona cut inside Butcher and steamed past Fenwick as if he didn't exist. Now his only obstacles were Shilton to his left and Butcher, regrouping, to his right. The keeper was dummied, and as Butcher lunged in desperation, Maradona drove the ball home.

'You have to say that's magnificent' wailed the BBC's Barry Davies to an awestruck audience who didn't need telling.

Bobby Robson had one roll of the dice left. Off came Steven and Reid, on came Waddle and Barnes, as the manager in desperation reverted to the wingers he had been forced to shun. In a tactical switch that might have backfired, Argentina fell back to protect their lead. Aided by opponents with no thought to attack, England now swarmed forward. Hoddle's free-kick was blocked by Pumpido. With ten minutes remaining Barnes' wizardry on the left produced the perfect cross. Lineker rose to claim it and the match boiled again.

It might have died in an instant of being reborn. A rampaging Argentine breakaway saw Tapia strike the foot of Shilton's post. When Fenwick, with another rush of blood, chopped down Valdano, most neutrals expected the red card. It stayed in the referee's pocket.

There was time for just one more 'if only'. An identical Barnes cross seemed set for an identical Lineker header. This time it was the player who finished up in the net, while the ball, with a mind of its own, stayed out. It would never have occurred to Lineker to palm the ball in. Had he done so, and the referee not seen it, one wonders whether Maradona would have led the protests.

Afterwards, one recalls the dignity of manager and players in defeat. Today, the whole match has somehow been condensed into Maradona's handball. At the time, it was conceded that no matter the manner of victory, it was deserved. Argentina were clearly the better side. England, it might be said, were squarely if not fairly beaten. Until two goals down, England had not had a whiff of a scoring chance. Besides, to be eliminated in such fashion heaped sympathy on those previously vilified. Bobby Robson could hold his head high. Maradona had got away with it, others would have tried, and England's demise was laid squarely at the door of referee and linesman. Bookmakers disavowed The Hand of God in another way, refunding stakes on punters who predicted a draw.

'Malvinas 2 Ingleses 1' screamed the tabloids of Buenos Aires.

| ARGENTINA (0) 2 | ENGLAND (0) 1 |
|---|---|
| Maradona 50, 54 | Lineker 80 |

ARGENTINA: Pumpido, Cuciuffo, Brown, Ruggeri, Olarticoechea, Batista, Giusti, Burruchaga (Tapia), Enrique, Valdano, Maradona.
ENGLAND: Shilton, Stevens (*of Everton*), Butcher, Fenwick, Sansom, Hoddle, Steven (Barnes), Reid (Waddle), Hodge, Lineker, Beardsley.

England were the only quarter-finalists to lose in normal time. The other three matches were all decided on penalties, disfiguring a World Cup that after half a century had still found no solution to the problem of drawn games. So England departed Mexico at the same stage as they had in 1970. There was less despondency this time, they were not defending the trophy, and their sights were correspondingly lower. Argentina would overcome Belgium in the semi-final (with the aid of another fulminating Maradona goal) and West Germany in the Final. Defeat by the eventual winners was some consolation for England, for who knows, they might have been proved the second best team in the tournament. FIFA placed England eighth.

For Tunisian referee, Ali Bennaceur, FIFA was unforgiving. His blind spot meant that his first World Cup match was also his last. As for Bobby Robson, his tournament had gone better than he could possibly have envisaged when Ray Wilkins was sent off against Morocco. Robson would stay in charge to lead England's quest for the World Cup in 1990. Leading his attack would be Gary Lineker, no longer just a rabbit-killer, as his six-goal haul amply proved. He was the leading goalscorer of Mexico '86.

---

*England appearances and goalscorers (substitute appearances in brackets)*
*World Cup qualifying rounds and final competition 1986*

| | Apps | Goals | | Apps | Goals |
|---|---|---|---|---|---|
| Sansom K * | 13 | 1 | Reid P | 4 | – |
| Shilton P *‡ | 13 | – | Hodge S | 3 (2) | – |
| Butcher T * | 10 | – | Woodcock A * | 3 (2) | 3 |
| Wilkins R *† | 9 | – | Beardsley P | 3 (1) | 1 |
| Lineker G | 8 (1) | 9 | Francis T *† | 2 (2) | – |
| Fenwick T | 8 | – | Martin A * | 2 | – |
| Hoddle G * | 8 | 1 | Williams S | 2 | – |
| Robson B * | 8 | 5 | Stevens G (*Spurs*) | 1 (4) | – |
| Stevens G (*Everton*) | 8 | – | Dixon K | 1 (1) | – |
| Hateley M | 7 (1) | 4 | Bracewell P | 1 | – |
| Steven T | 6 (1) | – | Duxbury M | 1 | – |
| Wright M | 6 | – | Mariner P *† | 1 | – |
| Waddle C | 5 (4) | 1 | Withe P * | 1 | – |
| Barnes J | 5 (2) | 2 | Chamberlain M | – (1) | – |
| Anderson V * | 4 | 1 | | | |

---

* Appeared in 1982 World Cup.                                    *29 players    28 goals*
† Appeared in 1978 World Cup.
‡ Appeared in 1974 World Cup.

# 11

# THE 1990 WORLD CUP

Time heals, and Maradona's felony was soon dismissed to the archives of sporting injustice. The British public had a royal wedding to look forward to, between Prince Andrew and Sarah Ferguson.

Not since Alf Ramsey had an England manager supervised more than one World Cup. It was a measure of Bobby Robson's qualified success in Mexico and his favoured standing within the FA that little energy was wasted trying to unseat him. Like a two-term American president, he won a second period more or less unopposed. The 1980s, for better or worse, would stand as the Bobby Robson era of English football.

His second period in office threatened to be more exacting than the first. The ongoing Heysel ban deprived his players of priceless European experience. By the time the new World Cup came round, the ban was in its fourth season. The consequences of this lost education were incalculable. The time would come when younger players brought into the squad would have had no experience of foreign styles, their first taste coming in internationals rather than the training ground of European club competition.

For certain key players, the prospect of indefinite banishment from Europe was one factor prompting migration abroad or to Scotland, whose clubs were not outlawed. Terry Butcher and Chris Woods decamped to Glasgow Rangers, Gary Lineker to Barcelona. Others were happy to remain domiciled, though seeking to move house. The lure of Anfield proved irresistible to Peter Beardsley and John Barnes, while Peter Shilton transferred to Derby County for the modest investment of £90,000. Not bad for an international goalkeeper still the pick of the pack.

Bobby Robson had better luck with his protracted bid to have league matches postponed before key World Cup eliminators, but by the time these came around his standing with the press and public had sunk to new depths. Having qualified without fuss for the 1988 European Championship – overcoming Turkey, Northern Ireland and Yugoslavia, whom England beat in Belgrade 4-1 – England set off for the finals in West Germany brimming with confidence. Alas, it all turned sour. There were shades of Portugal in

Monterrey when England lost 0-1 to Jack Charlton's emerging Republic of Ireland, shades of further misfortune when hitting the post twice in losing to Holland, and shades of despair when losing a third time, this time without excuse to the Soviet Union.

Never before had an England team finished bottom and pointless in any final tournament, and the press clamour for Robson's head verged on hysteria. Questions were even asked in the House of Commons about his suitability for the job. Seasoned commentators turned soothsayers, stating that they could foresee no England team in their lifetime reaching even the semi-finals of a major competition. The FA stood by the England manager, but these were, Robson declared, were the darkest days of his managerial life.

He could count his blessings. Southern England had been buffeted by the most destructive storm this century. A roll-on roll-off car ferry setting out from Zeebrugge with its car doors open capsized in the Channel drowning hundreds. In Gibraltar, the SAS gunned down three members of the IRA in broad daylight. The soldiers had the full support of Margaret Thatcher, now Britain's longest continuous serving prime minister this century, presiding over what she described as an era of great prosperity. She never said it, but she meant 'you've never had it so good'. Not everyone agreed. Passengers on the London Underground hijacked a train to protest against poor service. Africa's starving were grateful for the efforts and gimmicks of Comic Relief; red balls stuck to noses and car radiators were a mark of the time. So was the film *Fatal Attraction*, provoking fierce debate on the perils of adultery. *Crossroads*, the Birmingham soap opera, came to an end, while British publishing gaped at an unlikely best-seller, *A Brief History of Time*, by the wheelchair-bound Professor Stephen Hawking.

As the new qualifying campaign loomed, in the late summer of 1988, talk was of aeroplanes. The US cruiser *Vincennes* blasted an Iranian airliner out of the skies over the Gulf. More heroically, a West German youth, Matthias Rust aged nineteen, flew a light plane undetected by Russia's air-defence system across the Soviet Union and landed in Red Square. Drunk or mad, they said. In England, new laws permitted pubs to follow Scotland's and open and close when they pleased.

The Seoul Olympics went ahead without Sebastian Coe, forbidden to defend his 800 metres gold medals won in Moscow and Los Angeles. Ben Johnson won, then lost the 100 metres gold on drugs charges. Flo-Jo, with mane of black hair, swept to the ladies' sprint double. Her time in the 100 metres would have won gold in the men's final in 1952.

The Football League, newly celebrating its centenary, narrowly fought off pressures from the big clubs to break away and form a super-league. Their cause was not helped by the upstarts of Wimbledon beating mighty Liverpool in the FA Cup Final.

*Qualifying Group 2*

## ENGLAND v SWEDEN
*Wednesday, 18 October 1988*                    *Wembley – 65,628*

Better England qualified for all World Cups, but especially those in Europe, which offered more favourable odds. In 1990, the finals would be hosted by Italy. History showed that the challenge of Brazil and Argentina was emasculated whenever they competed in Europe. The Mediterranean climate had proved beneficial to England's chances in 1982, and it was hoped would do so again.

Having fought their way through a five-team group to reach Mexico, England now found themselves in one of three smaller groups. This was a mixed blessing, fewer fixtures offset against fewer qualifying places. In the previous qualifiers, those members of four-team groups knew beforehand that the palpitations of play-offs awaited those finishing second. With an eye to reduce fixtures, play-offs were now dispensed with. Instead, the two second-placed teams with the best records would qualify. One team finishing second would not. This meant that England, in addition to the stresses and strains of Group 2, needed to keep a nervy eye on the progress of Groups 1 and 4. Either that, or win Group 2 outright. England's opponents were Sweden, Poland, and Albania. First up, Sweden at Wembley.

Headlines that week had a tragic ring. The living quarters of the Piper Alpha oil platform, four storeys and 1,000 tons, were raised to the surface of the North Sea, three months after they toppled into the sea at a cost of 167 lives. Three and a half years after the event, the trial began in Brussels of twenty-six Liverpool supporters accused of manslaughter during the Heysel tragedy.

New York's 'Guardian Angels', complete with red berets, were promoting vigilante solutions to violence on London's Underground. They described their visit as 'a mission of peace'. Bond Street was equally important to Jason Bunn, reigning world Monopoly champion, who lost his title to a Japanese.

Japan, for the moment, had no claims on world football. Sweden, though more ambitious, were hard to assess, living equally with the greats and the smalls. They had climbed the heights in 1958, taking advantage of home soil to reach the World Cup Final. The following year they became only the second foreign team to win at Wembley. Since 1945 they had won three and lost three against England, a fair return, but not for a decade had they qualified for the finals of a major championship. Their one footballing triumph belonged to Gothenburg, who beat Dundee United in the Final of the 1986-87 UEFA Cup. In recent matches, the national side had recorded impressive wins over Spain, the Soviet Union, and West Germany, but when silverware, not pride, was at stake performances withered.

Sweden's biggest threat stemmed from their twin strikers, Ekström and Eskillson. It was a Johnny Ekström goal that had sunk England in a Stockholm friendly in September 1986, but both players had recently tried ploughing foreign fields (Ekström with Bayern Munich) and both had failed to settle. Neither would start the match.

Bobby Robson had taken the axe to several England stalwarts after the summer debacle in West Germany. Glenn Hoddle had won his last cap; so had Kenny Sansom, less through his own failings than because he had been pushed from Arsenal's first team by Nigel Winterburn. Team-mate Tony Adams, one of Robson's new breed of centre-half, would survive for the moment, but not for long. Viv Anderson, Dave Watson and Peter Reid were others who would play no more international football. Mark Wright must have feared the same fate, but after a long exile he would be rehabilitated. Meanwhile, Nottingham Forest were the flavour of the day. Brian Clough's exciting side would be rewarded with three caps against Sweden: Stuart Pearce at left-back, Neil Webb, Bryan Robson's new sidekick in midfield, and central defender Des Walker, who would start the game on the bench. The core of the side was that which prospered in Mexico but flopped in West Germany, with Beardsley now playing 'in the hole', in the vernacular, behind the front two, Lineker and Waddle. Only after the European Championship was the lacklustre Lineker diagnosed as suffering from hepatitis. He was still match-rusty, having played just once this season for Johann Cruyff's Barcelona.

Octobers, it will be recalled, generally smile on England while Septembers frown. England's last five October internationals had produced a goal tally of 24-0. Murphy's Law being what it is, against Sweden England flipped and flapped without effect. The game was forgettable, with few shots on goal, and most of them from the Swedes. At the heart of the Swedish defence, the prematurely grey Hysén caught the eye with his effortless interceptions and classy distribution. Shilton looked unexpectedly fallible in the second half, twice needing two attempts to deal with unexceptional shots. Bryan Robson and Neil Webb, meanwhile, were fully stretched containing Strömberg and Prytz (once of Glasgow Rangers), unable to venture forward themselves. Chants of 'what a load of rubbish' echoed round the stadium as England pushed forward in a late flurry. They came nearest with a Waddle shot that veered wide, and a Lineker 'goal' chalked off.

Never before had England failed to win their opening World Cup qualifier, and boos rained down on the England manager as he left the arena.

ENGLAND  (0) 0                    SWEDEN  (0) 0

ENGLAND: Shilton (Derby), Stevens (Rangers), Pearce (Forest), Webb (Forest), Adams (Arsenal) (*sub* Walker, Forest), Butcher (Rangers), Robson (Man U), Beardsley (Liverpool), Waddle (Spurs), Lineker (Barcelona), Barnes (Liverpool) (*sub* Cottee, Everton).
SWEDEN: Ravelli, R Nilsson (Schiller), Hysén, Larsson, Ljung, Thern, Strömberg, Prytz, J Nilsson, Holmqvist (Ekström), Pettersson.

## ALBANIA v ENGLAND
*Wednesday, 8 March 1989*                          *Tirana – 30,000*

That goalless draw was not the result England wanted, and Bobby Robson had to endure five months for the chance to override it, five months which saw the destruction of a Pam Am 'jumbo' over Lockerbie and the Ayatollah Khomeini issue a decree of death, a *fatwa*, against author Salman Rushdie for his allegedly blasphemous novel *The Satanic Verses*. England, meanwhile, scraped a 1-1 draw in Saudi Arabia, before stealing a late 2-1 win in Greece.

Like Sweden, Albania were World Cup newcomers to England. Unlike Sweden, they were no-hopers, winning only two of fifteen home internationals in the 1980s. The people lived in a never-never land of Stalinist isolation, in a land of almost no cars or telephones, attracting and welcoming almost nobody from outside. Each season Albania's teams came out of the hat in the European competitions, and each season their opponents did not know whether to rejoice at the prospect of a safe result, or curse Enver Hoxha, the everlasting Albanian leader, for the bureaucratic hassles about to be foisted upon them in visiting his joyless land. The national team did not know the meaning of 'friendlies', playing only two in the whole of the previous year.

Sweden has compounded their point at Wembley by taking two in Tirana. It was imperative that England match them; to fall behind the Swedes with a visit to Stockholm pending would dampen their chances of heading Group 2.

Glancing through the Under-21 England eleven which won 2-1 on the eve of the senior match, only one player – Paul Ince – could in years to come be congratulated on breaking through to the senior team.

In the Qemal Stafa Stadium, Albania's Minga might have flustered England within a minute, but Shilton's ample frame smothered the ball. England rallied and scored when Rocastle hooked the ball viciously across the goalmouth. One shot was charged down before Barnes pounced. The goal set the fires under Albania, who swept forward with enterprise and no little skill. Shehu, who unnerved England's defence every time he ran at them, skipped around Butcher and Pearce only to be foiled by Shilton's fingertips. England's equilibrium was restored by the magnificent Robson, up much of the night with a touch of food poisoning. Robson sealed Albania's fate by meeting Barnes' free-kick with a firm, far-post header. It was his twenty-fourth goal in his fiftieth international –

equalling Geoff Hurst's total – a prodigious return for a midfield player.

The player with least reason to smile was Gary Lineker. His eighth match without scoring, illness notwithstanding, marked his longest unproductive run.

The result kept the hounds off Bobby Robson's back for at least one more match. But even had England lost, and Robson bowed to the cry to step down, no one was available to take over. Leading contenders Graham Taylor and Terry Venables were both under contract with their clubs.

ALBANIA  (0) 0                           ENGLAND  (1) 2
                                         Barnes 16, Robson 63

ALBANIA: Mercini, Lekbello, Gega, Hodja, Zmijani, Josa, Millo, Jera, Demollari, Shehu, Minga.
ENGLAND: Shilton, Stevens, Pearce, Webb, Walker, Butcher, Robson, Rocastle, Waddle (Beardsley), Lineker (Smith), Barnes.

**ENGLAND v ALBANIA**
*Wednesday, 26 April 1989*                        *Wembley – 60,602*

In the days before the return fixture with Albania, English football was rocked by its latest and most costly tragedy. To Valley Parade and Heysel was now added Hillsborough, scene of the crushing to death of ninety-five Liverpool supporters. Anfield was in a state of such numbed shock that John Aldridge contemplated retirement, John Barnes could not face playing so soon, and ruled himself out of the Albania game, while Peter Beardsley was carefully monitored for signs of post-traumatic shock. Coincident with Hillsborough, on the other side of the world, a disgraced reformist, Hu Yaobang, died in a Shanghai hospital, setting in train a tide of upheaval that would shortly consume China. American comedienne Lucille Ball, star of countless episodes of *I Love Lucy*, died in the United States aged seventy-seven. Shortly before the match, 22,000 runners completed the ninth London marathon.

No Albanian national team had ever previously visited London. They toured the city open-mouthed, sight-seeing Big Ben, the Tower of London, Karl Marx's grave in Highgate, and lined up for a group photograph outside the British Museum, where Marx wrote *Das Kapital*.

Albania's team showed one surprise. With both senior goalkeepers unfit, and the Under-21 keeper in action the previous night, the job fell to seventeen-year-old Nallbani. Standing 6ft 2in, he could call upon no international experience, not even for the Under-21s.

Albania had recently lost to a late goal in Poland, so the proverbial cricket score in England's favour seemed far-fetched. Albania might be weak, but they weren't Turkey. The game's preliminaries included a minute's silence for the victims of Hillsborough and the drowning of the Albanian anthem by a chorus of 'You'll Never Walk Alone'.

It was a sprightly match, typified by Chris Waddle tormenting opponents left and right and setting up the opening goal for Gary Lineker after just five minutes. After a year without scoring, Lineker's joy was unrestrained. When Lineker fed Beardsley with a low cross to double the lead, England went into party mode. Their indiscipline almost cost them dear when Demollari's sweet volley flew past Shilton but was dubiously disallowed.

In the second half England knuckled down. Lineker set up another Beardsley goal, settling the doubts over the latter's mental fitness. The match, in retrospect, would stick in the memory for a second-half substitution. Paul Gascoigne had yet to start a match for England, never mind score. With the game safe he replaced David Rocastle and promptly manufactured a goal for Waddle. Not content, he set off on a marauding run, climaxed by a razor-sharp finish. Gascoigne's was undoubtedly the goal of the match.

The crowd went home smiling, but the manager had a weight on his mind.

'Gascoigne's as daft as a brush. He played in all the positions I told him not to. Maybe in future we should use two balls, one for Gascoigne, the other for the rest of the lads.'

ENGLAND   (2) 5                    ALBANIA   (0) 0
Lineker 5, Beardsley 12, 64,
Waddle 72, Gascoigne 88

ENGLAND: Shilton, Stevens (Parker), Pearce, Webb, Walker, Butcher, Robson, Rocastle (Gascoigne), Beardsley, Lineker, Waddle.
ALBANIA: Nallbani, Zmijani, Bubegi, Hodja, Gega, Jera, Shehu, Lekbello, Millo, Hasanpapa (Noga), Demollari.

**ENGLAND v POLAND**
*Saturday, 3 June 1989*                                    *Wembley – 69,203*

For weeks, Liverpool had scratched their heads, pondering whether or not to carry on in the FA Cup. They chose to do so, as their deceased supporters would surely have wished, and were rewarded by beating Everton 3-2 in the Final. But Anfield's agonies were not yet exhausted. As the rescheduled league season dragged into late May, Arsenal scored a last-minute clincher to take the championship on the greater number of goals scored. That same day, the death was announced of former Leeds and England manager Don Revie. The American evangelist, Billy Graham was back in town, with stadiums across London booked to hear God's message. One trusts he said a prayer for Terry Waite, passing his third birthday in captivity, somewhere in Lebanon.

The visit of Poland was a milestone in the career of Peter Shilton. It marked his 108th cap, bringing him level with Bobby Moore's English record. Shilton's career already extended through nineteen seasons, through five managers, and against forty different opponents. He had been beaten a paltry seventy times. If Ray Clemence had not been around in the late 'seventies, Shilton would now be approaching two hundred caps, unprecedented in world football. His next target was Pat Jennings' British record of 119 international appearances.

Since thumping Albania, England had indulged in a goalless draw with Chile at Wembley, prior to beating Scotland 2-0 at Hampden. England were now set to conclude their home fixtures in Group 2.

Only three Poles remained from the team trounced by England in Monterrey. Of these, giant sweeper Wójcicki made noises about seeking revenge. Another Pole, Lukasik, knew all about Gary Lineker, having man-marked him in the Cup-Winners' Cup when Barcelona faced Lech Poznan. Having lost to a last-minute goal in Sweden, Poland could not afford another defeat if they realistically hoped to qualify.

England created chances a-plenty. Lineker might have scored early on, but for a nasty foul by the Polish goalkeeper. The breakthrough was not long delayed, Lineker finishing off a move by scoring from an oblique angle. The game's decisive moment arrived shortly before the break, when Des Walker cleared Prusik's header off the line. Reprieved, England turned on the style in the second half. A sparkling move ended with Barnes side-footing a sweet goal, before a desperate back pass was intercepted by Lineker for Neil Webb to score a third.

As the players shook hands and exchanged shirts, it was early morning in Beijing, where guns were firing and tanks rolling into Tiananmen Square. In Iran, the Ayatollah Khomeini departed this earth, unleashing a tide of grief of epic proportions. With the media saturated by coverage of China, the England team slipped across to Copenhagen, to commemorate the centenary of Danish football. The matched ended 1-1.

ENGLAND  (1) 3                    POLAND  (0) 0
  Lineker 24, Barnes 69, Webb 82

ENGLAND: Shilton, Stevens, Pearce, Webb, Walker, Butcher, Robson, Waddle (Rocastle), Beardsley (Smith), Lineker, Barnes.
POLAND: Bako, Wijas, Wójcicki, Wdowczyk, Lukasik, Matysik, Prusik, Urban (Tarasciewicz), Furtok, Warzycha, Lesniak (Kosecki).

## SWEDEN v ENGLAND

*Wednesday, 6 September 1989*                    *Stockholm – 38,558*

England would conclude Group 2, at the dawn of the new league season, with testing fixtures in Sweden and Poland. They required two more points, bringing them up to nine, to make sure of qualification. That total would not guarantee winning Group 2, but it would ensure finishing second, and it could not be matched by *both* Romania and Denmark from Group 1.

Key England players had changed clubs in the summer. Gary Lineker had come home, to Spurs, as Chris Waddle left for Marseilles, for the improbable fee of £4.5 million. Neil Webb joined Manchester United from Nottingham Forest.

This, the first week of September, marked the fiftieth anniversary of the outbreak of World War II. West Germany, lodged in the same group as Wales and Holland, had sensibly arranged no fixture, for fear of provoking neo-Nazi outbursts. For days, the British public was bombarded with images and reminiscences from September 1939.

The week was also notable for the rare sight of Coventry City at the top of the English first division, and for a fresh outbreak of hooliganism by English fans abroad. One man was lost overboard on a North Sea ferry bound for Sweden. In anticipation of an unwanted invasion, the country embarked on the most extensive security measures in its history.

Sweden's football team had fallen away dramatically, plumbing the depths in the summer when losing 0-6 to Denmark and 2-4 to France. Their defence was clearly in disarray, and would need to stiffen considerably to withstand the threat posed by a rejuvenated Gary Lineker.

In Stockholm's Rasunda Stadium, England eschewed the precedent set by Chile, who had stormed off the pitch in Brazil when their goalkeeper faked being struck by a flare. They had hoped for a rematch. They got a ban when the blood on goalkeeper Roberto Rojas turned out to be self-inflicted. The blood pouring from Terry Butcher's head and reddening his white shirt was not. Butcher was *locum* skipper in the absence of Bryan Robson, out with bruised ribs, and sustained the injury in a fearful collision with Johnny Ekström – rehabilitated in the national side since his transfer to Cannes. Butcher refused to leave the pitch till half-time.

Since the spring of 1984, over a span of sixty-odd internationals, the England No. 11 shirt had invariably been worn either by John Barnes or Chris Waddle. Rarely did they both play together, but they had done so against Sweden at Wembley and they did in Stockholm. For such talented players, their output, measured solely in terms of goals scored or created, was modest. They were given little chance to shine in Stockholm, being effectively shut out by the Swedish deployment of two wide midfielders to buttress the full-backs. The supply lines to Lineker and Beardsley were consequently asphyxiated. Only once did Barnes project a decent cross, but Lineker's header was turned behind. For the most part, England were obliged to defend, and did not endear themselves with their long back-passes to Shilton. One, from Butcher, was from inside the Swedish half.

Prompted by Jonas Thern of Benfica, and enlivened by the arrival as substitute of Anders Limpár, Sweden looked the livelier team. Engqvist might have scored when the ball broke to him off Neil Webb, and again, three minutes from time. Des Walker, picking himself up from a thrilling tackle on Magnusson, undid his good work with a criminal back-pass. The astonished Magnusson could do no better than flip the ball into Shilton's grateful arms.

With the final whistle, England had gone more than six hours of football with Sweden without scoring. Butcher's head wound required further stitches, seventeen in all. He was lucky: his injuries would quickly heal and were masked by his pride. Neil Webb, however, had ruptured an Achilles tendon. He would be out of the game for six months and never be the same player again.

News that yet more trouble-makers had been rounded up after the game prompted the intervention of Margaret Thatcher. It might be prudent, she said, in so many words, if the FA considered withdrawing England from the World Cup.

SWEDEN  (0) 0                    ENGLAND  (0) 0

SWEDEN: Ravelli, R Nilsson, Hysén, Larsson, Ljung, Engqvist, Thern, Ingesson (Strömberg), J Nilsson (Limpár), Ekström, Magnusson.
ENGLAND: Shilton, Stevens, Pearce, Webb (Gascoigne), Walker, Butcher, Beardsley, McMahon, Waddle, Lineker, Barnes (Rocastle).

**POLAND v ENGLAND**
*Wednesday, 11 October 1989*                    *Katowice – 30,000*

The Iron Lady was being premature. England had not yet qualified for Italy, and their final opponents, Poland, would be trying their damnedest to obstruct them. Poland still had three games left, nothing less than three thumping wins would keep their hopes alive. To that extent England were unfortunate to have to travel to Katowice a fortnight before the Swedes, who might arrive to face opponents with nothing to play for.

Dipping behind the Iron Curtain was not without its risks in the autumn of 1989. The Soviet empire was crumbling. President Gorbachev's visit to East Berlin as the England party flew to Poland prompted massive pro-democracy demonstrations on the streets of the East German capital. The word 'Freedom' was to be heard echoing round Alexanderplatz. It is in troubled times like these that fantasies flourish. The Soviet press agency, Tass, reported in all seriousness that the city of Voronezh had been visited by a spacecraft manned by ten-feet-tall humanoids.

Michael Knighton would have felt ten feet tall had his attempts to take over Manchester United succeeded. More fortunate was Peter Short, a Scottish travel agent. Visiting the Northamptonshire town of Ashton, he heard about the world conker championships being staged in a local pub. He entered on the spur of the moment. And won.

In 1973, 105,000 Poles had packed the Slaski Stadium for the visit of England. Now, financial and political woes, coupled with disenchantment with Polish football, cut the gate by two thirds. Poland's four club representatives in Europe had been blown away in the first round, and only a sequence of improbable wins would keep the national team afloat.

Having scrapped eight of the side who lost to England in Mexico, another eight were pensioned off from the team flattened at Wembley. Urban, Wójcicki, and Matysik, were all omitted by new manager, Andrzej Strejlau, who coped with the exodus of his country's best players – including Dziekanowski to Celtic – by picking left-overs, three of them from his former club, Legia Warsaw.

Critical matches like this were no place for novices, and Bobby Robson sent out a side that had accumulated in excess of 450 caps. His players had never lost an away qualifier, in any competition, and this was hardly the time to forfeit that distinction. Experienced team or no, Bobby Robson would be left shell-shocked by Polish pace and invention. Playing with just three defenders, and with two wide men bearing down on each of England's overworked full-backs, Poland threatened from the start.

The wind and rain that clouded the Silesian coalfields was a poor theatre for Poland's verve. For forty-five minutes England could barely break out of their half, as Robert Warzycha and the mane-haired Ziober ran riot. As the interval approached, Shilton was called upon to make save after save, the most thrilling from Czachowski's dipping drive. Bryan Robson and Steve McMahon in midfield could spare no effort to support Lineker and Beardsley, who, as in Sweden, found themselves marooned up front chasing lost causes.

The second half began as the first, though the longer the game progressed the more Poland seemed to sense that fate was against them. England appeared to have drawn Poland's sting, so that their last, heart-stopping assault came almost out of the blue. The game was in its final minute and Shilton was set to boast the proud record of keeping six clean sheets in six World Cup qualifiers. Tarasciewicz, the ball at his feet, was fully thirty yards from goal, and innumerable red England shirts blocked his advance. His sudden shot swirled one way then the other before smashing against Shilton's crossbar.

The final whistle blew. England had qualified; Poland had not, missing out on the World Cup finals for the first time in twenty years. Bobby Robson was gracious enough to concede that not for two years had his team undergone such a trial.

Denied hope, Poland crumbled at home to Sweden, who thereby topped Group 2. England finished behind them, and had Tarasciewicz's shot been two inches lower, they would have been out, their place in Italy taken by Denmark. Such is the line between triumph and disaster.

POLAND  (0)                           ENGLAND  (0) 0

POLAND: Bako, Czachowski, Kaczmarek, Wdowczyk, R Warzycha, Nawrocki, Tarasciewicz, Ziober, Kosecki, Dziekanowski, K Warzycha (Furtok).
ENGLAND: Shilton, Stevens, Pearce, McMahon, Walker, Butcher, Robson, Rocastle, Beardsley, Lineker, Waddle.

---

*Qualifying Group 2*

| | | Home | | | | | Away | | | | |
|---|---|---|---|---|---|---|---|---|---|---|---|
| | P | W | D | L | F | A | W | D | L | F | A | Pts |
| SWEDEN | 6 | 2 | 1 | 0 | 5 | 2 | 2 | 1 | 0 | 4 | 1 | 10 |
| ENGLAND | 6 | 2 | 1 | 0 | 8 | 0 | 1 | 2 | 0 | 2 | 0 | 9 |
| Poland | 6 | 1 | 1 | 1 | 1 | 2 | 1 | 0 | 2 | 3 | 6 | 5 |
| Albania | 6 | 0 | 0 | 3 | 2 | 6 | 0 | 0 | 3 | 1 | 9 | 0 |

*Other group results*

| | | | | |
|---|---|---|---|---|
| Poland v Albania | 1-0 | | Sweden v Albania | 3-1 |
| Albania v Sweden | 1-2 | | Poland v Sweden | 0-2 |
| Sweden v Poland | 2-1 | | Albania Poland | 1-2 |

---

## World Cup finals – ITALY                    June-July 1990

Long before England sallied to the coalfields of Polish Silesia, gossip – emanating presumably from the corridors of FIFA – pointed to England being seeded in Italy and quarantined to the island outpost of Sardinia, much as they had (though not seeded) found themselves at the behest of Lady Luck shovelled out to Monterrey.

The bellow of frustration that accompanied Tarasciewicz's strike against Shilton's crossbar was not confined to Polish larynxes. It echoed from the corridors of FIFA, doubtless from the Cabinet Room at Number 10, and certainly from the good people of Sardinia, who must have wondered what they had done to deserve the English pestilence soon to descend on them.

FIFA's frustration was exacerbated by Sweden edging out England from the top of Group 2, for it threw their seeding principles into confusion. FIFA had hoped to retain the practice of 1986, seeding being based on performances in the previous World Cup. There was no difficulty with seeding Italy (hosts), Argentina (holders), West Germany (beaten finalists), and Belgium (semi-finalists). France, the other team to reach the last four in Mexico, would have been seeded in Italy, but they hadn't qualified. Two more seeds therefore remained to be drawn from the losing quarter-finalists. Of these, Mexico had found themselves banned for fielding over-aged players in an Under-20 tournament, Brazil claimed one of the seeding vacancies, leaving England and Spain to dispute the other. Both countries had reached the same stage in 1982 and 1986, but Spain, unlike England, had reached the finals in 1978, and Spain, unlike England, had topped their qualifying group this time round. Theirs, in other words, was the greater claim to be seeded. But security considerations outweighed those of equity, and Spain's protests were overruled. England were indeed headed for Sardinia, with the neighbouring island of Sicily staging those matches not involving Bobby Robson's team. For the second World Cup running, England found themselves deposited into Group F. F for 'far away', perhaps. The F-factor was not something of which England could be envious. England would play all three group matches in the Renato Sant 'Elia Stadium, built in 1970 to accommodate the then Italian champions, Luigi Riva's Cagliari.

It is curious how chance often conspires with collusion. With England having lost to the Irish Republic and then Holland in the finals of the European Championship, FIFA's magic balls now threw up the same two opponents, in the same order. Sardinia's security forces drew a deep breath, for Holland's hooligans were barely more civilised than England's. If prognostications were not heeded, Cagliari was set to become a war-zone. The draw offered one crumb of comfort for England. Instead of the Soviet Union in their final match, they would face Egypt. But remembering Morocco, even that seemed small mercy.

Much hinged, not just on the performances of Robson's team, but the behaviour of players and supporters in Italy. With prudent use of the carrot, UEFA had tentatively lifted the ban on English clubs for the new season. Whitehall, however, was sceptical, and Colin Moynihan, the Sports Minister, was thought to be looking for any excuse to keep the ban in place. At the very least, the army of fans *en route* for Italy knew the price to be exacted for their rowdiness.

The world had not stopped still in the first half of 1990. The United States had invaded Panama on the pretence of snatching General 'Pineapple' Noriega on drugs charges. Two Russian words had entered the English language: *glasnost* (openness) and *perestroika* (reconstruction). The Baltic states had became the latest to break from Moscow. Nelson Mandela had been released from a South African jail after twenty-eight years, and riots the length of

England spelled doom for the detested poll-tax.

Credit where credit is due: Bobby Robson's teams knew the art of qualifying for major events. Unbeaten again, this time without conceding a goal, it was now nine years since Greenwood's nightmare defeat in Oslo. Robson's failure against the Danes in 1983 remained his sole qualifying black spot. His record in various finals was less auspicious: absent in '84, chequered in '86, disastrous in '88. Italia '90 marked Bobby Robson's last opportunity to leave his stamp on English football.

His hopes for a build-up free from distraction were wrecked both by the gutter-press, with accusations about his private life, and his employers, who intimated that his services would not be required post-Italy. A third term was unthinkable, even if England won the World Cup. Manoeuvrings behind the scenes tied up Graham Taylor as Robson's successor, and PSV Eindhoven as Robson's new employer. Both appointments were ill-kept secrets, though for the sake of appearances neither was confirmed in public.

Robson's core players – Shilton, Butcher, Robson, Lineker, Beardsley, Barnes, and Waddle – had survived both Mexico and West Germany. Newcomers to the squad – eighteen came and went – were virginal in terms of foreign experience. The lifting of the UEFA ban, welcome as it was, would come too late to benefit Bobby Robson. In fact, the pressures to remain squeaky clean on the field could work against him, by impeding healthy aggression.

As with Mexico, England built a long winning sequence to take to the World Cup. They did not taste defeat after June 1988 until May 1990, a run of seventeen games that was ended abruptly by Uruguay at Wembley, just prior to departure for Sardinia. Since qualifying in Poland, England chalked up Wembley wins over Yugoslavia, Brazil, Czechoslovakia and Denmark, plus a draw with Italy, during a preparatory programme infinitely more testing than that in 1986.

Critics bemoaned the fact that England had not unearthed a single genuinely inventive talent since 1986. The best of the newcomers were all defenders. Stuart Pearce had for two years been ever-present at left-back but, as his *nomme de guerre* 'Psycho' hinted, here was a player of brutal tackles but few creative graces. Team-mate Des Walker excelled as a completely untypical British defender, lightning fast, a leech-like man-marker if necessary. Despite a compulsion to be rid of the ball the moment he won it, Walker's future seemed assured. By the time Ireland came around he had worn the No. 5 shirt sixteen times in succession, and he would clearly be a fixture in Italy.

At twenty-four, Walker was the second youngest player in the squad. The baby, in more ways than one, was the precocious, undisciplined, twenty-four year old Paul Gascoigne who, despite being as stable as a house of cards had already tempted Spurs into a £2 million investment to lure him from his native

The England squad before the Third Place play-off with Italy. (v Italy)

Newcastle. Gazza went into the World Cup with ten caps, half of them as substitute. He was equally adept at demolishing opponents and infuriating his manager, for here was raw talent, but so raw it could not easily be accommodated with ten others on the same side. Gascoigne was a live-wire, of roly-poly frame, poor eating habits, no great pace, volatile temperament, defensive naïveté, a player who provoked both referees and opponents, and who one sensed had better find himself pretty soon, for longevity à la Bryan Robson seemed improbable. A public campaign for Gascoigne's inclusion might have waned had he not turned on a virtuoso performance against Czechoslovakia, creating three goals and scoring a dazzling fourth, which caught his manager mouthing 'Brilliant, brilliant!' from the sidelines. That settled his place in the squad, though not necessarily the team, for Gascoigne's defensive shortcomings demanded that he be partnered by more resilient midfielders. It was customarily Bryan Robson who surged forward at every opportunity. Whoever played alongside Gascoigne had to sit back.

As for David Platt, Gascoigne was a veteran by comparison. Platt had started an international just once. An energetic, goalscoring midfielder, combining the best in Colin Bell and Martin Peters, he could hardly expect to figure much.

Perhaps most surprising call-up was that of Steve Bull, a crew-cutted lad who had never touched the rarefied heights of the second division, never mind the first, but who had banged in so many goals for Wolves that he found himself the first England player to be plucked from the third division since Peter Taylor. 'Bull-in-a-china-shop' captured the player precisely.

Otherwise, the squad was largely as you were. The partnership of Lineker and Beardsley had spluttered on and off for four years, seldom reaching the telepathic heights of 1986. Beardsley, to boot, had been out of action for almost two months. Butcher and Robson were in their thirties and Shilton had turned forty. Robson, as ever, was fighting to be fit. Having missed three months of the season following a hernia operation, he was now troubled, among other things, by a bruised heel and toe.

The squad was announced on leaving for Italy, prior to the final warm-up in Tunisia. There, Butcher's booking for head-butting an opponent stole more news-space than Bull's late leveller, which prevented back-to-back defeats.

| No | Name | Position | Club | Age | Caps | Goals |
|----|------|----------|------|-----|------|-------|
| 1 | Peter Shilton | Goalkeeper | Derby County | 40 | 117 | – |
| 2 | Gary Stevens | Full-back | Rangers | 27 | 38 | – |
| 3 | Stuart Pearce | Full-back | Nott'm Forest | 28 | 23 | 1 |
| 4 | Neil Webb | Midfield | Manchester U | 26 | 19 | 2 |
| 5 | Des Walker | Central defence | Nott'm Forest | 24 | 17 | – |
| 6 | Terry Butcher | Central defence | Rangers | 31 | 71 | 3 |
| 7 | Bryan Robson (c) | Midfield | Manchester U | 33 | 84 | 26 |
| 8 | Chris Waddle | Forward | Marseilles | 29 | 51 | 6 |
| 9 | Peter Beardsley | Forward | Liverpool | 29 | 39 | 7 |
| 10 | Gary Lineker | Forward | Tottenham | 29 | 50 | 31 |
| 11 | John Barnes | Forward | Liverpool | 26 | 52 | 10 |
| 12 | Paul Parker | Defender | QPR | 26 | 5 | – |
| 13 | Chris Woods | Goalkeeper | Rangers | 30 | 16 | – |
| 14 | Mark Wright | Central defence | Derby County | 26 | 23 | – |
| 15 | Tony Dorigo | Full-back | Chelsea | 24 | 3 | – |
| 16 | Steve McMahon | Midfield | Liverpool | 28 | 12 | – |
| 17 | David Platt | Midfield | Aston Villa | 23 | 4 | – |
| 18 | Steve Hodge | Midfield | Nott'm Forest | 27 | 21 | – |
| 19 | Paul Gascoigne | Midfield | Tottenham | 22 | 10 | 2 |
| 20 | Trevor Steven | Midfield | Rangers | 26 | 26 | 3 |
| 21 | Steve Bull | Forward | Wolves | 25 | 6 | 4 |
| 22 | David Seaman * | Goalkeeper | Arsenal | 26 | 3 | – |

| | | | | | | |
|---|---|---|---|---|---|---|
| * Seaman was replaced by Dave Beasant. | | | *Averages* | 27.5 | 31.4 | |

The squad was by some way the most experienced England had ever sent to compete for the World Cup, though this was largely accounted for by Shilton's 117 caps.

| World Cup | Ave age | Ave caps |
|-----------|---------|----------|
| 1950 | 28.2 | 9.5 |
| 1954 | 28.8 | 14.9 |
| 1958 | 25.2 | 12.5 |
| 1962 | 25.5 | 15.4 |
| 1966 | 26.5 | 23.0 |
| 1970 | 27.0 | 25.7 |
| 1982 | 28.0 | 26.5 |
| 1986 | 26.2 | 22.5 |
| 1990 | 27.5 | 31.4 |

## REPUBLIC OF IRELAND v ENGLAND

*Monday, 11 June 1990*                                    *Cagliari – 35,238*

Jack Charlton was a hero in Ireland long before he sent out his team to do battle with England in Cagliari. Appointed in February 1986 as the first non-Irish national manager, his halo had been fitted for size in the unlikely setting of Sofia, in November 1987, when Gary Mackay secured an improbable win for Scotland in Bulgaria. That result put Ireland through to their first ever major finals. One of England's World Cup-winning heroes in 1966, he was now poised to rival Saint Patrick in his adopted land. Playing to Irish, that is to say, English strengths, Charlton fashioned a side that infuriated purists – long balls pumped over the top to make defenders turn, allied to terrier-like harassment in midfield. The juxtaposition of Irish charm with such charmless football struck many as incongruous, like Wimbledon, famous for hoity-toity tennis and thumpy-bumpy football. Charlton was assisted in his team-building by elastic nationality requirements, picking players – some quipped – with no greater Irish connection than owning an Irish wolfhound. Such regulations, for example, enabled him to select Tony Cascarino: even Americans are said to be suspicious of presidential candidates whose name ends in 'o'! As for Ray Houghton, of Glasgow parents and Glasgow accent, he was one of several Liverpool players called upon. In days of old, Welsh and Irish teams would take the field with half their team plucked from first division reserves or from lower divisions. This handicap did not apply to Jack Charlton. With the exception of the vastly experienced Kevin Moran, playing with Blackburn in division two, Charlton's team to face England graced the top divisions in England, Scotland and Spain.

The Irish had performed famously in the European finals, beating England, drawing with the Soviet Union, and only losing to Holland, the champions-in-waiting, through a late, offside goal. Otherwise, who knows how far Ireland might have progressed. They had qualified for Italy with ease, linking arms with Spain and sprinting clear of a pack that included Northern Ireland.

Jack Charlton's success raised inevitable questions about his predecessors' lack of it. Prior to these, her first World Cup finals, Ireland's track record in the competition had been worse than that of almost anyone in Europe. Yet Ireland had been exporting her stars to England almost since the time of Henry VIII. Liam Brady, David O'Leary, Frank Stapleton, to name but three, were players from the top drawer who predated Charlton's arrival by many a year. Be that as it may, Ireland rolled into Italy on the back of an unbeaten run stretching back thirteen games with the loss of just two goals. The squad were well versed in the simplicities of Charlton's style, but with an average age of 28½ were the oldest in Italy. They arrived wearing the grin of urchins set on causing mischief at an upper-crust tea party, and no one had any doubts they could topple an apple-cart or two.

The opening matches had set the mood. Cameroon, with two players sent off, sensationally beat defending champions Argentina. Less sensationally, perhaps, Costa Rica toppled Scotland.

British football did not wish to start the tournament with two defeats against less-fancied opponents. Bobby Robson fielded seven of the side beaten by Ireland in Stuttgart. Not that that constituted much of a surprise. The twenty-two players all knew each other intimately. The introduction of Gascoigne, however, did bring a smile to Jack Charlton, as did the retention of Bryan Robson. The one, he felt, was too maverick, the other too old and battle-weary. At least, that's what Charlton *said*. His private thoughts we shall never know.

If the pre-match pep talks harped on courage and endurance, they might have drawn upon the example of Captain Tim Lancaster, flying holidaymakers to Malaga when his windscreen blew out. The pilot was sucked head-first through the gaping hole, exposed to temperatures of –30 degrees, with the cabin crew keeping desperate hold of his ankles. The co-pilot made an emergency landing at Southampton. Captain Lancaster survived.

It was as well his plane was not flying over Cagliari, for the stricken pilot might have had to contend with footballs bombarding his frostbitten torso. As it was, police helicopters circling above the stadium spent much of their time evading spherical projectiles soaring across their flight-paths.

The match in other words was ugly, the ball always in the sky, two sides indulging in brawn rather than brain. Even the conditions were archetypically British, squally, cloudy, cool. But England, playing against the wind, were favoured with an early goal. Waddle's one dangerous cross of the night lured Bonner suicidally from his goal-line. Lineker thrust back his shoulders and chested the ball past the keeper, hotly pursued by McCarthy and Morris, who were unable to prevent him shepherding it over the line. Lineker thereby matched Geoff Hurst's achievement of '66 and '70, scoring his team's last goal in one World Cup, and its first in the next.

As an attacking force that was the last seen of England, as ball and limbs were whacked indiscriminately with all the grace of a street fight. For England, it was now a case of guarding that precious lead. It might have been doubled on the hour when Waddle skipped past two players but was earthed by Moran. The West German referee shook his head. No penalty.

An electrical storm during the interval brought more thrills than the action that preceded it. The wind then died and rain came down, denying England their hoped-for second-half advantage. It was the substitutions of two players that turned the game on its head. Charlton introduced Alan McLoughlin to press forward from midfield. Tit-for-tat, Robson promptly sent on Steve McMahon. Almost McMahon's first act was to fumble the ball on the eighteen-yard line, and it bobbled to the Irishman best equipped to exploit the error. Kevin Sheedy's drive was low, true, and wide of Shilton's straining left hand. To compound his sins, McMahon was shortly booked.

'I sent him on to win us the game,' moaned Bobby Robson afterwards. 'Instead, he cost us it.' But at least England had not lost. Neither manager was too disheartened at the result, the first draw of the tournament to date. Those most unhappy were the neutrals – wondering how the British could endure, nay enjoy, such fare – and Greenpeace, thought to be protesting that British football was damaging the ozone layer. It was later confirmed that the ball had been in play for just forty-seven minutes out of the ninety.

REPUBLIC OF IRELAND  (0) 1      ENGLAND  (1) 1
  Sheedy 73                                   Lineker 8

IRELAND: Bonner (Celtic), Morris (Celtic), Staunton (Liverpool), McCarthy (Millwall), Moran (Blackburn), McGrath (Villa), Houghton (Liverpool), Townsend (Norwich), Aldridge (Real Sociedad) (*sub* McLoughlin, Swindon), Cascarino (Villa), Sheedy (Everton).
ENGLAND: Shilton, Stevens, Pearce, Gascoigne, Walker, Butcher, Waddle, Robson, Beardsley (McMahon), Lineker (Bull), Barnes.

**HOLLAND v ENGLAND**
*Saturday, 16 June 1990*                                    *Cagliari – 35,267*

The next day heralded the first shock of Group F. Nobody seriously thought Egypt could hold the Dutch. But they did, and they deserved more. Their spirited display worried both Bobby Robson and Jack Charlton, who could no longer be so cock-sure about the victory that would ensure qualification.

As for Holland, they'd been more daisies than tulips. They hadn't even qualified in 1982 and 1986, and were famous for snatching victories and defeats they did not deserve. If they suffered cruel luck in the World Cup Finals of both 1974 and 1978, their European triumph in 1988 was born of indubitable style married to prodigious good fortune. Thumped by the Soviet Union in their first match, Holland survived two dented goalposts in their second, against England, another against the Irish, and only qualified from their group by virtue of a late, offside goal against Jack Charlton's team. West Germany were overcome in the semi-final with the aid of a nonsensical penalty. The Soviets even missed a penalty in the Final. As they say, if your name is on the Cup, no mere footballers can wipe it off.

True, Dutch football had some magical players. Ruud Gullit (European Footballer of the Year, 1987) and Frank Rijkaard were dreadlocked Surinamese able to play in any position, while Marco van Basten (European Footballer of the Year, 1988 and '89) had some claim to be even better than Gary Lineker. This trio had just helped AC Milan retain the European Cup against Benfica, ensuring that Italian sympathies would be vested in Holland.

Another threesome – goalkeeper van Breukelen, van Aerle, and Wim Kieft, who would come on as substitute – were on the books of PSV Eindhoven, Bobby Robson's imminent employers. On the occasions their paths crossed his, the players were properly deferential, doffing their caps, so to speak.

Tactically, the Dutch were ready for anything: they could match England for muscle, if necessary, and outplay them for skill, for sure. Equally, they had the air of a team which knew their time had come, continuing to forge results not always merited by their performances. Egypt had shown that it might take more than just a superior team to beat them.

If Dutch fortunes had changed for the better, their ill-tempered internal squabblings had not. When had a Dutch squad not been riven by bickerings over money or player-power? This one was no more insouciant than its predecessors. The coach who guided Holland to the finals, Thijs Libregts, had been ousted by a mutiny of star players – Gullit prominent – but they were denied the replacement they demanded, Johann Cruyff. Rinus Michels, grand vizier of Dutch football, appointed Leo Beenhakker for the arduous task of healing the rifts and extracting the best.

Come match-day, the Queen had knighted Richard Hadlee in her Birthday Honours. Sir Richard had the honour to be the first cricketer knighted principally for his bowling. Like Ireland's footballers, Hadlee's New Zealand team had just held England to a comfortable draw. England's footballers, by this time, had all but closed the doors to the press, after groundless allegations that several players had enjoyed the favours of a hostess assigned to England's hotel. They also had a new goalkeeper. When David Seaman broke his thumb in training, FIFA permitted David Beasant to be flown out as a substitute.

England and Holland approached their match with added pressures. Both had not unreasonably hoped to have two points already in the bag, whereupon they might have settled for an uninspiring draw. Now they had everything to play for.

In a bid to outwit the other, both managers sprang surprises. For England, Paul Parker replaced Gary Stevens, and Beardsley was left out in favour of Mark Wright. Wright would have played in Mexico but for breaking his leg. Like Des Walker, he brought pace and skill to the defence, but his was a surprise recall. He hadn't been picked for two years, since shying off from the match with the Soviet Union in the European Championship.

This, Bobby Robson's last shot at the World Cup, may have brought out the gambling instinct, for Wright was asked to play sweeper, with Walker and Butcher man-marking in front of him. Never before in his eight-year reign had Robson employed a sweeper. It was he confessed, the biggest tactical surprise he had ever pulled.

The ploy almost came unstuck with the announcement of the Dutch team. With the exception of the now retired Arnold Muhren, Robson anticipated an unchanged line-up from that which had secured a hat-trick for van Basten in Düsseldorf. He had not reckoned on Beenhakker giving a debut to Aberdeen's Hans Gillhaus, playing him as a loose cannon on the left. Robson's intention had been for Walker and Butcher to man-mark in front of Mark Wright, but the inclusion of Gillhaus forced Butcher, in effect, to play *de facto* right-back, a position completely new to the left-sided stopper. Had Robson read Beenhakker's mind, Gary Stevens would have played instead. Now the England manager had to watch and wait.

In the event, Robson need not have fretted. The occasion proved too much for Gillhaus, and his preference for cutting inside rather than out played into Butcher's hands.

Butcher was not the only one to shine, for the match was as gripping as Ireland's had been wretched. Shilton's world record 120th cap was rewarded with a clean-sheet, but he would surely have surrendered that bonus for the win he and his team deserved. With Gascoigne looking the part in midfield and Walker nullifying the threat posed by van Basten, England looked a different outfit from that which had toiled against Ireland.

Not that the Dutch were mugs. They finished the first half in the ascendant, and with Bryan Robson struggling might have inflicted damage in the second. Playing with a pain-killing injection in his toe, Robson strained his Achilles tendon and was substituted by David Platt, to the frustration of Robson's natural deputy, Steve McMahon.

Though the match ended goalless, its most memorable moments were England's. Steve Bull, on for Waddle, flashed a header wide; Gascoigne wriggled past two defenders on the goal-line; Lineker 'scored', but had handled

Steve Bull feels the point of van Breukelen's knee. (v Holland)

the ball; and in the final minute Pearce also 'scored', but his free-kick had been indirect. The statistics showed that Holland forced thirteen corners to England's three, and had directed more shots at goal. But no one in the Dutch camp was prepared to dispute England's greater claim to a moral victory.

HOLLAND  (0) 0                    ENGLAND  (0) 0

HOLLAND: van Breukelen, van Aerle, Rijkaard, R Koeman, van Tiggelen, Wouters, Gullit, Witschge, van Basten, van't Schip (Kieft), Gillhaus.
ENGLAND: Shilton, Parker, Pearce, Wright, Walker, Butcher, Robson (Platt), Waddle (Bull), Gascoigne, Lineker, Barnes.

## EGYPT v ENGLAND
*Thursday, 21 June 1990*                    *Cagliari – 34,959*

The next day Ireland waged a sterile goalless draw with Egypt. Jack Charlton's denunciation of Egypt's negativity provoked outrage in Cairo and consternation in diplomatic circles. Charlton stood accused of affronting the Egyptian nation. He was quietly reminded: 'let him without stain cast the first stone.' Had not Charlton's Leeds team of the 'sixties specialised in cynicism?

Ireland's 0-0 draw also sent FIFA rushing to its book of rules and regulations. As in 1986, the four best third-placed teams would enter the second round. All four teams in Group F currently showed two draws and one goal. Should the final two matches, to be played concurrently, be identical draws, FIFA would be presented with an unprecedented blanket finish. Russian Roulette would separate the teams, and lots cast to determine all four group placings. Having three points and a neutral goal-difference, the team drawn out third was sure to survive; the team pulled out last would be on its way home.

There was little doubt that Egypt, having fought a rearguard action against Ireland, would do the same against England. If they could pull off another draw, they would finish the group stage unbeaten and – depending on results elsewhere – with better than even chances of progressing.

With other results coming in, the prize for topping Group F was a date with Belgium, with Colombia or Cameroon to follow. Finishing second was less appetising, being paired with Romania, with either Italy or Uruguay in the last eight. Squeezing through in third place might entail a clash with West Germany. The issue was simple: winning the match and the group would secure pole position.

This was the third World Cup in which England had faced Arab opponents, having beaten Kuwait 1-0 in 1982, and survived 0-0 against Morocco four years later. To date, England had never lost to a Third World nation, though they had come mighty close, most recently in Tunisia. It was doubtful that Egypt would even seek to score themselves; the real questions concerned England's ability to prise open a resolute and well-marshalled defence. England had won comfortably enough, 4-0 in Cairo, warming up for the 1986 World Cup, but in current circumstances that result was as misleading as a mirage. Ominously, Egypt had beaten Scotland, 3-1 at Pittodrie, in their final preparations for Italy, a result which perhaps explained why Scotland were now on their way home. The Scots had stood to survive as one of the best third-placed teams until Uruguay, scourge of 1986, scored an injury-time winner against South Korea.

With Bryan Robson fighting a losing battle with his fitness, he arranged for a faith healer to be flown out. It made no difference. He would not play. Nor would Butcher, dropped by Bobby Robson for club or country for the first time. Against his players' wishes, the manager reverted to a flat back four, and Mark Wright's claim to partner Walker outweighed Butcher's. Up front, Lineker played despite an infected toenail that prevented training. Steve Bull partnered him.

After the beer the champagne; now back to the beer. Another dreary match, no cohesion, no fluency, just eleven Egyptians back-peddling, two booked for time-wasting, cheered on by hundreds of Egyptian sailors in the stands. Hany Ramzi, the nominal sweeper, played so deep as to be a second goalkeeper.

Having created little, England scored. Walker was fouled by the touchline, and was being treated off the pitch when Gascoigne floated an inswinging free-kick that tempted Shobeir off his line. Mark Wright glanced the ball past the keeper and in via Yakan's head. It was Wright's first international goal. Egypt were equipped to starve the game, not resuscitate it, and presented England with few scares. With the final whistle Shobeir collapsed and had to be helped from the pitch in hysterics. Over in Sicily, Ireland's equaliser against the Dutch meant England had won Group F. FIFA's lucky dip would now contain just two, not the dreaded four teams. Ireland were placed second and Holland third. Ireland versus Romania, Holland versus the Germans. The luck of the Irish had staved off the luck of the Dutch.

EGYPT   (0) 0                          ENGLAND   (0) 1
                                                Wright 58

EGYPT: Shobeir, I Hassan, Yassein, H Ramzy, Yakan, A Ramzy, Youssef, Abdelghani, H Hassan, Abdelhamid (Abdelrahman), El Kas (Soliman).
ENGLAND: Shilton, Parker, Pearce, Gascoigne, Walker, Wright, McMahon, Waddle (Platt), Bull (Beardsley), Lineker, Barnes.

---

*Final positions – Group F*

|  | P | W | D | L | F | A | Pts |
|---|---|---|---|---|---|---|---|
| ENGLAND | 3 | 1 | 2 | 0 | 2 | 1 | 4 |
| REPUBLIC OF IRELAND | 3 | 0 | 3 | 0 | 2 | 2 | 3 |
| HOLLAND | 3 | 0 | 3 | 0 | 2 | 2 | 3 |
| Egypt | 3 | 0 | 2 | 1 | 1 | 2 | 2 |

---

**BELGIUM v ENGLAND**
*Tuesday, 26 June 1990*                                   *Bologna – 34,520*

It was proving a wretched, cynical World Cup, with fewer goals per game than any other. Group F's seven goals was even more miserly than Monterrey's nine. In future, steer clear of England and Group F, was the message relayed to the world. At least Sardinia and Sicily were done with the World Cup. Normality could return to the islands.

England were off to the mainland, up north to Bologna. The exodus of supporters trailing in their wake was marred by some 240 'fans' deported from Rimini, the largest mass deportation in Italian peacetime. Once again, UEFA's readmission of English clubs hung by a thread. The miscreants returned to a Britain enraptured by Luciano Pavarotti's *Nessun Dorma*, the first classical piece to storm the hit parade. The BBC used the record to introduce its World Cup programmes. Viewers evidently favoured BBC coverage, preferring the staid and stoic Desmond Lynam and Jimmy Hill to the slapstick of ITV's Rodney Marsh and Emlyn Hughes.

Further delights awaiting the deportees included an outbreak of crop-circle mania in Oxfordshire. Wimbledon had just commenced without Chris Evert or Jimmy Connors for the first time since 1972, and without a seeded Australian singles player since 1939. John McEnroe, seeded four, was a first round casualty, tumbling out to Derrick Rostagno. Across the capital, Philip Nelkon claimed the twentieth World Scrabble Championship. Unusual words included 'dzo', a hybrid cattle from the Himalayas. Not many people knew that.

Nor did many people know the names of six famous Belgians, to quote the cruel jibe. Poor downtrodden Belgium. The butt of endless Irish-type jokes from the French and Dutch. Belgians were even blamed for Waterloo – 175th anniversary just commemorated – though Belgium did not even exist in 1815. Footballing arguments had gone decisively in England's favour. Belgium's proximity had encouraged fixtures almost yearly through the 1920s. The two critical matches since 1945 had both ended all square, 4-4 in the 1954 World Cup, 1-1 in the 1980 European Championship. Seventeen meetings in total, with Belgium enjoying just the one victory, in 1936.

Guy Thys, their knowing manager, had been at the helm, off and on, since 1976, guiding the 'Red Devils' to the European Championship Final in 1980 (losing to West Germany), the second stage of the World Cup in 1982, and fourth place in 1986. John Lyall and Dave Sexton had run the eye over Belgium's progress in Italy. Skipper Jan Ceulemans, thirty-three, 6ft 2in tall, was a veteran of the 1980 draw with England, in which he scored, and was three times Belgian Footballer of the Year. That honour currently belonged to long-haired goalkeeper Michel Preud'homme, though he was not to everyone's taste. No nonsense Eric Gerets, thirty-six, was another on the books of PSV Eindhoven. He would now return to the side, having been sent off during the thrilling 3-1 win over Uruguay. But Belgium's jewel was undoubtedly Vincenzo 'Enzo' Scifo, now playing for Auxerre in France. Scifo had shone in Mexico as a twenty-two year old soloist, a leaner, swifter Gascoigne. Now in his prime, Shifo was expected to contribute much to England's downfall.

For his part, Bobby Robson was beset by problems of injury and loss of form to key players. In Mexico, his struggling captain had hung around for the good of the team: now he flew home for surgery, his third and last World Cup at an end. As for the lacklustre Barnes and Waddle, they were starting to sound like Matthews and Finney, outstandingly gifted but too often peripheral, both in position and performance. Rather than use one or the other, as was his want, Bobby Robson had taken to playing them both. And with good reason. Their recent club form had invited superlatives, Barnes being voted the Football Writers' Player of the Year, and Waddle inspiring Marseilles to the French championship. How could anyone leave out such talent?

Penalties beckon as David Platt swivels to score. (v Belgium)

Do unto Belgium as you would unto Holland. In other words, bring back a sweeper. Now that McMahon's Irish blunder had not proved costly, he was recalled and instructed to curb Scifo.

England were establishing themselves as the most schizophrenic team in Italy. Two dire matches and now two absorbing ones. That the match with Belgium yielded just one goal was down to goalposts and referee. The goalposts denied Belgium, the referee (or linesman) denied England. Belgium's fleetness of foot earned them a territorial advantage they retained throughout. Ceulemans skinned Wright but his shot came back off a post. At the other end, Lineker's pace down the line so befuddled the linesman that Barnes' scoring volley was erroneously flagged offside.

Parker, tormented by Versavel early on, grew in confidence, but still Belgium carried the greater threat. With McMahon AWOL, Scifo fired a skimmer from thirty yards, striking the base of Shilton's right post as Ceulemans had at the other end. Platt and Bull replaced McMahon, shattered, and Barnes, nursing his groin. For Belgium, ex-Spurs forward Nico Claesen stripped off, fancying his chances against the limping Walker. Gascoigne dived in on Scifo and was cautioned.

Extra time came and went. Poor Lineker, barely able to squeeze his swollen big toe into his boot, and training in slippers, hadn't managed a shot. There was barely a minute on the clock and penalties loomed when Gazza surged out of his own half, to be impeded by Gerets. Gascoigne might have played the free-kick square to exhaust the remaining seconds. Instead, at the urging of the bench, he chipped an angled ball over van der Elst and over Platt's shoulder. In a moment forever to be cherished in English football, Platt spun 360 degrees, anticlockwise, wrapping his foot around the dropping ball to hook an unstoppable volley past the amazed Preud'homme. The English Players' Player of the Year had beaten Belgium's. It was a special goal, Platt's first for England, and the Belgians sank to their knees in despair.

'This was the best team I ever had,' sighed Guy Thys. He had every right to be proud. Most football judges concurred that the better team had lost. But this crazy World Cup had thrown up five 'iffy' second-round winners. Argentina (v Brazil), Cameroon (v Colombia), Yugoslavia (v Spain), and Ireland, on penalties (v Romania) had also triumphed on questionable merit.

The next day a classic Belgian novel, translated into English, was published, title: *The Sorrow of Belgium*.

BELGIUM   (0) 0                    ENGLAND   (0) 1
                                            Platt 119
                                   *After extra time (0-0 after 90 minutes)*

BELGIUM: Preud'homme, Gerets, Clijsters, Demol, Grun, de Wolf, van der Elst, Scifo, Versavel (Vervoort), Degryse (Claesen), Ceulemans.
ENGLAND: Shilton, Parker, Pearce, Wright, Walker, Butcher, McMahon (Platt), Waddle, Gascoigne, Lineker, Barnes (Bull).

## CAMEROON v ENGLAND
*Sunday, 1 July 1990*                                    *Naples – 55,205*

As in 1986, England had reached the last eight. This time they were confronted not by Argentina but by Cameroon. On the face of it, this seemed an incalculable advantage. England had no direct experience of sub-Saharan, black African football, but it was generally the Arab African nations to the north that had been better schooled. Zaire's mortifying experience in 1974 had seen them bombarded by fourteen goals. Cameroon, themselves, had enjoyed a more impressive baptism. In 1982, in Spain, they had staged three creditable draws, but been squeezed out. African champions in 1984 and '88, they reached Italia '90 never having lost a match in the World Cup finals.

Coached by the Russian, Valeri Nepomniachi, Cameroon had been the talk of the championship since the opening day, when they beat Argentina with nine men. Cameroon exhibited, as the mood took them, mouth-watering skills coupled with – political correctness permitting – jungle brutality. That win over

Argentina made the defending champions, no slouches in thuggery, appear almost angelic by comparison. Massing's atrocious assault on Caniggia would have landed him in prison had he repeated it outside a football ground.

Cameroon topped Group B, losing just once (0-4), to the Soviet Union when qualification was assured. Cameroon had been distinctly inferior to the equally contradictory Colombians in the second round, and but for goalkeeper Higuita's hilarious dash from goal, where he was dispossessed by Roger Milla, Cameroon might not have survived. Milla was one of the bright lights of this mediocre tournament. African Footballer of the Year in 1976, he had played for some seasons in France before coming to wider notice in the 1982 finals as a mature thirty-year-old. Preferring an unorthodox spelling of his name, just to be different, he was now a sprightly thirty-eight, emerging from semi-retirement, and used exclusively as a super-sub for his remarkable speed over short distances. His four second-half introductions had already brought him four goals, which he celebrated with an ebullient, not to say erotic, dance with the corner flag. Cameroon's achievement, to date, in becoming the first African side to reach the quarter-finals had already prompted a FIFA directive. For the 1994 World Cup, African representation would be raised from two to three.

So much for the plusses. The debit column showed that Cameroon brought to the quarter-finals two red cards, eight yellows, and ninety fouls. Four of their best players were out, suspended. As Cameroon's magic was inseparable from their mayhem, few doubted fireworks would fly in Naples' San Paolo Stadium.

The Cameroon team were divided into amateurs and pros, domiciles and exiles – mostly decorating the French league, though goalkeeper N'Kono played in Spain with Español, and Mbouh in Switzerland with Chénois. Bobby Robson kept faith with the team that finished the match against Belgium. Not a few Little Englanders insisted that Cameroon's physical strength and individual talent were offset by their collective naïveté, and that England had a virtual bye into the semis where West Germany awaited.

From his hospital bed, Prince Charles doubtless switched on his TV expectantly. He had come a cropper falling off his polo pony and breaking his arm. Fears about the heir to the throne's well-being prompted renewed calls for him to give up polo, or turn to safer sports. Like tennis, perhaps. Wimbledon was in the grip of grunt-fever. Monica Seles' noisy exhalations were condemned as lacking decorum: besides, they affected the spectators' concentration.

High above, the Hubble space telescope continued to relay wonky pictures of distant galaxies. Had it realigned its lenses on Naples it would have witnessed a match to rank with the best in World Cup history.

The Cameroon 'Lions' emerged from the tunnel in their colourful red and green shirts singing gustily. Almost immediately Shilton had to save smartly from Omam Biyik. Cameroon's confidence should have been dented when

Stuart Pearce centred from the left; Platt's header was down and firm. This, his second priceless goal, marked the 100th of Italia '90.

There were those who wondered if Cameroon might cave in. Coming from behind was not yet among their noted accomplishments. But what transpired in the next hour would shock not only England, but football watchers everywhere. England hung on, somehow, till half-time, surviving several thunderous shots at Shilton's goal. When the teams reappeared, Roger Milla, shaven-haired, lined up for Cameroon, and Peter Beardsley for England. Platt was soon sent tumbling by the goalkeeper, but Mexican referee Codesal Mendez waved play on. Platt picked himself up, only to find Mendez pointing to the spot at the other end. Gascoigne, had upended the wily Milla, and Kunde scored with a penalty that Shilton almost reached.

Cameroon were already threatening to tear England asunder, and their second goal four minutes later did precisely that. The sweeper system may have worked against Holland and Belgium, but it was less appropriate against a team playing to no known system. Cameroon players were all over the place, one minute at left-back, the next at outside-right. England's back three, dragged hither and thither, were equally at sixes and sevens. The goal's architect was the indomitable Milla. Pulling defenders wide on the left, he threaded an exquisite pass into the path of the onrushing Ekeke. A chasm appeared at the heart of England's defence and Ekeke, himself a recent substitute, insolently chipped the ball over the advancing Shilton. It was a classic goal and England were on the ropes. Back in London, the noise bursting from the Cameroon Embassy alerted passers-by to the possibility of terrorist attack. The commotion might even have carried to the august halls of the Foreign Office, whose night-staff, secreted in front of a television, no doubt clapped politely and muttered darkly.

That goal put paid to England's chequered sweeper system. Off came Butcher, on went Trevor Steven, the second substitute. Wright promptly gashed his eye so severely that under normal circumstances he would have had to come off. Unable to head the ball, he pushed up into midfield. With Walker hobbling and Beardsley quite out of sorts, it was hard to envisage England's salvation. But rather than look for a third goal, Cameroon fell back, and that was their undoing. Platt fashioned a chance, but shot narrowly wide. Then, seven minutes from Armageddon, Gascoigne directed the ball to Lineker, who was swatted to the ground by Massing. Few penalties came any more clear-cut. It was England's first in the finals of the World Cup for twenty years, when Allan Clarke's beat Czechoslovakia in Mexico. That penalty had been immaterial to England's prospects. This one separated England from oblivion. A camera behind the goal dwelled on Lineker's face. Surely that was fear and uncertainty in his eyes. The camera was duped. Lineker swept the ball to N'Kono's left and England were alive.

Peter Shilton is down and England appear to be out as Ekeke chips Cameroon in front. (v Cameroon)

Only in extra time did England not look transparently second best. Cameroon had given their all. The first period was drawing to a close: another incisive through ball from Gazza, another burst from Lineker, and this time it was N'Kono himself who toppled England's saviour. One felt less nervous for Lineker this time. N'Kono duly dived left, but the ball was whacked straight and hard. 3-2, and Cameroon hardly threatened again.

'Some bye that was!' exploded Chris Waddle afterwards. Cameroon had had twenty-six shots and won six corners to England's fifteen shots and one corner.

England supporters rejoiced in reaching the semi-finals of the World Cup for the first time on foreign soil. For the rest of the world, there was only applause for Cameroon and tears at their going.

Roger Milla must have been doubly flattered, being honoured by his country and sought by the might of England. The honour was to be made Commander of the Order of Valour; the offer came from humble Walsall, of the fourth division.

CAMEROON  (0) 2
Kunde 62 pen, Ekeke 66

ENGLAND  (1) 3
Platt 25,
Lineker 83 pen, 105 pen
*After extra time (2-2 after 90 minutes)*

CAMEROON: N'Kono, Massing, Ebwelle, Kunde, Pagal, Tataw, M'Fede (Ekeke), Libiih, Makanaky, Maboang (Milla), Omam Biyik.

ENGLAND: Shilton, Parker, Pearce, Wright, Walker, Butcher (Steven), Platt, Waddle, Gascoigne, Lineker, Barnes (Beardsley).

## WEST GERMANY v ENGLAND
*Wednesday, 4 July 1990*                                    *Turin – 62,628*

As the dust settled, four giants of football, all previous winners of the World Cup, assembled for the semi-finals. Italy would face Argentina, hosts versus holders, while England would play West Germany in the latest instalment of their long-running saga. For England, no other country conjures up such deep-rooted or conflicting footballing emotions. The extra-time triumph in 1966; the agonising extra-time defeat in 1970. The records showed that since winning the World Cup, England had beaten their old adversary just twice in ten attempts – both in friendlies, and never when it mattered.

German coach Franz Beckenbauer was not being discourteous to his England counterpart when confessing that he preferred to face England than Cameroon. Better the devil you know. Cameroon provided obstacles that no opponents had yet fathomed.

Whether the German nation could devote its entire attention to some far off football field was open to question. The old certainties regarding East and West had disappeared in the blink of an eye. German economic union meant that the Deutschmark had just become legal tender in the East, and Checkpoint Charlie – that grim icon of the cold war – dismantled. Though no one could foresee it, before the year was out Germany would be reunited.

Could Bobby Robson succeed where others had failed? This was England's second World Cup semi-final, Germany's eighth in ten attempts since 1954. No other country could approach that kind of consistency. This would be Germany's sixty-seventh match in World Cup finals, surpassing the previous record held by Brazil. German football was seldom exhilarating in the manner of Italy's or Brazil's, but it was ruthlessly controlled and efficient. The Germans were unequalled at gauging the pace of a tournament, starting slowly, but building up a head of steam for the climax.

Franz Beckenbauer had assumed the reins in 1984. He was now two matches away from accomplishing that which had slipped away in the Final in Mexico, the honour of being only the second person (after Mario Zagalo) to win the World Cup both as player and manager. Of his players, five earned their living in Italy – Völler and Berthold with Roma, Brehme, Klinsmann and captain Matthäus with Internazionale. Matthäus was to Germany what Bryan Robson, in his prime, was to England. Klinsmann and Völler were strikers *extraordinaire*, doubly dangerous in tandem, while Andreas Brehme added new dimensions to the job of full-back. Brehme was a craftsman as much as a defender, a player who made Stuart Pearce, for all his strength, seem prehistoric. Beckenbauer's murderous keeper, Schumacher, villain of two previous World Cups, had given way to Cologne's Bodo Illgner.

Germany had found the net regularly in Italy, scoring thirteen goals to England's six. But only in the quarter-final with Czechoslovakia had they kept a clean sheet, and therein perhaps lay a glimmer of hope. Awaiting the winners in the Final were Argentina. Dreary, defensive Argentina, bereft of their blond star, Caniggia, and with Maradona just a ghost of himself. Oh for the chance to settle old scores. But first the little matter of Germany.

The match would be played in Turin, home of Juventus, raising fears that English no-goods would rub salt into the wounds of Heysel. England had been allowed just three days' recuperation from the Cameroon ordeal, taking over the hotel recently vacated by Brazil. John Barnes needed longer than three days to get fit, and was out. So, almost, was his infuriating twin, Chris Waddle. But Robson stuck with him, demanding that he reinforce the midfield and counter Littbarski, who had played against England in 1982. But Littbarksi would not play. His place went to the even faster Olaf Thon. The Marseilles wizard would need to attach his spurs. The sweeper system was retained, but this time with Butcher as the broom.

Cheered by a world record javelin throw in Stockholm by Steve Backley, the first Briton ever to set a world record in a field event, England set about proving the pundits wrong. For half an hour they were unrecognisable from the team hanging onto the coat-tails of Belgium and Cameroon. They tore into the Germans from the off, and Gascoigne's sweet volley tested Illgner at the foot of a post. Though striker Völler soon limped from the fray, replaced by Riedle, the loss did not impede the German effort. Indeed, the game tilted perceptibly towards Shilton's goal.

Half-time arrived with few chances created, few fouls committed, but with applause ringing around the stadium at the pulsating quality of the football.

Germany began the second half as they ended the first, but Shilton's goal had not been unduly threatened before the roof caved in. Pearce fouled Hässler. Thon touched the free-kick to Brehme, and as Paul Parker dashed from the wall Brehme's drive flew off him and looped cruelly beyond the stranded Shilton. A game of such grace hardly merited a more unworthy goal.

As with Cameroon, Butcher was hauled off, replaced again by Trevor Steven. As with Cameroon, just minutes remained when Lineker equalised. Parker's cross befuddled Augenthaler and Kohler and somehow squeezed beyond them to Lineker, who swept the ball through straining German legs and just inside Illgner's left post. Lineker's tenth goal in World Cup finals breathed life into flagging spirits.

The contest was as vibrant and finely balanced as any in the tournament.

After ninety minutes the sides were still deadlocked, but England appeared to have lost Gascoigne from the Final, should they get there. Gazza had clearly been marked for special attention. He would be fouled seven times on the night, by far the most of any player. He had lunged at Berthold and been booked by Brazilian referee José Ramiz Wright. It was his second caution in the competition. With tears streaming down his face Gascoigne fell apart. Lineker was seen yelling at the bench: 'Talk to him!' Gascoigne was still needed, and to his credit he pulled himself together. Extra time began with Waddle hitting one post, and ended with Buchwald banging the same. But there was no denying German supremacy now. This was their first extra period, England's third. Klinsmann missed a sitter, and England's only hope lay through the penalty shoot-out.

In London, even the House of Commons was hushed. The Rolling Stones' concert at Wembley had to contend with thousands listening through personal stereos, cheering and booing with each goal and each save. In view of the phoenix qualities demonstrated against Belgium and Cameroon, there were many who sensed that England's name was etched on the Cup. England won the toss and took the first kick. Efforts from Lineker, Beardsley and Platt were cancelled by bullets from Brehme, Matthäus, and Riedle. In tennis, 3-3 is a famously brittle score, with a break of serve often looming. And so it was in Turin. Pearce, normally so reliable, had been held back, but Illgner guessed right and the ball cannoned back off his legs. Thon put the Germans in front, and Waddle skied England's fifth kick over the bar. England were done, the Germans hysterical, though Matthäus wrapped a consoling arm around Waddle's shoulders.

A final 'if'. Had the shoot-out gone to sudden death, Gascoigne was first in line for England. With a different script, his could have been the final glory. Even with the script as it stood, this ranked as the match of the tournament. England looked better in defeat than they ever looked when beating Belgium and Cameroon.

In Mexico, three quarter-finals had been settled by penalties; in Italy, both semis. Such farce had no place in determining the champions of the world, and FIFA was already earnestly debating changes. The tally of corner kicks or cautions was mooted as standing in place of penalties. On both counts England would still have lost to Germany.

As millions of dejected British kettles went on, the resultant electricity surge was sufficient to illuminate Merseyside. It constituted the biggest drain on the national grid since 1984, following the final episode of *The Thorn Birds*.

WEST GERMANY  (0) 1*          ENGLAND  (0) 1
  Brehme 60                          Lineker 82
* West Germany won 4-3 on penalties  *After extra time (1-1 after 90 minutes)*

Lineker scores his tenth goal in World Cup finals. (v W Germany)

W GERMANY: Illgner, Brehme, Kohler, Augenthaler, Buchwald, Berthold, Matthäus, Hässler (Reuter), Thon, Völler (Riedle), Klinsmann.
ENGLAND: Shilton, Parker, Pearce, Wright, Walker, Butcher (Steven), Platt, Waddle, Gascoigne, Lineker, Beardsley.

## ITALY v ENGLAND
*Saturday, 7 July 1990*                                    *Bari – 51,426*

England grieved. They had played their best when it mattered, but it was not enough. But this was no cause for shame. Even those critics who argued that England could have gone out to Belgium, and should to Cameroon, conceded that Robson's men played like giants. The manager's last serious competitive match had lifted England to heights not equalled since 1966. The performance against West Germany invited comparisons with all-time great matches, like that with Brazil in 1970. For the third successive World Cup England had been k.o.'d in doubtful circumstances. In 1982 and 1990 they retired unbeaten. In 1986 they were put out by the 'Hand of God'. Then and now their conquerors went on to win the trophy.

England's would not be an early plane home, for a new experience awaited, the much-maligned play-off for third place. It was no consolation to both Italy and England that, but for an inch here and there, a penalty scored, a penalty saved, this could have been for real.

Having traversed the length and breadth of Italy in ten hectic days, it was back down south, to Bari. Robson shuffled his side for this semi-serious exhibition, playing Steven instead of Waddle and giving Dorigo a game at left-back to end Pearce's long run. Gascoigne was suspended. Neil Webb would appear as substitute, leaving only the reserve goalkeepers and the injured Hodge without a game in Italy.

Shilton had already confided that this, his 125th (his seventeenth in World Cup finals), would be his last international. His heirs in the wings had been mothballed too long. It would not be a glorious finale. Shilton was caught rolling the ball and was dispossessed by Baggio, who exchanged passes with 'Toto' Schillaci and – though clearly offside – opened the scoring. Platt's wonderful header from Dorigo's cross restored parity, only for Parker to impede Schillaci in the box. The Juventus striker duly scored his sixth goal of the tournament. The margin of defeat might have been yet worse. In injury time Berti ran from deep to plant a splendid header wide of Shilton. Absurdly, the linesman flagged for offside. No matter, England finished fourth overall.

The World Cup Final was an apology for a football match, deservedly won by West Germany, who mercifully overcame the wretched tactics of Argentina and reversed the result of 1986. Argentina finished the game with more players sent off – two – than accurate shots at goal – none.

The England players returned home to a reception they could never have anticipated. They also returned sporting the World Cup's Fair Play trophy, in recognition of receiving the fewest red and yellow cards and committing the fewest fouls in the competition. This accomplishment spoke volumes. Allied to the containment of the hooligan menace, it was enough to convince UEFA to welcome English clubs back into the fold. The cold war, said NATO, was officially over, and so were English football's cold years of isolation.

Bobby Robson's England epoch was at an end, as it was for Peter Shilton and Terry Butcher. At thirty-three, Bryan Robson's international career was on borrowed time. With the heart of the England team gone, new manager Graham Taylor would need to dig deep for replacements. Two – Paul Gascoigne and David Platt – had already announced themselves ready and able, though neither appeared in the International Journalists' World Team '90. Only one Englishman did, Des Walker, and he was among the substitutes.

| ITALY   (0) 2 | ENGLAND   (0) 1 |
|---|---|
| Baggio 70, | Platt 80 |
| Schillaci 85 pen | |

ITALY: Zenga, Baresi, Bergomi, De Agostini (Berti), Ferrara, Maldini, Vierchowod, Ancelotti, Giannini (Ferri), Baggio, Schillaci.
ENGLAND: Shilton, Stevens, Dorigo, Parker, Walker, Wright (Waddle), Platt, Steven, McMahon (Webb), Lineker, Beardsley.

*England appearances and goalscorers (substitute appearances in brackets)*
*World Cup qualifying rounds and final competition 1990*

| | Apps | Goals | | Apps | Goals |
|---|---|---|---|---|---|
| Lineker G * | 13 | 6 | Wright M * | 6 | 1 |
| Shilton P *†‡ | 13 | – | McMahon S | 5 (1) | – |
| Waddle C * | 12 (1) | 1 | Webb N | 5 (1) | 1 |
| Walker D | 12 (1) | – | Platt D | 3 (3) | 3 |
| Pearce S | 12 | – | Rocastle D | 3 (2) | – |
| Butcher T *† | 11 | – | Bull S | 1 (3) | – |
| Barnes J * | 9 | 2 | Steven T * | 1 (2) | – |
| Beardsley P * | 8 (3) | 2 | Adams A | 1 | – |
| Stevens G * | 8 | – | Dorigo T | 1 | – |
| Robson B *† | 7 | 1 | Smith A | – (2) | – |
| Gascoigne P | 6 (2) | 1 | Cottee A | – (1) | – |
| Parker P | 6 (1) | – | | | |

* Appeared in 1986 World Cup.                    *23 players    18 goals*
† Appeared in 1982 World Cup.
‡ Appeared in 1974 World Cup.

# 12

# THE 1994 WORLD CUP

When Graham Taylor stepped into the hot seat, he had no idea how hot it was to become. Like Bobby Robson before him, Taylor's was an appointment sealed and delivered in advance. Rival candidates like Terry Venables and Howard Kendall, however strong their applications appeared on paper, never appeared to sway the Football Association from its choice.

Nor was it seriously challenged by the public at large, for Graham Taylor's managerial record was outstanding. A third-rate full-back with Grimsby Town and Lincoln City, forced into premature retirement through injury, he had evolved into a first-rate young manager, whose rise took him from soccer basement to Wembley. The story began at Lincoln, whom Taylor – aged just thirty-one – guided to the fourth division championship on the back of a record seventy-four points and 111 goals. Lincoln were well placed in the third division when Elton John, casting around for the right man to revamp Watford, waved a blank cheque before his nose to tempt him back to the fourth division. The stay was brief. Successive promotions took Watford to the second division. By 1982 they were in the top flight; a year later they finished second to Liverpool; in 1984 they reached the FA Cup Final. Like Wimbledon in their wake, Watford had come a mighty long way.

In Taylor's opinion they could go no further. In 1987 he again dipped into a lower division to stoke the furnaces. Aston Villa were promoted at the first attempt. Two years later, in May 1990, they finished runners-up to Liverpool. But for the era of Anfield invincibility, Taylor would have brought champions' medals to two different clubs. He had won promotion five times and was widely perceived as one of – if not *the* – most gifted young managers in football. Where other England chiefs had confined their talents to just one club – *à la* Ramsey, Revie, Greenwood, Robson – here was a man who had proved he could do the business anytime, anywhere. No wonder the FA knew where to shop, and did not bother looking elsewhere.

Taylor was also good on TV. He was manifestly likeable, unlikely to incur animosity lightly. He was inarticulately articulate, like John Major, choosing his stock phrases fluently, and generally avoiding getting his wires crossed.

The doubts that persisted related to Taylor's preferred style of play. For more than a generation purists had been trying to wean English football away from the dreaded long-ball. Taylor appeared wedded to it, for it had served him well. His biggest challenge was to offset his inexperience as an international player with a playing style that, though it might suit club sides, might not suit national ones.

In this respect, his choice of assistant was both surprising and worrisome. Ideally, Taylor's number two should have filled the gaps in Taylor's armoury. Not that Lawrie McMenemy was a bad manager. Aside from an inglorious spell at Sunderland, he had turned Southampton into a useful and high-profile team. The problem was that Taylor's shortcomings were also McMenemy's. He, too, had not been much of a footballer, so that neither of them shared that crucial affinity with their players. The later introduction of Phil Neal as Third Man merely tinkered with the problem. Neal was an international all right, but his managerial achievements were modest, his Liverpool upbringing was hardly in tune with Taylor's, and he was rumoured to be a yes-man.

Taylor's first years at Lancaster Gate coincided with the shenanigans preceding the establishment in 1992 of the Premier League, and with FIFA's introduction of a major rule-change. Alarmed by the defensive drabness of Italia '90, it was decreed that back-passes to the goalkeeper were now to be outlawed. The law invited consternation and ridicule, but was soon generally accepted as a positive innovation.

Those early months were happy ones for the new England manager. His honeymoon lasted longer than most. Not for a year did he taste defeat, and even that was tolerable, as it came at the hands of the German world champions. But England's struggle to qualify for the finals of the 1992 European Championship suggested a darker future. Jack Charlton's Ireland played England off the pitch at Wembley, though they escaped with a 1-1 draw. Elimination was on the cards till late in the final qualifier in Poland, when Gary Lineker's volleyed equaliser put England through.

With Butcher and Shilton retired, Lineker had been Taylor's immediate choice as new England captain. This seemed an onerous extra burden on a player whose vital goals kept England afloat, the more so when it appeared that manager and captain seldom saw eye to eye; though, in fairness, Lineker kept scoring with the same happy abandon.

Taylor had, however, lost Paul Gascoigne, perpetrator of a hideous foul in the 1991 Cup Final. His transfer to Lazio was put on ice, so were his severed knee ligaments, and when he did return he never quite caught up with where he had left off.

Minus Gascoigne, England flew merrily off to Sweden for the European Championship. Though the team did not lose three in a row – as happened in 1988 – they once again propped up their group, contributing to dire goalless draws with Denmark and France, before taking the lead and losing to the hosts. Taylor compounded the sin of failure with the sin of inhumanity, substituting Lineker when England's golden boy was just one goal short of Bobby Charlton's all-time record of forty-nine. Lineker had been stuck on forty-eight for six matches, and was admittedly out of touch, but it was hard to see who else would score if he could not. Had the substitution brought victory, of course, England would have reached the semi-final and Taylor would have been spared the vilification that awaited him. But he had got it wrong, both tactically and personally. 'Swedes 2 Turnips 1' screamed a tabloid, and Taylor's relationship with the press would never be the same again.

Nor would Britain ever be the same again without Maggie Thatcher's withering eye. She had overseen England's performances in three World Cup finals, exceeding Harold Wilson's two. She departed the stage after Saddam Hussein's troops marched into Kuwait, but before he felt the full force of Operation Desert Storm, designed to make him pull out. In the midst of battle, beloved Alfred Wainwright, bard of England's lakeland fells, passed away. He had been a lifelong supporter of Blackburn Rovers, and died unsuspecting that the Kenny Dalglish revival lay around the corner.

Dalglish's earlier departure from Anfield heralded plummeting fortunes for Liverpool. This facilitated the emergence of Manchester United, for so long obscured by Anfield's shadow. No sooner were English clubs returned to Europe than Alex Ferguson's United snatched the Cup-Winners' Cup from Barcelona, eight years after Ferguson's Aberdeen secured the same trophy from those other Spanish giants, Real Madrid.

Flying even higher was Britain's first astronaut-ess. Helen Sharman had won a Soviet competition to promote international space cooperation, and lifted off with two Soviet cosmonauts in a Soyuz rocket. Had she dallied, the Soviet Union would have been no more.

These were years of celebration for British hostages seized in Lebanon in the mid- and late-1980s. First out was Brian Keenan, a year later John McCarthy, the campaign for whose release by Jill Morrell would make a lasting impact on British consciousness, then Jackie Mann. Finally, Terry Waite, taken in January 1987, was set free in November 1991. They returned to a Britain suffering the worst economic recession in half a century, the south of England bearing the brunt of the shut-downs, and obsessed by relations with the EEC. It was impossible to open a newspaper without encountering the dreaded word 'Maastricht'.

Britain had a new batch of sporting heroes. Scotland's Liz McColgan ran away with the 10,000 metres in the world championships. She would be queened British Sports Personality of 1991. The following summer, Linford Christie, Colin Jackson, and Sally Gunnell all returned from Barcelona adorned with Olympic gold medals.

The British music charts were hijacked by an unexpected hit. Bryan Adams, none of whose first seven discs made the top forty, stayed at No. 1 with *(Everything I do) I do it for you* for sixteen weeks. No one else in the rock era had ever been so high for so long.

Robert Maxwell, famed less for his chairmanship of Oxford United than for his shady business dealings, had been found floating in the sea off the Canary Islands. He was beyond the help of man or god. Or magic. The Magic Circle, founded in 1905 as an all-male preserve, cast off its sexist cloak and admitted women members for the first time.

Uncertainty awaited the newly independent republics of the former Soviet Union. Gorbachev had gone, toppled briefly by a coup, then by the disintegration of the union, which deprived him of any meaningful post. The new Russian chief was silver-haired Boris Yeltsin, presiding nervously over the remnants of the old empire. The former communist Yugoslavia also fell apart, leading to protracted conflicts between its ethnic constituents. The grotesque expression 'ethnic cleansing' was coined. The dismantling of Eastern Europe would have profound effects on sport, creating multitudes of small, independent states, all seeking separate affiliation to UEFA and FIFA.

This was bad news for European aspirants to the 1994 World Cup finals, to be held, controversially, in the United States, a country with no pedigree or even widespread interest in soccer. With Africa having already snatched one place from the Europeans, courtesy of Cameroon's exploits in 1990, this vastly inflated continent was now competing for just twelve places – plus Germany as defending champions. As recently as 1978, no European qualifying group comprised more than four nations. Now, all groups bar one had six teams, and that containing both Irelands had an unprecedented seven. England's opponents in Group 2 were named as Holland, Poland, Turkey, Norway and San Marino. The first three were being paired with England with incestuous frequency. Holland had been faced in the recent finals of both European Championship and World Cup; Poland in the qualifying rounds of each, plus the Mexico World Cup. England were now scheduled to face Poland seven times in seven years; Turkey, eight times in nine. With just two teams to qualify, England and Holland set off as overwhelming favourites, with Poland the team reckoned most liable to cause an upset.

*Qualifying Group 2*

## ENGLAND v NORWAY
*Wednesday, 14 October 1992*                    *Wembley – 51,441*

For a small country known more for its whale-hunters than its footballers, Norway had twisted the lion's tail in 1981, and now had an even greater capacity to do so again. That team of part-time no-hopers had evolved into one of hardened professionals. Its best players – like those of Denmark – constituted a diaspora, earning their crust throughout Europe. Eric Thorstvedt was long established as Spurs' goalkeeper. Gunnar Halle was steadfast in Oldham's defence, and in the months to follow others would be enticed across the North Sea.

Though presenting an incomparably greater threat than in 1981, Norway had still achieved nothing in the international arena. They had not qualified for the finals of a World Cup since 1938, nor come close. Lest we forget, they had finished bottom of the pile, despite beating England, in 1982, again in 1986, and in 1990 had crawled in fourth behind Yugoslavia, Scotland and France, beating only Cyprus. Though Denmark had flowered more or less overnight in the mid-eighties, Norway as yet showed few signs of becoming a second Denmark. BBC2's satirical football magazine, *Standing Room Only*, portrayed their manager, Egil Olsen, as a full-time 'professor of football', whose players willingly learned from female coaches and from the expertise of other sports. The Norwegians were renowned enthusiasts of the English game, and in their preference for zonal, rather than man-to-man marking, even played it the English way.

Norway had detonated Group 2 not with one bang, but two. First, they shredded San Marino 10-0. It was all very well to point at the opposition, but England had never reached World Cup double figures against anybody, not even Luxembourg. No one else would score ten against San Marino either.

A fortnight later, Norway defeated Holland 2-1, and Group 2 was thrown to the winds. The Dutch and English, not unreasonably, assumed their greatest threat would come from Poland. Norway's opening salvo turned Group 2 into a four-horse race. When Norway completed the double over San Marino, 2-0, just seven days before turning out at Wembley, they had six points nicely stowed away.

Norway needed to be stopped in their tracks before they started having ideas. Unfortunately, English football was in the grip of a recession as deep at that of the British economy. The national team had won just two of their last nine and none of their last four. They entered the match on the back of a 0-1 defeat in Spain, where their only consolation was the margin of humiliation. Norway were unbeaten in seven, but they surely harboured few hopes of salvaging anything from Wembley.

The team sent out to deflate them contained just four survivors from Italia '90 – Pearce, Walker, Platt, and Gascoigne. All but Pearce were now playing in Italy. Chris Woods, transferred to Sheffield Wednesday, had inherited Shilton's goalkeeper's jersey, fending off a stiff challenge from Arsenal's David Seaman. The Arsenal defenders Lee Dixon and Tony Adams – both capped, then discarded, by Bobby Robson – were recalled. Adams would partner Des

Walker, the muscle of the one linking with the pace of the other.

Taylor was happy to welcome back the prodigal son, Paul Gascoigne, for his first international in twenty months. Taking this risk with Gascoigne's physical, mental, and match fitness meant abandoning Taylor's preference for three central defenders. One would be sacrificed to stiffen the midfield. David Batty of Leeds and Paul Ince of Manchester United were both ferocious ball-winners, the latter – despite a sour demeanour – developing qualities that would soon be indispensable to his country. Out wide, there was no Barnes, Waddle, or anyone else. Width would be supplied not by wingers, but by others. The gloom cast by the international retirement of Gary Lineker seemed set to lighten, thanks to the prolific goalscoring of Alan Shearer for Blackburn and Ian Wright for Arsenal.

The match distracted attention from the five hundredth anniversary of Christopher Columbus' landing on the Bahamas, and from fears of further ozone depletion over Antarctica. Michael Heseltine announced the closure of thirty-one British mines, with 30,000 miners to be put out to grass. The Swiss horse, Sir Arkay, was destroyed on TV after slipping down a ramp and breaking its leg during the Horse of the Year Show at Wembley.

In Wembley's other, more famous stadium, Taylor's reshaped team soon found their feet. In driving rain the Italian connection of Platt and Gascoigne masterminded the midfield, creating early chances for Platt, himself, and Adams. Though Norway played with just one forward, Byornebye retaliated by shooting into the side netting.

Towards the end of the first half England's frustration prompted bookings for Ince and Gascoigne, who elbowed Nilsen in the face and was fortunate not to be sent off. His more legitimate contributions fully vindicated Taylor's judgment in recalling him. Gascoigne would be named 'man of the match'.

Fears that this might turn out to be one of those nights were eased when Pearce's free-kick was met by David Platt, whose header took a devious route into goal. It was Platt's fifth goal in seven games, during which time no other England player had scored. A Shearer header was then nodded off the line. But suddenly Rekdal, destroyer of Holland, uncorked a shot from indecent range that speared high and wide of Chris Woods.

Afterwards, neither manager glossed over the unfairness of the result. Taylor described his team's showing as the most consistently attacking performance of his managership. Egil Olsen conceded that England had played better and were unlucky not to win. Norway, he said, had been unable to cope with England's pressured, long-ball style, that denied his players time and space.

The statistics supported these assessments. England mustered six shots on target against two, and manufactured forty crosses against nineteen. (They also committed eighteen fouls to Norway's eleven.)

Holland were no less frustrated. On the same evening they found themselves two goals down at home to Poland, but pulled back to all-square. If there was any doubt beforehand, there was none now. England and Holland would have their work cut out.

ENGLAND (0) 1                    NORWAY (0) 1
  Platt 55                         Rekdal 76

ENGLAND: Woods (Sheff W), Dixon (Arsenal) (*sub* Palmer, Sheff W), Pearce (Forest), Batty (Leeds), Walker (Sampdoria), Adams (Arsenal), Platt (Juventus), Gascoigne (Lazio), Shearer (Blackburn) I Wright (Arsenal) (*sub* Merson, Arsenal), Ince (Man U).
NORWAY: Thorstvedt, Nilsen, Pedersen (Berg), Bratseth, Bjornebye, Ingebrigtsen, Mykland (Flo), Rekdal, Halle, Sorloth, Jakobsen.

**ENGLAND v TURKEY**
*Wednesday, 18 November 1992*                    *Wembley – 42,984*

England welcomed Turkey to Wembley in a world blessed with a new American president, Clinton, and a world headed for destruction. The Comet Swift-Tuttle was predicted to strike the Earth on 14 August 2116, following what would be the forty-fifth World Cup finals. Norwich City had made a runaway start to the first ever FA Carling Premiership. The publishing world was saturated with memoirs of the Gulf War, written by generals and captured pilots, and the tabloids were saturated with details of Mandy Smith's divorce from Rolling Stone Bill Wyman.

A survey of national stereotypes had concluded that Germans were perceived as the most ruthless of peoples, the French the most stylish, Italians and Spanish the most lazy and untrustworthy, and the British the most boring. A survey of film critics sought to establish the greatest film of all time. As with previous polls, Orson Welles' *Citizen Kane* (1941) ran away with the nomination, though on this occasion John Ford's *The Searchers*, with John Wayne, was voted fifth.

A survey of the meanest English footballers would probably include Vinnie Jones on the list. He was digging deep into his pockets after being fined a record £20,000 for his part in the video 'Soccer's Hard Men'.

One could be reasonably sure Taylor was not thinking of calling up Vinnie Jones in the search for two points against goal-battered Turkey. Sooner or later Turkey were sure to evade defeat by England and to score against them. They had so far tried and failed six times. They had come closest during the European qualifiers the previous year, losing by the odd goal home and away, and at Wembley being deprived of a goal by the crossbar. Coach Sepp Piontek had triumphed at Wembley when managing Denmark, and now uttered predictable noises about football being a funny game, liable to spring surprises at any time. To date, his team had gone down 0-1 in Poland, but beaten San Marino 4-1. Ominously, Turkey's Under-21 side now defeated England's 1-0 at Leyton Orient. Even more ominously, Piontek predicted that Norway and Holland would qualify from Group 2.

English football had been deflated by the early exit of its clubs from European competition, and by the air of uncertainty injected by that home draw with Norway. Graham Taylor saw no reason to change his team, and but for an injury to David Batty – replaced by Carlton Palmer – he would not have done so. A heavy cold might have sidelined Gascoigne. He was told to wrap up warm and turned up for training wearing fourteen shirts and fourteen pairs of shorts.

Turkey's decade-long search for a goal nearly ended when Walker's error set up Hakan. Woods saved with his legs, but Unal hit the ball back against the bar. The likely effects of a Turkish goal remained hypothetical, for Gascoigne shortly put England ahead, skirting round a challenge after the ball had broken off Bulent.

Gascoigne was already directing every English move, and it was his free-kick that set up the second goal. Ian Wright crossed for Shearer to squeeze ahead of his marker with a firm diving header.

Ugur's lob gave Turkey hope, before Pearce's deflected free-kick put the game beyond their reach. England had one further treat in store. The rare sighting of Des Walker in the opponents' half was exceeded by his despatch of an even rarer cross. Gascoigne finished it off with a delicate waltz around the goalkeeper.

Once again, the irrepressible Gazza was nominated man of the match. In the spirit of generosity, he declined to accept the £3,000 award.

The match had the saddest of sequels. The High Court ruled that after three and a half years, Tony Bland, the last surviving victim of Hillsborough, should have his feeding tube disconnected and be allowed to die with dignity.

ENGLAND (2) 4                    TURKEY (0) 0
    Gascoigne 16, 61, Shearer 29,
    Pearce 59

ENGLAND: Woods, Dixon, Pearce, Palmer, Walker, Adams, Platt, Gascoigne, Shearer, Wright, Ince.
TURKEY: Hayrettin, Recep, Bulent, Gokhan, Ogun, Orhan, Hami (Riza), Unal, Mehmet (Ugur), Oguz, Hakan.

## ENGLAND v SAN MARINO
*Wednesday, 17 February 1993*                    *Wembley – 51,154*

Having to play San Marino was like asking Manchester United to face a school-kiddies eleven, as was once memorably arranged for *Jim'll Fix it*. On that occasion, to the signature tune of *Match of the Day*, an honourable 3-3 draw resulted. The real thing was unlikely to end so cosily.

San Marino – area: 240 square miles, pop: 24,000 – was Europe's oldest independent republic. She had acquired separate membership of FIFA in 1988, long before the break-up of Eastern Europe added a further plague of new members. Previously, Cyprus, Malta and Luxembourg were considered Europe's small fry. Each was guaranteed to give San Marino a pasting.

San Marino's list of accomplishments would not have been out of keeping in a black comedy. The team had lost all its previous twelve matches, and scored just two goals. It had recently lost to the youth team of an Italian fourth division side, and was said to be contemplating a lap of honour if England beat them by no more than five goals. San Marino's assortment of butchers, bakers and candlestick makers included a goalkeeper, Benedettini, a travel agent by trade, who drove the team coach. Sweeper Guerra was a student of politics and sometime painter. The players earned no salaries from international football, and were said to be mightily impressed by the training facilities offered to them by Yeading FC of the Diadora League. William Hill offered odds of 66-1 against San Marino beating England, reputedly the longest odds ever quoted for a football match.

The only professionals in their side played in the Italian second and fourth divisions. The former, Bonini, now with Bologna, was the team's one formerly great player. Now thirty-three, he had graced Juventus' midfield in the Heysel European Cup Final against Liverpool.

If Norway could put ten past San Marino, there was no knowing what damage England might inflict. Nor had they any sensible yardstick to go by. Scotland, in the recent European Championship qualifiers, had encountered stiffer resistance, winning just 4-0 at home, 2-0 away.

Graham Taylor made four changes. Stuart Pearce and Ian Wright were both nursing groin strains, while Alan Shearer – like Gascoigne before him – had fallen foul of cruciate ligament damage to his knee. He would not play again till the autumn. John Barnes was recalled, and a first cap given to QPR's Les Ferdinand. A late developer, Ferdinand had played at Wembley for Southall in the 1986 FA Vase Final, before being despatched to Turkish side Besiktas on loan. Only since Roy Wegerle's transfer to Blackburn had he held down a regular place at Loftus Road. Late in the day, Paul Ince called off to attend to his unwell son, allowing David Batty to step in. David Platt assumed the captaincy from Pearce.

The match was overshadowed by the murder hunt for the killers of two-year-old James Bulger, found mutilated on a railway line in Liverpool, and the ongoing trial of nurse Beverley Allitt, charged with murdering three babies and one child.

Michael Jackson insisted to Oprah Winfrey that he had done nothing to lighten his skin, but was suffering from a bleaching disease; England's cricketers slumped to their heaviest Test defeat in India (by an innings and twenty-two runs in Madras); Mick Hucknall of Simply Red was voted best male artist at the Annual Brits Awards; Ian Porterfield of Chelsea became the first Premier League manager to be sacked; and the inimitable Roy of the Rovers, having thrilled readers young and old in the *Tiger* since 1954, and in his own comic since 1976, finally hung up his boots.

Had Taylor been asked beforehand to name a respectable score, he would probably have settled for six. He got them, in the end. Midway through the first half everything looked on course. Taylor's new captain had scored twice with headers, though San Marino protested with justice that the second had been cleared before it crossed the line.

It was always expected that once England scored the floodgates would open. Instead, the score registered 2-0 for half the match. It was deep into the second half before Platt secured his hat-trick, by which time the crowd were subjecting John Barnes to taunts and boos every time he touched the ball, which was seldom.

The crowd might have turned their derision on Gascoigne, who was totally snuffed out by Zanotti, a player from the Italian seventh division. The job of marking Gazza should have fallen to Marco Mazza, but he didn't fancy it.

With fifteen minutes to play, San Marino were holding out for a famous 0-3 defeat. But then Palmer's header made it four, Platt five, and Ferdinand netted a wobbly sixth to lodge himself on England's list of World Cup goalscorers.

Platt, one short of Malcolm Macdonald's record five (v Cyprus, 1975), was set up to equal the record with a late penalty, which he fluffed. Served him right for his earlier illegitimate header.

ENGLAND (2) 6          SAN MARINO (0) 0
Platt 13, 23, 66, 80,
Palmer 75, Ferdinand 85

ENGLAND: Woods, Dixon, Dorigo, Palmer, Walker, Adams, Platt, Gascoigne, Ferdinand, Barnes, Batty.
SAN MARINO: Benedettini, Muccioli, Gennari, Zanotti, Canti, Guerra, Manzaroli, M Mazza, Bacciocchi (P Mazza), Bonini, Francini (Matteoni).

**TURKEY v ENGLAND**
*Wednesday, 31 March 1993*                                    *Izmir – 60,000*

Here we go again. Turkey for the eighth time. They hadn't scored yet, but for how much longer could the English goal lead such a charmed life. The cumulative score since 1984 was now 27-0 in England's favour, figures likely to give even a saint an inferiority complex. Heaven forbid, Turkey had recently failed to score against San Marino, providing the tiny republic with its first 'point' in its history.

English soccer was still mourning the death of Bobby Moore. Tofik Bakhramov's death was less publicised, but he was known to Moore and everyone else as 'the Russian linesman', who doubtfully awarded Geoff Hurst his second goal in 1966.

Away from football, Joan Caws, seven-times winner, sought to defend her Women's World Draughts Championship in Weston-Super-Mare; Cambridge overturned all predictions to win the 139th Varsity Boat Race; Emma Thompson received her 'best actress' Oscar for *Howard's End*; Jayne Torvill and Christopher Dean announced their intention to skate at the 1994 Winter Olympics; and John Major celebrated his fiftieth birthday. Aston Villa's arthritic Irishman, Paul McGrath collected the PFA's Player of the Year, with Paul Ince in second place.

Chelsea's Dennis Wise had scored the only goal on England's most recent visit to Izmir. Wise was no longer part of Taylor's plans, and somebody else had to conjure up the necessary goals. Les Ferdinand had joined Alan Shearer on the injury list, as had Sheffield Wednesday's David Hirst. That left Ian Wright to carry the burden, though after seven games he was still searching for his first England goal. QPR's versatile Andy Sinton filled Pearce's role at left-back.

Maybe the bolt of lightning that struck the team's plane on its flight to Izmir was intended to shake up the Arsenal striker. If so, it failed. Wright achieved little in a brutish match whose main accomplishment was that it finished with its full complement of twenty-two players. The contest commenced with a nasty lunge by Platt on Mehmet and steadily deteriorated.

The Turks who crowded the tiers of the Ataturk Stadium wished to see nothing as much as a Turkish goal. Unfortunately for them, all they got was an English one. After Wright was upended on the touchline, Barnes' free-kick was converted by a stooping Platt header. The goal worsened the atmosphere both on the pitch and off it. Dixon was booted on the shin, and had to be replaced at half-time by Nigel Clough. Up in the gods, Turkish thugs rained coins in the direction of Chris Woods.

England were looking to escape to the dressing room unscathed when, six minutes into first-half injury time, they scored a welcome second goal. Turkey had just switched goalkeepers. Engin had damaged a hand colliding with Platt and Adams and been substituted by Hayrettin, who had kept goal at Wembley. The newcomer had yet to touch the ball when his defence froze in the face of Ince's cross. Gascoigne was all alone as he dived to direct a slow-motion looping header over Hayrettin's head.

That goal knocked much of the aggro from the match, which resumed in an atmosphere of sullen peevishness rather than all-out war. Players continued to kick lumps out of one another, and Platt was cautioned for knocking the ball out of Hayrettin's hands, but the result was never in doubt and Turkey seldom threatened to break their duck.

Chris Woods returned to the changing room to patch up his head, split by a coin, and Gascoigne to contemplate his own personal fall from grace. Two splendid games had been succeeded by two apologetic ones. He looked short of pace and anything but fit.

Three healthy wins and a dozen goals without reply had eased the pain of the dropped point against Norway. The leeway had been made up: England joined the Norwegians on seven points.

TURKEY   (0) 0               ENGLAND   (2) 2
                                         Platt 6, Gascoigne 45

TURKEY: Engin (Hayrettin), Recep (Hami), Ogun, Alli Guncar, Tugay, Bulent, Feyyaz, Unal, Mehmet, Oguz, Orhan.
ENGLAND: Woods, Dixon (Clough), Sinton, Palmer, Walker, Adams, Platt, Gascoigne, Barnes, Wright (Sharpe), Ince.

## ENGLAND v HOLLAND
*Wednesday, 28 April 1993*                          *Wembley – 73,163*

Dutch football was on the ebb. Domestic attendances were down, PSV Eindhoven were no longer winning European Cups, and the country's best players continued to migrate. In the World Cup qualifiers, defeat in Norway, a home draw with Poland, an 'iffy' win in Turkey, had seen Holland knocked off the pace. Defeat at Wembley would leave them with a mountain to climb.

Of the Dutch team that fought an enthralling draw in Cagliari in 1990, only Rijkaard, Wouters, Gullit, and Witschge remained. The side had been largely dismembered after losing on penalties to Denmark in the European Championship. Of those survivors, Gullit had fitness problems, physically and mentally, Rijkaard likewise. Van Aerle and van Basten were long-term absentees. Hard-man Wouters would doubtless try to leave his mark on Gazza.

The current side was managed by Dick Advocaat, who looked on screen, with his bald crown and trench-coat, somewhere between a monk and a spiv.

He made room for Gascoigne's Lazio team-mate, Aron Winter, who knew Gazza's foibles better than anyone in the England camp. But Advocaat also had an ace up his sleeve. Dennis Bergkamp, a quiet, fair, twenty-three-year-old, had the poise of a ballet dancer and the speed of a whippet. Leading scorer in Holland for the past two seasons, he too was joining the national exodus. Internazionale had agreed to pay £8 million for his goals. His international tally to date was twelve from twenty games. A deep-lying forward like so many on the continent, like so few in Britain, Bergkamp was known in Dutch as 'schadaw spits' – the shadow striker. As a child, his heroes were said to be Glenn Hoddle and Tottenham Hotspur.

Meanwhile, the City of London was reeling from the shock of a one-ton IRA bomb; the Texas town of Waco from the violent end to the siege of the Branch Davidians; and cricket from a plethora of rule and fashion changes – two runs docked for a no ball, four-day county cricket, fifty overs on Sundays, and pyjamas as kit. Brian Clough had announced his retirement. He had set his sights on managing England; instead, his Nottingham Forest team had fallen through the trap-door. Forest hoped to rise again, Zambia had nowhere to rise to, after seventeen of her national squad perished in a plane crash in the Atlantic.

What wouldn't Graham Taylor have given for a repeat score of the Under-21s, 3-0 winners over Holland? Knowing his team had to attack, and that the Dutch defence was its Achilles heel, Taylor picked the boldest team he could, which coincidentally was England's first to contain five black outfield players. He resisted the campaign to 'bring back Waddle', aware that the player (back in England, with Sheffield Wednesday) had failed to set Wembley alight in the Coca-Cola Cup Final with Arsenal. With his regular left-backs injured, Taylor fielded Arsenal's Martin Keown. Despite the barracking he took against San Marino, John Barnes kept his place.

Barnes' critics were glad he did. The game had barely kicked-off when Witschge body-checked Paul Ince. The free-kick was to the right of centre, several yards outside the eighteen-yard line. Platt and Gascoigne dummied the kick, leaving it to Barnes, who curled it over the wall and high to de Goey's left. It was the start of dreams. For the next half-hour Holland could not distinguish night from day. Platt bulged the side-netting before England extended their lead. Gazza and Platt were involved, the ball broke to Ferdinand who, with time and room, struck the far post. Ferdinand should have scored; he could hardly plead ill-fortune. On the contrary, the ball could have rebounded anywhere, but it flew back at Platt, who, having started the move finished it off, poking it back into the empty net.

Breaks like that win and lose matches, and England must have thought this was their day. The Dutch must have thought likewise, but rather than give up the ghost hit back with a sublime goal. There seemed no danger as Wouters lobbed the ball down the inside-right channel. It was dropping over Bergkamp's head. By the time schadaw spits had brought it under control, Adams would have been breathing down his neck. So, taking a leaf from David Platt against Belgium, he hit it on the turn and on the drop. The ball changed direction in the flick of a boot and sailed over Woods' head. On the run of play, the goal was scarcely deserved, but no one was going to quibble over its merit.

Realising that his team were being outgunned, Advocaat made changes for the second half. He introduced full-back de Wolf, pushed Rijkaard into midfield and Bergkamp further forward. The restructuring made no dent in English supremacy, though Wouters' elbow inflicted a nasty dent in Gascoigne's cheekbone, belated revenge for Gazza's mickey-taking in Cagliari. He went off for X-rays, replaced by Paul Merson. Ruud Gullit made a forlorn exit, having been short-changed by Keown, and even the most optimistic Dutch fan must have feared the game was up.

It might have been had England been awarded a penalty when de Boer kicked the ever-threatening Ferdinand, and had Des Walker not suffered a rush of blood as 'overdrive' Overmars rushed past him. Even in hot pursuit, Walker hadn't a prayer. He would have had to wait just four more minutes before swapping shirts, but he was evidently impatient. Bearing down on the penalty area he grabbed at Overmars' shirt, a professional foul, but could do nothing to impede his opponent's flight. Both players were still entwined as they crossed the eighteen-yard line, by which time Walker virtually had Overmars' shirt off his back. Though the initial offence had occurred outside, the flying Dutchman had bravely stayed on his feet, and the penalty was as incontestable as it was foolhardy. By rights, Walker should have gone, but Danish referee Mikkelsen generously settled for the penalty, despatched sweetly by Gullit's substitute, van Vossen.

Pulling back two-goal deficits against, first, Poland, and now England, was a useful habit, but Dick Advocaat was honest enough to admit his team had deserved nothing, that England's pressure had stopped his team playing. Taylor was honest enough to say that he felt like crying.

The Queen felt like crying, too. Windsor Castle had gone up in smoke. Her Majesty was opening up Buckingham Palace to fund the restoration.

ENGLAND   (2) 2                    HOLLAND   (1) 2
  Barnes 2, Platt 24                    Bergkamp 35, van Vossen 86 pen

ENGLAND: Woods, Dixon, Keown, Palmer, Walker, Adams, Platt, Gascoigne (Merson), Ferdinand, Barnes, Ince.
HOLLAND: de Goey, Blind, de Boer, Wouters, Witschge, Winter, Bergkamp, Rijkaard, Bosman (de Wolf), Gullit (van Vossen), Overmars.

## POLAND v ENGLAND
*Saturday, 29 May 1993*                                    *Katowice – 60,000*

Poor England. Poor Halifax, bottom of the league and now out of it. For the Shaymen, salvation seemed impossible. For England, it required goals and points from end of season trips to Poland and Norway. As things stood, England needed to cancel out those dropped home points at home to Norway and Holland by drawing the returns. That would put everything down to goal-difference. But that equation ignored Poland, as always late starters in World Cup qualifiers, and for that reason afforded exaggerated respect as potential dark horses. In truth, any side that scraped 1-0 home wins over both Turkey and, yes, San Marino was unlikely to trouble the big boys.

With regard to the palaver at Tottenham, no one knew who the big boys were any more. The partnership of Alan Sugar and Terry Venables was dream ticket turned nightmare. Both men were in court over Venables' sacking. The same fate awaited Bernard Tapie, whose Marseilles had just won the European Cup amid allegations of match-fixing.

Graham Taylor was having his obituaries prepared. Should England fail against Poland, the world might awake to the headline 'Pole-axed'; should they fail in Oslo, perhaps to Monty Python's 'stuffed Norwegian Blue'.

The beleaguered manager was not helped by injuries to Les Ferdinand, bad back, and Ian Wright, whose painful toe and ankle would relegate him to the bench. It was a gamble, introducing an untried player in a match of this importance, but Tottenham's Teddy Sheringham had finished the season with twenty-nine goals. He had pressed his case ahead of Newcastle's Andy Cole, who showed the way by scoring twice in a 4-1 victory for the Under-21s. Gascoigne was permitted by Lazio to play only if he protected his cheekbone by wearing a *Phantom of the Opera* face-mask. Ince was missing, having collected two yellow cards. QPR's David Bardsley was a late stand-in for Lee Dixon.

With games in hand, Poland harboured sufficient hopes to entice 60,000 to pack the Slaski Stadium. Manager Andrzej Strejlau was shrewd enough to bill England as 'the fourth best country in the world'. Victory would keep Poland on course for the USA: the country needed some comfort in that post-Iron Curtain era of anxious hope and economic frustration. The players did not endear themselves to their countrymen when – in a nation whose average wage was perhaps £50 a week – they allegedly demanded a £4,000-per-man win bonus.

England had taken a quick-fire lead against the Dutch; Poland should have reciprocated against the English. Marek Lesniak speared England's back line, scampered past Walker as though he wasn't there, and with the goal at his mercy shot wide. One could hear Taylor's intake of breath from the press-box.

Nor did matters improve. A Sheringham header that floated past was small beer compared with the champagne raids on Woods' goal. England might have been three behind by the time Poland belatedly opened their account. Barnes, without looking, played a doomed pass near his own goal. Adamczuk left Walker for dead and made no mistake in lobbing over Woods. With two blunders in two games, Des Walker was in danger of throwing away his hard-won reputation as England's outstanding central defender.

Chris Woods kicked the ball straight at Lesniak, but redeemed himself with a fine save. Gascoigne once again looked out of his depth (he would suffer Taylor's post-match indictment of having a 'refuelling problem'). Taylor pulled off Carlton Palmer and threw on Ian Wright in the hope that, sore toe or no, he would score a priceless goal. David Platt, uncertain of his first-team place at Juventus, dropped back to midfield.

Lady Luck smiled on Taylor and Wright. With the game drifting away, Polish keeper Bako fumbled Wright's shot and the ball bobbled into the net. Wright was off the mark, Taylor was off the bench, and England were off the hook.

POLAND (1) 1                  ENGLAND (0) 1
Adamczuk 35                   Wright 84

POLAND: Bako, Kozminski, Szewczyk, Czachowski, Adamczuk, Kosecki, Swierczewski, Brzeczek, Lesiak, Lesniak (Wegrzyn), Furtok.
ENGLAND: Woods, Bardsley, Dorigo, Palmer (Wright), Walker, Adams, Platt, Gascoigne (Clough), Sheringham, Barnes, Ince.

**NORWAY v ENGLAND**
*Wednesday, 2 June 1993*                              *Oslo – 22,500*

Scheduling two vital World Cup eliminators four days apart at the fag end of the season, when English soccer appetites were at their lowest, was never likely to bring the best out of Taylor's boys. Their worst performance so far, in Katowice, had, in the event, not proved costly. They surely could not play so badly in Norway!

Thankfully, the press was deflected by several prominent anniversaries. The Queen had been on the throne for forty years. Her coronation coincided with the first ascent of Mount Everest, now reduced to a rubbish heap. It was also the semi-centenary of the Hungarian, Lazlo Biro's, invention of the ball-point pen, which consigned to antiquity the old dip-pen and the fountain pen. The Epsom Derby was won by Commander in Chief, beating the odds-on favourite Tenby into tenth place. Swindon Town had been promoted to the Premier League through the play-offs, but manager Glenn Hoddle was set for Chelsea.

For reasons of his own, Graham Taylor threw his previous tactics into the melting pot and produced not a genie but a monster. Again, he would happily have settled for the Under-21s' result, a 1-1 draw (Cole netting once more), and miscalculated in thinking Norway were of the same opinion. Though keeping his line-up under wraps, Taylor gambled on a team to assist Norway achieve that aim. Playing Gary Pallister in a three-man defence behind a four-man midfield that included Manchester United's Lee Sharpe in place of Barnes, he opted for an untried front duo of Sheringham and Ferdinand supported by the lacklustre Gascoigne. As for the one-time Maoist, Egil Olsen, he found himself managing a team almost more English than England's. In addition to Thorstvedt (earning his seventy-sixth cap) and Gunnar Halle, Stig Bjornebye was now with Liverpool, and by the new season Swindon Town and Sheffield United would have signed up Jan Fjortoft and the towering Jostein Flo.

The match confronted Taylor with his nemesis. His players were unsure about their instructions, foisted upon them with just a day to spare, and they ran around like headless chickens. Alas for Taylor, Norway wanted not one point but two. By half-time the corner-count was 9-0 in their favour, but it seemed as though they would be deprived of the lead their adventurous play merited. The interval was just three minutes away, and the nearest Norway had come was through Fjortoft's glancing header, well saved by Woods. But then Des Walker – disillusioned in Italy and negotiating to come home – perpetrated his third critical error in three matches. He felled Fjortoft on the left touchline and stayed to backchat the referee rather than take up position. Fjortoft sprinted forward, collected Halle's quickly-taken free-kick, and of a sudden alarm-bells flashed. On the bench Taylor was heard to squeal 'they've taken it!'. Fjortoft was permitted an uninterrupted run into the box. He pulled the ball back to Leonhardsen, who scuffed his shot but sent it looping inside the near post as Woods dived to his far.

Norway must have anticipated an English backlash after the break. Instead, they quickly found themselves further ahead. Mykland's long pass forward caught Walker squeezed between two Norwegians. Bohinen collected on the left and scored emphatically with his right foot.

The introduction of Wright and Clough for Sheringham and Walker salvaged little in the way of respect, never mind goals. Platt, Ferdinand and Wright all missed when they could have scored, but these late gestures were cancelled out by Sorloth and Bohinen who might reasonably have added to Norway's tally.

Norway could not believe how easy their victory had been. What must have hurt Taylor more than anything was his players' apparent lack of fight. He admitted 'I got it wrong. We, the players and I, made a pig's ear of it. The lack of passion was unbelievable. I'm here to be shot at and I have no defence.' The tabloids were in no mood to be merciful, vying for the ultimate put-down:

'Vike off now, Taylor,' 'Norse manure,' 'Oslo-rans,' 'Taylor's dummies'. A poll showed John Major to be the most unpopular prime minister since polls began. Taylor might have qualified as the most unpopular England manager.

The season was dead. England's cricketers were about to be savaged by Australia's, and Taylor could reflect on the task ahead. Norway followed up their win with a draw in Holland, and seemed set fair for USA. England and Holland were nip and tuck for second place. Each had to play Poland, San Marino, and each other. Should both fail against Poland, the Poles could leapfrog over them.

|           | P | W | D | L | F  | A  | Pts |
|-----------|---|---|---|---|----|----|-----|
| Norway    | 7 | 5 | 2 | 0 | 20 | 3  | 12  |
| England   | 7 | 3 | 3 | 1 | 16 | 6  | 9   |
| Holland   | 7 | 3 | 3 | 1 | 17 | 8  | 9   |
| Poland    | 5 | 3 | 2 | 0 | 8  | 3  | 8   |
| Turkey    | 8 | 1 | 1 | 6 | 7  | 17 | 3   |
| San Marino| 8 | 0 | 1 | 7 | 1  | 32 | 1   |

NORWAY  (1) 2                    ENGLAND  (0) 0
  Leonhardsen 42, Bohinen 48

NORWAY: Thorstvedt, Halle, Pedersen, Bratseth (Nilsen), Bjornebye, Leonhardsen, Rekdal, Mykland, Bohinen, Flo, Fjortoft (Sorloth).
ENGLAND: Woods, Dixon, Pallister, Palmer, Walker (Clough), Adams, Platt, Gascoigne, Ferdinand, Sheringham (Wright), Sharpe.

**ENGLAND v POLAND**
*Wednesday, 8 September 1993*                    *Wembley – 71,220*

A new season, new hopes. Nigel Short was daring to become the first Englishman to win the (albeit breakaway) world chess championship. Up against him was the greatest ever player, Garry Kasparov. Algeria's Noureddine Morceli had knocked two seconds off Steve Cram's eight-year-old world mile record. Cricket witnessed two astonishing victories over Sussex: Essex beat them in a four-day match that amassed a record aggregate 1,808 runs; while in the Nat West Final, Warwickshire chased Sussex's record total of 321 and got there off the last ball. Lovers of birdsong were distressed to learn that the song thrush was disappearing from our gardens and being replaced by magpies. The buzzword in computers was the arrival of 'virtual reality'.

The virtual reality of Poland was that they had come to draw and would play with a five-man midfield. Polish football was in chaos. Seven of the team had changed clubs since the 1-1 draw in Katowice.

Graham Taylor had to go for broke. Chris Woods had looked ill at ease in goal for some time, and had conceded a soft winner to Arsenal in the FA Cup Final. He stepped down for Arsenal's David Seaman. Taylor also brought in two fresh full-backs. Though Nottingham Forest were playing in the Endsleigh League, Stuart Pearce, having missed eight internationals through injury, was recalled as captain. Liverpool's promising Rob Jones had recovered from a stress fracture of the shin just in time to be sent off against Coventry. That did not stop him winning his second cap. Des Walker paid the price for his disastrous string of errors. An England regular for nearly five years, he was replaced by Arsenal's Tony Adams. Paul Ince played through the pain of a damaged shoulder. Strikers Ferdinand and Wright boasted just one goal each.

The tone of the evening was set from the first minute. Gascoigne brought a good save from Bako, and shook his fist at the crowd to whip them up. They needed little encouragement, for they were soon rewarded with an incisive goal. Platt's angled ball pierced the enemy nerve centre. Ferdinand sprinted between two defenders, killed the ball with his first touch, and despatched it cleanly with his second.

That goal settled any nerves and permitted England to play with the verve and panache that spectators demanded. Ferdinand's pace looked likely to steal a goal at any stage, Gascoigne looked sharp, and both Pallister and Wright might have extended the lead before the interval. Only in the closing stages of that first half did England momentarily falter. Robert Warzycha had not yet played in Everton's first team this season. He had not forgotten the route to goal, and his twenty-five yarder was touched over by Seaman. Potentially more damaging were bookings meted out to Jones and Gascoigne. Jones had swiped at Swierczewski's ankles, while Gascoigne clattered Czachowski from behind. This, his second yellow card of the qualifiers, meant he would sit out the crucial match in Holland. Worse might have followed. Gascoigne elbowed Adamczuk and should have begun the long walk, especially as he recklessly booted the ball away when penalised.

Any fears that England might squander their advantage were laid to rest in the opening spell of the second half. Jones pumped in a long free-kick, Ferdinand hung in the air to flick it on, and Gascoigne chested the ball into space and hooked an unstoppable volley. Four minutes later Sharpe touched a free-kick to Gascoigne, who teed it up for Pearce to blast round the wall. Poland sagged like a burst balloon. Two long range shots was all they could manage in ninety minutes. England's pride had been restored and with it their hopes of USA. Dutch manager Dick Advocaat slipped away wearing a frown.

England's home fixtures were now complete. Looking back, they had done little wrong in any of them. They had piled on the goals, and, but for late and ill-deserved equalisers by Norway and Holland, would have had a maximum ten points to show.

This match was England's seventh with Poland in the World Cup, from which nine points had been harvested. No other nation has been faced so frequently, or presented England with so many points. Who said Poland were England's bogey-team?

ENGLAND  (1) 3                    POLAND  (0) 0
Ferdinand 6, Gascoigne 49,
Pearce 53

ENGLAND: Seaman, Jones, Pearce, Ince, Pallister, Adams, Platt, Gascoigne, Ferdinand, Wright, Sharpe.
POLAND: Bako, Czachowski, Lesiak, Kosminski, Adamczuk (Bak), Kosecki, R Warzycha, Brzeczek, Swierczewski, Furtok (Ziober), Lesniak.

## HOLLAND v ENGLAND
*Wednesday, 13 October 1993*                    *Rotterdam – 48,000*

Two weeks later the Poles lost in Oslo, guaranteeing Norway's qualification while effectively extinguishing the Polish threat. That same evening, Holland smashed seven goals past San Marino, wiping out England's slender advantage in goal-difference.

Now, all roads led to Rotterdam, to the home of Feyenoord. Ever since the schedule for Group 2 had been laid down, this fixture had stood out. Had all gone to plan, it might not have assumed momentous overtones. Both the English and the Dutch might already have had one foot in America. Norway had put paid to that. Two of football's foremost nations were now scrabbling for one remaining place. Both sides were level on points, but Holland's goal-difference was better by three. Victory for either side would probably seal the coffin of the loser. Should the match be drawn, England would be the happier, for one further fixture remained. The Dutch would have to win in Poland, but would be overtaken by a five-goal England victory over San Marino.

Nigel Short boosted English morale when he won his first match against Kasparov, admittedly at the sixteenth attempt; a sixty-year-old Venezuelan violin-maker became the oldest man to conquer Everest; and Benn and Eubank filled Old Trafford for their (drawn) long-awaited boxing rematch.

Judge me on my World Cup record, Taylor had said, and one couldn't be fairer than that. His choice of team, however, provoked fresh howls of outrage, condemning him in the public mind should he lose. Mind you, of the five changes he announced, three were enforced. Paul Gascoigne, suspended, was set to miss his first qualifier. That excused Taylor the dilemma of whether to play him, but confronted him with another, who to pick in his place. Against the instincts of many, he opted for Carlton Palmer rather than Andy Sinton, whose breadth of play had earned him a summer transfer to Sheffield Wednesday. Stuart Pearce (hamstring) failed a late fitness test, surrendering his place and his driving leadership to the more attack-minded but less defensively stubborn Tony Dorigo. Les Ferdinand (also hamstring) was replaced by Alan Shearer, back in harness but hardly reattuned to international football.

Taylor's two voluntary changes were at right-back – where Paul Parker, out of the side for two years, was considered a safer bet than the inexperienced Rob Jones – and in the accommodation of Arsenal's Paul Merson, at best an occasional international footballer. Merson's dropped club-mate, Ian Wright, would keep the bench warm.

For Holland, of course, the match was no less critical than for England. Dick Advocaat was managing only on an interim basis, expecting to hand over to Barcelona's Johann Cruyff should Holland reach the finals. The heart of the current side – Gullit, Rijkaard, Wouters, Ronald and Erwin Koeman – were all the wrong side of thirty, and van Basten not far off. Defeat by England would probably spell the end of the international road for all of them. Van Basten, unfit, and Gullit, sulking, would in any case be missing against England.

News from outside the stadium was not good. Skirmishes between Dutch and English fans were breaking out all over Rotterdam. Hundreds had been arrested. ITV showed the match live, though had it been played at Wembley, it would have been snapped up by Sky for a minority audience. The viewing multitudes chuckled at the splash of orange on the screen, orange wigs, orange war-paint, orange flags, flares, even the pitch seemed orange.

Those same viewers witnessed a furious opening assault by the Dutch. Three times Marc Overmars powered past Dorigo. The Leeds full-back resorted to a crude lunge, for which he was booked. But Seaman experienced nothing like the danger to his goal that de Goey was shortly to face. Merson set Platt through on the keeper, but the shot was parried. Merson cut inside de Wolf to shoot wide. Then, in the space of sixty seconds midway through the half England might have scored thrice. Dorigo's twenty-five-yard free-kick bounced back off a post. Adams' follow-up was blocked for a corner, from which Platt's stooping header was frantically hacked away.

Five minutes before the interval Holland received the butt of the game's first crucial incident. Rijkaard scored a neat goal, wrongly chalked off for offside. Those who, after the match, would savage the match officials forget that, with the keener eyes demanded of them, England would, and should, have trailed at half-time.

Though the critics' choice, Sinton, reappeared instead of Palmer, Holland began the second half as ominously as they had the first. Bergkamp ran forty yards to plant a shot that Seaman was equal to.

For Ronald Koeman – missing through injury at Wembley, and relegated to the substitutes' bench at Barcelona – his lack of pace at the back was always

The moment England died. Koeman brings down David Platt but is not sent off. (v Holland)

likely to be critically exposed. It was his one transparent weakness, but was well masked provided he enjoyed defensive cover. That cover was missing as Sinton's weighted pass sent Platt clear. Homing on his prey diagonally from behind, Koeman wrestled Platt to the floor. The English bench rose as one, for England's future might well rest on German referee Assenmacher's dual verdicts, free-kick or penalty, red card or yellow. Both decisions went against England. The free-kick was proper, the offence clearly outside. The caution was not, for Koeman should have been expelled. It had been a textbook professional foul. Koeman would miss the next game, but, alas, not the rest of this.

With a different script, England might have ridden their misfortune. But within two minutes Ince impeded Wouters in the danger zone outside England's box. The free-kick was dead centre, and tailor-made for Holland's specialist taker, Ronald Koeman. His drive cannoned into Ince, who had encroached, and who was promptly booked. That dread feeling in the pit of the stomach as Koeman stepped back for a second attempt even infiltrated the TV commentary box. Brian Moore articulated the fears of millions as Seaman positioned himself too far to one side. 'He's going to flip one now!' Moore screamed, as much to Seaman as to his audience. Moore had correctly read Koeman's mind as the Dutchman – who should have been peeling off his kit in the changing room – cheekily flicked the ball over the wall and into the space vacated by Seaman.

Even then England were not done. Within four minutes Merson's free-kick from infinitely greater range struck the inside of de Goey's post and flew across the goal-line. Seaman brilliantly foiled Holland seconds later, but his intervention only briefly postponed a second Dutch goal. Bergkamp set off like an express train, and looked to have controlled the ball with his hand before wrong-footing a defender and drilling a low shot of no great power inside Seaman's post. On another day, the goalkeeper might have prevented both goals.

These cumulative setbacks caused Taylor to forget his good manners. He stalked the touchline, brushing aside a FIFA official, raging – as seen in a later, riveting, television documentary – that the referee had got him the sack. As microphones were thrust under his nose at the end, he was clearly an angry man. Koeman was on his mind, so was Walker's penalty at Wembley. It did not occur to him that Walker had also escaped marching orders. In that sense, the refereeing had been consistent, if doubly wrong. In earlier matches, too, Paul Gascoigne could consider himself fortunate not to have been sent off twice. Nor was Taylor in the mood to reflect on Rijkaard's perfectly good first-half goal. Had it been at the other end, he would have moaned long and hard. In the wider sense, too, if justice is to miscarry, better that it favours the superior team. It had in the case of Maradona's hand of God; it did now in Rotterdam.

'He's going to flip one now!' David Seaman flaps at Ronald Koeman's retaken free kick. (v Holland)

The end is nigh. 'The referee has got me the sack.' (v Holland)

It's not all over yet, Taylor insisted, and he was right. But now he needed assistance from the Poles and a torrent of goals against San Marino.

HOLLAND  (0) 2                    ENGLAND  (0) 0
  R Koeman 61, Bergkamp 68

HOLLAND: de Goey, de Wolf, R Koeman, F de Boer, Rijkaard, Wouters, E Koeman, Bergkamp, Overmars (Winter), R de Boer (van Gobbel), Roy.
ENGLAND: Seaman, Parker, Dorigo, Ince, Pallister, Adams, Platt, Palmer (Sinton), Shearer, Merson (Wright), Sharpe.

## SAN MARINO v ENGLAND
*Wednesday, 17 November 1993*                    *Bologna – 2,378*

Wednesday, 17 November was the closing date for European applications to the World Cup. Across the continent battles would be fought, tears shed, champagne drunk. France and Denmark would be among the unlikely names to reach for the handkerchiefs, the Irish Republic to swig nectar. England would be grabbing the tissues too, unless …

Bergkamp's 'killer' goal looked set to kill England. Assuming they managed to beat San Marino, Holland had to avoid defeat in Poland. Should the Dutch lose by one goal, England had to win by seven to go through. When asked which was the more attainable objective, drawing in Poland or winning by *seven* away to San Marino, Taylor answered, tongue in cheek, the latter.

In the modern era, asking any international side to score seven goals away from home to another was asking much. Though Holland had done precisely that to San Marino, England – even at Wembley – had fallen one short. Had they lost in Rotterdam by one goal, their target now would have been a more attainable five. Five-goal margins in soccer are infinitely more common than seven-goal ones, which belong in the freakish, once-in-a-lifetime bracket.

The equation was further complicated by the collapse of the Polish team. Since losing at Wembley and in Oslo in September they had fallen apart, crushed 0-3 at home to Norway and providing the Turks with a rare win. Four defeats in a row had knocked the stuffing out of them and knocked their manager out of a job. Most of Poland's expatriate stars could not be bothered to travel and ruled themselves out of the side. A makeshift outfit – looking ahead to the next World Cup – was likely to put up only token resistance. To stiffen their resolve, a British tabloid was said to be offering the Poles £10,000 per man should they pull off a victory. Either way, England had to plan for the unexpected. *If* Holland should fall flat on their faces, England had to capitalise. They had to complete the job in hand without reference to happenings elsewhere.

Taylor's quest for seven goals required a do-or-die, kamikaze approach. He could hardly send out a bread-and-butter eleven. The whole team needed to be recast and redirected. Blackburn's Stuart Ripley was brought in for his first cap with the specific brief – get those crosses in. Ferdinand was fit and would play; Shearer had strained his back and would not.

San Marino did not play their home internationals at 'home' but to the north, in the Italian city of Bologna, in a stadium holding a special place in English affections. It was in the Renata Dall'Ara arena that David Platt scored that never-to-be-forgotten winner against Belgium in 1990. Then, England had been watched by 34,000; now, by a mere 2,378, the smallest audience for an England international this century.

Back home, a Modern Doomsday Book had just been compiled. Using satellite photography, it confirmed the dramatic shrinkage of Britain's ponds, hedgerows, plant varieties and woodland.

Taylor's Doomsday Book was signed and sealed eight seconds after the kick-off in San Marino. He might have thought he had suffered every setback, every cruel lash of every whip. But when Pearce fluffed a simple back-pass, enabling Gualtieri to prod the ball past an astonished Seaman, he must have presumed a kind of madness had been let loose. San Marino had scored the quickest goal in the history of international football. To read 'San Marino 1

England 0' was simply not possible – not just improbable, *impossible*. That the scorer should share the name (different spelling) as the Argentine general who ordered the invasion of the Falkland Islands, added to the sense of unreality.

After twenty minutes San Marino were still in front, and England, rattled and incohesive, had created little. Far from banging in the eight goals now necessary, they must have begun to dread the unthinkable.

A long-range Ince goal – his first for his country – put England back on course. San Marino's obliging goalkeeper conceded three goals anyone else would have saved, and in injury time Ian Wright netted England's 199th World Cup goal to complete the easiest personal quartet he could have imagined. It was all academic, of course. Not only had a seven-goal winning margin proved beyond England, but Holland were seldom in trouble, beating Poland 3-1. So England were left stranded on ninety-seven World Cup games, denied the three group fixtures in the United States to bring up the ton. Afterwards all talk was of Davide Gualtieri and Nicola Bacciocchi, who had had the audacity to thump Seaman's post. San Marino – two goals in seventeen internationals, and one of those a penalty – had been a hair's breadth from scoring twice for the first time.

It was all too much for the BBC, who pulled the plug on the latter stages and switched to covering Wales v Romania. The cameras were no talisman. Wales also lost. For the first time since the war, Britain would not be represented in the finals of the World Cup.

Over a ten-match campaign, a quarter of a league season, England had finished third. They had taken just one point apiece off the two teams above them. Taylor's frustration at Holland's late Wembley equaliser was now shown to be baseless. Had England won that match 2-1, they would still have finished third. There was no escaping it, the national team had been found wanting. San Marino's manager, Giorgio Leoni, was scathing in his comparison between English and Dutch football: 'England's play is faster, but you can see what they are going to do.'

In due course, Graham Taylor resigned. A thoroughly decent man, he had undoubtedly done his best, but fallen well short of the standards set by his predecessor. He had inherited a side one penalty kick away from the World Cup Final, and left it palpably short of quality and depth. The magic he wrought at Sincil Bank and Vicarage Road did not work on the international plane. But though Taylor had failed as a manager, he never failed as a man. The shameful hostility of the tabloids had one unprecedented and regrettable consequence. No one in his right mind was going to put his head on the block and suffer what Taylor had suffered. When asked about taking the job, all the obvious candidates shied away. And who could blame them. Not for several months was it clear who would lead England into the new era. The man who emerged, the man who said 'yes', was Terry Venables.

SAN MARINO  (1) 1                ENGLAND  (3) 7
  Gualtieri 1                         Ince 22, 73, Wright 34, 46, 78, 90,
                                      Ferdinand 38

SAN MARINO: Benedettini, Valentini (Gobbi), Gennari, Zanotti, Canti,
Guerra, Manzaroli, delle Valle, Bacciocchi (P Mazza), Bonini, Gualtieri,
ENGLAND: Seaman, Dixon, Pearce, Ince, Pallister, Walker, Platt, Ripley,
Ferdinand, Wright, Sinton.

---

*Qualifying Group 2*

| | | | Home | | | | Away | | | | |
|---|---|---|---|---|---|---|---|---|---|---|---|
| | P | W | D | L | F | A | W | D | L | F | A | Pts |
| NORWAY | 10 | 5 | 0 | 0 | 18 | 2 | 2 | 2 | 1 | 7 | 3 | 16 |
| HOLLAND | 10 | 3 | 2 | 0 | 13 | 3 | 3 | 1 | 1 | 16 | 6 | 15 |
| England | 10 | 3 | 2 | 0 | 16 | 3 | 2 | 1 | 2 | 10 | 6 | 13 |
| Poland | 10 | 2 | 1 | 2 | 4 | 7 | 1 | 1 | 3 | 6 | 8 | 8 |
| Turkey | 10 | 3 | 0 | 2 | 9 | 8 | 0 | 1 | 4 | 2 | 11 | 7 |
| San Marino | 10 | 0 | 1 | 4 | 1 | 19 | 0 | 0 | 5 | 1 | 27 | 1 |

*Other group results*

| | | | |
|---|---|---|---|
| Norway v San Marino | 10-0 | Norway v Turkey | 3-1 |
| Norway v Holland | 2-1 | Poland v San Marino | 1-0 |
| Poland v Turkey | 1-0 | San Marino v Poland | 0-3 |
| San Marino v Norway | 0-2 | Holland v Norway | 0-0 |
| Holland v Poland | 2-2 | Norway v Poland | 1-0 |
| Turkey v San Marino | 4-1 | San Marino v Holland | 0-7 |
| Turkey v Holland | 1-3 | Poland v Norway | 0-3 |
| Holland v Turkey | 3-1 | Turkey v Poland | 2-1 |
| San Marino v Turkey | 0-0 | Turkey v Norway | 2-1 |
| Holland v San Marino | 6-0 | Poland v Holland | 1-3 |

*England appearances and goalscorers (substitute appearances in brackets)*
*World Cup qualifying rounds 1994*

| | Apps | Goals | | Apps | Goals |
|---|---|---|---|---|---|
| Platt D * | 10 | 7 | Seaman D | 3 | – |
| Adams A * | 9 | – | Dorigo A * | 3 | – |
| Ince P | 8 | 2 | Shearer A | 3 | 1 |
| Walker D * | 8 | – | Sinton A | 2 (1) | – |
| Gascoigne P * | 8 | 4 | Batty D | 2 | – |
| Palmer C | 7 (1) | 1 | Sheringham T | 2 | – |
| Woods C | 7 | – | Merson P | 1 (2) | – |
| Dixon L | 7 | – | Bardsley D | 1 | – |
| Wright I | 5 (3) | 5 | Jones R | 1 | – |
| Ferdinand L | 5 | 3 | Parker P * | 1 | – |
| Pearce S * | 4 | 2 | Keown M | 1 | – |
| Pallister G | 4 | – | Ripley S | 1 | – |
| Barnes J *† | 4 | 1 | Clough N | – (3) | – |
| Sharpe L | 3 (1) | – | | | |

---

\* Appeared in 1990 World Cup.               *27 players     26 goals*
† Appeared in 1986 World Cup.

---

## Appendix 1
Clubs supplying players in World Cups 1950-94 (includes qualifying rounds and final stages)

| | Club | Caps | Players | Caps | Other clubs |
|---|---|---|---|---|---|
| 1 | **Manchester Utd** | 118 | Robson B | 20 | +7 WBA |
| | | | Charlton R | 18 | |
| | | | Coppell S | 11 | |
| | | | Byrne R | 8 | |
| | | | Ince P | 8 | |
| | | | Wilkins R | 8 | +3 Chelsea, +9 Milan |
| | | | Stiles N | 6 | |
| | | | Taylor T | 6 | |
| | | | Aston J | 5 | |
| | | | Edwards D | 4 | |
| | | | Pallister G | 4 | |
| | | | Sharpe L | 4 | |
| | | | Hill G | 3 | |
| | | | Greenhoff B | 2 | |
| | | | Pearson Stuart | 2 | |
| | | | Webb N | 2 | +4 Forest |
| | | | Connelly J | 1 | +1 Burnley |
| | | | Duxbury M | 1 | |
| | | | Parker P | 1 | +7 QPR |
| | | | Pearson Stan | 1 | |
| | | | Pegg D | 1 | |
| | | | Rowley J | 1 | |
| | | | Viollet D | 1 | |
| | | | *23 players* | | |
| 2 | **Liverpool** | 101 | Barnes J | 13 | +7 Watford |
| | | | Thompson P | 12 | |
| | | | Beardsley P | 11 | +4 Newcastle |
| | | | Clemence R | 11 | +1 Spurs |
| | | | McDermott T | 9 | |
| | | | Hughes E | 8 | |
| | | | Neal P | 8 | |
| | | | Hunt R | 6 | |
| | | | Keegan K | 6 | +1 Hamburg, +5 South'pton |
| | | | McMahon S | 6 | |
| | | | A'Court A | 3 | |
| | | | Hughes L | 3 | |
| | | | Callaghan I | 2 | |
| | | | Kennedy R | 2 | |
| | | | Jones R | 1 | |
| | | | *15 players* | | |

| 3 | **Arsenal** | 87 | Sansom K | 22 | |
| | | | Adams A | 10 | |
| | | | Rix G | 8 | |
| | | | Wright I | 8 | |
| | | | Dixon L | 7 | |
| | | | Woodcock A | 7 | +4 Cologne |
| | | | Rocastle D | 5 | |
| | | | Anderson V | 4 | +2 Forest |
| | | | Ball A | 3 | +4 Blackpool, +4 Everton |
| | | | Merson P | 3 | |
| | | | Seaman D | 3 | |
| | | | Storey P | 3 | |
| | | | Smith A | 2 | |
| | | | Keown M | 1 | |
| | | | Mariner P | 1 | +13 Ipswich |
| | | | *15 players* | | |

| 4 | **Tottenham** | 82 | Hoddle G | 11 | |
| | | | Waddle C | 11 | +2 Newcastle, +9 Marseilles |
| | | | Lineker G | 9 | +1 Leic,+8 Everton,+4 Barc |
| | | | Gascoigne P | 8 | +8 Lazio |
| | | | Greaves J | 7 | +2 Chelsea |
| | | | Peters M | 6 | +5 West Ham |
| | | | Stevens G A | 5 | |
| | | | Chivers M | 4 | |
| | | | Mullery A | 4 | |
| | | | Norman M | 4 | |
| | | | Ramsey A | 4 | |
| | | | Sheringham T | 2 | |
| | | | Smith R | 2 | |
| | | | Baily E | 1 | |
| | | | Brooks J | 1 | |
| | | | Clarke H | 1 | |
| | | | Clemence R | 1 | +11 Liverpool |
| | | | Ditchburn E | 1 | |
| | | | *18 players* | | |

| 5 | **Wolverhampton** | 55 | Wright W | 20 | |
| | | | Flowers R | 8 | |
| | | | Mullen J | 6 | |
| | | | Williams B | 5 | |
| | | | Bull S | 4 | |
| | | | Slater W | 4 | |
| | | | Clamp E | 3 | |
| | | | Wilshaw D | 3 | |

|  |  |  | Broadbent P | 1 | |
|--|--|--|-------------|---|--|
|  |  |  | Hancocks J | 1 | |

*10 players*

| 6 | **Nott'm Forest** | 50 | Pearce S | 16 | |
|---|-------------------|----|----------|-----|--|
|  |  |  | Walker D | 13 | +7 Sampdoria, +1 Sheff Wed |
|  |  |  | Shilton P | 9 | +2 Leic, +13 So'ton, +13 Derby |
|  |  |  | Webb N | 4 | +2 Man Utd |
|  |  |  | Clough N | 3 | |
|  |  |  | Anderson V | 2 | +4 Arsenal |
|  |  |  | Francis T | 2 | +3 Birm,+6 Man C,+4 Samp |
|  |  |  | Birtles G | 1 | |

*8 players*

| 7 | **Ipswich Town** | 49 | Butcher T | 14 | +11 Rangers |
|---|------------------|----|-----------|-----|-------------|
|  |  |  | Mariner P | 13 | +1 Arsenal |
|  |  |  | Mills M | 13 | |
|  |  |  | Beattie K | 3 | |
|  |  |  | Osman R | 3 | |
|  |  |  | Gates E | 2 | |
|  |  |  | Whymark T | 1 | |

*7 players*

| 8 | **Everton** | 48 | Lineker G | 8 | +1 Leic,+4 Barc, +9 Spurs |
|---|-------------|----|-----------|---|---------------------------|
|  |  |  | Stevens M G | 8 | +8 Rangers |
|  |  |  | Steven T | 7 | +3 Rangers |
|  |  |  | Wilson R | 6 | +5 Huddersfield |
|  |  |  | Ball A | 4 | +4 Blackpool, +3 Arsenal |
|  |  |  | Reid P | 4 | |
|  |  |  | Labone B | 3 | |
|  |  |  | Newton K | 3 | |
|  |  |  | Wright T | 2 | |
|  |  |  | Bracewell P | 1 | |
|  |  |  | Cottee A | 1 | |
|  |  |  | Latchford R | 1 | |

*12 players*

| 9 | **West Ham** | 40 | Moore R | 17 | |
|---|--------------|----|---------|-----|--|
|  |  |  | Brooking T | 9 | |
|  |  |  | Hurst G | 6 | |
|  |  |  | Peters M | 5 | +6 Spurs |
|  |  |  | Martin A | 3 | |

*5 players*

| 10 | **Southampton** | 38 | Shilton P | 13 | +2 Leic, +9 Forest, +13 Derby |
|----|-----------------|----|-----------|-----|-------------------------------|
|  |  |  | Watson D | 6 | +3 Man City |
|  |  |  | Wright M | 6 | +6 Derby |

|  |  |  | Channon M | 5 |  |
|---|---|---|---|---|---|
|  |  |  | Keegan K | 5 | +6 Liverpool, +1 Hamburg |
|  |  |  | Williams S | 2 |  |
|  |  |  | Paine T | 1 |  |
|  |  |  | *7 players* |  |  |
| 11 | **Sheffield Wed** | 33 | Palmer C | 8 |  |
|  |  |  | Springett R | 8 |  |
|  |  |  | Woods C | 7 |  |
|  |  |  | Swan P | 4 |  |
|  |  |  | Quixall A | 2 |  |
|  |  |  | Sinton A | 2 | +1 QPR |
|  |  |  | Fantham J | 1 |  |
|  |  |  | Walker D | 1 | +13 Forest, +7 Sampdoria |
|  |  |  | *8 players* |  |  |
| 12 | **Leeds United** | 32 | Charlton J | 7 |  |
|  |  |  | Cherry T | 5 |  |
|  |  |  | Cooper T | 4 |  |
|  |  |  | Hunter N | 4 |  |
|  |  |  | Clarke A | 3 |  |
|  |  |  | Dorigo A | 3 | +1 Chelsea |
|  |  |  | Madeley P | 3 |  |
|  |  |  | Batty D | 2 |  |
|  |  |  | Barnes P | 1 | +1 Man City, +1 WBA |
|  |  |  | *9 players* |  |  |
| 13 | **Derby County** | 29 | Shilton P | 13 | +2 Leic, +9 Forest, +13 So'ton |
|  |  |  | Wright M | 6 | +6 Southampton |
|  |  |  | McFarland R | 5 |  |
|  |  |  | Mozley B | 2 |  |
|  |  |  | Todd C | 2 |  |
|  |  |  | Hector K | 1 |  |
|  |  |  | *6 players* |  |  |
| 14 | **Blackpool** | 28 | Armfield J | 8 |  |
|  |  |  | Matthews S | 7 |  |
|  |  |  | Mortensen S | 6 |  |
|  |  |  | Ball A | 4 | +4 Everton, +3 Arsenal |
|  |  |  | Johnstone H | 2 |  |
|  |  |  | Garrett T | 1 |  |
|  |  |  | *6 players* |  |  |
| 14 | **West Brom** | 28 | Robson B | 7 | +20 Man Utd |
|  |  |  | Robson R | 7 |  |
|  |  |  | Howe D | 4 |  |
|  |  |  | Kevan D | 4 |  |

|    |                      |    |            |    |                          |
|----|----------------------|----|------------|----|--------------------------|
|    |                      |    | Astle J    | 2  |                          |
|    |                      |    | Allen R    | 1  |                          |
|    |                      |    | Barnes P   | 1  | +1 Man City, +1 Leeds    |
|    |                      |    | Nicholls J | 1  |                          |
|    |                      |    | Rickaby S  | 1  |                          |
|    |                      |    | *9 players* |   |                          |
| 16 | **Manchester City**  | 25 | Bell C     | 7  |                          |
|    |                      |    | Francis T  | 6  | +3 Birm, +2 Forest, +3 Samp |
|    |                      |    | Lee F      | 3  |                          |
|    |                      |    | Watson D   | 3  | +6 Southampton           |
|    |                      |    | Marsh R    | 2  |                          |
|    |                      |    | Royle J    | 2  |                          |
|    |                      |    | Barnes P   | 1  | +1 Leeds, +1 WBA         |
|    |                      |    | Tueart D   | 1  |                          |
|    |                      |    | *8 players* |   |                          |
| 16 | **QPR**              | 25 | Fenwick T  | 8  |                          |
|    |                      |    | Parker P   | 7  | +1 for Man Utd           |
|    |                      |    | Ferdinand L | 5 |                          |
|    |                      |    | Bardsley D | 1  |                          |
|    |                      |    | Bowles S   | 1  |                          |
|    |                      |    | Clement D  | 1  |                          |
|    |                      |    | Francis G  | 1  |                          |
|    |                      |    | Sinton A   | 1  | +2 for Sheff Wed         |
|    |                      |    | *8 players* |   |                          |
| 18 | **Blackburn**        | 23 | Douglas B  | 11 |                          |
|    |                      |    | Clayton R  | 5  |                          |
|    |                      |    | Eckersley W | 3 |                          |
|    |                      |    | Shearer A  | 3  |                          |
|    |                      |    | Ripley S   | 1  |                          |
|    |                      |    | *5 players* |   |                          |
| 19 | **Glasgow Rangers**  | 22 | Butcher T  | 11 | +14 Ipswich              |
|    |                      |    | Stevens M G | 8 | +8 Everton               |
|    |                      |    | Steven T   | 3  | +7 Everton               |
|    |                      |    | *3 players* |   |                          |
| 20 | **Fulham**           | 20 | Haynes J   | 14 |                          |
|    |                      |    | Cohen G    | 6  |                          |
|    |                      |    | *2 players* |   |                          |
| 21 | **AC Milan**         | 17 | Wilkins R  | 9  | +3 Chelsea, +8 Man Utd   |
|    |                      |    | Hateley M  | 8  |                          |
|    |                      |    | *2 players* |   |                          |

| 22 | **Preston** | 16 | Finney T | 16 | |
|----|----|----|----|----|----|
| | | | *1 player* | | |

| 23 | **Aston Villa** | 15 | Platt D | 6 | +7 Juventus, +3 Sampdoria |
|----|----|----|----|----|----|
| | | | Hodge S | 5 | |
| | | | Withe P | 2 | |
| | | | Gidman J | 1 | |
| | | | Morley A | 1 | |
| | | | *5 players* | | |

| 23 | **Chelsea** | 15 | Bentley R | 3 | |
|----|----|----|----|----|----|
| | | | Wilkins R | 3 | +8 Man Utd, +9 Milan |
| | | | Dixon K | 2 | |
| | | | Greaves J | 2 | +7 Spurs |
| | | | Osgood P | 2 | |
| | | | Bonetti P | 1 | |
| | | | Brabrook P | 1 | |
| | | | Dorigo A | 1 | +3 Leeds |
| | | | *8 players* | | |

| 25 | **Sampdoria** | 14 | Walker D | 7 | +13 Forest, +1 Sheff Wed |
|----|----|----|----|----|----|
| | | | Francis T | 4 | +3 Birm, +2 Forest,+6 Man C |
| | | | Platt D | 3 | +6 Villa, +7 Juventus |
| | | | *3 players* | | |

| 26 | **Birmingham** | 13 | Merrick G | 6 | |
|----|----|----|----|----|----|
| | | | Hall J | 4 | |
| | | | Francis T | 3 | +2 Forest,+6 Man C,+4 Samp |
| | | | *3 players* | | |

| 26 | **Portsmouth** | 13 | Dickinson J | 12 | |
|----|----|----|----|----|----|
| | | | Froggatt J | 1 | |
| | | | *2 players* | | |

| 28 | **Newcastle** | 12 | Beardsley P | 4 | +11 Liverpool |
|----|----|----|----|----|----|
| | | | Broadis I | 4 | |
| | | | Milburn J | 2 | |
| | | | Waddle C | 2 | +11 Spurs, +9 Marseilles |
| | | | *4 players* | | |

| 29 | **Huddersfield** | 11 | Wilson R | 5 | +6 Everton |
|----|----|----|----|----|----|
| | | | Staniforth R | 4 | |
| | | | McGarry W | 2 | |
| | | | *3 players* | | |

| 30 | **Bolton** | 10 | Banks T | 4 | |
|----|----|----|----|----|----|
| | | | Lofthouse N | 4 | |

|    |    |    |                |    |                                    |
|----|----|----|----------------|----|------------------------------------|
|    |    |    | Hassall H      | 1  |                                    |
|    |    |    | Langton R      | 1  |                                    |
|    |    |    | *4 players*    |    |                                    |
| 31 | **Leicester**     | 9 | Banks G     | 6 | +3 Stoke                           |
|    |    |    | Shilton P      | 2  | +9 Forest,+13 So'ton,+13 Derb      |
|    |    |    | Lineker G      | 1  | +8 Everton,+4 Barc,+9 Spurs        |
|    |    |    | *3 players*    |    |                                    |
| 31 | **Marseilles**    | 9 | Waddle C    | 9 | +2 Newcastle, +11 Spurs            |
|    |    |    | *1 player*     |    |                                    |
| 33 | **Middlesbrough** | 8 | Mannion W   | 3 |                                    |
|    |    |    | McNeil M       | 3  |                                    |
|    |    |    | Peacock A      | 2  |                                    |
|    |    |    | *3 players*    |    |                                    |
| 33 | **Lazio**         | 8 | Gascoigne P | 8 |                                    |
|    |    |    | *1 player*     |    |                                    |
| 35 | **Burnley**       | 7 | McDonald C  | 4 |                                    |
|    |    |    | Pointer R      | 2  |                                    |
|    |    |    | Connelly J     | 1  | +1 Man Utd                         |
|    |    |    | *3 players*    |    |                                    |
| 35 | **Juventus**      | 7 | Platt D     | 7 | +6 Villa, +3 Sampdoria             |
|    |    |    | *1 player*     |    |                                    |
| 35 | **Stoke City**    | 7 | Banks G     | 3 | +6 Leicester                       |
|    |    |    | Franklin C     | 3  |                                    |
|    |    |    | Chamberlain M  | 1  |                                    |
|    |    |    | *3 players*    |    |                                    |
| 35 | **Watford**       | 7 | Barnes J    | 7 | +13 Liverpool                      |
|    |    |    | *1 player*     |    |                                    |
| 39 | **Barcelona**     | 4 | Lineker G   | 4 | +1 Leic, +8 Everton, +9 Spurs      |
|    |    |    | *1 player*     |    |                                    |
| 39 | **Cologne**       | 4 | Woodcock A  | 4 | + 7 Arsenal                        |
|    |    |    | *1 player*     |    |                                    |
| 39 | **Sheffield Utd** | 4 | Hodgkinskon A | 3 |                                  |
|    |    |    | Currie A       | 1  |                                    |
|    |    |    | *2 players*    |    |                                    |

| 42 | **Bristol City** | 3 | Atyeo J | 3 | |
| | | | *1 player* | | |
| 43 | **Luton Town** | 2 | Owen S | 1 | |
| | | | Streten B | 1 | |
| | | | *2 players* | | |
| 43 | **Internazionale** | 2 | Hitchens G | 2 | |
| | | | *1 player* | | |
| 43 | **Sunderland** | 2 | Shackleton L | 1 | |
| | | | Watson W | 1 | |
| | | | *2 players* | | |
| 46 | **Brighton** | 1 | Foster S | 1 | |
| | | | *1 player* | | |
| 46 | **Hamburg** | 1 | Keegan K | 1 | +6 Liverpool, +5 South'pton |
| | | | *1 player* | | |
| 46 | **Real Madrid** | 1 | Cunningham L | 1 | |
| | | | *1 player* | | |
| | *48 clubs* | *1155* | | | |

# Appendix 2

England World Cup goalscorers 1950-94 (includes qualifying rounds and final stages)

| Name | Goals | Apps | Name | Goals | Apps |
|------|-------|------|------|-------|------|
| Lineker, Gary | 15 | 22 | Pointer, Ray | 2 | 2 |
| Platt, David | 10 | 16 | Smith, Bobby | 2 | 2 |
| Charlton, Bobby | 9 | 18 | Clarke, Allan | 2 | 3 |
| Robson, Bryan | 9 | 27 | Edwards, Duncan | 2 | 4 |
| Taylor, Tommy | 8 | 6 | Kevan, Derek | 2 | 4 |
| Lofthouse, Nat | 6 | 4 | Mullen, Jimmy | 2 | 6 |
| Hurst, Geoff | 5 | 6 | Ince, Paul | 2 | 8 |
| Wright, Ian | 5 | 8 | Peters, Martin | 2 | 11 |
| Woodcock, Tony | 5 | 11 | Finney, Tom | 2 | 16 |
| Keegan, Kevin | 5 | 12 | Pearce, Stuart | 2 | 16 |
| Mariner, Paul | 5 | 13 | Waddle, Chris | 2 | 22 |
| Gascoigne, Paul | 5 | 16 | Allan, Ronnie | 1 | 1 |
| Barnes, John | 5 | 20 | Froggatt, Jack | 1 | 1 |
| Rowley, Jack | 4 | 1 | Nicholls, John | 1 | 1 |
| Atyeo, John | 4 | 3 | Tueart, Dennis | 1 | 1 |
| Mortensen, Stan | 4 | 6 | Viollet, Dennis | 1 | 1 |
| Hateley, Mark | 4 | 8 | Connelly, John | 1 | 2 |
| Greaves, Jimmy | 4 | 9 | Hitchens, Gerry | 1 | 2 |
| Milburn, Jackie | 3 | 2 | Pearson, Stuart | 1 | 2 |
| Wilshaw, Dennis | 3 | 3 | Royle, Joe | 1 | 2 |
| Broadis, Ivor | 3 | 4 | Bentley, Roy | 1 | 3 |
| Channon, Mike | 3 | 5 | Mannion, Wilf | 1 | 3 |
| Ferdinand, Les | 3 | 5 | Shearer, Alan | 1 | 3 |
| Hunt, Roger | 3 | 6 | Hunter, Norman | 1 | 4 |
| Flowers, Ron | 3 | 8 | Mullery, Alan | 1 | 4 |
| Brooking, Trevor | 3 | 9 | Anderson, Viv | 1 | 6 |
| McDermott, Terry | 3 | 9 | Webb, Neil | 1 | 6 |
| Haynes, Johnny | 3 | 14 | Bell, Colin | 1 | 7 |
| Beardsley, Peter | 3 | 15 | Palmer, Carlton | 1 | 8 |
| Francis, Trevor | 3 | 15 | Hoddle, Glenn | 1 | 11 |
| Hassall, Harold | 2 | 1 | Wright, Mark | 1 | 12 |
| Pearson, Stan | 2 | 1 | Sansom, Kenny | 1 | 22 |
| Kennedy, Ray | 2 | 2 | (own goals) | 2 | |
| | | | *Total* | *199* | |

**Appendix 3**

England World Cup goalkeepers 1950-94 (includes qualifying rounds and final stages)

| Name | World Cups | Apps | Goals | Ave per match |
|---|---|---|---|---|
| Shilton, Peter | 1974, '82, '86, '90*** | 37 | 16 | 0.43 |
| Banks, Gordon | 1966,* '70 | 9 | 4 | 0.44 |
| Williams, Bert | 1950 | 5 | 3 | 0.60 |
| Woods, Chris | 1994 | 7 | 6 | 0.86 |
| Clemence, Ray | 1974, '78, '82 | 12 | 12 | 1.00 |
| Springett, Ron | 1962 | 8 | 8 | 1.00 |
| Hodgkinson, Alan | 1958 | 3 | 3 | 1.00 |
| Seaman, David | 1994 | 3 | 3 | 1.00 |
| McDonald, Colin | 1958 | 4 | 5 | 1.25 |
| Merrick, Gil | 1954* | 6 | 12 | 2.00 |
| Ditchburn, Ted | 1958 | 1 | 2 | 2.00 |
| Streten, Bernard | 1950 | 1 | 2 | 2.00 |
| Bonetti, Peter | 1970* | 1 | 3 | 3.00 |
| *Extra time matches* | Totals | 97 | 79 | |

## Appendix 4
England World Cup captains 1950-94 (includes qualifying rounds and final stages)

| Captain | World Cups | Captain | W | D | L |
|---|---|---|---|---|---|
| Billy Wright | 1950, '54, '58 | 20 | 11 | 5 | 4 |
| Bryan Robson | 1986, '90 | 15 | 6 | 8 | 1 |
| Bobby Moore | 1966, '70, '74 | 13 | 8 | 2 | 3 |
| Johnny Haynes | 1962 | 7 | 3 | 2 | 2 |
| Kevin Keegan | 1978, '82 | 7 | 4 | 0 | 3 |
| Mick Mills | 1982 | 6 | 4 | 2 | 0 |
| David Platt | 1994 | 6 | 2 | 2 | 2 |
| Peter Shilton | 1986, '90 | 5 | 3 | 0 | 2 |
| Terry Butcher | 1990 (Swe A, Bel, Cam, W Ger) | 4 | 2 | 2 | 0 |
| Stuart Pearce | 1994 (Nor H, Turk H, Pol H, San A) | 4 | 3 | 1 | 0 |
| Emlyn Hughes | 1978 (Lux A, Italy H) | 2 | 2 | 0 | 0 |
| Phil Thompson | 1982 (Nor H, Rom A) | 2 | 1 | 0 | 1 |
| Ray Wilkins | 1986 (N Ire H&A) | 2 | 1 | 1 | 0 |
| Jimmy Armfield | 1962 (Lux H) | 1 | 1 | 0 | 0 |
| Martin Peters | 1974 (Pol H) | 1 | 0 | 1 | 0 |
| Gerry Francis | 1978 (Fin A) | 1 | 1 | 0 | 0 |
| Dave Watson | 1982 (Rom H) | 1 | 0 | 1 | 0 |

## Appendix 5
England's full World Cup record 1950-94 (includes qualifying rounds and final stages)

|  | P | W | D | L | F | A | Pts |
|---|---|---|---|---|---|---|---|
| Poland | 7 | 3 | 3 | 1 | 11 | 4 | 9 |
| Luxembourg | 4 | 4 | 0 | 0 | 20 | 1 | 8 |
| Turkey | 4 | 4 | 0 | 0 | 19 | 0 | 8 |
| Northern Ireland | 4 | 3 | 1 | 0 | 13 | 3 | 7 |
| Finland | 4 | 3 | 1 | 0 | 12 | 3 | 7 |
| Wales | 4 | 3 | 1 | 0 | 10 | 3 | 7 |
| Portugal | 4 | 2 | 1 | 1 | 5 | 3 | 5 |
| Romania | 5 | 1 | 3 | 1 | 3 | 3 | 5 |
| San Marino | 2 | 2 | 0 | 0 | 13 | 1 | 4 |
| Albania | 2 | 2 | 0 | 0 | 7 | 0 | 4 |
| Denmark | 2 | 2 | 0 | 0 | 9 | 3 | 4 |
| France | 2 | 2 | 0 | 0 | 5 | 1 | 4 |
| Scotland | 2 | 2 | 0 | 0 | 5 | 2 | 4 |
| Czechoslovakia | 2 | 2 | 0 | 0 | 3 | 0 | 4 |
| Republic of Ireland | 3 | 1 | 2 | 0 | 7 | 3 | 4 |
| Argentina | 3 | 2 | 0 | 1 | 5 | 3 | 4 |
| Hungary | 3 | 2 | 0 | 1 | 5 | 3 | 4 |
| Switzerland | 3 | 2 | 0 | 1 | 5 | 3 | 4 |
| West Germany * | 4 | 1 | 2 | 1 | 7 | 6 | 4 |
| Belgium | 2 | 1 | 1 | 0 | 5 | 4 | 3 |
| Norway | 4 | 1 | 1 | 2 | 6 | 5 | 3 |
| Paraguay | 1 | 1 | 0 | 0 | 3 | 0 | 2 |
| Chile | 1 | 1 | 0 | 0 | 2 | 0 | 2 |
| Mexico | 1 | 1 | 0 | 0 | 2 | 0 | 2 |
| Cameroon | 1 | 1 | 0 | 0 | 3 | 2 | 2 |
| Egypt | 1 | 1 | 0 | 0 | 1 | 0 | 2 |
| Kuwait | 1 | 1 | 0 | 0 | 1 | 0 | 2 |
| Sweden | 2 | 0 | 2 | 0 | 0 | 0 | 2 |
| Italy | 3 | 1 | 0 | 2 | 3 | 4 | 2 |
| Holland | 3 | 0 | 2 | 1 | 2 | 4 | 2 |
| Austria | 1 | 0 | 1 | 0 | 2 | 2 | 1 |
| Bulgaria | 1 | 0 | 1 | 0 | 0 | 0 | 1 |
| Morocco | 1 | 0 | 1 | 0 | 0 | 0 | 1 |
| Soviet Union | 2 | 0 | 1 | 1 | 2 | 3 | 1 |
| Spain | 2 | 0 | 1 | 1 | 0 | 1 | 1 |
| Uruguay | 2 | 0 | 1 | 1 | 2 | 4 | 1 |
| Brazil | 3 | 0 | 1 | 2 | 1 | 4 | 1 |
| United States | 1 | 0 | 0 | 1 | 0 | 1 | 0 |
| *38 nations* | *97* | *52* | *27* | *18* | *199* | *79* | *131* |

* 1990 semi-final taken as 1-1

|  | | | | | | | |
|---|---|---|---|---|---|---|---|
| World Cup finals | 41 | 18 | 12 | 11 | 55 | 38 | 48 |
| World Cup qualifiers | 56 | 34 | 15 | 7 | 144 | 41 | 83 |
| Home record in qualifiers | 27 | 19 | 8 | 0 | 81 | 15 | 46 |
| Away record in qualifiers | 29 | 15 | 7 | 7 | 63 | 26 | 37 |

## Appendix 6

England appearances and goalscorers in the World Cup 1950-94
(includes qualifying rounds and final stages)

| Apps | Player | 1950 | | 1954 | | 1958 | | 1962 | | 1966 | | 1970 | | 1974 | | 1978 | | 1982 | | 1986 | | 1990 | | 1994 | |
|---|---|---|---|---|---|---|---|---|---|---|---|---|---|---|---|---|---|---|---|---|---|---|---|---|---|
| | | A | G | A | G | A | G | A | G | A | G | A | G | A | G | A | G | A | G | A | G | A | G |
| 37 | Shilton, Peter | | | | | | | | | | | | | 2 | | | | 9 | | 13 | | 13 | | | |
| 27 | Robson, Bryan | | | | | | | | | | | | | | | | | 12 | 3 | 8 | 5 | 7 | 1 | | |
| 25 | Butcher, Terry | | | | | | | | | | | | | | | | | 4 | | 10 | | 11 | | | |
| 22 | Lineker, Gary | | | | | | | | | | | | | | | | | | | 9 | 9 | 13 | 6 | | |
| 22 | Sansom, Kenny | | | | | | | | | | | | | | | | | 9 | | 13 | 1 | | | | |
| 22 | Waddle, Chris | | | | | | | | | | | | | | | | | | | 9 | 1 | 13 | 1 | | |
| 21 | Walker, Des | | | | | | | | | | | | | | | | | | | | | 13 | | 8 | |
| 20 | Barnes, John | | | | | | | | | | | | | | | | | | | 7 | 2 | 9 | 2 | 4 | 1 |
| 20 | Wilkins, Ray | | | | | | | | | | | | | | | 3 | | 8 | | 9 | | | | | |
| 20 | Wright, Billy | 6 | | 6 | | 8 | | | | | | | | | | | | | | | | | | | |
| 18 | Charlton, Bobby | | | | | | | 8 | 6 | 6 | 3 | 4 | | | | | | | | | | | | | |
| 17 | Moore, Bobby | | | | | | | 4 | | 6 | | 4 | | 3 | | | | | | | | | | | |
| 16 | Finney, Tom | 6 | | 5 | 1 | 5 | 1 | | | | | | | | | | | | | | | | | | |
| 16 | Gascoigne, Paul | | | | | | | | | | | | | | | | | | | | | 8 | 1 | 8 | 4 |
| 16 | Pearce, Stuart | | | | | | | | | | | | | | | | | | | | | 12 | | 4 | 2 |
| 16 | Platt, David | | | | | | | | | | | | | | | | | | | | | 6 | 3 | 10 | 7 |
| 16 | Stevens, M Gary | | | | | | | | | | | | | | | | | | | 8 | | 8 | | | |
| 15 | Beardsley, Peter | | | | | | | | | | | | | | | | | | | 4 | 1 | 11 | 2 | | |
| 15 | Francis, Trevor | | | | | | | | | | | | | | | 3 | 1 | 8 | 2 | 4 | | | | | |
| 14 | Haynes, Johnny | | | | | 7 | 2 | 7 | 1 | | | | | | | | | | | | | | | | |
| 14 | Mariner, Paul | | | | | | | | | | | | | | | 2 | 1 | 11 | 4 | 1 | | | | | |
| 13 | Mills, Mick | | | | | | | | | | | | | | | 3 | | 10 | | | | | | | |
| 12 | Clemence, Ray | | | | | | | | | | | | | 2 | | 6 | | 4 | | | | | | | |
| 12 | Dickinson, Jim | 5 | | 6 | | 1 | | | | | | | | | | | | | | | | | | | |
| 12 | Keegan, Kevin | | | | | | | | | | | | | 2 | | 5 | 4 | 5 | 1 | | | | | | |
| 12 | Thompson, Phil | | | | | | | | | | | | | | | 2 | | 10 | | | | | | | |
| 12 | Wright, Mark | | | | | | | | | | | | | | | | | | | 6 | | 6 | 1 | | |
| 11 | Ball, Alan | | | | | | | | | 4 | | 4 | | 3 | | | | | | | | | | | |
| 11 | Coppell, Steve | | | | | | | | | | | | | | | 1 | | 10 | | | | | | | |
| 11 | Douglas, Bryan | | | | | 3 | | 8 | | | | | | | | | | | | | | | | | |
| 11 | Hoddle, Glenn | | | | | | | | | | | | | | | | | 3 | | 8 | 1 | | | | |
| 11 | Peters, Martin | | | | | | | | | 5 | 1 | 4 | 1 | 2 | | | | | | | | | | | |
| 11 | Wilson, Ray | | | | | | | 5 | | 6 | | | | | | | | | | | | | | | |
| 11 | Woodcock, Tony | | | | | | | | | | | | | | | | | 6 | 2 | 5 | 3 | | | | |
| 10 | Adams, Tony | | | | | | | | | | | | | | | | | | | | | 1 | | 9 | |
| 10 | Steven, Trevor | | | | | | | | | | | | | | | | | | | 7 | | 3 | | | |
| 9 | Banks, Gordon | | | | | | | | | 6 | | 3 | | | | | | | | | | | | | |
| 9 | Brooking, Trevor | | | | | | | | | | | | | | | 4 | 1 | 5 | 2 | | | | | | |
| 9 | Greaves, Jimmy | | | | | | | 6 | 4 | 3 | | | | | | | | | | | | | | | |
| 9 | McDermott, Terry | | | | | | | | | | | | | | | 1 | | 8 | 3 | | | | | | |
| 9 | Watson, Dave | | | | | | | | | | | | | | | 3 | | 6 | | | | | | | |

| No | Name | 1950 A | 1950 G | 1954 A | 1954 G | 1958 A | 1958 G | 1962 A | 1962 G | 1966 A | 1966 G | 1970 A | 1970 G | 1974 A | 1974 G | 1978 A | 1978 G | 1982 A | 1982 G | 1986 A | 1986 G | 1990 A | 1990 G | 1994 A | 1994 G |
|---|---|---|---|---|---|---|---|---|---|---|---|---|---|---|---|---|---|---|---|---|---|---|---|---|---|
| 8 | Armfield, Jimmy | | | | | | | 8 | | | | | | | | | | | | | | | | | |
| 8 | Byrne, Roger | | | 4 | | 4 | | | | | | | | | | | | | | | | | | | |
| 8 | Fenwick, Terry | | | | | | | | | | | | | | | | | | | 8 | | | | | |
| 8 | Flowers, Ron | | | | | | | 8 | 3 | | | | | | | | | | | | | | | | |
| 8 | Hateley, Mark | | | | | | | | | | | | | | | | | | | 8 | 4 | | | | |
| 8 | Hughes, Emlyn | | | | | | | | | | | | | 4 | | 4 | | | | | | | | | |
| 8 | Ince, Paul | | | | | | | | | | | | | | | | | | | | | | | 8 | 2 |
| 8 | Neal, Phil | | | | | | | | | | | | | | | 1 | | 7 | | | | | | | |
| 8 | Palmer, Carlton | | | | | | | | | | | | | | | | | | | | | | | 8 | 1 |
| 8 | Parker, Paul | | | | | | | | | | | | | | | | | | | | | 7 | | 1 | |
| 8 | Rix, Graham | | | | | | | | | | | | | | | | | 8 | | | | | | | |
| 8 | Springett, Ron | | | | | | | 8 | | | | | | | | | | | | | | | | | |
| 8 | Wright, Ian | | | | | | | | | | | | | | | | | | | | | | | 8 | 5 |
| 7 | Bell, Colin | | | | | | | | | | | 3 | | 4 | 1 | | | | | | | | | | |
| 7 | Charlton, Jack | | | | | | | | | 6 | | 1 | | | | | | | | | | | | | |
| 7 | Dixon, Lee | | | | | | | | | | | | | | | | | | | | | | | 7 | |
| 7 | Matthews, Stan | 1 | | 3 | | 3 | | | | | | | | | | | | | | | | | | | |
| 7 | Robson, Bobby | | | | | 3 | | 4 | | | | | | | | | | | | | | | | | |
| 7 | Woods, Chris | | | | | | | | | | | | | | | | | | | | | | | 7 | |
| 6 | Anderson, Viv | | | | | | | | | | | | | | | | | 2 | | 4 | 1 | | | | |
| 6 | Cohen, George | | | | | | | | | 6 | | | | | | | | | | | | | | | |
| 6 | Hunt, Roger | | | | | | | | | 6 | 3 | | | | | | | | | | | | | | |
| 6 | Hurst, Geoff | | | | | | | | | 3 | 4 | 3 | 1 | | | | | | | | | | | | |
| 6 | Merrick, Gil | | | 6 | | | | | | | | | | | | | | | | | | | | | |
| 6 | McMahon, Steve | | | | | | | | | | | | | | | | | | | | | 6 | | | |
| 6 | Mortensen, Stan | 6 | 4 | | | | | | | | | | | | | | | | | | | | | | |
| 6 | Mullen, Jimmy | 2 | | 4 | 2 | | | | | | | | | | | | | | | | | | | | |
| 6 | Stiles, Norbert | | | | | | | | | 6 | | | | | | | | | | | | | | | |
| 6 | Taylor, Tommy | | | 2 | | 4 | 8 | | | | | | | | | | | | | | | | | | |
| 6 | Webb, Neil | | | | | | | | | | | | | | | | | | | | | 6 | 1 | | |
| 5 | Aston, Jack | 5 | | | | | | | | | | | | | | | | | | | | | | | |
| 5 | Channon, Mike | | | | | | | | | | | | | 1 | | 4 | 3 | | | | | | | | |
| 5 | Cherry, Trevor | | | | | | | | | | | | | | | 5 | | | | | | | | | |
| 5 | Clayton, Ronnie | | | | | 5 | | | | | | | | | | | | | | | | | | | |
| 5 | Ferdinand, Les | | | | | | | | | | | | | | | | | | | | | | | 5 | 3 |
| 5 | Hodge, Steve | | | | | | | | | | | | | | | | | | | 5 | | | | | |
| 5 | McFarland, Roy | | | | | | | | | | | | | 4 | | 1 | | | | | | | | | |
| 5 | Rocastle, David | | | | | | | | | | | | | | | | | | | | | 5 | | | |
| 5 | Stevens, Gary A | | | | | | | | | | | | | | | | | | | 5 | | | | | |
| 5 | Williams, Bert | 5 | | | | | | | | | | | | | | | | | | | | | | | |
| 4 | Banks, Tommy | | | | | 4 | | | | | | | | | | | | | | | | | | | |
| 4 | Broadis, Ivor | | | 4 | 3 | | | | | | | | | | | | | | | | | | | | |
| 4 | Bull, Steve | | | | | | | | | | | | | | | | | | | | | 4 | | | |
| 4 | Chivers, Martin | | | | | | | | | | | | | 4 | | | | | | | | | | | |
| 4 | Cooper, Terry | | | | | | | | | | | 4 | | | | | | | | | | | | | |

| | | 1950 | | 1954 | | 1958 | | 1962 | | 1966 | | 1970 | | 1974 | | 1978 | | 1982 | | 1986 | | 1990 | | 1994 | |
|---|---|---|---|---|---|---|---|---|---|---|---|---|---|---|---|---|---|---|---|---|---|---|---|---|---|
| | | A | G | A | G | A | G | A | G | A | G | A | G | A | G | A | G | A | G | A | G | A | G | A | G |
| 4 | Dorigo, Tony | | | | | | | | | | | | | | | | | | | | | 1 | | 3 | |
| 4 | Edwards, Duncan | | | | | 4 | 2 | | | | | | | | | | | | | | | | | | |
| 4 | Hall, Jeff | | | | | 4 | | | | | | | | | | | | | | | | | | | |
| 4 | Howe, Don | | | | | 4 | | | | | | | | | | | | | | | | | | | |
| 4 | Hunter, Norman | | | | | | | | | | | 1 | | 3 | 1 | | | | | | | | | | |
| 4 | Kevan, Derek | | | | | 4 | 2 | | | | | | | | | | | | | | | | | | |
| 4 | Lofthouse, Nat | | | 4 | 6 | | | | | | | | | | | | | | | | | | | | |
| 4 | McDonald, Colin | | | | | 4 | | | | | | | | | | | | | | | | | | | |
| 4 | Mullery, Alan | | | | | | | | | | | 4 | 1 | | | | | | | | | | | | |
| 4 | Norman, Maurice | | | | | | | 4 | | | | | | | | | | | | | | | | | |
| 4 | Pallister, Gary | | | | | | | | | | | | | | | | | | | | | | | 4 | |
| 4 | Ramsey, Alf | 4 | | | | | | | | | | | | | | | | | | | | | | | |
| 4 | Reid, Peter | | | | | | | | | | | | | | | | | | | 4 | | | | | |
| 4 | Sharpe, Lee | | | | | | | | | | | | | | | | | | | | | | | 4 | |
| 4 | Slater, Bill | | | | | | | 4 | | | | | | | | | | | | | | | | | |
| 4 | Staniforth, Ron | | | 4 | | | | | | | | | | | | | | | | | | | | | |
| 4 | Swan, Peter | | | | | | | 4 | | | | | | | | | | | | | | | | | |
| 3 | A'Court, Alan | | | | | 3 | | | | | | | | | | | | | | | | | | | |
| 3 | Atyeo, John | | | | | 3 | 4 | | | | | | | | | | | | | | | | | | |
| 3 | Barnes, Peter | | | | | | | | | | | | | | | 1 | | 2 | | | | | | | |
| 3 | Beattie, Kevin | | | | | | | | | | | | | 3 | | | | | | | | | | | |
| 3 | Bentley, Roy | 3 | 1 | | | | | | | | | | | | | | | | | | | | | | |
| 3 | Clamp, Eddie | | | | | 3 | | | | | | | | | | | | | | | | | | | |
| 3 | Clarke, Allan | | | | | | | | | | | 1 | 1 | 2 | 1 | | | | | | | | | | |
| 3 | Clough, Nigel | | | | | | | | | | | | | | | | | | | | | | | 3 | |
| 3 | Eckersley, Bill | 1 | | 2 | | | | | | | | | | | | | | | | | | | | | |
| 3 | Franklin, Cornelius | 3 | | | | | | | | | | | | | | | | | | | | | | | |
| 3 | Hill, Gordon | | | | | | | | | | | | | | | 3 | | | | | | | | | |
| 3 | Hughes, Laurie | 3 | | | | | | | | | | | | | | | | | | | | | | | |
| 3 | Hodgkinson, Alan | | | | | 3 | | | | | | | | | | | | | | | | | | | |
| 3 | Labone, Brian | | | | | | | | | | | 3 | | | | | | | | | | | | | |
| 3 | Lee, Francis | | | | | | | | | | | 3 | | | | | | | | | | | | | |
| 3 | Madeley, Paul | | | | | | | | | | | | | 2 | | 1 | | | | | | | | | |
| 3 | Mannion, Wilf | 3 | 1 | | | | | | | | | | | | | | | | | | | | | | |
| 3 | Martin, Alvin | | | | | | | | | | | | | | | | | 1 | | 2 | | | | | |
| 3 | McNeil, Mick | | | | | | | 3 | | | | | | | | | | | | | | | | | |
| 3 | Merson, Paul | | | | | | | | | | | | | | | | | | | | | | | 3 | |
| 3 | Newton, Keith | | | | | | | | | | | 3 | | | | | | | | | | | | | |
| 3 | Osman, Russell | | | | | | | | | | | | | | | | | 3 | | | | | | | |
| 3 | Seaman, David | | | | | | | | | | | | | | | | | | | | | | | 3 | |
| 3 | Shearer, Alan | | | | | | | | | | | | | | | | | | | | | | | 3 | 1 |
| 3 | Sinton, Andy | | | | | | | | | | | | | | | | | | | | | | | 3 | |
| 3 | Storey, Peter | | | | | | | | | | | | | 3 | | | | | | | | | | | |
| 3 | Wilshaw, Dennis | | | 3 | 3 | | | | | | | | | | | | | | | | | | | | |
| 2 | Astle, Jeff | | | | | | | | | | | 2 | | | | | | | | | | | | | |
| 2 | Batty, David | | | | | | | | | | | | | | | | | | | | | | | 2 | |
| 2 | Callaghan, Ian | | | | | | | | | 1 | | | | | | 1 | | | | | | | | | |

| No. | Player | 1950 A | 1950 G | 1954 A | 1954 G | 1958 A | 1958 G | 1962 A | 1962 G | 1966 A | 1966 G | 1970 A | 1970 G | 1974 A | 1974 G | 1978 A | 1978 G | 1982 A | 1982 G | 1986 A | 1986 G | 1990 A | 1990 G | 1994 A | 1994 G |
|---|---|---|---|---|---|---|---|---|---|---|---|---|---|---|---|---|---|---|---|---|---|---|---|---|---|
| 2 | Connelly, John | | | | | | | 1 | 1 | 1 | | | | | | | | | | | | | | | |
| 2 | Dixon, Kerry | | | | | | | | | | | | | | | | | | | 2 | | | | | |
| 2 | Gates, Eric | | | | | | | | | | | | | | | | | 2 | | | | | | | |
| 2 | Greenhoff, Brian | | | | | | | | | | | | | | | 2 | | | | | | | | | |
| 2 | Hitchens, Gerry | | | | | | | 2 | 1 | | | | | | | | | | | | | | | | |
| 2 | Johnstone, Harry | | | 2 | | | | | | | | | | | | | | | | | | | | | |
| 2 | Kennedy, Ray | | | | | | | | | | | | | | | 2 | 2 | | | | | | | | |
| 2 | Marsh, Rodney | | | | | | | | | | | | | 2 | | | | | | | | | | | |
| 2 | McGarry, Bill | | | 2 | | | | | | | | | | | | | | | | | | | | | |
| 2 | Milburn, Jackie | 2 | 3 | | | | | | | | | | | | | | | | | | | | | | |
| 2 | Mozley, Bertram | 2 | | | | | | | | | | | | | | | | | | | | | | | |
| 2 | Osgood, Peter | | | | | | | | | | | 2 | | | | | | | | | | | | | |
| 2 | Peacock, Alan | | | | | | | 2 | | | | | | | | | | | | | | | | | |
| 2 | Pearson, Stuart | | | | | | | | | | | | | | | 2 | 1 | | | | | | | | |
| 2 | Pointer, Ray | | | | | | | 2 | 2 | | | | | | | | | | | | | | | | |
| 2 | Quixall, Albert | | | | | 2 | | | | | | | | | | | | | | | | | | | |
| 2 | Royle, Joe | | | | | | | | | | | | | | | 2 | 1 | | | | | | | | |
| 2 | Sheringham, Teddy | | | | | | | | | | | | | | | | | | | | | | | 2 | |
| 2 | Smith, Alan | | | | | | | | | | | | | | | | | | | | | 2 | | | |
| 2 | Smith, Bobby | | | | | | | 2 | 2 | | | | | | | | | | | | | | | | |
| 2 | Todd, Colin | | | | | | | | | | | | | 2 | | | | | | | | | | | |
| 2 | Williams, Steve | | | | | | | | | | | | | | | | | | | 2 | | | | | |
| 2 | Withe, Peter | | | | | | | | | | | | | | | | | 1 | | 1 | | | | | |
| 2 | Wright, Tommy | | | | | | | | | | | 2 | | | | | | | | | | | | | |
| 1 | Allen, Ronnie | | | 1 | 1 | | | | | | | | | | | | | | | | | | | | |
| 1 | Baily, Eddie | 1 | | | | | | | | | | | | | | | | | | | | | | | |
| 1 | Bardsley, David | | | | | | | | | | | | | | | | | | | | | | | 1 | |
| 1 | Birtles, Gary | | | | | | | | | | | | | | | | | 1 | | | | | | | |
| 1 | Bonetti, Peter | | | | | | | | | | | 1 | | | | | | | | | | | | | |
| 1 | Bowles, Stan | | | | | | | | | | | | | | | 1 | | | | | | | | | |
| 1 | Brabrook, Peter | | | | | 1 | | | | | | | | | | | | | | | | | | | |
| 1 | Bracewell, Paul | | | | | | | | | | | | | | | | | | | 1 | | | | | |
| 1 | Broadbent, Peter | | | | | 1 | | | | | | | | | | | | | | | | | | | |
| 1 | Brooks, Johnny | | | | | 1 | | | | | | | | | | | | | | | | | | | |
| 1 | Chamberlain, Mark | | | | | | | | | | | | | | | | | | | 1 | | | | | |
| 1 | Clarke, Harry | | | 1 | | | | | | | | | | | | | | | | | | | | | |
| 1 | Clement, Dave | | | | | | | | | | | | | | | 1 | | | | | | | | | |
| 1 | Cottee, Tony | | | | | | | | | | | | | | | | | | | | | 1 | | | |
| 1 | Cunningham, Laurie | | | | | | | | | | | | | | | | | 1 | | | | | | | |
| 1 | Currie, Tony | | | | | | | | | | | | | 1 | | | | | | | | | | | |
| 1 | Ditchburn, Ted | | | 1 | | | | | | | | | | | | | | | | | | | | | |
| 1 | Duxbury, Mike | | | | | | | | | | | | | | | | | | | 1 | | | | | |
| 1 | Fantham, John | | | | | | | 1 | | | | | | | | | | | | | | | | | |
| 1 | Foster, Steve | | | | | | | | | | | | | | | | | 1 | | | | | | | |
| 1 | Francis, Gerry | | | | | | | | | | | | | | | 1 | | | | | | | | | |
| 1 | Froggatt, Jack | 1 | 1 | | | | | | | | | | | | | | | | | | | | | | |
| 1 | Garrett, Tom | | | 1 | | | | | | | | | | | | | | | | | | | | | |
| 1 | Gidman, John | | | | | | | | | | | | | | | 1 | | | | | | | | | |

| | | 1950 | | 1954 | | 1958 | | 1962 | | 1966 | | 1970 | | 1974 | | 1978 | | 1982 | | 1986 | | 1990 | | 1994 | |
|---|---|---|---|---|---|---|---|---|---|---|---|---|---|---|---|---|---|---|---|---|---|---|---|---|---|
| | | A | G | A | G | A | G | A | G | A | G | A | G | A | G | A | G | A | G | A | G | A | G | A | G |
| 1 | Hancocks, John | 1 | | | | | | | | | | | | | | | | | | | | | | | |
| 1 | Hassall, Harold | | | 1 | 2 | | | | | | | | | | | | | | | | | | | | |
| 1 | Hector, Kevin | | | | | | | | | | | | 1 | | | | | | | | | | | | |
| 1 | Jones, Rob | | | | | | | | | | | | | | | | | | | | | | | | 1 |
| 1 | Keown, Martin | | | | | | | | | | | | | | | | | | | | | | | | 1 |
| 1 | Langton, Bob | 1 | | | | | | | | | | | | | | | | | | | | | | | |
| 1 | Latchford, Bob | | | | | | | | | | | | | | | 1 | | | | | | | | | |
| 1 | Morley, Tony | | | | | | | | | | | | | | | | | 1 | | | | | | | |
| 1 | Nicholls, John | | | 1 | 1 | | | | | | | | | | | | | | | | | | | | |
| 1 | Owen, Syd | | | 1 | | | | | | | | | | | | | | | | | | | | | |
| 1 | Paine, Terry | | | | | | | | | 1 | | | | | | | | | | | | | | | |
| 1 | Pearson, Stan | 1 | 2 | | | | | | | | | | | | | | | | | | | | | | |
| 1 | Pegg, David | | | | | | 1 | | | | | | | | | | | | | | | | | | |
| 1 | Rickaby, Stan | | | 1 | | | | | | | | | | | | | | | | | | | | | |
| 1 | Ripley, Stuart | | | | | | | | | | | | | | | | | | | | | | | | 1 |
| 1 | Rowley, Jack | 1 | 4 | | | | | | | | | | | | | | | | | | | | | | |
| 1 | Shackleton, Len | 1 | | | | | | | | | | | | | | | | | | | | | | | |
| 1 | Streten, Bernard | 1 | | | | | | | | | | | | | | | | | | | | | | | |
| 1 | Tueart, Dennis | | | | | | | | | | | | | | | 1 | 1 | | | | | | | | |
| 1 | Viollet, Dennis | | | | | | | 1 | 1 | | | | | | | | | | | | | | | | |
| 1 | Watson, Willie | 1 | | | | | | | | | | | | | | | | | | | | | | | |
| 1 | Whymark, Trevor | | | | | | | | | | | | | | | 1 | | | | | | | | | |
| | (own goals) | | | | | | | | | | | | | | | | | | | 2 | | | | |

| | 1950 | 1954 | 1958 | 1962 | 1966 | 1970 | 1974 | 1978 | 1982 | 1986 | 1990 | 1994 |
|---|---|---|---|---|---|---|---|---|---|---|---|---|
| *97 games* | *6* | *6* | *8* | *8* | *6* | *4* | *4* | *6* | *13* | *13* | *13* | *10* |
| *199 goals* | *16* | *19* | *19* | *21* | *11* | *4* | *3* | *15* | *19* | *28* | *18* | *26* |
| *203 different players* | *25* | *23* | *26* | *20* | *15* | *19* | *18* | *33* | *29* | *29* | *23* | *27* |
| *1155 caps* | *66* | *66* | *88* | *88* | *66* | *52* | *45* | *74* | *158* | *165* | *166* | *121* |

**Appendix 7**
Results of World Cup finals 1930-1990

## URUGUAY – 1930

| *Pool I* | | P | W | D | L | F | A | Pts |
|---|---|---|---|---|---|---|---|---|
| France v Mexico | 4-1 | ARGENTINA | 3 | 3 | 0 | 0 | 10 | 4 | 6 |
| Argentina v France | 1-0 | Chile | 3 | 2 | 0 | 1 | 5 | 3 | 4 |
| Chile v Mexico | 3-0 | France | 3 | 1 | 0 | 2 | 4 | 3 | 2 |
| Chile v France | 1-0 | Mexico | 3 | 0 | 0 | 3 | 4 | 13 | 0 |
| Argentina v Mexico | 6-3 | | | | | | | | |
| Argentina v Chile | 3-1 | | | | | | | | |

| *Pool II* | | P | W | D | L | F | A | Pts |
|---|---|---|---|---|---|---|---|---|
| Yugoslavia v Brazil | 2-1 | YUGOSLAVIA | 2 | 2 | 0 | 0 | 6 | 1 | 4 |
| Yugoslavia v Bolivia | 4-0 | Brazil | 2 | 1 | 0 | 1 | 5 | 2 | 2 |
| Brazil v Bolivia | 4-0 | Bolivia | 2 | 0 | 0 | 2 | 0 | 8 | 0 |

| *Pool III* | | P | W | D | L | F | A | Pts |
|---|---|---|---|---|---|---|---|---|
| Romania v Peru | 3-1 | URUGUAY | 2 | 2 | 0 | 0 | 5 | 0 | 4 |
| Uruguay v Peru | 1-0 | Romania | 2 | 1 | 0 | 1 | 3 | 5 | 2 |
| Uruguay v Romania | 4-0 | Peru | 2 | 0 | 0 | 2 | 1 | 4 | 0 |

| *Pool IV* | | P | W | D | L | F | A | Pts |
|---|---|---|---|---|---|---|---|---|
| United States v Belgium | 3-0 | UNITED STATES | 2 | 2 | 0 | 0 | 6 | 0 | 4 |
| United States v Paraguay | 3-0 | Paraguay | 2 | 1 | 0 | 1 | 1 | 3 | 2 |
| Paraguay v Belgium | 1-0 | Belgium | 2 | 0 | 0 | 2 | 0 | 4 | 0 |

*Semi-finals*
Argentina v United States     6-1          Uruguay v Yugoslavia          6-1

*Final*
Uruguay v Argentina     4-2

## ITALY – 1934

*1st Round*
| | |
|---|---|
| Italy v United States | 7-1 |
| Germany v Belgium | 5-2 |
| Spain v Brazil | 3-1 |
| Sweden v Argentina | 3-2 |
| Czechoslovakia v Romania | 2-1 |
| Austria v France | 3-2 (aet) |
| Switzerland v Holland | 3-2 |
| Hungary v Egypt | 4-2 |

*2nd Round*
| | |
|---|---|
| Germany v Sweden | 2-1 |
| Italy v Spain | 1-1  1-0 (replay) |
| Austria v Hungary | 2-1 |
| Czechoslovakia v Switz'land | 3-2 |

*Semi-finals*
Czechoslovakia v Germany   3-1          Italy v Austria                1-0

*Third/Fourth play-off*                  *Final*
Germany v Austria     3-2                 Italy v Czechoslovakia     2-1 (aet)

## FRANCE – 1938

| 1st Round | | 2nd Round | |
|---|---|---|---|
| Switzerland v Germany | 1-1 4-2 (replay) | Sweden v Cuba | 8-0 |
| Cuba v Romania | 3-3 2-1 (replay) | Italy v France | 3-1 |
| Hungary v Dutch E Indies | 6-0 | Hungary v Switzerland | 2-0 |
| France v Belgium | 3-1 | Brazil v Czechoslovakia | 1-1 2-1 (replay) |
| Czechoslovakia v Holland | 3-0 (aet) | | |
| Brazil v Poland | 6-5 (aet) | | |
| Italy v Norway | 2-1 (aet) | | |

*Semi-finals*

| Italy v Brazil | 2-1 | Hungary v Sweden | 5-1 |
|---|---|---|---|

| *Third/Fourth play-off* | | *Final* | |
|---|---|---|---|
| Brazil v Sweden | 4-2 | Italy v Hungary | 4-2 |

## BRAZIL – 1950

### Pool I

| | | | P | W | D | L | F | A | Pts |
|---|---|---|---|---|---|---|---|---|---|
| Brazil v Mexico | 4-0 | BRAZIL | 3 | 2 | 1 | 0 | 8 | 2 | 5 |
| Yugoslavia v Switzerland | 3-0 | Yugoslavia | 3 | 2 | 0 | 1 | 7 | 3 | 4 |
| Yugoslavia v Mexico | 4-1 | Switzerland | 3 | 1 | 1 | 1 | 4 | 6 | 3 |
| Brazil v Switzerland | 2-2 | Mexico | 3 | 0 | 0 | 3 | 2 | 10 | 0 |
| Brazil v Yugoslavia | 2-0 | | | | | | | | |
| Switzerland v Mexico | 2-1 | | | | | | | | |

### Pool II

| | | | P | W | D | L | F | A | Pts |
|---|---|---|---|---|---|---|---|---|---|
| Spain v United States | 3-1 | SPAIN | 3 | 3 | 0 | 0 | 6 | 1 | 6 |
| England v Chile | 2-0 | England | 3 | 1 | 0 | 2 | 2 | 2 | 2 |
| United States v England | 1-0 | Chile | 3 | 1 | 0 | 2 | 5 | 6 | 2 |
| Spain v Chile | 2-0 | United States | 3 | 1 | 0 | 2 | 4 | 8 | 2 |
| Spain v England | 1-0 | | | | | | | | |
| Chile v United States | 5-2 | | | | | | | | |

### Pool III

| | | | P | W | D | L | F | A | Pts |
|---|---|---|---|---|---|---|---|---|---|
| Sweden v Italy | 3-2 | SWEDEN | 2 | 1 | 1 | 0 | 5 | 4 | 3 |
| Sweden v Paraguay | 2-2 | Italy | 2 | 1 | 0 | 1 | 4 | 3 | 2 |
| Italy v Paraguay | 2-0 | Paraguay | 2 | 0 | 1 | 1 | 2 | 4 | 1 |

### Pool IV

| | | | P | W | D | L | F | A | Pts |
|---|---|---|---|---|---|---|---|---|---|
| Uruguay v Bolivia | 8-0 | URUGUAY | 1 | 1 | 0 | 0 | 8 | 0 | 2 |
| | | Bolivia | 1 | 0 | 0 | 1 | 0 | 8 | 0 |

### Final Pool

| | | *Final Positions* | | | | | | | |
|---|---|---|---|---|---|---|---|---|---|
| Uruguay v Spain | 2-2 | 1 URUGUAY | 3 | 2 | 1 | 0 | 7 | 5 | 5 |
| Brazil v Sweden | 7-1 | 2 Brazil | 3 | 2 | 0 | 1 | 14 | 4 | 4 |
| Uruguay v Sweden | 3-2 | 3 Sweden | 3 | 1 | 0 | 2 | 6 | 11 | 2 |
| Brazil v Spain | 6-1 | 4 Spain | 3 | 0 | 1 | 2 | 4 | 11 | 1 |
| Sweden v Spain | 3-1 | | | | | | | | |
| Uruguay v Brazil | 2-1 | | | | | | | | |

## SWITZERLAND – 1954

### Pool I

| | | | P | W | D | L | F | A | Pts |
|---|---|---|---|---|---|---|---|---|---|
| Yugoslavia v France | 1-0 | BRAZIL | 2 | 1 | 1 | 0 | 6 | 1 | 3 |
| Brazil v Mexico | 5-0 | YUGOSLAVIA | 2 | 1 | 1 | 0 | 2 | 1 | 3 |
| France v Mexico | 3-2 | France | 2 | 1 | 0 | 1 | 3 | 3 | 2 |
| Brazil v Yugoslavia | 1-1 (aet) | Mexico | 2 | 0 | 0 | 2 | 2 | 8 | 0 |

### Pool II

| | | | P | W | D | L | F | A | Pts |
|---|---|---|---|---|---|---|---|---|---|
| Hungary v South Korea | 9-0 | HUNGARY | 2 | 2 | 0 | 0 | 17 | 3 | 4 |
| W Germany v Turkey | 4-1 | W GERMANY | 2 | 1 | 0 | 1 | 7 | 9 | 2 |
| Hungary v W Germany | 8-3 | Turkey | 2 | 1 | 0 | 1 | 8 | 4 | 2 |
| Turkey v South Korea | 7-0 | South Korea | 2 | 0 | 0 | 2 | 0 | 16 | 0 |
| W Germany v Turkey | 7-2 (play-off) | | | | | | | | |

### Pool III

| | | | P | W | D | L | F | A | Pts |
|---|---|---|---|---|---|---|---|---|---|
| Austria v Scotland | 1-0 | URUGUAY | 2 | 2 | 0 | 0 | 9 | 0 | 4 |
| Uruguay v Czechoslovakia | 2-0 | AUSTRIA | 2 | 2 | 0 | 0 | 6 | 0 | 4 |
| Austria v Czechoslovakia | 5-0 | Czechoslovakia | 2 | 0 | 0 | 2 | 0 | 7 | 0 |
| Uruguay v Scotland | 7-0 | Scotland | 2 | 0 | 0 | 2 | 0 | 8 | 0 |

### Pool IV

| | | | P | W | D | L | F | A | Pts |
|---|---|---|---|---|---|---|---|---|---|
| England v Belgium | 4-4 (aet) | ENGLAND | 2 | 1 | 1 | 0 | 6 | 4 | 3 |
| Switzerland v Italy | 2-1 | SWITZERLAND | 2 | 1 | 0 | 1 | 2 | 3 | 2 |
| England v Switzerland | 2-0 | Italy | 2 | 1 | 0 | 1 | 5 | 3 | 2 |
| Italy v Belgium | 4-1 | Belgium | 2 | 0 | 1 | 1 | 5 | 8 | 1 |
| Switzerland v Italy | 4-1 (play-off) | | | | | | | | |

### Quarter-finals

| | | | |
|---|---|---|---|
| W Germany v Yugoslavia | 2-0 | Austria v Switzerland | 7-5 |
| Uruguay v England | 4-2 | Hungary v Brazil | 4-2 |

### Semi-finals

| | | | |
|---|---|---|---|
| W Germany v Austria | 6-1 | Hungary v Uruguay | 4-2 (aet) |

### Third/Fourth play-off

| | | Final | |
|---|---|---|---|
| Austria v Uruguay | 3-1 | W Germany v Hungary | 3-2 |

## SWEDEN – 1958

### Pool I

| | | | P | W | D | L | F | A | Pts |
|---|---|---|---|---|---|---|---|---|---|
| W Germany v Argentina | 3-1 | W GERMANY | 3 | 1 | 2 | 0 | 7 | 5 | 4 |
| N Ireland v Czechoslovakia | 1-0 | N IRELAND | 3 | 1 | 1 | 1 | 4 | 5 | 3 |
| W Germany v Czecho'vakia | 2-2 | Czechoslovakia | 3 | 1 | 1 | 1 | 8 | 4 | 3 |
| Argentina v N Ireland | 3-1 | Argentina | 3 | 1 | 0 | 2 | 5 | 10 | 2 |
| W Germany v N Ireland | 2-2 | | | | | | | | |
| Czechoslovakia v Argentina | 6-1 | | | | | | | | |
| N Ireland v Czechoslovakia | 2-1 (play-off, aet) | | | | | | | | |

*Pool II*

| | | | P | W | D | L | F | A | Pts |
|---|---|---|---|---|---|---|---|---|---|
| France v Paraguay | 7-3 | FRANCE | 3 | 2 | 0 | 1 | 11 | 7 | 4 |
| Yugoslavia v Scotland | 1-1 | YUGOSLAVIA | 3 | 1 | 2 | 0 | 7 | 6 | 4 |
| Yugoslavia v France | 3-2 | Paraguay | 3 | 1 | 1 | 1 | 9 | 12 | 3 |
| Paraguay v Scotland | 3-2 | Scotland | 3 | 0 | 1 | 2 | 4 | 6 | 1 |
| France v Scotland | 2-1 | | | | | | | | |
| Yugoslavia v Paraguay | 3-3 | | | | | | | | |

*Pool III*

| | | | P | W | D | L | F | A | Pts |
|---|---|---|---|---|---|---|---|---|---|
| Sweden v Mexico | 3-0 | SWEDEN | 3 | 2 | 1 | 0 | 5 | 1 | 5 |
| Hungary v Wales | 1-1 | WALES | 3 | 0 | 3 | 0 | 2 | 2 | 3 |
| Wales v Mexico | 1-1 | Hungary | 3 | 1 | 1 | 1 | 6 | 3 | 3 |
| Sweden v Hungary | 2-1 | Mexico | 3 | 0 | 1 | 2 | 1 | 8 | 1 |
| Sweden v Wales | 0-0 | | | | | | | | |
| Hungary v Mexico | 4-0 | | | | | | | | |
| Wales v Hungary | 2-1 (play-off) | | | | | | | | |

*Pool IV*

| | | | P | W | D | L | F | A | Pts |
|---|---|---|---|---|---|---|---|---|---|
| England v Soviet Union | 2-2 | BRAZIL | 3 | 2 | 1 | 0 | 5 | 0 | 5 |
| Brazil v Austria | 3-0 | SOVIET UNION | 3 | 1 | 1 | 1 | 4 | 4 | 3 |
| England v Brazil | 0-0 | England | 3 | 0 | 3 | 0 | 4 | 4 | 3 |
| Soviet Union v Austria | 2-0 | Austria | 3 | 0 | 1 | 2 | 2 | 7 | 1 |
| Brazil v Soviet Union | 2-0 | | | | | | | | |
| England v Austria | 2-2 | | | | | | | | |
| Soviet Union v England | 1-0 (play-off) | | | | | | | | |

*Quarter-finals*

| | | | |
|---|---|---|---|
| France v N Ireland | 4-0 | W Germany v Yugoslavia | 1-0 |
| Sweden v Soviet Union | 2-0 | Brazil v Wales | 1-0 |

*Semi-finals*

| | | | |
|---|---|---|---|
| Brazil v France | 5-2 | Sweden v W Germany | 3-1 |

| *Third/Fourth play-off* | | *Final* | |
|---|---|---|---|
| France v W Germany | 6-3 | Brazil v Sweden | 5-2 |

## CHILE – 1962

*Group 1*

| | | | P | W | D | L | F | A | Pts |
|---|---|---|---|---|---|---|---|---|---|
| Uruguay v Colombia | 2-1 | SOVIET UNION | 3 | 2 | 1 | 0 | 8 | 5 | 5 |
| Soviet Union v Yugoslavia | 2-0 | YUGOSLAVIA | 3 | 2 | 0 | 1 | 8 | 3 | 4 |
| Yugoslavia v Uruguay | 3-1 | Uruguay | 3 | 1 | 0 | 2 | 4 | 6 | 2 |
| Soviet Union v Colombia | 4-4 | Colombia | 3 | 0 | 1 | 2 | 5 | 11 | 1 |
| Soviet Union v Uruguay | 2-1 | | | | | | | | |
| Yugoslavia v Colombia | 5-0 | | | | | | | | |

*Group 2*

| | | | P | W | D | L | F | A | Pts |
|---|---|---|---|---|---|---|---|---|---|
| Chile v Switzerland | 3-1 | W GERMANY | 3 | 2 | 1 | 0 | 4 | 1 | 5 |
| W Germany v Italy | 0-0 | CHILE | 3 | 2 | 0 | 1 | 5 | 3 | 4 |
| Chile v Italy | 2-0 | Italy | 3 | 1 | 1 | 1 | 3 | 2 | 3 |
| W Germany v Switzerland | 2-1 | Switzerland | 3 | 0 | 0 | 3 | 2 | 8 | 0 |

| W Germany v Chile | 2-0 |
| Italy v Switzerland | 3-0 |

*Group 3*

| Brazil v Mexico | 2-0 | BRAZIL | 3 | 2 | 1 | 0 | 4 | 1 | 5 |
| Czechoslovakia v Spain | 1-0 | CZECHOSLOVAKIA | 3 | 1 | 1 | 1 | 2 | 3 | 3 |
| Brazil v Czechoslovakia | 0-0 | Mexico | 3 | 1 | 0 | 2 | 3 | 4 | 2 |
| Spain v Mexico | 1-0 | Spain | 3 | 1 | 0 | 2 | 2 | 3 | 2 |
| Brazil v Spain | 2-1 |
| Mexico v Czechoslovakia | 3-1 |

*Group 4*

| Argentina v Bulgaria | 1-0 | HUNGARY | 3 | 2 | 1 | 0 | 8 | 2 | 5 |
| Hungary v England | 2-1 | ENGLAND | 3 | 1 | 1 | 1 | 4 | 3 | 3 |
| England v Argentina | 3-1 | Argentina | 3 | 1 | 1 | 1 | 2 | 3 | 3 |
| Hungary v Bulgaria | 6-1 | Bulgaria | 3 | 0 | 1 | 2 | 1 | 7 | 1 |
| Argentina v Hungary | 0-0 |
| England v Bulgaria | 0-0 |

*Quarter-finals*

| Yugoslavia v W Germany | 1-0 | Chile v Soviet Union | 2-1 |
| Brazil v England | 3-1 | Czechoslovakia v Hungary | 1-0 |

*Semi-finals*

| Brazil v Chile | 4-2 | Czecho'vakia v Yugoslavia | 3-1 |

*Third/Fourth play-off* | | *Final* |

| Chile v Yugoslavia | 1-0 | Brazil v Czechoslovakia | 3-1 |

---

## ENGLAND – 1966

*Group 1*

| | | | P | W | D | L | F | A | Pts |
|---|---|---|---|---|---|---|---|---|---|
| England v Uruguay | 0-0 | ENGLAND | 3 | 2 | 1 | 0 | 4 | 0 | 5 |
| France v Mexico | 1-1 | URUGUAY | 3 | 1 | 2 | 0 | 2 | 1 | 4 |
| Uruguay v France | 2-1 | Mexico | 3 | 0 | 2 | 1 | 1 | 3 | 2 |
| England v Mexico | 2-0 | France | 3 | 0 | 1 | 2 | 2 | 5 | 1 |
| Uruguay v Mexico | 0-0 |
| England v France | 2-0 |

*Group 2*

| W Germany v Switzerland | 5-0 | W GERMANY | 3 | 2 | 1 | 0 | 7 | 1 | 5 |
| Argentina v Spain | 2-1 | ARGENTINA | 3 | 2 | 1 | 0 | 4 | 1 | 5 |
| Spain v Switzerland | 2-1 | Spain | 3 | 1 | 0 | 2 | 4 | 5 | 2 |
| Argentina v W Germany | 0-0 | Switzerland | 3 | 0 | 0 | 3 | 1 | 9 | 0 |
| Argentina v Switzerland | 2-0 |
| W Germany v Spain | 2-1 |

*Group 3*

| | | | | | | | | |
|---|---|---|---|---|---|---|---|---|
| Brazil v Bulgaria | 0-0 | PORTUGAL | 3 | 3 0 0 | 9 | 2 | 6 |
| Portugal v Hungary | 3-1 | HUNGARY | 3 | 2 0 1 | 7 | 5 | 4 |
| Hungary v Brazil | 3-1 | Brazil | 3 | 1 0 2 | 4 | 6 | 2 |
| Portugal v Bulgaria | 3-0 | Bulgaria | 3 | 0 0 3 | 1 | 8 | 0 |
| Portugal v Brazil | 3-1 | | | | | | |
| Hungary v Bulgaria | 3-1 | | | | | | |

*Group 4*

| | | | | | | | | |
|---|---|---|---|---|---|---|---|---|
| Soviet Union v North Korea | 3-0 | SOVIET UNION | 3 | 3 0 0 | 6 | 1 | 6 |
| Italy v Chile | 2-0 | NORTH KOREA | 3 | 1 1 1 | 2 | 4 | 3 |
| Chile v North Korea | 1-1 | Italy | 3 | 1 0 2 | 2 | 2 | 2 |
| Soviet Union v Italy | 1-0 | Chile | 3 | 0 1 2 | 2 | 5 | 1 |
| North Korea v Italy | 1-0 | | | | | | |
| Soviet Union v Chile | 2-1 | | | | | | |

*Quarter-finals*

| | | | |
|---|---|---|---|
| England v Argentina | 1-0 | Portugal v North Korea | 5-3 |
| W Germany v Uruguay | 4-0 | Soviet Union v Hungary | 2-1 |

*Semi-finals*

| | | | |
|---|---|---|---|
| W Germany v Soviet Union | 2-1 | England v Portugal | 2-1 |

*Third/Fourth play-off*    *Final*

| | | | |
|---|---|---|---|
| Portugal v Soviet Union | 2-1 | England v W Germany | 4-2 (aet) |

---

## MEXICO – 1970

*Group 1*

| | | | P | W D L | F | A | Pts |
|---|---|---|---|---|---|---|---|
| Mexico v Soviet Union | 0-0 | SOVIET UNION | 3 | 2 1 0 | 6 | 1 | 5 |
| Belgium v El Salvador | 3-0 | MEXICO | 3 | 2 1 0 | 5 | 0 | 5 |
| Soviet Union v Belgium | 4-1 | Belgium | 3 | 1 0 2 | 4 | 5 | 2 |
| Mexico v El Salvador | 4-0 | El Salvador | 3 | 0 0 3 | 0 | 9 | 0 |
| Soviet Union v El Salvador | 2-0 | | | | | | |
| Mexico v Belgium | 1-0 | | | | | | |

*Group 2*

| | | | | | | | |
|---|---|---|---|---|---|---|---|
| Uruguay v Israel | 2-0 | ITALY | 3 | 1 2 0 | 1 0 | 4 |
| Italy v Sweden | 1-0 | URUGUAY | 3 | 1 1 1 | 2 1 | 3 |
| Uruguay v Italy | 0-0 | Sweden | 3 | 1 1 1 | 2 2 | 3 |
| Israel v Sweden | 1-1 | Israel | 3 | 0 2 1 | 1 3 | 2 |
| Sweden v Uruguay | 1-0 | | | | | |
| Israel v Italy | 0-0 | | | | | |

*Group 3*

| | | | | | | | |
|---|---|---|---|---|---|---|---|
| England v Romania | 1-0 | BRAZIL | 3 | 3 0 0 | 8 3 | 6 |
| Brazil v Czechoslovakia | 4-1 | ENGLAND | 3 | 2 0 1 | 2 1 | 4 |
| Romania v Czechoslovakia | 2-1 | Romania | 3 | 1 0 2 | 4 5 | 2 |
| Brazil v England | 1-0 | Czechoslovakia | 3 | 0 0 3 | 2 7 | 0 |
| Brazil v Romania | 3-2 | | | | | |
| England v Czechoslovakia | 1-0 | | | | | |

*Group 4*

| | | | P | W | D | L | F | A | Pts |
|---|---|---|---|---|---|---|---|---|---|
| Peru v Bulgaria | 3-2 | W GERMANY | 3 | 3 | 0 | 0 | 10 | 4 | 6 |
| W Germany v Morocco | 2-1 | PERU | 3 | 2 | 0 | 1 | 7 | 5 | 4 |
| Peru v Morocco | 3-0 | Bulgaria | 3 | 0 | 1 | 2 | 5 | 9 | 1 |
| W Germany v Bulgaria | 5-2 | Morocco | 3 | 0 | 1 | 2 | 2 | 6 | 1 |
| W Germany v Peru | 3-1 | | | | | | | | |
| Bulgaria v Morocco | 1-1 | | | | | | | | |

*Quarter-finals*

| | | | |
|---|---|---|---|
| Uruguay v Soviet Union | 1-0 (aet) | Brazil v Peru | 4-2 |
| Italy v Mexico | 4-1 | W Germany v England | 3-2 (aet) |

*Semi-finals*

| | | | |
|---|---|---|---|
| Italy v W Germany | 4-3 (aet) | Brazil v Uruguay | 3-1 |

*Third/Fourth play-off* | | *Final* | |
|---|---|---|---|
| W Germany v Uruguay | 1-0 | Brazil v Italy | 4-1 |

---

## WEST GERMANY– 1974

*Group 1*

| | | | P | W | D | L | F | A | Pts |
|---|---|---|---|---|---|---|---|---|---|
| W Germany v Chile | 1-0 | E GERMANY | 3 | 2 | 1 | 0 | 4 | 1 | 5 |
| E Germany v Australia | 2-0 | W GERMANY | 3 | 2 | 0 | 1 | 4 | 1 | 4 |
| W Germany v Australia | 3-0 | Chile | 3 | 0 | 2 | 1 | 1 | 2 | 2 |
| E Germany v Chile | 1-1 | Australia | 3 | 0 | 1 | 2 | 0 | 5 | 1 |
| E Germany v W Germany | 1-0 | | | | | | | | |
| Chile v Australia | 0-0 | | | | | | | | |

*Group 2*

| | | | P | W | D | L | F | A | Pts |
|---|---|---|---|---|---|---|---|---|---|
| Brazil v Yugoslavia | 0-0 | YUGOSLAVIA | 3 | 1 | 2 | 0 | 10 | 1 | 4 |
| Scotland v Zaire | 2-0 | BRAZIL | 3 | 1 | 2 | 0 | 3 | 0 | 4 |
| Brazil v Scotland | 0-0 | Scotland | 3 | 1 | 2 | 0 | 3 | 1 | 4 |
| Yugoslavia v Zaire | 9-0 | Zaire | 3 | 0 | 0 | 3 | 0 | 14 | 0 |
| Scotland v Yugoslavia | 1-1 | | | | | | | | |
| Brazil v Zaire | 3-0 | | | | | | | | |

*Group 3*

| | | | P | W | D | L | F | A | Pts |
|---|---|---|---|---|---|---|---|---|---|
| Holland v Uruguay | 2-0 | HOLLAND | 3 | 2 | 1 | 0 | 6 | 1 | 5 |
| Sweden v Bulgaria | 0-0 | SWEDEN | 3 | 1 | 2 | 0 | 3 | 0 | 4 |
| Holland v Sweden | 0-0 | Bulgaria | 3 | 0 | 2 | 1 | 2 | 5 | 2 |
| Bulgaria v Uruguay | 1-1 | Uruguay | 3 | 0 | 1 | 2 | 1 | 6 | 1 |
| Holland v Bulgaria | 4-1 | | | | | | | | |
| Sweden v Uruguay | 3-0 | | | | | | | | |

*Group 4*

| | | | P | W | D | L | F | A | Pts |
|---|---|---|---|---|---|---|---|---|---|
| Italy v Haiti | 3-1 | POLAND | 3 | 3 | 0 | 0 | 12 | 3 | 6 |
| Poland v Argentina | 3-2 | ARGENTINA | 3 | 1 | 1 | 1 | 7 | 5 | 3 |
| Argentina v Italy | 1-1 | Italy | 3 | 1 | 1 | 1 | 5 | 4 | 3 |
| Poland v Haiti | 7-0 | Haiti | 3 | 0 | 0 | 3 | 2 | 14 | 0 |

Argentina v Haiti        4-1
Poland v Italy           2-1

*Pool A*

| Brazil v E Germany     | 1-0 | HOLLAND      | 3 | 3 | 0 | 0 | 8 | 0 | 6 |
| Holland v Argentina    | 4-0 | Brazil       | 3 | 2 | 0 | 1 | 3 | 3 | 4 |
| Holland v E Germany    | 2-0 | East Germany | 3 | 0 | 1 | 2 | 1 | 4 | 1 |
| Brazil v Argentina     | 2-1 | Argentina    | 3 | 0 | 1 | 2 | 2 | 7 | 1 |
| Holland v Brazil       | 2-0 |              |   |   |   |   |   |   |   |
| Argentina v E Germany  | 1-1 |              |   |   |   |   |   |   |   |

*Pool B*

| Poland v Sweden        | 1-0 | W GERMANY    | 3 | 3 | 0 | 0 | 7 | 2 | 6 |
| W Germany v Yugoslavia | 2-0 | Poland       | 3 | 2 | 0 | 1 | 3 | 2 | 4 |
| Poland v Yugoslavia    | 2-1 | Sweden       | 3 | 1 | 0 | 2 | 4 | 6 | 2 |
| W Germany v Sweden     | 4-2 | Yugoslavia   | 3 | 0 | 0 | 3 | 2 | 6 | 0 |
| Sweden v Yugoslavia    | 2-1 |              |   |   |   |   |   |   |   |
| W Germany v Poland     | 1-0 |              |   |   |   |   |   |   |   |

*Third/Fourth play off*            *Final*
Poland v Brazil          1-0       W Germany v Holland      2-1

## ARGENTINA – 1978

*Group 1*

| | | | P | W | D | L | F | A | Pts |
|---|---|---|---|---|---|---|---|---|---|
| Italy v France      | 2-1 | ITALY     | 3 | 3 | 0 | 0 | 6 | 2 | 6 |
| Argentina v Hungary | 2-1 | ARGENTINA | 3 | 2 | 0 | 1 | 4 | 3 | 4 |
| Italy v Hungary     | 3-1 | France    | 3 | 1 | 0 | 2 | 5 | 5 | 2 |
| Argentina v France  | 2-1 | Hungary   | 3 | 0 | 0 | 3 | 3 | 8 | 0 |
| France v Hungary    | 3-1 |           |   |   |   |   |   |   |   |
| Italy v Argentina   | 1-0 |           |   |   |   |   |   |   |   |

*Group 2*

| W Germany v Poland  | 0-0 | POLAND    | 3 | 2 | 1 | 0 | 4 | 1  | 5 |
| Tunisia v Mexico    | 3-1 | W GERMANY | 3 | 1 | 2 | 0 | 6 | 0  | 4 |
| Poland v Tunisia    | 1-0 | Tunisia   | 3 | 1 | 1 | 1 | 3 | 2  | 3 |
| W Germany v Mexico  | 6-0 | Mexico    | 3 | 0 | 0 | 3 | 2 | 12 | 0 |
| Poland v Mexico     | 3-1 |           |   |   |   |   |   |    |   |
| W Germany v Tunisia | 0-0 |           |   |   |   |   |   |    |   |

*Group 3*

| Austria v Spain   | 2-1 | AUSTRIA | 3 | 2 | 0 | 1 | 3 | 2 | 4 |
| Brazil v Sweden   | 1-1 | BRAZIL  | 3 | 1 | 2 | 0 | 2 | 1 | 4 |
| Austria v Sweden  | 1-0 | Spain   | 3 | 1 | 1 | 1 | 2 | 2 | 3 |
| Brazil v Spain    | 0-0 | Sweden  | 3 | 0 | 1 | 2 | 1 | 3 | 1 |
| Spain v Sweden    | 1-0 |         |   |   |   |   |   |   |   |
| Brazil v Austria  | 1-0 |         |   |   |   |   |   |   |   |

### Group 4

| Match | Score | | P | W | D | L | F | A | Pts |
|---|---|---|---|---|---|---|---|---|---|
| Peru v Scotland | 3-1 | PERU | 3 | 2 | 1 | 0 | 7 | 2 | 5 |
| Holland v Iran | 3-0 | HOLLAND | 3 | 1 | 1 | 1 | 5 | 3 | 3 |
| Scotland v Iran | 1-1 | Scotland | 3 | 1 | 1 | 1 | 5 | 6 | 3 |
| Holland v Peru | 0-0 | Iran | 3 | 0 | 1 | 2 | 2 | 8 | 1 |
| Peru v Iran | 4-1 | | | | | | | | |
| Scotland v Holland | 3-2 | | | | | | | | |

### Group A

| Match | Score | | P | W | D | L | F | A | Pts |
|---|---|---|---|---|---|---|---|---|---|
| W Germany v Italy | 0-0 | HOLLAND | 3 | 2 | 1 | 0 | 9 | 4 | 5 |
| Holland v Austria | 5-1 | Italy | 3 | 1 | 1 | 1 | 2 | 2 | 3 |
| Italy v Austria | 1-0 | W Germany | 3 | 0 | 2 | 1 | 4 | 5 | 2 |
| Holland v W Germany | 2-2 | Austria | 3 | 1 | 0 | 2 | 4 | 8 | 2 |
| Holland v Italy | 2-1 | | | | | | | | |
| Austria v W Germany | 3-2 | | | | | | | | |

### Group B

| Match | Score | | P | W | D | L | F | A | Pts |
|---|---|---|---|---|---|---|---|---|---|
| Brazil v Peru | 3-0 | ARGENTINA | 3 | 2 | 1 | 0 | 8 | 0 | 5 |
| Argentina v Poland | 2-0 | Brazil | 3 | 2 | 1 | 0 | 6 | 1 | 5 |
| Poland v Peru | 1-0 | Poland | 3 | 1 | 0 | 2 | 2 | 5 | 2 |
| Argentina v Brazil | 0-0 | Peru | 3 | 0 | 0 | 3 | 0 | 10 | 0 |
| Brazil v Poland | 3-1 | | | | | | | | |
| Argentina v Peru | 6-0 | | | | | | | | |

### Third/Fourth play-off
Brazil v Italy            2-1

### Final
Argentina v Holland            3-1 (aet)

---

## SPAIN – 1982

### Group 1

| Match | Score | | P | W | D | L | F | A | Pts |
|---|---|---|---|---|---|---|---|---|---|
| Italy v Poland | 0-0 | POLAND | 3 | 1 | 2 | 0 | 5 | 1 | 4 |
| Peru v Cameroon | 0-0 | ITALY | 3 | 0 | 3 | 0 | 2 | 2 | 3 |
| Italy v Peru | 1-1 | Cameroon | 3 | 0 | 3 | 0 | 1 | 1 | 3 |
| Poland v Cameroon | 0-0 | Peru | 3 | 0 | 2 | 1 | 2 | 6 | 2 |
| Poland v Peru | 5-1 | | | | | | | | |
| Italy v Cameroon | 1-1 | | | | | | | | |

### Group 2

| Match | Score | | P | W | D | L | F | A | Pts |
|---|---|---|---|---|---|---|---|---|---|
| Algeria v W Germany | 2-1 | W GERMANY | 3 | 2 | 0 | 1 | 6 | 3 | 4 |
| Austria v Chile | 1-0 | AUSTRIA | 3 | 2 | 0 | 1 | 3 | 1 | 4 |
| W Germany v Chile | 4-1 | Algeria | 3 | 2 | 0 | 1 | 5 | 5 | 4 |
| Austria v Algeria | 2-0 | Chile | 3 | 0 | 0 | 3 | 3 | 8 | 0 |
| Algeria v Chile | 3-2 | | | | | | | | |
| W Germany v Austria | 1-0 | | | | | | | | |

### Group 3

| Match | Score | | P | W | D | L | F | A | Pts |
|---|---|---|---|---|---|---|---|---|---|
| Belgium v Argentina | 1-0 | BELGIUM | 3 | 2 | 1 | 0 | 3 | 1 | 5 |
| Hungary v El Salvador | 10-1 | ARGENTINA | 3 | 2 | 0 | 1 | 6 | 2 | 4 |
| Argentina v Hungary | 4-1 | Hungary | 3 | 1 | 1 | 1 | 12 | 6 | 3 |
| Belgium v El Salvador | 1-0 | El Salvador | 3 | 0 | 0 | 3 | 1 | 13 | 0 |

Belgium v Hungary        1-1
Argentina v El Salvador  2-0

*Group 4*

| England v France | 3-1 | ENGLAND | 3 | 3 | 0 | 0 | 6 | 1 | 6 |
|---|---|---|---|---|---|---|---|---|---|
| Czechoslovakia v Kuwait | 1-1 | FRANCE | 3 | 1 | 1 | 1 | 6 | 5 | 3 |
| England v Czechoslovakia | 2-0 | Czechoslovakia | 3 | 0 | 2 | 1 | 2 | 4 | 2 |
| France v Kuwait | 4-1 | Kuwait | 3 | 0 | 1 | 2 | 2 | 6 | 1 |
| France v Czechoslovakia | 1-1 | | | | | | | | |
| England v Kuwait | 1-0 | | | | | | | | |

*Group 5*

| Spain v Honduras | 1-1 | N IRELAND | 3 | 1 | 2 | 0 | 2 | 1 | 4 |
|---|---|---|---|---|---|---|---|---|---|
| Yugoslavia v N Ireland | 0-0 | SPAIN | 3 | 1 | 1 | 1 | 3 | 3 | 3 |
| Spain v Yugoslavia | 2-1 | Yugoslavia | 3 | 1 | 1 | 1 | 2 | 2 | 3 |
| Honduras v N Ireland | 1-1 | Honduras | 3 | 0 | 2 | 1 | 2 | 3 | 2 |
| Yugoslavia v Honduras | 1-0 | | | | | | | | |
| N Ireland v Spain | 1-0 | | | | | | | | |

*Group 6*

| Brazil v Soviet Union | 2-1 | BRAZIL | 3 | 3 | 0 | 0 | 10 | 2 | 6 |
|---|---|---|---|---|---|---|---|---|---|
| Scotland v New Zealand | 5-2 | SOVIET UNION | 3 | 1 | 1 | 1 | 6 | 4 | 3 |
| Brazil v Scotland | 4-1 | Scotland | 3 | 1 | 1 | 1 | 8 | 8 | 3 |
| Soviet Union v New Zealand | 3-0 | New Zealand | 3 | 0 | 0 | 3 | 2 | 12 | 0 |
| Soviet Union v Scotland | 2-2 | | | | | | | | |
| Brazil v New Zealand | 4-0 | | | | | | | | |

*Group A*

| Poland v Belgium | 3-0 | POLAND | 2 | 1 | 1 | 0 | 3 | 0 | 3 |
|---|---|---|---|---|---|---|---|---|---|
| Soviet Union v Belgium | 1-0 | Soviet Union | 2 | 1 | 1 | 0 | 1 | 0 | 3 |
| Soviet Union v Poland | 0-0 | Belgium | 2 | 0 | 0 | 2 | 0 | 4 | 0 |

*Group B*

| W Germany v England | 0-0 | W GERMANY | 2 | 1 | 1 | 0 | 2 | 1 | 3 |
|---|---|---|---|---|---|---|---|---|---|
| W Germany v Spain | 2-1 | England | 2 | 0 | 2 | 0 | 0 | 0 | 2 |
| England v Spain | 0-0 | Spain | 2 | 0 | 1 | 1 | 1 | 2 | 1 |

*Group C*

| Italy v Argentina | 2-1 | ITALY | 2 | 2 | 0 | 0 | 5 | 3 | 4 |
|---|---|---|---|---|---|---|---|---|---|
| Brazil v Argentina | 3-1 | Brazil | 2 | 1 | 0 | 1 | 5 | 4 | 2 |
| Italy v Brazil | 3-2 | Argentina | 2 | 0 | 0 | 2 | 2 | 5 | 0 |

*Group D*

| France v Austria | 1-0 | FRANCE | 2 | 2 | 0 | 0 | 5 | 1 | 4 |
|---|---|---|---|---|---|---|---|---|---|
| Austria v N Ireland | 2-2 | Austria | 2 | 0 | 1 | 1 | 2 | 3 | 1 |
| France v N Ireland | 4-1 | N Ireland | 2 | 0 | 1 | 1 | 3 | 6 | 1 |

*Semi-finals*

Italy v Poland        2-0          W Germany v France        3-3 (aet)
                                   (W Germany won on penalties)

| *Third/Fourth play-off* | | *Final* | |
|---|---|---|---|
| Poland v France | 3-2 | Italy v W Germany | 3-1 |

## MEXICO – 1986

### Group A

| | | | P | W | D | L | F | A | Pts |
|---|---|---|---|---|---|---|---|---|---|
| Bulgaria v Italy | 1-1 | ARGENTINA | 3 | 2 | 1 | 0 | 6 | 2 | 5 |
| Argentina v South Korea | 3-1 | ITALY | 3 | 1 | 2 | 0 | 5 | 4 | 4 |
| Italy v Argentina | 1-1 | BULGARIA | 3 | 0 | 2 | 1 | 2 | 4 | 2 |
| South Korea v Bulgaria | 1-1 | South Korea | 3 | 0 | 1 | 2 | 4 | 7 | 1 |
| Argentina v Bulgaria | 2-0 | | | | | | | | |
| Italy v South Korea | 3-2 | | | | | | | | |

### Group B

| | | | P | W | D | L | F | A | Pts |
|---|---|---|---|---|---|---|---|---|---|
| Mexico v Belgium | 2-1 | MEXICO | 3 | 2 | 1 | 0 | 4 | 2 | 5 |
| Paraguay v Iraq | 1-0 | PARAGUAY | 3 | 1 | 2 | 0 | 4 | 3 | 4 |
| Mexico v Paraguay | 1-1 | BELGIUM | 3 | 1 | 1 | 1 | 5 | 5 | 3 |
| Belgium v Iraq | 2-1 | Iraq | 3 | 0 | 0 | 3 | 1 | 4 | 0 |
| Paraguay v Belgium | 2-2 | | | | | | | | |
| Mexico v Iraq | 1-0 | | | | | | | | |

### Group C

| | | | P | W | D | L | F | A | Pts |
|---|---|---|---|---|---|---|---|---|---|
| France v Canada | 1-0 | SOVIET UNION | 3 | 2 | 1 | 0 | 9 | 1 | 5 |
| Soviet Union v Hungary | 6-0 | FRANCE | 3 | 2 | 1 | 0 | 5 | 1 | 5 |
| Soviet Union v France | 1-1 | Hungary | 3 | 1 | 0 | 2 | 2 | 9 | 2 |
| Hungary v Canada | 2-0 | Canada | 3 | 0 | 0 | 3 | 0 | 5 | 0 |
| France v Hungary | 3-0 | | | | | | | | |
| Soviet Union v Canada | 2-0 | | | | | | | | |

### Group D

| | | | P | W | D | L | F | A | Pts |
|---|---|---|---|---|---|---|---|---|---|
| Brazil v Spain | 1-0 | BRAZIL | 3 | 3 | 0 | 0 | 5 | 0 | 6 |
| Algeria v N Ireland | 1-1 | SPAIN | 3 | 2 | 0 | 1 | 5 | 2 | 4 |
| Spain v N Ireland | 2-1 | Northern Ireland | 3 | 0 | 1 | 2 | 2 | 6 | 1 |
| Brazil v Algeria | 1-0 | Algeria | 3 | 0 | 1 | 2 | 1 | 5 | 1 |
| Spain v Algeria | 3-0 | | | | | | | | |
| Brazil v N Ireland | 3-0 | | | | | | | | |

### Group E

| | | | P | W | D | L | F | A | Pts |
|---|---|---|---|---|---|---|---|---|---|
| Uruguay v W Germany | 1-1 | DENMARK | 3 | 3 | 0 | 0 | 9 | 1 | 6 |
| Denmark v Scotland | 1-0 | W GERMANY | 3 | 1 | 1 | 1 | 3 | 4 | 3 |
| Denmark v Uruguay | 6-1 | URUGUAY | 3 | 0 | 2 | 1 | 2 | 7 | 2 |
| W Germany v Scotland | 2-1 | Scotland | 3 | 0 | 1 | 2 | 1 | 3 | 1 |
| Uruguay v Scotland | 0-0 | | | | | | | | |
| Denmark v W Germany | 2-0 | | | | | | | | |

### Group F

| | | | P | W | D | L | F | A | Pts |
|---|---|---|---|---|---|---|---|---|---|
| Morocco v Poland | 0-0 | MOROCCO | 3 | 1 | 2 | 0 | 3 | 1 | 4 |
| Portugal v England | 1-0 | ENGLAND | 3 | 1 | 1 | 1 | 3 | 1 | 3 |
| England v Morocco | 0-0 | POLAND | 3 | 1 | 1 | 1 | 1 | 3 | 3 |
| Poland v Portugal | 1-0 | Portugal | 3 | 1 | 0 | 2 | 2 | 4 | 2 |

England v Poland          3-0
Morocco v Portugal        3-1

*Second Round*

| | | | |
|---|---|---|---|
| Mexico v Bulgaria | 2-0 | Brazil v Poland | 4-0 |
| W Germany Morocco | 1-0 | France v Italy | 2-0 |
| Belgium v Soviet Union | 4-3 (aet) | Argentina v Uruguay | 1-0 |
| Spain v Denmark | 5-1 | England v Paraguay | 3-0 |

*Quarter-finals*

W Germany v Mexico    0-0 (aet. W Germany won on penalties)
Belgium v Spain       1-1 (aet. Belgium won on penalties)
France v Brazil       1-1 (aet. France won on penalties)
Argentina v England   2-1

*Semi-finals*

W Germany v France    2-0      Argentina v Belgium    2-0

*Third/Fourth play-off*          *Final*
France v Belgium      4-2      Argentina v W Germany    3-2

## ITALY – 1990

*Group A*

| | | | P | W | D | L | F | A | Pts |
|---|---|---|---|---|---|---|---|---|---|
| Italy v Austria | 1-0 | ITALY | 3 | 3 | 0 | 0 | 4 | 0 | 6 |
| Czechoslovakia v USA | 5-0 | CZECHOSLOVAKIA | 3 | 2 | 0 | 1 | 6 | 3 | 4 |
| Italy v United States | 1-0 | Austria | 3 | 1 | 0 | 2 | 2 | 3 | 2 |
| Czechoslovakia v Austria | 1-0 | United States | 3 | 0 | 0 | 3 | 2 | 8 | 0 |
| Italy v Czechoslovakia | 2-0 | | | | | | | | |
| Austria v United States | 2-1 | | | | | | | | |

*Group B*

| | | | | | | | | | |
|---|---|---|---|---|---|---|---|---|---|
| Cameroon v Argentina | 1-0 | CAMEROON | 3 | 2 | 0 | 1 | 3 | 5 | 4 |
| Romania v Soviet Union | 2-0 | ROMANIA | 3 | 1 | 1 | 1 | 4 | 3 | 3 |
| Argentina v Soviet Union | 2-0 | ARGENTINA | 3 | 1 | 1 | 1 | 3 | 2 | 3 |
| Cameroon v Romania | 2-1 | Soviet Union | 3 | 1 | 0 | 2 | 4 | 4 | 2 |
| Argentina v Romania | 1-1 | | | | | | | | |
| Soviet Union v Cameroon | 4-0 | | | | | | | | |

*Group C*

| | | | | | | | | | |
|---|---|---|---|---|---|---|---|---|---|
| Brazil v Sweden | 2-1 | BRAZIL | 3 | 3 | 0 | 0 | 4 | 1 | 6 |
| Costa Rica v Scotland | 1-0 | COSTA RICA | 3 | 2 | 0 | 1 | 3 | 2 | 4 |
| Brazil v Costa Rica | 1-0 | Scotland | 3 | 1 | 0 | 2 | 2 | 3 | 2 |
| Scotland v Sweden | 2-1 | Sweden | 3 | 0 | 0 | 3 | 3 | 6 | 0 |
| Brazil v Scotland | 1-0 | | | | | | | | |
| Costa Rica v Sweden | 2-1 | | | | | | | | |

*Group D*

| Colombia v UAE | 2-0 | W GERMANY | 3 | 2 | 1 | 0 | 10 | 3 | 5 |
| W Germany v Yugoslavia | 4-1 | YUGOSLAVIA | 3 | 2 | 0 | 1 | 6 | 5 | 4 |
| Yugoslavia v Colombia | 1-0 | COLOMBIA | 3 | 1 | 1 | 1 | 3 | 2 | 3 |
| W Germany v UAE | 5-1 | United Arab Emirates | 3 | 0 | 0 | 3 | 2 | 11 | 0 |
| W Germany v Colombia | 1-1 | | | | | | | | |
| Yugoslavia v UAE | 4-1 | | | | | | | | |

*Group E*

| Belgium v South Korea | 2-0 | SPAIN | 3 | 2 | 1 | 0 | 5 | 2 | 5 |
| Spain v Uruguay | 0-0 | BELGIUM | 3 | 2 | 0 | 1 | 6 | 3 | 4 |
| Spain v South Korea | 3-1 | URUGUAY | 3 | 1 | 1 | 1 | 2 | 3 | 3 |
| Belgium v Uruguay | 3-1 | South Korea | 3 | 0 | 0 | 3 | 1 | 6 | 0 |
| Spain v Belgium | 2-1 | | | | | | | | |
| Uruguay v South Korea | 1-0 | | | | | | | | |

*Group F*

| England v Rep Ireland | 1-1 | ENGLAND | 3 | 1 | 2 | 0 | 2 | 1 | 4 |
| Egypt v Holland | 1-1 | REP IRELAND | 3 | 0 | 3 | 0 | 2 | 2 | 3 |
| England v Holland | 0-0 | HOLLAND | 3 | 0 | 3 | 0 | 2 | 2 | 3 |
| Egypt v Rep Ireland | 0-0 | Egypt | 3 | 0 | 2 | 1 | 1 | 2 | 2 |
| England v Egypt | 1-0 | | | | | | | | |
| Rep Ireland v Holland | 1-1 | | | | | | | | |

*Second Round*

| Cameroon v Colombia | 2-1 (aet) | Argentina v Brazil | 1-0 |
| England v Belgium | 1-0 (aet) | Yugoslavia v Spain | 2-1 (aet) |
| Czechoslovakia v Costa Rica | 4-1 | Italy v Uruguay | 2-0 |
| W Germany v Holland | 2-1 | Rep Ireland v Romania | 0-0 (aet) |
| | | (Rep Ireland won on penalties) | |

*Quarter-finals*

| England v Cameroon | 3-2 (aet) | Italy v Rep Ireland | 1-0 |
| W Germany v Czecho'vakia | 1-0 | Argentina v Yugoslavia | 0-0 (aet) |
| | | (Argentina won on penalties) | |

*Semi-finals*

| Argentina v Italy | 1-1 (aet. Argentina won on penalties) |
| W Germany v England | 1-1 (aet. W Germany won on penalties) |

*Third/Fourth play-off*      *Final*

| Italy v England | 2-1 | W Germany v Argentina | 1-0 |